Library of
Davidson College

The Decline and Fall of Virgil in Eighteenth-Century Germany

In the early modern period, the culture of Rome, with Virgil as its greatest figure, was the model for emulation. But in eighteenth-century Europe, a shift occurred in favor of Greece, a trend that was most pronounced in Germany. Led by Winckelmann, German poets and thinkers extolled Greek art, dismissing all Roman art as derivative and Virgil as second rate and incapable of understanding true beauty. The export of this new view of Virgil and, more generally, Roman culture to the rest of Europe in the nineteenth century soon made it the reigning dogma, and it formed the point of departure for Virgil scholarship in the twentieth century. This, however, did not prevent German poets from using Virgil, although neither they nor later scholars called attention to it. Virgil has a continued, unexamined presence in the epic and idyll of Klopstock, Wieland, Goethe, and Novalis. This comparative investigation of the relation of modernity to antiquity through Virgil and his twofold reception provides a new perspective on this issue.

Geoffrey Atherton is assistant professor in the Department of German Studies at Connecticut College.

Studies in German Literature, Linguistics, and Culture

The Decline and Fall of Virgil in Eighteenth-Century Germany

The Repressed Muse

Geoffrey Atherton

CAMDEN HOUSE

Copyright © 2006 Geoffrey Atherton

All Rights Reserved. Except as permitted under current legislation,
no part of this work may be photocopied, stored in a retrieval system,
published, performed in public, adapted, broadcast, transmitted,
recorded, or reproduced in any form or by any means,
without the prior permission of the copyright owner.

First published 2006
by Camden House

Camden House is an imprint of Boydell & Brewer Inc.
668 Mt. Hope Avenue, Rochester, NY 14620, USA
www.camden-house.com
and of Boydell & Brewer Limited
PO Box 9, Woodbridge, Suffolk IP12 3DF, UK
www.boydellandbrewer.com

ISBN: 1–57113–306–2

Library of Congress Cataloging-in-Publication Data

Atherton, Geoffrey, 1965–
 The decline and fall of Virgil in eighteenth-century Germany: the repressed muse / Geoffrey Atherton.
  p. cm. — (Studies in German literature, linguistics, and culture)
 Includes bibliographical references and index.
 ISBN 1–57113–306–2 (hardcover ; alk. paper)
 1. German literature — 18th century — History and criticism.
 2. Virgil — Influence. 3. Virgil — Appreciation — Germany.
 4. Aesthetics, German — 18th century. I. Title. II. Series: Studies in German literature, linguistics, and culture (Unnumbered)

PT295.A75 2006
830.9'351—dc22

2005022909

A catalogue record for this title is available from the British Library.

This publication is printed on acid-free paper.
Printed in the United States of America.

parentibus optimis carissimisque

Contents

Preface	ix
Acknowledgments	xvii
List of Abbreviations	xix
1: Virgil: A Pentheus to the Germans in the Eighteenth Century?	1
2: Virgil Both Read and Unread	63
3: Virgil the Rhapsode	96
4: Theorizing Genre: From Pastoral to Idyll	136
5: The German Idyll and the Virgilian Muse	198
Conclusion: Proximity and Estrangement	281
Works Cited	289
Index	307

Preface

AT THE BEGINNING OF THE EIGHTEENTH CENTURY Virgil enjoyed a position of unparalled authority in the literary culture of Germany as well as Europe more generally. Virgil's preeminence in the highest of the recognized genres of poetic composition, the epic, was unquestioned, and in the popular and luxuriant pastoral, his language, his motifs, and his image of Arcadia (his own innovation) pervaded the artistic consciousness of the age. Yet by the century's close Virgil had been not merely dethroned but also degraded as the poet who had failed to compose anything that could creditably be called a poem. This fall from grace was not confined to Virgil alone but extended to the assessment of the entire Roman literary achievement: Virgil became *the* failed poet, and Latin literature *the* failed national literature. To explain this shift requires an examination of its relation to the wider concerns of the German Enlightenment and the contemporaneous rise of German philhellenism. The primary aim of this book is to explain this repudiation of Virgil and the Latins in Germany during the eighteenth century and the understanding of antiquity it bequeathed to the nineteenth and twentieth centuries. The book's other objective is to show that, despite Virgil's official dethronement and dismemberment, German writers of the period in epic and pastoral literature continued to harken to the Virgilian muse, although they were increasingly disinclined to acknowledge it after the century's midpoint.

The familiarity with Virgil in the original that all educated Germans had from their schooling contributed mightily to this continued presence. The intimate acquaintance with his works accounts, to a large extent, for the passages alluded to that recur so frequently — a selection not much changed in the twentieth century — but it accounts neither for their context nor for their interpretation; for these, we must return to the eighteenth century's larger interests. Nor does the firsthand knowledge German intellectuals and writers had of the Virgilian texts retard their progressive estrangement from him during the period. Old acquaintance held little charm before the intoxicating thrill of the new, in this case, the discovery of an apparently more authentic antiquity in ancient Greece.[1] Homer and the Greeks — these were the century's passion: by its end, Virgil and the Latins were, with few exceptions, the objects of embarrassment, silence, and even outright scorn. The subsequent scholarly tradition, at first sharing too closely these sentiments, was slow to investigate the larger claims made on behalf of the Greeks by virtually all the leading

German literary and intellectual figures in the eighteenth century.[2] Indeed, the preference was not merely to concentrate on the wealth of materials about the Greeks readily at hand in writers and intellectuals from the period, but also, on occasion, to do so through the claim of a Greek and German elective affinity, a connection of soul, or "das griechische Reich deutscher Nation."[3]

Friedrich Nietzsche (1844–1900) first administered a comprehensive shock to the notion of an easy communion between Greek and German. Nonetheless, the impulse in literary studies for a general reevaluation of the eighteenth century's animating belief in its Greek creation came from outside Germany: from England, in the form of E. M. Butler's landmark study, *The Tyranny of Greece over Germany* (1935). Postwar scholarship has made Butler's insights its own, thoroughly reevaluating the eighteenth century's relation to Greece while continuing to explore further aspects of it.[4] It has, however, stopped short of reexamining the relation of eighteenth-century poets and thinkers to the Latins. The present study addresses this point by investigating the views of these poets and thinkers and the uses to which they put the foremost Latin poet, Virgil. It examines the supercession of a Latin by a Greek model not from the more familiar perspective of what the new vision of Greece portends for German culture, but rather by examining the virtual removal of the Latin literary works from the German canon. The point bears repetition that as long as Latin retained its central role in the curriculum of the nineteenth-century Gymnasium, Virgil remained a school text, but, if the Germans still read him, they did so now with little favor and appreciation.

Much of the more general imperative driving the reception of Virgil during the eighteenth century stems from the rise of German philhellenism after its midpoint. The reception of Rome's foremost poet forms the pendant piece to that of Homer and the Greeks. In the course of the eighteenth century, Virgil and the Romans come to form the paradigmatic and negative contrary to the emerging view of Greece. This development, like that of German philhellenism, shapes the literary historiography of the Romantics. Further, again like German philhellenism, the reassessment of the Latin heritage contributes to the formulation of a national cultural identity. However, while the intensity of German Graecomania was expressed in such notions as a special affinity of soul, no such general acknowledgment exists for the corresponding vehemence of the rejection of the Latin world. Yet this vehemence is no less striking, and no less in want of explanation, than the ardency of German philhellenism. It animates the categorical statements on Virgil and Latin culture in literary and intellectual discussions just as it militates against any open engagement with the poet. The vehemence of this rejection necessitates a larger framework for its proper understanding no less than the fervency of German philhellenism does for its full appreciation.

This larger framework is sketched in chapter 1 by exploring three related contexts. The first larger context is that of the critical tradition associated with Virgil and the crucial role of history within it. History is at work in this tradition in a number of senses. It is present in the recognition that the image of Virgil to emerge in twentieth-century scholarship (more so in the earlier than in the latter part of the century) responds to the expectations inherited from the eighteenth century. Further, the image of Virgil in the mind of eighteenth-century writers and intellectuals, both the characteristics commonly associated with the poet and the methods used to elaborate them, stems largely from the French *Querelle des anciens et des modernes*. And finally, the *Querelle* also strikingly introduces the question of history more directly. It does so in the recognition that earlier ages do not necessarily regard in the same light the "universal principles" so dear to the Enlightenment. This difficulty would be of little urgency if the Enlightenment did not regard its own culture both as descended from and also as participating in antiquity. But this belief was central to the age and it required the development of a means for understanding the processes of historical change. This understanding would allow the later period both to figure satisfactorily to itself the transformations leading to the present while fully acknowledging historical difference, and also to affirm the universality of its own fundamental beliefs, or at least assure itself that this development was not contrary to them.

The second larger context to affect the reading of Virgil was the Enlightenment's preoccupation with nature. The contrast between nature on the one hand and civilization or culture on the other gained a sharper focus as the century advanced. In the Enlightenment view, the genius was that rare individual still capable of harkening to nature's call, despite the deformities of culture; the state of nature embodied a humanity at peace with itself in nature before the advent of the ills society brings. Fortunately, ancient Greece offered the image of a people thought to have reconciled this alienation within historical time. Consequently, Homer and the Greeks became the historical proof of this idyllic concept of nature and were indissolubly linked to the more general preoccupation with nature. Within the rich mass of literature from the eighteenth century inspired by this common preoccupation, the idyll or pastoral came for a brief period to offer the age an adequate imaginative depiction of the state of nature. The idyll lives from the desire of the present for a purer simpler state, although this desire may not itself become directly or too manifestly the subject of idyll, a tension that Friedrich Schiller (1759–1805) would memorably fix with the theoretical pairing of naive and sentimental. The desire for a happier, more naive condition in an idyllic nature reduced but did not entirely banish sentimental reflection on this earlier state or doubts about its veracity. Awkwardly for this concept of idyllic nature, the rich storehouse of the pastoral tradition from which it draws is perhaps more heavily stocked with items from the poems of Virgil than from any other poet. They provide powerful evocations of Arcadia and love amenable to a naive assimilation to the idyll of the eighteenth century, yet they also present a repertory of technique for just such sentimental reflection hostile to true naivety. Three strands combine in the German idyll of the eighteenth century: a naive nature under the aegis of ancient Greece for its achievement in reconciling culture to nature, the developing and increasingly anxious tension between the naive and the sentimental, and finally a literary tradition too heavily dependent on the Virgilian texts. To the eighteenth century, Virgil himself appeared to have recognized the appeal of nature but fatefully to have preferred an egregiously sentimental cultivation of his talent and thus to have abandoned his genius and art.

The final larger context concerns the articulation of a German identity in the eighteenth century. The discovery of a new Greece in the decades after 1750 and the claim of a peculiar German affinity for its spirit not only invested original German productions with added authority, but also diminished the prestige of French neo-classical models. The French under Louis XIV had laid claim to Augustan Rome, proclaiming themselves its modern successors. Now Greece would displace Rome as the true "antiquity"; Rome became rather the model for the "false" imitation of nature, the suppression of one's own voice in favor of that of another, the example of a failed national literature. These sentiments militated powerfully against an appreciation of the foremost poet of the Latin tradition, Virgil; indeed, he must become its most conspicuous failure. The Jena Romantics, the Schlegel brothers, expressed these views most clearly. They drew the conclusions for the assessment of Virgil that their predecessors' arguments suggested but had not always stated explicitly. An awareness of the similarity of the position of Rome and Germany added vehemence to their statements. Both nations found themselves confronted with an enormously rich, varied, and prestigious cultural tradition in the face of which both felt decidedly inferior. These cultural traditions, in the one case that of Greece, in the other that of France, also threatened to smother their first attempts to strike out on their own. Thus we may recognize that the severity of the Schlegel brothers' statements about Virgil as the preeminent Latin poet owes as much to fear as it does to scorn.

These larger concerns set and define the use and value of Virgil as a figure, a model, and an ideal to which one may appeal. They most emphatically do not determine what actual use passages, themes, and techniques so often handled and read may come to have. It does not follow from the slaying of the father figure that the offspring exhibit none of his traits, loath though they may be to acknowledge them. Such was the case with Virgil in the eighteenth century. So deeply ingrained was Virgil in the educated and literary culture of the time that he came unbidden to the mind of the writer. It is, to repeat, not a matter of Virgil as a figure, a paradigm;

it is rather a matter of certain sets of themes, of particular phrases or techniques. They depended for their continued influence on the means of their transmission. The repetitive and canonical occurrence in specific contexts prised Virgilian elements from the Virgilian texts. By losing their unduly close Virgilian association they continued to exert an influence. Such a process accounts for the otherwise odd presence of a Virgilian hermeneutic in the interpretation of the Laocoon statue by Johann Joachim Winckelmann (1717–68), for a Virgilian tincture in German epic, and, most productively, in the German idyllic tradition.

Although much of this study deals with the eclipse of Virgil before the rising "Sonne Homer," in Johann Gottfried von Herder's (1744–1803) phrase, it should not be forgotten that this misrepresents the century as a whole. It reflects the bias of literary and intellectual historiography. The canonical figures of German intellectual and literary life all come from the latter half of the century, from the period when Graecomania reached its zenith. Christoph Martin Wieland (1733–1813), Johann Wolfgang von Goethe (1749–1832), Friedrich Hölderlin (1770–1843), Novalis (1772–1801), and Friedrich Schlegel (1772–1829): none evinces any strong attachment to Virgil. Schiller, with his translations from Virgil as a mature poet, stands as the exception to this general rule. In the first half of the century, however, German opinion conformed more closely to that elsewhere in Europe. The first stirrings of a reappraisal of Homer in the Quarrel of the Ancients and the Moderns succeeded in dissuading neither the age of Louis XIV from favorably comparing its accomplishments to those of Rome under Augustus, nor England in the first decades of the eighteenth century from hailing an Augustan Age of its own. Germany hailed no such comparable age, even though such individual figures as the philosopher and mathematician Gottfried Wilhelm Leibniz (1646–1716), Albrecht von Haller (1707–77), poet, scientist and father of medical physiology, and the dramatist and critic Gotthold Ephraim Lessing (1729–81) all held Virgil in high regard. The great change occurred after the middle decades of the century and acquired inexorable momentum from Winckelmann's embrace of Greece as the sole model for artistic achievement.

When explicit statements thus argue for an increasing distance from the Latin poet, understanding the context of transmission becomes crucial for assessing the continued presence of Virgilian themes and wording. Consequently, the greater portion of this study concentrates on establishing some of these paths of transmission, as the assessment of any more significant Virgilian reception depends on them. Chapter 2 begins with just such an example of the continued susceptibility to Virgilian formulations although the temper of the time argued against it. It examines Winckelmann's famous dictum, "a noble simplicity and quiet grandeur," "eine edle Einfalt und stille Größe," not in its wording, but in his application of it to the Laocoon statue. To a more modern eye the statue seems to exemplify almost anything other than a noble simplicity and a quiet grandeur. The interpretative tradition resting on the Virgilian narrative prepares the connection for Winckelmann between the statue and the statement. However, because of the stages of its transmission, in which the material was refashioned and adapted to new purposes and concerns along the way, its Virgilian origins became obscure.

The chapter continues by looking at the reading of Virgil in the schools as they established which selections were read and how they were understood. It examines Virgil's place in the curriculum, which was a formidable one, since no one, neither the boneheaded nor those without a taste for it, could escape an enforced familiarity with Virgil, if he (and the gender here is accurate) were privileged enough to complete his schooling. Virgil's status as the school text *par excellence* made him the early neo-humanist Christian Gottlob Heyne's (1729–1812) choice as a demonstration piece to illustrate the new techniques of the neo-humanist reading of texts. Heyne also conceived his project of a new Virgil edition (1767–75) in full consciousness of the ferment caused by the works of such as Lessing and Winckelmann. Such was the success of his commentary in advancing the new approach to textual evidence that his edition became the Virgil edition of the century. It secured international fame for Heyne and made him one of the founding figures of German neo-humanism; one of his occasional students, Friedrich August Wolf (1759–1824) is credited with the establishment of modern classical studies. It has also, to the best of my knowledge, made his Virgil the progenitor of all subsequent modern Virgil editions.

The third chapter turns to the consideration of the field most closely associated with Virgil, namely, that of epic. Epic, though much cultivated in the eighteenth century, lives more from cultural authority than from any more popular enthusiasm. The interests of poetics and the residual humanism of the schools in rhetoric largely determined the reading of Virgil in the classroom and thus of the appearance of Virgilian stylistic traits in subsequent epic. Likewise, the preference in the schools for certain books and passages from the *Aeneid* also accounts for the hold they continued to have on the imagination and consequently their presence in the mock heroic or comic epic.

The remaining two chapters, 4 and 5, turn to the site of the strongest Virgilian engagement: the idyll. Although the idyll is now a defunct genre, it enjoyed widespread popularity in the eighteenth century, beginning with Salomon Gessner's (1730–88) *Idyllen* of 1756. Of equal or perhaps even greater vigor are the century's accompanying theoretical considerations of the genre. Chapter 4 concentrates on these deliberations because they preserve a certain set of Virgilian associations while shaping them to suit the newer interests in nature and grafting on to the idyll a preference for nature in the Greek guise of Theocritus. As with the Laocoon tradition, the theoretical debate preserves a certain Virgilian influence while facilitating its distancing from the texts themselves. Chapter 5 then looks at the evidence for a continued presence of Virgil in idyllic literature, broadly conceived. As one or another instance may seem forced, I have given a large number in order to demonstrate that there are sufficient occurrences to warrant some explanation of their presence. This explanation revolves around the developing tension between the naive and the sentimental, both in the theoretical debate and in the literary production. The idyll acts as a vehicle that provides the imagination with images of nature and its close relation to ancient Greece that seem adequate to the theoretical expectations of nature and antiquity. However, the growing suspicion less of the pastoral world's veracity than of its attainability, its relation to the present, results in the demand that wherever the naive is deemed to be present, the sentimental must be absent, although the dynamic tension between the two is the necessary precondition for the naive. In the articulation of this pastoral world and of its inner dynamic we may trace a perceptible, though attenuated, Virgilian strand.

Notes

[1] Modern scholarship dealing with Virgil in a general way in the eighteenth century is slight. It tends to reiterate at regular intervals the conclusion that Virgil is of steadily diminishing importance to the writers in the eighteenth century. In 1995, Maria Erxleben finds herself confirming Anton Gail's opinion of half a century previously: Erxleben, "Goethe und Vergil," in *Vergil: Antike Weltliteratur in ihrer Entstehung und Nachwirkung*, ed. Johannes Irmscher (Amsterdam: Hakkert, 1995), 131–48. Gail had set out to document the engagement of German authors with Latin literature, but found little enough to document. With the exception of the elegy, the title of Gail's essay indicates his findings: "Im Schatten der Griechen: Die augusteische Dichtung, vor allem Vergil und Horaz im deutschen Schriftum um 1800," in *On Romanticism and the Art of Translation: Studies in Honor of Edwin Hermann Zeydel*, ed. Gottfried F. Merkel (Princeton: Princeton UP, 1956), 141–62. Gail concludes: "Vergils jahrhundertealte anregende Funktion verblasste vor dem Originalgenie Homers" (160). Slightly earlier Wolfgang Schadewaldt had arrived at a similar conclusion in his essay "Goethes Beschäftigung mit der Antike," the afterword to Ernst Grumach's encyclopaedic collection of Goethe's references to ancient authors, *Goethe und die Antike* (Berlin: Walter de Gruyter & Co., 1949), 2: 971–1050. The "Antike" referred to is generally Greek antiquity. With regard to Goethe's view of the Latin heritage, Schadewaldt notes Goethe's agreement with the prevailing attitude of his day in Germany and his not always "segensreich" break with the common European Latin tradition (978). Grumach's collection and Schadewaldt's essay far surpass an earlier survey by William Jacob Keller who, nonetheless, arrived in 1916 at a similar conclusion in his study "Goethe's Estimate of the Greek and Latin Writers," *Bulletin of the University of Wisconsin*, Philology

and Literature Series 6 (1916), 1–129. Earlier studies largely amount to compilations of "An- und Nachklänge," sometimes suggestive, sometimes not, but as a whole lacking a connective interpretation: Oskar Brosin, *Parallelstellen aus modernen Dichtern zu Virgils Aeneis*, Progr. Nr. 163 (Liegnitz: H. Krumbhaar, 1880) and Theodor Oesterlen, "Vergil in Schillers Gedichten," in *Studien zu Vergil und Horaz* (Tübingen: 1885).

[2] The focus on Homer gave rise to general studies such as Georg Finsler's *Homer in der Neuzeit von Dante bis Goethe* (Leipzig & Berlin: 1912). Jacob Friedrich Braitmeier provides an earlier treatment of some of the same ground, "Über die Schätzung Homers und Virgils von C. Scaliger bis Herder," in *Korrespondenz-Blatt für Gelehrten und Realschulen Württembergs*, 32 (1885): 454–68, 502–3; 33 (1886): 84–92, 121–29, 271–94, 364–73, and 525–33. See Volker Riedel's massive study of the German relation to antiquity from the Renaissance to the present for a more general overview and in the excellent bibliography a sense of the scope of scholarly engagement with the topic as well as more generally of the preponderance of the interest in relations to Greece: *Antikerezeption in der deutschen Literatur vom Renaissance-Humanismus bis zur Gegenwart* (Stuttgart: Metzler, 2000). For a shorter account of this phenonemon in this period see Joachim Wohlleben, "Germany 1750–1830," in *Perceptions of the Ancient Greeks*, ed. K. J. Dover (Oxford: Blackwell, 1992), 170–202.

[3] Walther Rehm, *Griechentum und Goethezeit: Geschichte eines Glaubens* (Leipzig: Dieterich'sche Verlagsbuchhandlung, 1936), 16; also 12 & 18. Rehm's account proved very successful, with three reprintings, one in 1938, and two after the war in 1952 and 1968. See also Riedel, *Antikerezeption*, 112.

[4] See Riedel, *Antikerezeption*, 430–53.

Acknowledgments

IT IS MY PLEASURE TO THANK the many friends and colleagues who have given freely of their support and encouragement during the writing of this book. In particular I should like to express my gratitude to Theodore Ziolkowski for the interest he has shown in this work and the kindness and criticism he has shown throughout. For the generous financial support that made much of the research for this book possible, I should also like to express my thanks to the Social Sciences and Humanities Research Council of Canada and to the German Academic Exchange Service. And finally I should like to thank the staff of the Prussian State Library in Berlin for their kind assistance with my many requests.

G. A.
July 2005

Abbreviations

The following abbreviations have been used in the text:

Aen.   *Aeneid,* by Publius Vergilius Maro. In *Opera,* ed. R. A. B. Mynors. Oxford: Oxford UP, 1969. Cited according to book and verse number. Translations are from W. F. Jackson Knight's translation (Baltimore: Penguin, 1958) unless otherwise noted.

Ec.   *Eclogues,* by Publius Vergilius Maro. In *Opera,* ed. R. A. B. Mynors. Oxford: Oxford UP, 1969. Cited according to eclogue and verse number. Translations are from C. Day Lewis's translation (London: Jonathan Cape, 1963) unless otherwise noted.

Ge.   *Georgics,* by Publius Vergilius Maro. In *Opera,* ed. R. A. B. Mynors. Oxford: Oxford UP, 1969. Cited according to Georgic and verse number. Translations are from J. W. Mackail's translation (New York: Random House, 1934) unless otherwise noted.

GKA   Winckelmann, Johann Joachim. *Geschichte der Kunst des Alterthums.* Wiener Ausgabe 1934. Repr. Darmstadt: Wissenschaftliche Buchgesellschaft, 1972.

GSW   Goethe, Johann Wolfgang. *Sämtliche Werke nach Epochen seines Schaffens.* Edited by Karl Richter with the assistance of Herbert G. Göpfert, Norbert Miller, and Gerhard Sauder. (Münchener Ausgabe.) 21 vols. Munich: Hanser, 1985–98.

HW   Herder, Johann Gottfried. *Werke.* Edited by Martin Bollacher, Jürgen Brummack, Christoph Bultmann, Ulrich Gaier, Gunter E. Grimm, Hans Dietrich Irmscher, Rudolf Smend, and Johannes Wallmann. 10 vols. Frankfurt am Main: Deutscher Klassiker Verlag, 1985–2000.

NGW   Winckelmann, Johann Joachim. *Gedanken über die Nachahmung der griechischen Werke in der Malerei und Bildhauerkunst.* Edited by Ludwig Uhland. Stuttgart: Reclam, 1990.

NKS   Nietzsche, Friedrich. *Sämtliche Werke.* Kritische Studienausgabe. Edited by Giorgio Colli und Mazzino Montinari. 1967–77. 15 vols. Repr. Munich: Deutscher Taschenbuch Verlag; Berlin; New York; de Gruyter, 1999.

O   Heyne, Christian Gottlob, ed. *Opera*, by Publius Vergilius Maro. 2nd rev. ed. 4 vols. Leipzig: Caspar Fritsch, 1787–89.

*Sch*W   Schiller, Johann Christoph Friedrich. *Werke*. Nationalausgabe, im Auftrag des Goethe- und Schiller-Archivs, des Schiller-Nationalmuseums und der Deutschen Akademie. Gen. ed. Julius Petersen and Gerhard Fricke. 35 vols. Weimar: Böhlaus Nachfolger, 1943–.

1: Virgil: A Pentheus to the Germans in the Eighteenth Century?

Virgil and Parnassus

PENTHEUS, KING OF THEBES by descent from Cadmus and Harmonia, resisted the encroachment into his dominion of a new god, Dionysus, and his worship but the citizens, led by his mother Agave, were much attracted to this new deity and his cult. They abandoned the city to celebrate the novel rites in the countryside and on the mountains. Pentheus, still resisting but curious, followed the Bacchants and climbed a tree to observe in secret the strange and intrusive rituals. There he was discovered and torn limb from limb by an enraged band of Bacchants led by Agave. Flaunting the head, she returned to the city where the madness fell from her eyes and she became aware of the enormity of what she had done. She and the entire royal family were condemned to leave Thebes and wander as outcasts, while the city was left leaderless and decapitated.

The story of Pentheus serves as an analogy for the reception of Virgil in Germany during the eighteenth century. By then Virgil had been the sovereign of the poetic kingdom by long tenure and honorable descent; Parnassus, the haunt of the Muses, was, in one version of the myth, where the fateful confrontation between Pentheus and the new god of ecstasy and sponsor of a novel kind of poetry had taken place. The record of the dethronement of Virgil, the old lord of the poetic kingdom, and all it meant for the Germans of the time can be considered in three ways. Virgil as sovereign is the lord of epic, the primary literary genre. He is first deprived of his preeminence in this field as the understanding of the genre and its claims to priority are reshaped. But the underlying source of the dissatisfaction with the old order of the poetic kingdom is deeper than literary culture and lies in the recognition and discovery of a new and powerful deity — Nature. The assimilation of this new deity, with Homer as its high priest, is realized only with the dismemberment (the sparagmos) and partition of the Virgilian legacy; only later in the twentieth century do the Germans recognize what the dethronement of Virgil meant both for literature and for themselves.

To turn to the first of these analogies, Parnassus, the poetic kingdom, Virgil's realm: the record of this kingdom is largely historical and that in three senses of the word for the purposes of this investigation. In the first sense it follows the history of poetics. The construction of the poetic throne that Virgil occupied began well before his time through the codification of the literary canon by the scholar poets in Alexandria with epic as the most prestigious of literary creations and, after Homer's tour de force, the most difficult too. Virgil, and Latin literature more generally with the Neoterics, the "new poets," took his bearings from the writings of the Alexandrians. Virgil framed his *Aeneid* within this context in the hope of achieving for Latin literature a successful epic, the mark of which is its acceptance as *the* national poem. And so it was received at the time. Even during its composition the epic became famous. Suetonius, Virgil's biographer, reports that Augustus commanded the poet to read from the unfinished epic. And when Virgil died unexpectedly in 19 B.C., Augustus countermanded Virgil's deathbed order that the incomplete epic be destroyed. Roman delight at Virgil's achievement, even as he was composing it, is palpable in the famous lines by Propertius from 26 B.C.:

> *Cedite Romani scriptores, cedite Grai:*
> *nescioquid maius nascitur Iliade.* (2.34.65–66)[1]

> [Give way, Roman, yield, Greek writers:
> I know of something being born greater than the Iliad.]

The paths of criticism that Propertius laid out here have long remained valid, not simply for the *Aeneid* but for Virgil as a whole. In the subsequent intellectual and literary tradition, Virgil became first the writer of an epic, the *Aeneid*, before all else, while secondly the measure of epic was the comparison to Homer. The comparison naturally did not remain static as subsequent ages' understanding of Homer and familiarity with him likewise underwent change. Homer retained respect as the acknowledged father of poetry but as a figure retreated behind Virgil in later antiquity and the Middle Ages, until the early modern period unabashedly granted Virgil sole possession of the poetic throne.[2] Already a little over a century after Virgil's death, Quintilian, when writing about the education of the young, placed him virtually level with Homer for all practical purposes and in stature, of all the poets, either Greek or Latin, second only to Homer himself, but not at all by much (*haud dubie proximus*, 10. 1. 86, see also 12. 11. 26). By the Renaissance, the humanist Marco Vida (c. 1485–1566), the author of the Renaissance poetics *De arte poetica* for the instruction of the young (1527), dispensed with such timidity and exclaimed:

> *Unus hic ingenio præstanti, gentis Achivæ*
> *Divinos vates longe superavit, & arte,*
> *Aureus, immortale sonans. stupet ipsa, pavetque,*
> *Quamvis ingentem miretur Græcia Homerum.*[3]

> [There is one excelling in talent, and in art
> golden, in sound immortal, surpassing by far
> the divine bards of the Greeks. Hellas stands pale
> and amazed, even though it marvels at great Homer.]

He finished with the admonishment that it is illicit for a poet to hope to better Virgil (*sperare nefas sit vatibus ultra;* 1.177).

In addition to becoming the epitome of the poet, the figure of Virgil also acquired other attributes. As was often the case with great men, portents of future distinction accompanied his birth. Popular lore soon added various mythical elements so that Virgil eventually became a magician.[4] As Homer before him, Virgil also became a sage, a philosopher with insight and knowledge into all areas of human endeavor. For the Middle Ages the culmination of this process is most familiar from Dante. Virgil could guide Dante through Hell and Purgatory not only because the rhapsode was a philosopher of universal knowledge, but also because his epic told the tale of the founding of the worldly universal city, the precursor to the universal religion with its seat under the pope in Rome. Although Virgil for later antiquity, and for the Middle Ages as well as for the Renaissance, acquired a significance that far exceeded the narrower scope of epic, the foundation for this growth was laid in the status of epic and the *Aeneid*.

Of more immediate relevance, the poetics of the early modern period continued to grant epic pride of place among the genres. Thus whenever a critic wished to state his general views on poetry, he had inevitably to give an account of its most important genre, epic. The continued relevance of this tradition for German criticism in the early decades of the eighteenth century may be seen in Gottsched's poetics. On the strength of his poetics, the *Critische Dichtkunst*, first published in 1730, Johann Christoph Gottsched (1700–1766) became the literary arbiter of the early Enlightenment in the German-speaking world for the next two decades. He introduces his chapter on epic with the sentence: "Nunmehro kommen wir an das rechte Hauptwerk und Meisterstück der ganzen Poesie, ich meyne an die Epopee oder an das Heldengedicht."[5]

The other important parameter for the reception of Virgil, which we may similarly trace back to antiquity, was Virgil's close association with the Augustan settlement of the civil wars and the effective end of the Republic with the establishment of the Principate after the battle of Actium in 31 B.C. Virgil extolled the return of peace, the benefits of good government, and the dependence of these on the political order. In his final poem, the *Aeneid*, he became the poet of the new imperial dispensation under Augustus. As all of Virgil's three poems, the *Eclogues*, the *Georgics* and, above all, the *Aeneid*, provide support for this tendency; it seems a constant of his development and thus the name Virgil evokes, in addition to the immediate association with epic, the attendant notion of poet together with prince engaging in a single national enterprise. While modern scholars of what is sometimes called the "Harvard School" of Virgilian criticism have recently called into question the degree to which Virgil's undoubted association with and proximity to the Augustan establishment may also be taken for wholehearted support for Augustus and his policies — the theory of Virgil's two voices first put forward by Adam Parry in 1963[6] — for the period we are investigating it is the Virgil of the Augustan reading that dominates.[7] For the eighteenth century, both parts of the fourth-century Servius's pithy summary of Virgil's purposes in writing the *Aeneid* remain valid without further ado: *intentio Vergilii haec est: Homerum imitari et Augustum laudare a parentibus* (Virgil's purpose is this: to imitate Homer and to praise Augustus through his ancestors).[8]

At the outset of the eighteenth century, the Germans regarded Virgil no differently than did the rest of Europe in the early modern period: Virgil, both the poet and his texts, are the epitome of literary achievement according to the canons of taste and humanistic learning. In the late Renaissance Julius Caesar Scaliger (1484–1558) had carried the exaltation of Virgil to such lengths that his treatment of poets in book V of his *Poetices libri septem* (1561) became unbalanced. Roughly half the book is devoted to the comparison of Virgil with other poets, and of this, again roughly half is devoted to the comparison with Homer, much to Homer's detriment. Scaliger too exemplifies the dominance of epic and of the epic poets in the poetological thinking of the time. He begins his consideration of poets by announcing that we must start by comparing the Greek and Latin poets, but passes straightaway to the essential comparison: *Ac primum quidem primos, Homerum atque Vergilium* (but first the foremost among them, Homer and Virgil).[9] At the comparison's conclusion Scaliger states the lesson budding young poets should draw from it: *Cuius exemplum regula principium finis esse debet nobis Maro* (4:300; For us, Virgil [i.e. Publius Vergilius Maro] must be the model and rule, the beginning and the end). He continues by paraphrasing a quip reported by Cicero that poets do not seem to use a language ordinary mortals can understand so that it becomes: other writers, apart from Virgil, use some language other than the language of poetry (4:300–302). So immoderate is Scaliger's partiality for Virgil that his latest editors coin for it the term "Maronolatrie."[10]

Elsewhere, in the early modern period, Virgil enjoyed an immense prestige as well. In 1687 in the France of Louis XIV, Charles Perrault (1628–1703) announced in the poem, *Le Siècle de Louis le Grand* — the poem that opened the literary feud known as the *Querelle des anciens et des modernes* — that he approached the ancients "sans plier les genoux" (not on bended knee). In keeping with the cliché of his age, he picked Augustan Rome as the paradigmatic time in antiquity for the point of comparison with the France of Louis XIV.[11] Since citing the Augustan age was simply a shorthand means of referring to all that is best in antiquity by referring to its zenith, Perrault was also at liberty to consider whatever was deemed praiseworthy in the Greek half of antiquity. He made use of this liberty to castigate Homer among the poets while conceding that Virgil "mérite des Autels" (is deserving of altars).[12] Praise for antiquity came to settle on Rome while the Greeks came to be the favored object of reproach.

Similarly in England it was a mark of Virgil's stature that John Dryden (1631–1700), the preeminent poet of Restoration England, devoted his later years to the translation of all of Virgil's three poems (1697), a task presumably merited for one whom he called "my Divine Master."[13] We may again see the primacy of epic in Dryden's different treatment of the prefatory material for each of the three poems. For the first two, the *Eclogues* and the *Georgics*, he wrote perfunctory dedications to the patron, only six or seven pages in length, and largely encomiastic in nature, and left the task of writing more substantial introductory essays for these poems to others. The *Aeneid*, however, he reserved for himself; he felt his dedication was by itself a sufficient introduction and it runs to some eighty pages in length.

In Germany, the literary opinion of the philosopher and mathematician Leibniz, a figure of universal genius and the only German of his age to attract attention beyond the boundaries of the Holy Roman Empire, also conforms to this pattern. Among his numerous other activities he also found time to read works of literature. Two of his favorite authors were Horace and Virgil, and from the latter he could quote lengthy passages until the end of his life.[14] In the *Anmerckungen bey den Neuen Zeitungen gelehrter Sachen vom Jahr 1715*, his criticisms of François de Fénelon's (1651–1715) *Télémaque* (1699) led him to reflect on Homer and Virgil:

> Mit dem Homero kan es beßer angehn, weil ich selbst dafür halte, daß Homerus die Götter und Helden lächerlich vorgestellet, indem er nicht wie Virgilius für einen Augustum etwas Majestatisches [*sic*], sondern für den griechischen Pöbel, denen er seine aufsaze vorgelesen, etwas lustiges machen wollen. Inzwischen zeigt er an vielen ohrten seinen großen Geist, und schwinget sich hoch wenn er will.[15]

In keeping with the notion that reflection on epic inevitably entails a consideration of Virgil with reference to Homer, we see in Leibniz the dominance of Virgil's position: namely, the discussion of Homeric epic occurs under the presumption of Virgilian epic as the standard. Whatever the value of the specific comment on Virgil in Leibniz and others, the name of Virgil serves as shorthand for a writer to indicate his position on the contentious literary issues of the day and on matters of taste and morals.

However far such general deliberations may take us from the sphere of epic, the Virgil on whom they are hung remains the Virgil of epic, the Virgil of the *Aeneid*. The recognition that Virgil's reputation and the broader claims on his behalf stem from epic and its critical tradition should not, however, obscure the fact that the eighteenth century encountered Virgil in other cultural and intellectual milieus. In the eighteenth century, as in previous ages, there were many "Virgils" at work, not only one. In addition to Virgil the cultural figure of grand epic and its sweeping literary and cultural historiography, there is also the Virgil of the *Eclogues* and the *Georgics*, of pastoral and didactic poetry, the Virgil of the schoolboy, of language learning, and of rhetoric. To some extent, these Virgils overlap, although the Virgil of the literary tradition remains the dominant one in the sense that the changes that occur there in the estimation of Virgil, whether he is a good or a bad poet, and on what grounds, determine Virgil's overall reputation in the eighteenth century. The other Virgils, however, existing within distinct yet related traditions, ensure that Virgil continues to be a powerful influence. They function, to continue the analogy to Pentheus, once the head is removed, as dismembered limbs.

Leibniz's passage also introduces the second sense of the word historical, that is, the problem of history that comes to light as one of the results of the *Querelle des anciens et des modernes*. Leibniz's Homer sits there in his wig and powder and condescends to the common folk. Unfortunately his poems became as rude or as "lächerlich" as they were. His gods, as Plato had not failed to note, were disreputable and offensive to pious feeling, and his heroes were, for a later age, brutal and entirely too common for their noble stature — Achilles abandons the Greek army to slaughter, abuses the corpse of Hector, and prepares his own meals, while Odysseus lives with a swineherd and disguises himself as a beggar, and so on. Virgil, on the other hand, possessed a high moral purpose and the dignity to match — therefore his epic is better. If, however, one begins to suspect that Homer does not sit there in wig and powder, what he does wear and how his garb is to be determined become pressing matters.

The celebrated *Querelle* that began dramatically with Perrault's reading of his poem, *Le Siècle de Louis le Grand* before the French Academy in 1687 and the umbrage of Nicolas Boileau (1636–1711) was, in truth, but a further, though heated, round in the long-standing dispute about the relation of the modern cultures to antiquity, principally Latin antiquity.[16] In some ways it is the lesser known, second round of the *Querelle* in 1714 in France, also called the *Querelle d'Homère* because of its narrower focus on Homer, and with Madame Anne de Dacier (1654–1720) for the ancients and Antoine Houdar(t) de la Motte (1672–1731) for the moderns, that interests us more. This is not so because the nature of the arguments they and others put forward on behalf of their respective sides are substantially new, indeed they are compilations of earlier positions, but rather because the compilation clarifies and makes succinct the nature of the historical problem the Enlightenment finds itself confronted with when it reads Homer. The champions of the ancients rested their argument on the weight of two thousand years of authority that the works of the ancients provided the timeless model for all subsequent nations and times. Their opponents, the moderns, compared instead the advances of their own time, particularly in the sciences, and asked whether such advances might not be found in other fields of endeavor. They postulated a notion of progress from the comparison of their time to antiquity but one that implicitly required a more precise historical undergirding in order to explain what the nature of this progress is and how it is deemed to occur over time. Simply enumerating the achievements of the contemporary age states the end result of the historical process for the moment; it does not explain how it has come to be.

However, both sides, ancient and modern, met on the grounds of the shared conviction that the increasingly rationalist canons of taste and nature remain universally valid. History was a question of the degree to which a given age or culture succeeds in realizing these standards, an essentially cyclical view of history. From this perspective, Perrault's comparison of "le siècle de LOUIS au beau siècle d'Auguste" was eminently reasonable. Similarly, the comparison of two authors, in our case Homer and Virgil, but also many others both ancient and modern, was a standard form of criticism. However, precisely what was understood under "la politesse" or "le bon goût" was taken largely from the world of the Baroque court, that of Louis XIV. Consequently, when the moderns turned to the ancients their gaze came to rest more on Greeks rather than Romans since the works of Homer or of Theocritus provided many instances that could neither be squared with the canons of taste nor the expectations of nature, except under the supposition that it was a rude and savage nature, and not one to be imitated. The ancients, for their part, had little to offer in response; abuse of the interrogators and the insistence that two and a half thousand years of continuous tradition cannot be wrong — "Tous les Geants, j'appelle ainsi tous les grands hommes depuis vingt-cinq ou vingt-six siecles [*sic*] bien-loin de déclarer la guerre à Homere, l'ont honoré, l'ont respecté, l'ont reconnu generalement [*sic*] pour le Pere [*sic*] de la Poësie [*sic*],"[17] (all the giants, this is what I call all the great men who, far from declaring war on Homer, have for the past twenty five or six centuries honored, respected, and generally recognized him as the father of poetry) — are not arguments.

More promising is the observation that the ancient authors wrote for audiences and circumstances different than those of today. This may accurately describe the ancient author's situation, yet it does little to address the nub of the moderns' problem. It neither offers a means for understanding the presuppositions that shape the ancient author's different world, nor establishes a method for discerning the processes of change that would eventually result in the contemporary world, nor, finally, does it reconcile this historical change to the age's espousal of universal principles.[18] On the one side, the ancients can appear as parrots who simply cite the authorities, while on the other, the moderns, particularly de la Motte, emerge as philistines.

Once the heat of the debate recedes, a "both . . . and" compromise results as the anonymous article on Homer (1735) in the vast half-Baroque, half-Enlightenment encyclopedia, Zedler's *Universal-Lexikon*, illustrates:

> Uberhaupt ist gewiß, daß Homerus in Beschreibung so wohl derer Götter, als Menschen, sich nach denen Sitten seiner Zeiten gerichtet, da eine gewiße, rohe und wilde Art, mit grosser Stärke und Unerschrockenheit begleitet, die vortrefflichste Tugend und Vollkommenheit ausmachen muste. Wenn man also dieses Dichters Beschreibungen gegen unsere heutige Sitten und Lebens-Art, oder auch wohl gegen die gesunde Vernunft halten will, muß man an ihm nothwendig sehr viel auszusetzen finden.[19]

Somewhat schizophrenically, the two sides fall neatly into two separate sentences, each containing key terms of the Enlightenment. While there are failings in Homer's descriptions of gods and men, these do not belong properly to the most excellent virtue, "vortreffliche Tugend," and thus to perfection, "Vollkommenheit," but rather to the "wildness" or "savageness" (since "wild" contains both meanings) with which the imagination of the Homeric age pictured them. Equally, in the second sentence, sound reason, "gesunde Vernunft," or, as it is glossed, the "Sitten," "les mœurs," the manners of our age, must necessarily "notwendig" take exception to these failings. Yet when the age "removes" the traits and actions offensive to sound reason, little remains of the Homeric hero worth endorsing. The hopeful connection between the two sentences, the "wenn man also," suggests a logical progression from one sentence to the next where contradiction would be closer to the mark.

The problem is not solvable in the terms posed and must await further developments in the eighteenth century's historical understanding. The eighteenth century will take up the task with great gusto and produce innumerable histories on all manner of topics as well as reflections on history.[20] It will also engage figures from across the intellectual spectrum as well as some of the best known figures of the century, such as Giambattista Vico (1668–1744), Voltaire (1694–1778), David Hume (1711–76), Edward Gibbon (1737–94), Herder, and Schiller. In the uneasy truce that follows the *Querelle* (uneasy because it leaves unsolved the pressing questions it broaches), the two sides will engage in the common historical enterprise so that the older labels become confused. With respect to the question of the relation to ancient literature, the fruits of this development in Germany will emerge most forcefully at the century's close in the writings of Schiller and Friedrich Schlegel. Schiller in *Über naive und sentimentale Dichtung* (1795–96) and Schlegel in *Über das Studium der Griechischen Poesie* (1797), both attempt aesthetic systems based on modes rather than on the genres of older poetics. Both present traits, attributes that are historically grounded and become concepts through which particular times, poets and literary forms are to be understood.[21]

Quite apart from its far-ranging implications for many topics, one of the consequences of this larger matter of the elaboration of historical understanding in the eighteenth century was the emergence of a new Greece, radically different from and opposed to the Latin world so familiar to the Renaissance and the Baroque era. For them, Greek and Latin were two halves of the one antiquity: what the Greeks began, the Latins continued and brought to completion. We may thus equally well speak of the creation of a new Greece, since it is only with the deepening historical sense that the contours of the new Greece could emerge from behind the Latin shadow and take on firmer shape and color. It requires a sense of how to give substance to the notion that an earlier age fashioned its view of the world according to different presuppositions. It involves the reading of texts less for edification than for information about the world of their composition and also the development of methods to weigh and critique the new information extracted. And finally it necessitates a new purpose, soon found in the notion of a "nation" and its continuous or progressive cultural life. The relevance of all this to Virgil is that it results in the wholesale reconceptualization and reordering of the comparison to Homer such that, particularly in German eyes, Virgil will increasingly become a distant, embarrassing, and failed figure. Just as the development of a more historical and favorable appreciation of Homer only occurred through a reexamination of Greek culture more generally, a similar and opposite reappraisal of Latin culture accompanies the German estrangement from Virgil.

The third sense here of the word historical is more narrowly the history of Virgilian scholarship. So long as Virgil sits on his poetic throne and forms a central part of the grand literary tradition, intellectuals concerned about cultural matters and writers interested in taking part in wider-ranging aesthetic arguments will have an opinion about Virgil. Once, however, Virgil is evicted from the throne, a process that only occurred by degrees, culminating at the end of the eighteenth century, concern for him is committed increasingly to the care of scholars. The reason for introducing this matter of Virgilian scholarship now is twofold.

In his most recent book on Virgil, Richard Thomas begins with an exploration of how any private reader's attitude, shaped in part by his age, informs his reading of the poet.[22] By acknowledging his, Thomas's, motives, he wishes to assist his reader in better assessing the arguments and evidence he adduces in support of his position for an oppositional reading of Virgil — in opposition, that is, to an Augustan reading, be it strong or soft. My view of Virgil is dependent on twentieth-century Virgilian scholarship, since it is this view of the twentieth-century Virgil that brings into relief the older eighteenth-century figure. The frequent instances on which I have occasion to refer to twentieth-century scholarship serve not as a corrective to the eighteenth century's view of Virgil; they are the means rather of throwing the German eighteenth century's response to Virgil into sharper focus, of indicating hermeneutic potentialities within Virgil. This approach risks so distorting the eighteenth century's view of Virgil and ours of its reconstruction here that it might render the whole enterprise worthless. Whether this is the case the reader must judge from what follows. As a more general comment I would note that the initial impulse for twentieth-century Virgilian scholarship comes from and is shaped by the long digestion and popularization in the nineteenth century of the view of Virgil that first crystallized at the end of the eighteenth century in Germany.

Modern Virgilian scholarship starts with Richard Heinze's book *Virgils epische Technik* in 1903.[23] In the first half of the century, the "European School" of interpretation is largely a German affair with such names as Eduard Norden (1903), Theodor Haecker (1931), Friedrich Klingner (1943), Viktor Pöschl (1950), and Karl Büchner (1955). They tended to lay stress on Virgil's vision of Rome, its restoration of peace, of *humanitas* and *ordo* after the social and political upheavals of a century of intermittent civil war from the Gracchi brothers in 133 B.C. to Augustus's triumph at the battle of Actium in 31 B.C. It calls for no great insight to divine a partial motivation for the concentration on Virgil as a hopeful voice in response to the catastrophes of German history in the first half of the twentieth century and the need of the early Federal Republic to emphasize the return of order and stability in the humane and liberal traditions of the Enlightenment.[24] Nor does it surprise to learn that those who invest Virgil with the weight and scope of the title "Vater des Abendlandes"[25] occupy the conservative side of the political spectrum, though they run its gamut from liberal and Christian humanists such as Theodor Haecker to supporters of fascism such as Hans Oppermann.[26]

The powerful restatements of this view in the aftermath of the Second World War: in the second of the many editions of Klingner's *Römische Geisteswelt* (1952), in Büchner's book-length article on Virgil for the Pauly-Wissowa *Realencyclopädie* (1955), and in Vinzenz Buchheit's *Vergil über die Sendung Roms* (1963), did not have to wait long for a response. It came from America (the "Harvard School" referred to above) and deliberated on the significance of troubling details. It examined such questions as the hesitation of the Golden Bough, the magical key for Virgil's entry into the underworld, in falling into Aeneas's outstretched hand, or the meaning of his exiting the underworld though the Gate of Ivory, the gate of false dreams, after Anchises' "Heldenschau" of the heroes of Roman history, or the interpretation of Aeneas's killing of Turnus with *furiis* (12. 946), that is, justified wrath or fury to the point of madness. It arrived at the view that Virgil was pessimistic about the realization of the ideals and hopes he had vested in the Augustan imperial settlement in the *Aeneid:* "It is this perception of Roman history as a long Pyrrhic victory of the human spirit that makes Virgil his country's truest historian."[27] To indicate with the single word "Vietnam" the contemporary source for the critics' skepticism oversimplifies wider and longer maturing cultural shifts, though it does point to its trenchant emergence in America in the sixties and seventies. Though the intervening decades may have taken the heat from the difference of opinion, they have done nothing to remove its geographical distinctness. The Harvard School remains largely an interest of English-language scholarship: however, British scholarship tends to take a middle position toward it, and even within American Virgilian scholarship itself, it was always but one strand. The title, for example, of Brook Otis's 1964 book, *Virgil: A Study in Civilized Poetry* speaks for itself. German scholarship, however, has by and large remained unconvinced. Thomas acknowledges only Werner Suerbaum among the Germans as having taken up pessimistic perspectives,[28] while the Suerbaum of 1999 characterizes the earlier Suerbaum of 1981 as "mit Sympathien für den pessimistischen 'Harvard'-Vergil."[29]

A neat inverse relation obtains between historical circumstance and interpretation in these two schools: the brightest, most hopeful Augustan Virgil arises from a society beset by all manner of turmoil and about to experience its darkest hour, while the most pessimistic Virgil of doom emerges from a society that, though the sixties and Vietnam represent a turning point in the post-War era, nonetheless enjoyed a comparatively stable political and social order and, arguably, unparalleled prosperity in the decades after the Second World War. The distinctive mark of twentieth-century Virgilian reception would seem to be that it does not conform to the historical principle of Virgilian reception that Robert Graves notes: "whenever a golden age of stable government, full churches, and expanding wealth dawns among the Western nations, Virgil always returns to supreme favour."[30]

The comment on the dispute in the latest edition of *The Oxford Classical Dictionary*, "Naturally, simple appeal to the text or its historical setting cannot settle which of these approaches is adopted," points oddly to a shared attitude to the text and its historical setting that marks both sides as the offspring of Heinze.[31] Heinze wrote in response to the received view in his day of Virgil as Homer's plagiarist, a clever versifier of no originality, the inventor of at most a hero who was a prig and a milksop, and the source of much maudlin gloom. This view in turn stems from German Romanticism, with such as August Wilhelm Schlegel (1767–1845). He, a scholar and theorist, while deliberating in his *Vorlesungen über schöne Literatur und Kunst* at Berlin (1801–4) and pondering Virgil's manifold borrowings from other poets, both Greek and Latin, could only shake his head and consider the poet a "geschickter Mosaikarbeiter"[32] or "ein eklektischer Poet" whose "zusammengeflicktes System" deprived the borrowed material of its "eigentliche Bedeutung."[33]

To refute such views as this in Germany, Heinze published a dry, dense, and meticulous book of several hundred pages devoted to the subject of Virgil's epic technique. The effect of the book, and the source of the immense stimulus it gave to Virgilian studies, is the restoration of a perspective from which Virgil's epic style is anything but a patchwork quilt. The question of its "true meaning" once again becomes a legitimate object of criticism. Heinze specifically omitted the last areas of unusual talent the eighteenth century had conceded to Virgil, namely, language and meter, in order to look instead at the exact construction of the Virgilian narrative. He restores the adjective "learned" to the understanding of Virgil's style, but not, as previously, as simply a matter of rhetoric and grammar.[34] He concludes that Virgil's cobbling together is entirely too extensive and artistically controlled for it to be the product of incompetence.

The question is then, what is this competence, and what does one make of it? To supply this want, numerous others follow in Heinze's wake, for example, Karl Büchner, Theodor Haecker, Friedrich Klingner, and Viktor Pöschl, to mention only a few names. They undertook the task with the advantage of the new analytical tools at their disposal: changed conceptions of the artist and his relation to his work and society, a hundred years of intensive classical scholarship, and, for urgent motive, the shattering effect of the First World War on the intellectual presuppositions and social order of their age. With all these advantages, they are quick to take on what have now become for them the lingering shibboleths of the older criticism. The American school follows in these footsteps to very different conclusions, as we have seen. Michael Putnam, for example, when situating his study of the *Aeneid* (1965) begins with Heinze and passes on to Pöschl so that the reader will have clearly before him his, Putnam's, point of departure.[35] The combined effect of all this work modifies or refutes the earlier estimation of Virgil on every point.

What both sides share is a common method. Heinze disregards the established modes of criticism. He does not engage in source criticism, nor does he wish to regard the author as giving utterance to the life of a people's national culture in the fashion of the Romantics such as A. W. Schlegel, nor does he aspire to demonstrate the author's original genius through aesthetic considerations. These methods he rejects as entirely too subjective and prefers instead the less malleable verities of the historical method: "Dies Buch will nicht Werturteile fällen, sondern historische Tatsachen."[36] Loosely the two halves of his book correspond to the terms "textual analysis" and "inventory of technique." The extended analyses of passages from the *Aeneid* provide the basis for the more generalized conclusions about the elements of Virgil's technique in the second half. Their summarizing character also brings to the fore, in addition to Virgil's aesthetic concerns, "die politischen und moralischen Tendenzen des Dichters auf die Gestaltung des Gedichts."[37] In comparison to what will follow after

Heinze, the final chapter devoted to Virgil's larger aims is modest. Yet his demonstration of the text's detailed construction at many levels, the inventory of Virgil's technique, and his linking of it to Virgil's relation to his historical setting is an approach that remains fundamental to later scholars. Further, the sense of the text's construction and of its entanglement with historical circumstance in Heinze and others reflects, though soberly, the literary modernism then taking shape. Changes in notions of originality and creativity, as well as of allusion, reference, and thus of signification, foster a perspective in which the Neoteric poets appear much more strikingly modern. As the century proceeds, Virgil acquires an increasingly modernist hue. Renewed interrogation of the text drives the successive advances in Virgilian scholarship: that is, attention to allusion and context, structure, symbolism, word patterns, metaphorical usage, narratology, focalization, and subjective style; all lead to a new appreciation of Virgilian language and intertextuality. For example, W. R. Johnson, from whose book *Darkness Visible* (1976) the designations "Harvard" and "European" school come, resorts in passing to such terms as "impressionism" and "expressionism" to capture his sense of Virgilian style. As he obviously does not intend us to read Virgil as either an "impressionist" or an "expressionist,"[38] these terms merely express a sense of Virgil's approximation to a modernist sensibility of a text and its possible functioning.

The second reason for introducing the topic of Virgilian scholarship here is the connection to the eighteenth century alluded to above. The observation that German enthusiasm for Greece occurs simultaneously and in tandem with its estrangement from the Latin heritage has become a relative commonplace. And so too has the notion that this estrangement distinguishes subsequent German intellectual and cultural development from other European cultures. This does not suggest that other nations' estimation of Greek and Latin culture does not also undergo change; it does. Rather, just as the intensity and scope of Hellenism is greatest in Germany and therefore distinctive of it, so too is the derision of Roman achievements. Writing for *Die Zeit*'s special literary supplement for the 2001 Frankfurt book fair, the largest in Germany, Gustav Seibt observes: "Die deutsche Griechenlandmanie war eine geistige Revolution. Sie löste die deutsche Nationalliteratur aus dem kosmopolitisch-europäischen Zusammenhang der lateinischen Überlieferung heraus."[39] Seibt's observation echoes similar comments made by German Virgilian scholars of half a century ago and more.

In passing, these scholars invariably noted the peculiarity of the German attitude towards Virgil and fix its origin in the eighteenth century. Hans Oppermann (1930) views the preference for Homer as a trait of the Germanic peoples generally. Consequently Virgil's displacement is not to be considered as, "sein persönliches Schicksal."[40] Rudolf Borchardt (1930) comments that the cultivation of Virgil remained unbroken in the lands of the Roman Empire. Its old imperial border separating "das Freie Germanien" from the Latin world doubles as a cultural border some seventeen hundred years later when that latter-day "Freie Germanien . . . hat folgerichtig . . . Vergil den Hellenismus und Homer entgegengestellt und sich von ihm losgesprochen."[41] Theodor Haecker (1931) takes umbrage at this earlier method of interpretation: "Eine bloß philologisch-ästhetische Erklärung Vergils und seines Werkes ist ein Falsum, eine Zersetzung des Ganzen, ausgeführt durch zersetzte Geister."[42] The origin of this misapprehension he finds in the German eighteenth century and a defect not of the object beheld, but of the eye of the beholder.[43] The classicist Friedrich Klingner also regards it as all of a piece. If at the turn of the twentieth century Virgil stood at a point "am fernsten" from the Germans, then it is only the distant reflex of a change that began "in der Zeit Herders, Goethes und Niebuhrs."[44] If Herder and Goethe were "mehr oder weniger kühl" towards a poet they preferred left on the shelf, the generation that followed was even more so. "Humboldt, die Romantiker, auch Friedrich August Wolf sind Virgil ohne weiteres abgeneigt."[45] One could add to this list with ease. However, neither the puzzlement at the animadversions of the eighteenth century would change, nor the reasons for it increase. All confirm the change in the eighteenth century and observe the absence of a Virgilian presence in the writers and intellectuals of the final decades of the century. They regard the turn from the Latin poets as integral to the construction of German identity. The use of Latin literature, first, to throw into bold contrast the unique qualities of Greek genius and, second, to emphasize its remove from the Greek, reflects the effort of the Germans to give to themselves their own unique voice. They fail however to give due measure to the lack of difference between Rome and Greece in the eighteenth century. Their remarks presuppose that the eighteenth century thought it self-evident that a choice was to be made between Greece and Rome. It is rather that the eighteenth century is about to discover that the quantitative difference between the two halves of antiquity is also a qualitative difference of increasingly greater and radical significance. In this process the contrast to Rome facilitates the delineation of the newly recovered Greek cultural artifacts. Only then does the need for a choice become clear.

As style has both figured in the revival of Virgilian studies in the twentieth century, through its reassessment by Heinze, and has always been a central element in the estimation of the poet and his works, it provides a ready means for approaching the eighteenth century. In Germany during the eighteenth century the conception of Virgilian style grew progressively narrower. Formerly it offered evidence of Virgil's insight into the human condition and his relevance to the wider community; now it became instead the evidence for his lack of a poetic sensibility and of any deeper significance. Virgil's style seemed increasingly only a rather mechanical application of rhetoric: brilliant perhaps in the virtuosity with which Virgil exploited in Latin the full range of rhetorical devices and developed the resources of the language, but in the end testifying to nothing more than its own linguistic dexterity. What remained to Virgil is an understanding of literary creation as simply a formal exercise. Because of his undoubted skill, it excites a certain emotion, though one empty of signification as no larger purpose animates it.

As we began with Leibniz, we shall at first stay with German philosophers, since they offer a useful antidote to the uniformity and linearity that the following summary of eighteenth-century German views of Virgil of necessity falsely lends to them. Immanuel Kant (1724–1804), in the *Beobachtungen über das Gefühl des Schönen und Erhabenen* (1764), elucidates his views on the artistic quality of the feeling engendered by the representation of vice with the remark, "Überhaupt ist der Held des Homers schrecklich erhaben, des Virgils seiner dagegen edel."[46] Kant's judgment illustrates the view then current from the *Querelle*. Both Achilles and Aeneas may be great heroes. Achilles displays great martial prowess, yet combines it with great cruelty and is therefore "schrecklich" in his sublimity, while Aeneas, by placing his prowess in the service of *pietas*, gives an example of virtue and is thus "edel" in his sublimity. Nor does Kant's estimation of Virgil seem to undergo any radical change with time. He discusses in the introduction to the *Logik* (1800) the dangers before those who pursue "Gelehrsamkeit" and the "Bildung des Geschmacks," and notes that these two pursuits of "Wissenschaft" may degenerate into "Pedanterie und Galanterie." For an antidote to these evils he prescribes "die wahre Popularität." However, to acquire that popularity,

> muß man die Alten lesen, z. B. Cicero's philosophische Schriften, die Dichter Horaz, Virgil u. s. w., unter den Neuern Hume, Schaftsbury u. a. m. Männer, die alle vielen Umgang mit der verfeinerten Welt gehabt haben, ohne den man nicht populär sein kann. Denn wahre Popularität erfordert viele praktische Welt- und Menschenkenntniß, Kenntniß von Begriffen, dem Geschmacke und den Neigungen der Menschen, worauf bei der Darstellung und selbst der Wahl, schicklicher, der Popularität angemessener Ausdrücke beständige Rücksicht zu nehmen ist. (*GS*, 8: 47)

These words betray Kant's age. The language, the associations, the heroes, all come from the middle decades of the eighteenth century. Latin authors can still do duty for the whole of antiquity; there is no need to distinguish the Greeks from them. The English seem to be the sole inhabitants of modernity; one can safely omit any mention of the nation beset by gallantry, France. The polish of worldly refinement as the basis of true popularity, the emphasis on the practical experience of the world of affairs, and, as the final seal of this "Bildung," an elegant diction, are all precepts with which Lord Chesterfield (1694–1773) could concur. They point back to Kant's formative years in the zenith of the German Enlightenment before German

Classicism and Romanticism under the influence of the French Revolution had caused either a thoroughgoing revision of the Enlightenment's ideals or the exploration of new ones.

Yet if Kant represents the received wisdom of this age, it is also in this very selfsame time that one finds the first clear indications of a change. Winckelmann, casting about in 1755 for some means of articulating his vision of the beauty embodied in the Laocoon statue, hit upon the idea of telling his readers what it is not. The true Greek beauty of nature is exactly *not* the beauty that Virgil perceived in it. The small pamphlet, *Gedanken über die Nachahmung der griechischen Werke in der Malerei und der Bildhauerkunst*, with its categorical assurance that the way to greatness lay in the imitation of the Greeks, and a visit to Athens, marked the beginning of the German infatuation with all things Greek and also of a reevaluation of every facet of Greek culture.

Of equal interest is the corollary that Latin culture, here represented by Virgil, must also be reexamined to allow the specifically Greek achievement to emerge from the more general idea of antiquity. It is an undertaking that proceeds not by exploring what is peculiar to the Roman world, but rather according to a method that seeks to show that it does not possess those attributes so prized in the Greek world.[47] The activity of definition moves as much by the comprehension of what something is "not" as by what it is. Latin literature does duty as the paradigmatic contrary to Greek literature, as hate does to love; and there is no interest in what hate might be, beyond detailing the ways in which it is not love.

So sweeping a change occurs only by degrees. Lessing confessed that his feelings of affront at Winckelmann's cavalier treatment of Virgil first moved him to write what became the *Laokoon oder Über die Grenzen der Malerei und Poesie* (1766). And later still, in the 1790s, Schiller admits that he returned seriously to the translation of Virgil to counter the general disrepute into which Virgil had fallen as result of Alois Blumauer's *Virgils Aeneis travestiert* (1784–88). Both of these statements are essentially reactions, in itself an indication that an intellectual interest in the Latin poet was of sufficient oddity to require a defense. One can hardly imagine so unequivocal an assertion in Germany as Voltaire's in France in 1733, "*Homère a fait Virgile*, dit-on; si cela est, c'est sans doute son plus bel ouvrage" (They say, "Homer made Virgil"; if this is so, then it is without doubt his most beautiful work).[48]

Before the middle of the eighteenth century almost every German poet of note either admitted directly that Virgil was integral to his creative work or did so indirectly through the sincerest form of flattery. Although the urbane early Enlightenment poet Friedrich von Hagedorn (1708–54) preferred Horace, he was not opposed to Virgil; the young Pietistic poet Immanuel Jakob Pyra (1715–44) both translated from the *Aeneid* and remained unable to conceive of an epic free of the Virgilian form; Haller, despite his Calvinist doubt about the utility of poetry, deemed Virgil the best poet and the *Georgics* the greatest poem ever; Johann Peter Uz (1720–96), the most reflective of the Anacreontic poets, made skillful use of Virgilian motifs; Gessner also adopted a number of topoi from Virgil in his development of the modern idyll; Maler Müller (1749–1825) and Wieland on occasion rewrote significant portions from the Virgilian poems; a conflation of the *Eclogues* and the *Georgics* formed the basis of Johann Heinrich Voss's (1751–1826) idylls; Goethe, too, was not above suggestive reworkings of Virgilian material; and finally, perhaps most oddly, Novalis can find a Romantic use for Virgil. In this progression there is a clear movement from an explicit engagement and imitation to an implicit and unacknowledged one.

Following the modest Virgilian efflorescence in the earlier part of the century, the precipitous descent to insignificance in the second half is all the more striking; Aristotle could not have found a more exemplary instance of peripeteia. No vast body of literature with a self-evident kinship to the Virgilian corpus proclaims itself. A perusal of the works of Friedrich Gottlieb Klopstock (1724–1803) and Wieland yields no hoard of similarities and allusions, despite the German authors' familiarity with the Virgilian poems: Klopstock adorned his letters as a fashionable young man of literary sophistication with references to Virgil, and Wieland read Latin at the age of eight and Virgil better than his teacher at thirteen.[49] Presumably, Schiller and Gottfried August Bürger (1747–94) offer slightly surer ground, as they were both translators of Virgil and poets in their own right. Indeed, in Schiller's case, he was even a vehement defender of Virgil against the universal ridicule that he attracted as a result of the success of Blumauer's parody of the *Aeneid*. Because of this evident interest in Virgil, the expectation of discovering among such translators and poets as these a more subtle and nuanced reception of Virgil might seem not rash. Bürger employed some words and images from the Dido episode in his *Lenore* (1774) just as Schiller returned to the Laocoon episode; yet overall they are largely silent. Virgil's relative absence in these, his greatest supporters, illustrates that the increasing German distance from Virgil has deeper causes than the merely cyclical movement of literary fashion.

It fell, however, to others, to the Jena Romantics at the century's close, to give the most forceful expression to the new estimation of Virgil. Caroline von Schlegel wrote of the *Aeneid*, after having become acquainted with it for the first time through Voss's 1799 translation, "Niemals habe ich es mir so schlecht denken können. Erstlich dünkt es mich ganz und gar nicht episch — . . . Und das ist dem Homer nachgebildet?"[50] Friedrich Schlegel early on followed the lead of Winckelmann in his manner of argumentation: Greek literature, because it is nature in the round, fully formed, divided into its parts, and yet still a whole, is the measure of all literature, and this perfection of beauty can be grasped viscerally in the imperfection of the Latins. In the Alexandrian period, after the close of classical Greek culture, as the young Schlegel argued in *Von den Schulen der griechischen Poesie* (1794), "Gelehrsamkeit" had come to replace "Schönheit" as the guiding principle of art: "Die Werke der Alexandriner sind zwar trocken, schwerfällig, tot, ohne inneres Leben, Schwung und Größe."[51] While he conceded to this style a certain aesthetic merit, he deemed it ultimately insufficient to nurture creations of true beauty. And, unfortunately for the poets of the Golden Age of Latin Literature, "Der Stil Ovids, Properzens, Virgils ist," he wrote, "im ganzen Alexandrinisch" (*KFS* 1:15). A certain borrowed style is the only trait in Latin literature worthy of notice, though quite why one should exert oneself to remark something of such aesthetic inconsequence does not emerge.

In the choice of style, Schlegel merely took up the last remnant of the older poetics of the Enlightenment and turned it from a source of praise to a cause of blame. Earlier, style had become (although its implications were variously understood) the last means by which a genuine enthusiasm and appreciation for Virgil seemed possible to the Enlightenment. The Virgilian poem in which they found whatever they envisaged under the ideal of style most perfectly realized was the *Georgics*. The *Eclogues*, Virgil's earlier, first set of poems, were of dubious morality, their politics suspect, the pernicious specter of Allegory hung about them; Virgil consistently refused to adhere to the generic limitations of the bucolic, and nature did not emerge from them pure, but obscured, deformed and, worst of all, mannered. True the later *Aeneid* did possess the same musical beauty in its meter as the *Georgics*. Yet its faults were numerous and grave; it suffered from the ballast of plagiarism, pedantry, and a general poverty of invention. It labored in addition under lackluster characters (Dido excepted), the glorification of war, and generic heterogeneity. And finally it praised the destruction of republican freedom under the Principate. In short, nothing could recommend the poem to one who sought genuine feeling, beautifully articulated in a work of creative genius. "Gelehrsamkeit" had polluted the wellsprings of Latin poetry.

The *Georgics*, however, seemed to speak of the taming and beneficial ordering of nature, of the possibility of living in a golden age within it, and did so in a language of perfect harmony and beauty. Joseph Addison (1672–1719), in his introductory essay to Dryden's translation of the *Georgics* (1697), considered it the best of Virgil's poems. After him, England in the eighteenth century succumbed to a Georgic rapture.[52] In Germany, Haller was not slow to follow suit, in which opinion Lessing and Heyne, Virgil's editor in Germany, soon joined him. In Goethe's youthful enthusiasms, Virgil had no place and, when later he found some place for him, the poem to elicit commendation is the *Georgics*. He praised the style of the poem, and, comparing Voss's German verses with the Latin original, found them lacking "den geistigen Abdruck des himmelreinen und schönen Virgils."[53] His praise of Virgil as pure and beautiful was typical of the judgments on the style and general impression of the *Georgics*.

This gradual reduction of the interpretative approach to the Virgilian œuvre to that of style, largely grounded on the *Georgics*, resulted in far too slender a basis for the support of a towering reputation once the consideration of a work's style ceded first place to the pursuit of its elusive spirit according to the temperament of its people and age. Friedrich Schlegel was consistent in working out the implications of this change. While he might in 1794 be prepared to grant an excellence of style to the Alexandrian poets, in *Über das Studium der griechischen Poesie* from the years 1795–97 he was unable to extend that same appreciation of style to Virgil (for Horace, there is an ambiguous exception). He can excuse, but not justify, the excessive admiration for Virgil. He collects and selects from the Greek cornucopia with taste and diligence, yet, "Das Ganze ist ein Stückwerk ohne lebende Organisation und schöne Harmonie, er kann dennoch für den höchsten Gipfel des gelehrten künstlichen Zeitalters der alten Poesie gelten" (*KFS* 1:349). The tepidness of this praise emerges with the further qualification: "Er ist in diesem an sich unvollkommen Stil zwar nicht schlechthin vollkommen, aber doch der trefflichste" (*KFS* 1:349). The work he may have in mind as he wrote this general description is unclear, as the claim can be argued from any of Virgil's poems. Nonetheless, the *Aeneid* seems the most likely candidate. The earlier Renaissance poetics had decreed Virgil the greatest poet, far above Homer, and the *Aeneid* the greatest poem; now Schlegel will make of him the least of poets, and of the *Aeneid*, the greatest of failures.

As time passed, Schlegel merely refined his opinion to render it more consistent and, by the same token, more devastating. In the *Geschichte der Poesie der Griechen und Römer* (1798), he argues that Virgil "an sich aber ist . . . weder vollendet noch klassisch. Die ÄNEIDE ist kein reines, ächtes Epos. Das Rhetorische und Tragische hat man im ganzen und im einzelnen oft bemerkt, und die lyrischen Stellen bieten sich auch sichtbar und zahlreich genug dar" (*KFS* 1:490). From this, one might grasp what true epic is — by inversion. The serene flow of true epic's narrative forbids sophistical linguistic dexterity, and does not permit the awesome, one-sided passion of the stage or the emotional intensity of the lyrical voice.

Virgil's concentration on these aspects makes of his epic a prototype for a second, derivative and false kind of epic: "Mit einem Wort: Virgil hat das Epos rhetorisirt, er hat die erste Epopöe auf den Effekt gemacht. Hiermit ist schon das unpoetische Fundament ausgesprochen."[54] What is different from Homer is non-epic. By reading Virgil to discover that he is not Homer, the high opinion of Homer is confirmed, and proven. The value of reading Racine to prove that he is not Shakespeare seems dubious, and ultimately beside the point; further, that such a method could ever recommend — let alone impose — itself is a matter of some puzzlement.

Yet it is precisely in this manner that Schlegel proceeds. Its force is felt into the twentieth century, though somewhat mitigated by the distinction between primary and secondary epic. Primary epic is epic by anonymous hands, composed from oral sources; secondary epic is the epic of a single author, conscious of working within a written literary tradition. The distinction remains only a scholarly palliative so long as the conviction persists that artificial epic, not springing from the same soil, is not proper epic. C. S. Lewis's preface to Milton (1954) speaks to his sense of its prevalence: "Partly as the result of romantic primitivism a silly habit has grown up of making Homer a kind of norm by which Virgil is to be measured."[55]

In the 1812 lectures on the *Geschichte der Alten und Neuen Literatur*, Friedrich Schlegel returns to the subject of Virgil and the *Aeneid* once again. As in accordance with the principles of Romantic literary historiography at least some scintilla of a people's spirit must shine through in its literature, no matter how foreign to it that garb may be, he acknowledges that the *Aeneid* is "mit Recht Nationalgedicht der Römer" (*KFS* 6:80) because of the quintessential spirit of Roman patriotism that it exudes. No sooner said than hedged. In talent and enthusiasm, Virgil yields to Lucretius and Ovid; the poem is a "vollkommnes Dichterwerk" (*KFS* 6:80), it lacks harmony, the acquired art does not agree with the poet's native talent; language, representation (Darstellung), and structure are deficient. In the eleventh and twelfth lectures Schlegel extends his sights to include the baneful influence of Virgil through the ages; Camões, Tasso, Milton, and Klopstock have all suffered from a deleterious familiarity with Virgil.

Increasingly Schlegel's view of Virgil becomes an adjunct to the writing of literary history. With Schlegel's views on Greek literature long since worked out and metamorphosed into a principle for the organization of literary history, Latin ceases to be the medium through which he works back to reach Athens. It becomes instead the supreme paradigm of a ruined "Nationalpoesie," a poetry that adopts a poetic method alien to its native spirit and so fails to find its own, unique voice (*KFS* 6:130–31). Roman literature stands as a "warnendes Beispiel" (*KFS* 11:136) to the successive ages — the French, sadly, among the modern nations, have, in his opinion, most conspicuously neglected to heed this warning.[56] These thoughts he had earlier detailed with respect to Virgil in *Europa* 1803 (*KFS* 5:38–39). "Da zeigt sich denn ein eignes Phänomen; den hervorgebrachten Werken ist, weil sie nicht gelungen, der Name von Gedichten und Kunstwerken vielleicht mit Recht abzusprechen, . . . Unter diese Klasse der mit ungünstigen Umständen kampfenden und dadurch interessanten Dichter gehört Virgilius" (*KFS* 5:38).[57] The compliment of interesting failure is more apparent than real. If a poet fails to produce works recognizable as poems, then by what right may he lay claim to the title of poet? If the songbird does not sing, how does one know it is a songbird? Virgil becomes in effect a mute nightingale. Schlegel had expressed himself less circumspectly only a few pages beforehand: "ihm selbst [Vergil] mag seine hohe Absicht wohl eine Stelle unter den Dichtern verdienen, wenn gleich sein Werk nicht gelten darf" (*KFS* 5:30). "Mag" does not indicate a suggestion put forward with great conviction. These remarks complete the German dismemberment of Virgil as a poet and through him, in large measure, the Germans' alienation from the Roman experience and ultimately from insight into their own condition.

Schlegel's radical views, or some modified form of them, prevailed in Germany for a century. Barthold Georg Niebuhr (1776–1831), Schlegel's contemporary, detailed in the first volume of his *Römische Geschichte* the "ungünstigen Umstände" with which Virgil wrestled so unhappily, but it is in his lectures delivered at Bonn that Niebuhr distilled the Romantic view for wider consumption. In a few short pages, not only Virgil but the entire literature of the Augustan age are dismissed. With the death of Cicero and Caesar, literature went into decline, and of Virgil:

> Seine Eklogen sind eine nichts weniger als glückliche Nachahmung des Theokrit, sie wollen auf römischem Boden etwas schaffen was nicht da ist. . . . Glücklicher ist sein Lehrgedicht über den Landbau, es hält sich auf einer mittleren Stufe, man kann nichts anderes als Löbliches davon sagen. Die ganze Aeneis ist von Anfang bis zu Ende ein mißlungener Gedanke, . . . Virgil gehört zu den merkwürdigen Beispielen, wie man seinen Beruf verfehlen kann, sein wahrer Beruf war die Lyrik: . . . .[58]

Niebuhr gave the lectures from 1828 to 1829, but they were only pieced together from notes and published from 1846 to 1848, by which time they were a helpful summary of the self-evident in Germany.[59]

To an extent, other European nations followed the German lead. They adopted the preference for Greek poetry and found themselves somewhat embarrassed by the Latin poet. Nonetheless, that knowledge did not interrupt a continued, if mostly more subdued, relation to Roman antiquity. The French literary critic Charles Augustin Sainte-Beuve (1804–69), untouched by the change of opinion, felt the figure of Virgil merited a study in 1857 because "c'est un poëte qui, en France, n'a pas cessé d'être dans l'usage et dans l'affection de tous" (he is a poet who has never ceased in France to be in everyone's affections and frame of reference).[60] He restates the preference of French Classicism for the Latin poets: if he had to abandon all of the Latin world and "l'antique patrie" (the ancient homeland), he would keep Horace as a friend and Virgil, "c'est le maître et l'ami encore" (he is the master and yet a friend).[61] For poets it was a different matter. Victor Hugo, knowing in 1827 that it was neither feasible nor fashionable for one of a romantic temperament to confess a partiality for Virgilian verse, declared, "Virgile n'est que la lune d'Homère" (Virgil is only Homer's moon).[62] Nonetheless, familiarity exacts its own tribute. For the poet in him, only a decade later, in 1837, the moon proved itself an idol of sufficient poetic divinity for a mortal to honor: "Virgile! ô poète! ô mon maître divin!" (O Virgil! O poet! My divine master!).[63]

In England, Samuel Taylor Coleridge (1772–1834) agreed with the German Romantics, whose writings he knew well.[64] The French writer, the Marquis d'Argens (1704–71), expressed great admiration for the pathos in a few lines from the *Aeneid* (*Aen*. 6.863–64),[65] that Coleridge considered, using the customary concessions made to style, "beautiful, especially in metre and composition"; yet, he continued, "what one deep feeling that goes to the human heart? I see not one."[66] Later in life, in 1824, he repeated the same opinion: that Virgil is a poet of great technical mastery, but with nothing to say: "If you take from Virgil his diction and metre, what do you leave him?"[67] John Conington and Henry Nettleship, Virgil's English commentators in the nineteenth century, expressed almost every reservation possible about Virgil as an artist and his poems as works of art, but they did not let these scruples prevent them from producing an edition of Virgil long to remain unsurpassed in English.[68] William Young Sellar saw fit to produce a weighty tome on Virgil for the mid-Victorian period in 1877 and his readers saw fit to require of him many editions of it.[69] Tennyson confessed himself bewitched by the Virgilian music from his first acquaintance with it and, in the poem "To Virgil" from 1881, wrote the oft repeated line, "Wielder of the stateliest measure/ever moulded by the lips of man."[70] It is the last of the poem's encomiums and yet this is the feature Tennyson has admired the longest; the lines preceding it read: "I salute thee, Mantovano,/I have loved thee since my day began." Again for the want of any more theoretical justification, the final preoccupation of the Enlightenment resurfaces — style.

The eighteenth century also transmitted a few other concerns to the nineteenth, which the new century then molded according to its own interests and tastes. The eighteenth century's preference for the *Georgics* bequeathed the notion of a sensibility on Virgil's part for external nature, which runs through all his works, even if, with his false concept of the poet, he was unable to develop it: "In the Georgics and the Aeneid, as well as in the Eclogues, Virgil shows a great susceptibility to the beauty and power of nature."[71] The other concern from the eighteenth century is the problem of Virgilian pathos. The eighteenth century's hostility to the Virgilian use of rhetoric arose in part from the abuse of poetic language it seemed to represent. Virgil's poetic language aroused feeling for which the eighteenth century could discover no convincing interpretation, though it too remained susceptible to its presence in Virgil's verse. The nineteenth century was less troubled by a need to account for the presence of such pathos in Virgil's language, preferring instead often to revel in it. According to Williams,[72] it is Sainte-Beuve who transforms the line from the *Aeneid, sunt lacrimae rerum et mentem mortalia tangunt* (1.462; there is pity for a world's distress, and a sympathy for a short-lived humanity; 41), into the *locus classicus* of the tear-drenched Virgil.[73] For a century given to the rigors of duty the concomitant need to expatiate on the emotional costs need hardly surprise. Niebuhr prefigures both these elements with his belief that Virgil missed his calling by failing to write lyric, since lyric was the forum for the individual to give vent to feeling and nature. Both these elements also figure in Tennyson's appreciation of Virgil. He is for him the "Landscape lover, lord of language" and also "Thou majestic in thy sadness at the doubtful doom of human kind."

In Germany, in contrast, during the nineteenth century silence reigns. The kind of general study of Virgil for the broader public that Sainte-Beuve had produced for French readers in 1857 and Sellar for the English in 1877 would not appear in Germany until 1930, when Walter Wili published his *Vergil*.[74] However, in compensation there belongs to the repressed the fitting irony of return. Thus the study of Virgil takes its next original turn in Germany with Heinze and the inversion once again of what was previously inverted, namely, the evaluation of style.

Nature, the New God

If Virgil's kingdom was the realm of poetry, then the new god against whom he offended so resolutely and grievously was nature. The concept of nature, though hardly the unique possession of the Enlightenment, acquired a ubiquity in the literature and thought of the time, as well as new accents. It approached deification in the saying of Spinoza *deus sive natura* or, to phrase the matter from the opposite perspective, nature became a secularized god. It became the source of morality as well as the muse and principle of poetry. The state of nature, that is an ideal human existence lived in harmony with nature before the advent of civil society, for which view Jean-Jacques Rousseau (1712–78) became the spokesman, exercised an immense power over the imagination in Germany. Hölderlin, in the poem to Rousseau of the same name, compared him not merely to the prophet without honor in his own country but also to a tree that has outgrown its native soil:

> Des Lebens Überfluß, das Unendliche,
>   Das um ihn [den Baum] . . . und dämmert, er faßt es nie.
> Doch lebts in ihm und gegenwärtig,
>   Wärmend und wirkend, die Frucht entquillt ihm.[75]

The simile is most apposite in the image of the tree as rooted in and sustained by the flux of life but fated with its branches never to be able to "touch" the infinite of the sun and the wind, though it is the interaction with them that causes the tree to bear its fruit. The image catches the paradoxical character of sentiment in the eighteenth century. Feeling permits us to perceive the world around us at the same time that, as the medium of relation, it does not allow us to grasp the totality of the nature that it presents as everywhere around us. The result of the awareness of this experience is the condition of "Sehnsucht" or "yearning."

We may observe the same features as well as the tendency to transpose religious features onto the communion with nature in Goethe's *Die Leiden des jungen Werthers* (1774). Werther describes in the second letter the experience of an intense communion with nature, which, though somewhat long, is worth citing in its entirety:

> Wenn das liebe Tal um mich dampft, und die hohe Sonne an der Oberfläche der undurchdringlichen Finsternis meines Waldes ruht, und nur einzelne Strahlen sich in das innere Heiligtum stehlen, ich dann im hohen Grase am fallenden Bache liege, und näher an der Erde tausend mannigfaltige Gräschen mir merkwürdig werden; wenn ich das Wimmeln der kleinen Welt zwischen Halmen, die unzähligen, unergründlichen Gestalten der Würmchen, der Mückchen näher an meinem Herzen fühle, und fühle die Gegenwart des Allmächtigen, der uns nach seinem Bilde schuf, das Wehen des Alliebenden, der uns in ewiger Wonne schwebend trägt und erhält; mein Freund! wenn's dann um meine Augen dämmert, und die Welt um mich her und der Himmel ganz in meiner Seele ruhn wie die Gestalt einer Geliebten — dann sehne ich mich oft und denke: ach könntest du das wieder ausdrücken, könntest du dem Papiere das einhauchen, was so voll, so warm in dir lebt, daß es würde der Spiegel deiner Seele, wie deine Seele ist der Spiegel des unendlichen Gottes! — mein Freund — aber ich gehe darüber zugrunde, ich erliege unter der Gewalt der Herrlichkeit dieser Erscheinungen.[76]

The whole passage is but one sentence. It is of the "wenn-dann" pattern but with a tricolonic protasis before we finally reach the "dann" clause of the apodosis. Its cumbersome length insists not only on the totality of the whole experience but also indicates the vast and often contradictory impulses of the mystic experience Werther tries to squeeze out onto the paper. The first portion describes the bright sunlight above the treetops with only a few rays piercing the impenetrable darkness of the canopy into the inner sanctuary. It recalls the effect of light entering a Gothic church, a topic on Goethe's mind at the time as illustrated by the little essay "Von deutscher Baukunst" (1773) on the Gothic cathedral with its reference to such churches as "Bäume Gottes" (*GSW* 1/2:415).[77] We move vertically from the bright open infinity of the sky to the dark enclosed miniature infinity of the world of insects. The organ of perception sensible of the continuous sweep of this motion is the heart, to which is likewise granted the feeling of the unifying force at work behind the discrete instances. The word "fühlen" is used of both. The more traditional religious language of our creation "nach seinem Bilde" assures us of some form of identity with this force, while Pietistic vocabulary also appears, "ruhn," "Spiegel," "einhauchen," and so on. The principal activity of this infinite is love; it is the

"Alliebende." Its sustaining effect is bliss, "Wonne," to which Werther responds in like manner with the image of "Erde" and "Himmel" as his beloved. If we translate the pair as the earth and the sky, then we have the entire physical world, or, if we translate it as heaven and earth, then we have the finite and the infinite. The final consequence of this for Werther is his exhaustion before the continual effort to grasp his beloved, to possess it as at once finite and infinite. He thus succumbs, "erliegen," an end that acquires a darker tone with the use of the word "Gewalt," "power, force, or violence," particularly when conjoined with the rest of the phrase "der Herrlichkeit dieser Erscheinungen." *In nuce* the sentence foreshadows the course of the novel.

This nature is less an external nature, that is, a simple landscape or setting, than it is an internal nature, intimately implicated with the sentimental subject and present to it through the medium of feeling. Kant, if we may read him as a commentator on *Werther*, more soberly but with great rigor underscores some of the consequences for this view of nature and its relation to the sentimental subject. In the third critique, the *Critique of Judgment* (1790), he insists on the right, indeed the necessity for the individual to experience for himself in nature a moment of this identity of the individual with the infinite. This is the beautiful and the most complete form of it. Consequently, representations of it must appear lesser and derivative before it, as appears in Werther's oft repeated frustration at his inability to paint in either words or drawings an adequate representation. The "Naturschöne," as Kant designates the first kind of experience, stands above the "Kunstschöne," the second kind, a conclusion by no means accepted if we think of such as Schiller or Hegel for whom the realm of art is an expression of freedom.

The branch of literature in which the century most assiduously cultivated this sense of nature and that enjoyed an enormous, though short-lived, vogue in Germany was the idyll. The importance for it of the distinction between a "Naturschöne" and a "Kunstschöne" and its relation to nature and the sentimental subject was that the quest in the eighteenth century for an adequate artistic representation of the direct communion with nature proceeded increasingly by insisting on the representation as the direct expression of it. References to artistic contrivance, to an end to the experience on the horizon, to the rupture of its illusion, or to some larger perspective beyond, became progressively less acceptable and finally inimical to the idyll. Like Werther, who was driven to madness and suicide to escape the acuteness of the contradiction, the idyll as a genre collapsed under the weight of the tension. Artificial in its origins, it became unbearably insipid, though not before it imparted a mode capable of assimilation to other literary forms and impulses, to such genres as the idyllic or bourgeois epic, a phenomenon of the late eighteenth century, and the "Dorfgeschichte" of the nineteenth century (by Adalbert Stifter, for instance).

The distinctive German idyll began with the appearance and instant success of Gessner's *Idyllen* in 1756 and ended its short career as a well-defined genre with the *Idyllen* of Voss in 1801 (although almost all of the poems were written in the 1770s and 80s and published earlier). Of greater interest and of greater vigor were the theoretical debates that accompanied the literary production. The debate on the pastoral began its German phase with Gottsched's chapter, "Schäfergedichte," — the term "Idylle" would only establish itself in the wake of Gessner's success — in his *Critische Dichtkunst* of 1730. The starting point of the German debate owed much to the earlier French reformulation of the pastoral through such figures as the Jesuit scholar and poet René Rapin (1621–87) and Bernard le Bovier de Fontenelle (1657–1757), the highly effective champion of Enlightenment rationality. It soon, however, became an issue of some heat and contributed to the development of aesthetic thought. This debate is perhaps best known from the appearance it made in Schiller's *Über naive und sentimentale Dichtung*, where, of the poetic forms belonging to the sentimental, only the idyll has a section with its own title "Die Idylle." Explicit in the debate on the idyll is the degree to which harmonious human life in nature — harmonious because inner human nature seems to correspond to a providential external nature without the need of the intermediary externalized reflection provided by civilization — proceeds according to the instinct laid down in feeling and its spontaneous pursuit. The idyll functions in this sense as a secularized Garden of Eden, with the signal difference that following your inborn nature does not lead to the sampling of a forbidden fruit. Indeed the inhabitants of this world do not suffer from any of the doubts that plague Werther, namely, the insidious fear that they may fail to grasp the ideal they sense about them. The suggestion that one of the idyll's denizens may harbor such existential suspicions is sufficient to destroy the properly idyllic character. Equally problematic is any doubt the poet may cast on his depiction through any distancing device or other artistic contrivance. Naturally what life the genre displays it owes precisely to its ability in some fashion to acknowledge this delicate tension, either directly through its own devices or through drawing on the readers' expectations, even though these avenues are contested by the theory.

The other dominant trend of the theory is the idyll's increasing historicization or realism. Realism does not mean the desire to represent the life of contemporary rural folk, although there are sharp elements of such realism in both Maler Müller and Voss, as much as it does the attempt to find in rural life examples of just such an easy communion with nature. Real in the sense that we are removed from shepherds bearing Greek names in an imaginary landscape and transported to a scene recognizably similar in its main features to life today and historical in the sense that the depictions confirm the notion that such a mode of existence forms part of our world today. We may trace by degrees in the theory the progression from the unreal world of Gessner's Grecian shepherds through young love and the family to the smaller human community of the village. The sense of where the boundary between the idyllic and the non-idyllic worlds falls eventually extends to include even the society of the small provincial town in Goethe's *Hermann und Dorothea* (1797), at which point the idyll is ready to dissolve into the "Dorfgeschichte."

As the location of the idyll changes, so too do the inhabitants of the idyllic world. In addition to simple country folk, adolescents, women, and children come increasingly to the fore. *Werther* again serves to illustrate this last point. Shortly after Werther's episode in the Gothic sanctuary of the woods, he happens upon another such moment of rapture, this time more in the manner of a tableau he beholds, and one into which he afterwards succeeds, to some degree, in inserting himself. While taking coffee in the open air outside an inn house beneath a linden tree, Werther sees one very small boy sitting on the ground clasping in front of him one still smaller boy. He describes the elder boy thus: "und ungeachtet der Munterkeit, womit er aus seinen schwarzen Augen herumschaute, ganz ruhig saß" (*GSW* 2/2:357, the letter of May 26). The spectacle of such tender solicitude in one so young, of a child caring for a babe, and the touch of a Winckelmannian dynamic stillness, "Munterkeit" and "Ruhe," unleashes a flood of comment on Werther's part about nature, the proper feeling toward it, and also the relation of civilization and art to it. When the mother returns to collect the children, Werther addresses her. His intervention both diminishes the scene's idyllic quality as we learn of the family's circumstances and also places Werther himself into the idyllic world. He frequently assures us of his ambiguous citizenship in it with such comments as in the letter of May 15 ("Die geringen Leute des Ortes kennen mich schon und lieben mich, besonders die Kinder"; *GSW* 2/2:353), which insist on his affinity with the idyll's inhabitants.

The relevance of the idyll to the reception of Virgil is its proximity to the *Eclogues* and, as the idyll moves closer to the village community, to the *Georgics* as well. These poems, particularly the *Georgics*, do contain some elements of the kind of nature the sentimental reader so fervently sought. Yet they also exhibit much else besides that perplexed and antagonized the sentimental reader's expectations. Like Pentheus with Dionysius, Virgil seems to evince a certain affinity with the new god of nature but then wilfully to deny it and, in his poems, even to deform it. The *Eclogues* especially are obviously highly mannered, elegant, and refined poems and, though they may powerfully evoke Arcadia and love, they are full of tropes, devices, references to contemporary figures, politics, grand prophecy, and creation stories. They introduce topics and a critical distance that are indigestible to the eighteenth century. The *Georgics* too have a heterogeneous character, but because of their didactic tone they are more accessible, which accounts, in part, for their greater popularity. Those portions that tell of the farmer's failures or of a nature hostile to human wants and labor are overlooked in favor of those that portray rather a rhythm of life and labor consonant with nature: in effect the famous "Praises" (all from just one of the four Georgics), of Italy, of spring, and especially of the country life. The reading of both these works in the light of an idyllic nature tends to conflate the poems so that the nature portrayed in the idyll acquires increasingly Georgic features. The *Eclogues*, despite their difficulties, maintain their association with the idyllic world through the indelible image of Arcadia in them. Furthermore, the *Eclogues* are such a cornucopia of devices for figuring the ideal world of nature so deeply ingrained in the European pastoral tradition and so familiar through their entrenched position in the educational system, that they force themselves on the imagination. However, they may only do so once they are cleansed of their overly close association with Virgil: to continue the Pentheus analogy, once the poet's limbs are dismembered so that their origin is obscured, only then may they be employed elsewhere. The means of this cleansing of the limbs is the pastoral theory. As the idyll becomes the scene of the most intensive engagement with the Virgilian corpus it will concern us greatly in the latter chapters.

There is yet a further sense of the word "historical" with respect to the idyll that requires mention here. Pastoral as the song of shepherds is by long tradition held to have been the first and most primitive form of poetry. This belief finds support in the notion that humans first led the life of pastoralists before the introduction of agriculture and permanent settlements, from which hamlets in turn there insensibly sprang larger towns and eventually cities with their urban culture and the state. In this view of history, the pastoral is as old as epic, indeed it in truth precedes epic since the lesser, simpler form gives rise to the larger, more complex form. We may trace its association with the Virgilian poems back to antiquity and the fourth-century A.D. commentary by Donatus, who tells us that the pastoral's origins go back to the most ancient of times, *a priscis temporibus*, depict the manner of life first lived on earth, *ab ea vita, quae prima in terris fuit*, and further that it offers an image of a golden age, *speciem aurei saeculi*, in which opinion Scaliger also follows.[78] Humans as shepherds in the first age is such a commonplace image that Herder, when describing the origin of language from the everyday objects that surround the earliest humans, seizes on the bleating sheep to show how sounds led to language: "Aber horch! das Schaf blöcket! . . . 'Ha! sagt der lernende Unmündige, . . ., nun werde ich dich wieder kennen — Du blöckst!"[79]

This view of human history is confirmed by biblical history. The books of Moses, the oldest books of the Bible, relate not merely the tale of the Garden and the expulsion of Adam and Eve from it but also the form of life that replaces it, the age of the Patriarchs, the age of the shepherd. As the closest age of fallen man to life in Eden, it is also the closest historical approach for humans to the golden age. All of these associations are present to the eighteenth century as it considers the idyll: "Poetisch würde ich sagen, es sey eine Abschilderung des güldenen Weltalters; auf christliche Art zu reden aber: eine Vorstellung des Standes der Unschuld, oder doch wenigstens der patriarchalischen Zeit, vor und nach der Sündflüth."[80] Werther again offers an example of the proximity of the two to the imagination. In the novel's third and fifth letters (May 12 and 15), Werther writes of a well in a shaded spot just outside of town: "Wenn ich da sitze, so lebt die patriarchalische Idee so lebhaft um mich wie sie alle, die Altväter am Brunnen Bekanntschaft machen und freien" (*GSW* 2/2:352). After this pointed comment he relates an instance of biblical postfiguration in the letter of May 15, where he meets a bashful young maiden at the well and assists her with her water jug, a similar situation to that related in Genesis 24: 13–20.

A further consequence of this assimilation of the pastoral to a wider historical scheme is that it brings Homer into its purview; he becomes a figure of idyllic nature. In common with the pastoral, Homer, the archaic age, his epics and heroes also descend from this earliest age. The shared meter, the dactylic hexameter, seems to prove the two literary forms' kinship while their subject matter would at first glance argue for their difference. Kings, armies, and battles, like the affairs of states, do not fit into the pastoralist age. The *Iliad* with its heroes and war may be the Homer that preoccupies the considerations of the critical tradition in its comparison of Homer and Virgil. It is not however this Homer who catches the imagination of the eighteen century.

Temporally epic may come at the end of the earliest age and the idyll at its beginning, but as they both give expression to the same age, one spirit animates them. Both are viewed as documents of the closest historical approach to the age of innocence, the state of nature, the golden age. This is the Homer who captivates. And it is the Homer of the *Odyssey* who can be more easily assimilated to idyllic nature. There is much less blood and gore, and there are many more episodes of adventure and scenes of everyday and domestic life. Famously the first book of *Werther*, the "happy" book, stands under the aegis of Homer. He is Werther's constant companion and consolation (May 13, *GSW* 2/2:353, and August 28, *GSW* 2/2:396), and Werther takes Homer with him in more than the simply physical sense when he goes off on his ramblings about the countryside. In the letter describing the two peasant children, in which Werther is sitting in the open air in front of the inn house, seated at a table and drinking his most unpastoral coffee, he is also reading his Homer, which, by indicating the mood in which he will read the scene of nature before him, also instructs the reader in the proper manner of reading. In the case of the two places in the novel where more than simply the name of Homer occurs and we can tell what passage in Homer Werther has in mind, both are from the *Odyssey* and both equate some action or moment in Werther's life to the Homeric age.[81] Of the first he enthuses: "Es ist nichts, das mich so mit einer stillen, wahren Empfindung ausfüllte als die Züge patriarchalischen Lebens, die ich, Gott sei Dank, ohne Affektation in meine Lebensart verweben kann" (June 21, *GSW* 2/2:372). The vicarious means of access to this earlier age is sentimental feeling schooled in nature, for only this ensures that the moment is without affectation, that is, it is naive.

The premise underlying Werther's confidence is that the nature present to Homer and the nature present to the eighteenth century is the same. The differences of time or rather of history are simply the accretions of civilization that the proper cultivation of feeling can slough off. Werther's successes in inserting himself into the idyllic are however noticeably tenuous and transitory. His need to assure himself of the moment's authenticity through the comparison to antiquity and to remark on the moment only indicates his estrangement from it. Were he truly to live in the idyllic world according to the dictates of his sentiments, he would not need confirmation from an outside source of its veracity, nor would such a comparison make any sense to him. It is, however, the central problem of the idyll in the eighteenth century.

Nonetheless the joining here of idyll and epic fosters the conflation of the two genres that soon appears in the "bürgerliches" oder "idyllisches Epos" of first Voss's *Luise* (1795) and then of Goethe with his *Hermann und Dorothea* (1797). Considerably more remarkable than the poem itself was the reaction to *Hermann und Dorothea*. Wilhelm von Humboldt (1767–1835) proposed to erect on its slight frame a complete aesthetic system of several hundred pages. August Wilhelm Schlegel declared that "das einzige Mittel" to understand the poem was through the understanding of Homeric epic.[82] It is not just *a* means to understand the poem: it is, he argues, the *only* means that does it justice. The burden of his argument is that the only possible remaining form of true epic in the eighteenth century is that of such works as *Hermann und Dorothea*. The task he sets himself in the essay is to mold and transform the Homeric epic, by means of successive theoretical characterizations, in such a way that the necessary Homeric outcome becomes Goethe's epic. In essence, *Hermann und Dorothea* is what Homer would write today.

Yet anyone holding it in one hand and the *Iliad* in the other would be hard put to understand the similarity. Schlegel grants that the contents of Goethe's poem bear little resemblance to Homeric epic. A provincial lad falls in love with a refugee lass, fleeing the upheavals of the French Revolution. Although he knows his parents will disapprove, he resolves to marry her and takes her home — his first act of maturity. At home his resolve and love triumph over his parents' bourgeois prejudice. Its similarity to the spirit of Homer turns for Schlegel on Goethe's successful replication of the essence of "d[er] Erzählungsweise des alten Homerus."[83] Essence indicates not that Goethe's technique functions in all respects like that of Homer but rather that they are identical in their effect. The artistic representation of *Hermann und Dorothea* provokes in the sentimental subject the same conviction as it did in Werther, namely, that true idyllic nature is present in feeling for the sentimental subject and that this truth of nature is identical to that of the Greeks. What emerges from this aesthetic reflection is "das Würdige und Große in der menschlichen Natur... ohne einseitige Vorliebe."[84] To imitate the Greeks means to create in their spirit on the assurance that the nature revealed to the sentimental subject remains constant in its effects and so permits us to overcome the separation of time.

For Virgil, this renders him chargeable with two grievous offenses against nature. In the first instance, the more the *Eclogues* and the *Georgics*, the two poems to fall within the purview of the idyll for the eighteenth century, seem to afford a kinship of feeling for nature with Arcadia and the golden age, the more objectionable is Virgil's abundant recourse to devices that only make palpable to the sentimental subject his estrangement from nature. In the second item of the charge, it is the gift of genius to gain such access to nature and the task of the poet, above all in the poetry closest to nature, to give an aesthetic representation of it that elicits a similar response in the reader so that this person too may have an intimation of "das Würdige and Große der menschlichen Natur ohne einseitige Vorliebe." By signally refusing to do this, Virgil is guilty of offenses both against idyllic nature and against a poet's true nature, against his own genius.

Disicienda poetae membra

The third and final point of the comparison to Pentheus touches on the story's emotional and psychological elements. To leave aside the matter of the Euripidean gods, Euripides apportions blame to both Pentheus and the citizens of Thebes for Pentheus's death. Each suffers from his own kind of blindness. Pentheus, on the one hand, precipitates his own death by his adamant refusal to acknowledge his attraction to the Dionysian while the full scope of the deed's horror and the citizens' complicity in it is made clear by the role of Pentheus's mother in his dismemberment. One member of the royal family heads the refusal of the city to accept Dionysus while another member of the royal family leads the citizenry in his worship. The tragedy is thus both familial and civic. For a modern reader these two sides capture the drama's psychological compulsion. Similarly, the German reception of Virgil during the eighteenth century does not merely concern, nor progress along, the lines of scholarly interpretations and dispassionate arguments developed reciprocally for and against; rather, it is motivated by a strong and passionate interest, not all of whose motivations are either immediately apparent, nor logically connected. It is this element that the Pentheus analogy allows us to underscore.

The ardency of the Germans' attachment to all things Greek arises in part from the need to discover an antiquity that would authorize their own cultural production and facilitate the articulation of a distinctive German identity. France had laid so comprehensive a claim to the Latin heritage through the insistent comparison of "le siècle de LOUIS au beau siècle d'Auguste" that Rome's utility for this purpose to the Germans was exhausted.[85] Indeed for them Rome acquires a distinctly French mien; Rome's virtues and strengths are those elaborated in the *Querelle*. The comparison of France to Augustan Rome emphasizes precisely those accomplishments that the Germans increasingly and most keenly feel themselves to lack in the latter half of the eighteenth century.[86] They could not point to a nation unified into a state, reaching its apogee under a great monarch, whose greatness one could easily discern in the nation's military and political preeminence and in the universally acknowledged brilliance of its literary and intellectual culture. French cultural prestige only exacerbates the animus against Rome.[87] This Rome can offer Germans of the eighteenth century little comfort; indeed this Rome, if it is the apogee of antiquity, must appear as a positive impediment. Its claim to normative status cannot remain unchallenged.

Rome, however, would be a matter of only moderate importance if its would-be modern exemplar, France, were simply one nation among many, and, of equal importance, if the Germans were not so sensible of their own lack of a grand, golden cultural past.[88] Of the other nation states with which the Germans compare themselves in the eighteenth century, England, and to a lesser degree Spain, both could boast an established literary and intellectual tradition, while Italy, the other nation of modernity that was not a state, could pride itself on a cultural florescence in the Renaissance much envied by such as France and England. The preeminence of the French language and culture in Germany during the eighteenth century provoked an increasingly strong reaction as the century progressed.[89] Restoration and Augustan England might hope to emulate French successes, but the political circumstances of France and Germany were sufficiently different that they militated against such easy emulous rivalry between nations. At first Frederick the Great's successful defiance of the great powers in the Seven Years' War met with great enthusiasm. Yet it was tempered by the fact that he was not only the king of so illiberal a country as Prussia, but also the Francophile *non plus ultra*. He spoke and wrote French in preference to his native German, and in 1780 he published, in French, a survey of German literature, detailing its faults, as its title indicates: *De la littérature allemande, des défauts qu'on peut lui reprocher, quelles en sont les causes, et par quels moyens on peut les corriger* (On German Literature, the faults one may criticize, what their causes are, and by what means one may correct them).

The prominence of France on the modern stage and Rome on the ancient stage counsels an alternative strategy. By finding competing actors, representing different styles of acting, one may challenge the dominance of both and make space for further voices on the stage. What occurs, to quote Müsil, is a parallel action: the displacement of Rome by Greece on the ancient stage, and, on the modern stage, the reduction of France to a more mortal stature through the discovery of the English and Shakespeare. The discovery of a Greek antiquity, distinguished by its radical difference from Rome, acts as a proxy fight to the similar quarrel in the modern world. The parallel is somewhat unbalanced as the proxy fight shows greater virulence and consequence than the modern one. It should not be understood from this that the desire for a distinctive German cultural identity either causes the changes leading to modern philhellenism or constitutes the sole motive for interest in the multitudinous issues in which its pursuit is enmeshed; it does, however, provide some explanation for the intensity of the feeling both for Greece and against Rome.[90] For the exploration of some of the tensions in the vehement statements about Rome or France, the use of a psychological analogy such as the Pentheus story offers a further means of approaching the issue of national identity.[91] To read such statements in the light of the more chauvinistic and xenophobic attitudes of nineteenth-century nationalism and of three Franco-German wars within seventy years would be to impose on the idea of "nation" in the eighteenth century a "nationalistic" sense that it cannot be made to bear without some violence.[92]

To return to Pentheus and the question of psychology: in the eighteenth century we may regard France as playing the elder sibling to Germany's younger sibling. So enormously successful is the elder sibling that the younger feels completely overshadowed. The elder seems to have excelled in every field of endeavor and taken every prize so that there appears to be no outlet left for the younger sibling's talents. The unqualified approval of the family's patriarch, Virgil, for the elder sibling's attainments only compounds the younger's sense of inadequacy. So deeply rooted is this sense that the younger not merely finds a cousin, England, to set up against the overbearing rival, but also casts about for a new patriarch, Greece, who, it claims, is the true patriarch. Such a maneuver can naturally only be accomplished by metaphorically slaying the reigning patriarch. The Penthean Virgil must be dismembered. It is this necessity that the emended Horatian tag that heads this section seeks to encapsulate. It is not that Virgil begins the century as the poet and his scattered limbs, but rather that the Germans of the eighteenth century feel driven to dismember the poet as the century progresses.

However, while the metaphorical desire to slay the father may point to the child's wish to establish its difference and independence from the parent, it also underscores the similarity between child and parent, though the child may not be disposed to acknowledge any such shared traits and, indeed, may even fear their possible presence. This other aspect is equally useful for the examination of the German relation to Virgil in the eighteenth century. The Thebans cannot suffer the loss of their king and royal family without injury to themselves, nor can the Germans excise Virgil from their literary canon, and by inference the Latin heritage more generally, without closing their eyes to the affinities long association have left. Thus Virgil's increasingly scattered limbs may appear in disguised or unacknowledged form, or so it will be the burden of this argument to show, in Winckelmann, in the German idyllic tradition, and above all and perhaps most curiously, but most fittingly, in the Jena Romantics, as it is the Schlegel brothers who give the most succinct and complete expression to the German estrangement from Virgil.

These, however, are particular instances of the limbs, whereas the more immediate purpose here is to establish a general framework for this dismemberment by examining the constitutive dynamic tension of German philhellenism between the normative and the historical view of Greece from the perspective on Roman history that accompanies it.[93] Rome and Latin culture acquire an intermediary position between the Greek past and the German present in a fashion that not merely and most obviously reflects inversely the emerging vision of Greece but also the articulation of a German voice and its reaction to French influence. Such animus by no means suggests that other motivations are not at work in the rise of German philhellenism or the history of Rome, though it does explain why it became a matter of quite such importance to the Germans. It is a strand among many, but nevertheless a strand.

The observation made earlier that it is the cultivation of taste or the "Bildung" of sentimental feeling that affords the individual a glimpse into nature as well as into the artifacts of ancient Greece may indicate the imaginative means for bridging the gap of time, though it hardly does justice to the enormous sense of excitement and discovery that it unleashes. Nor does it convey the intense German identification with ancient Greece that was the well-known hallmark of German philhellenism's originator Winckelmann.[94] This rings out in the categorical statement in his pamphlet *Gedanken über die Nachahmung:* "Der einzige Weg für uns, groß, ja, wenn es möglich ist, unnachahmlich zu werden, ist die Nachahmung der Alten."[95] The pamphlet's enormous effect is hardly attributable to its wide circulation, as only fifty to sixty copies were printed, although its success led to a reprinting in the following year. The editors of the text in the Deutscher Klassiker Verlag (1995) note that, despite the small print run, Winckelmann's comment about its "unglaublichen Beyfall" "hält indes jeder sachlichen Überprüfung stand."[96] Many reasons may be adduced for its success from the essay's pungent and pithy prose and to the intriguing medley of opinions and ideas it manages to combine: nature, genius, sublimity, beauty, "Bildung," the remarkable idea that a construct of art is the surest teacher of nature, the nomination of Greece to this post of teacher, the recognition of Greece as a secular *praeceptor humanitatis* to the Germans, and a historical conception of culture, all of which are presented with great verve and learning; nonetheless, its success would seem to owe at least as much to its timeliness.[97] The sentiments the essay expressed so forcefully struck a deep and responsive chord. Its vision of Greece and its urgent importance to the present fired the imagination and helped in Germany to propel with added urgency the reexamination and reevaluation of every aspect of Greek culture. The fervor embraced not merely writers and intellectual figures but also scholars in the classical disciplines who were shortly to give definitive shape to modern classical scholarship, such as Friedrich August Wolf.

A reappraisal on this scale could only be conducted if accompanied by a great and ardent passion, as only so sweeping an inner transformation of the self could bridge the gulf of time that separates the moderns from the cultural monuments of antiquity and permit these artifacts to speak afresh to the modern world. The shades of the dead demand a libation of blood to restore their voice to them. A sense of "Bildung," more radical by far than Kant's, is required for this new project. For the age, so complete a "Bildung" occurred first, and spontaneously, according to Goethe, in the person of Winckelmann: "Eine solche antike Natur war, insofern man es nur von einem unsrer Zeitgenossen behaupten kann, in Winckelmann wieder erschienen."[98] The exhilaration and sense of intellectual discovery may propel and accompany the emergence of a Greece very different from that known to the sixteenth or seventeenth centuries, yet it also makes this Greece, in part, anachronistic and ahistorical by the very strength of the imaginative identification.[99] This Greece comes to embody the noblest aspirations of the Enlightenment. The brilliance of A. W. Schlegel's review of Goethe's *Hermann und Dorothea* is the intricate set of arguments that take the reader from the Homeric world to the present and join them under "das Würdige und Große in der menschlichen Natur" so that we may fairly regard Goethe as Homer speaking German. Eventually, the one-sidedness of this Apollonian Greece summons an equally vehement and passionate disavowal from the most unlikely quarter, from among the ranks of German classical philologists, with Nietzsche and the publication of his *Die Geburt der Tragödie* in 1872. If Nietzsche's reflections and their importance to the twentieth century indicate that they do not bear simply on classical studies, they also testify to the fact that the earlier philhellenism was deeply and firmly interwoven into many more matters than the mere scholarly study of Greece. The critique of it could only occur as part of a reevaluation much wider in scope.

To lay too much stress on the ahistorical element involved in the normative view of Greece would be simply to make it a rather crass restatement of the "ancien" side of the *Querelle*. It neglects the other equally powerful element of German philhellenism, historicism.[100] German philhellenism represents rather the digestion of the compromise between the normative and the historical views in which the *Querelle* ended and a response to it. Historicism is the other powerful and contradictory strand and likewise present in Winckelmann. To buttress his unequivocal claims he avails himself of historical argument. Ancient Greece, and nowhere else, through the serendipitous operation of climate and culture produces a people in whom the propensity toward the beautiful becomes so pronounced that it becomes endemic among them.[101] This insight confers a unique status on the ancient Greeks that is not simply the repetition of the old argument from the *Querelle* that honor is owed to the ancients for they were first, they were the inventors of epic, rhetoric, and so on. They are rather not the creators of artifacts, but the purveyors of an attitude, an accomplishment of culture, aesthetic representation: "Der gute Geschmack ... hat sich angefangen zuerst under dem griechischen Himmel zu bilden" (*NGW*, 4). Individual poets, philosophers, or artists thus become those figures who take up, crystallize, and give expression to that feeling for the beautiful that everywhere surrounds them in life, which is Winckelmann's chief concern. Likewise their products all bear the same distinguishing feature since they do not give expression to a primarily individual insight but a collective accomplishment: "Das allgemeine vorzügliche Kennzeichen der griechischen Meisterstücke ist endlich eine edle Einfalt und eine stille Größe" (*NGW*, 20).

In his later *Geschichte der Kunst des Altertums* (1764) Winckelmann sets about turning this insight into historical argument. It permits him to regard the jumbled mass of artifacts, styles, and sundry information contained in the records as manifestations of the one animating principle, this sense for the beautiful. It provides a definition of relevance that he may then apply to his evidence.[102] Laying out a doctrine of the genesis, growth, maturity, and eventual decline of the aesthetic feeling provides a means for establishing a chronology for the artifacts and their styles. The novelty of regarding artistic artifacts as reflective of a larger culture is immediately apparent if we consider the previous method of comparison that prevailed in the discussion of epic. If the critic wished to discuss epic, he broached the question of what epic was by comparing Homer and Virgil. Winckelmann may now approach a work of art by considering where it fits in the development of a style or attitude, what new features it brings to light, what further developments it might give rise to or whether and in what sense it might represent a certain end or culmination.

By turning to history to approach his vision of the ideal, Winckelmann also makes it beholden to history. The more he ties the work of art to its historical background and demonstrates the way in which it arises from and responds to a specific set of historical circumstances, the greater the sense of it as a unique unrepeatable moment of history. It implicitly calls into question the validity of the conviction that only the imitation of the Greeks will assure the modern of greatness. This tension is, however, constitutive of German philhellenism. The relation of norm to history in

German philhellenism is similar to that of naive and sentimental in the idyll. Although the naive will represent the longed-for condition because of its greater proximity to nature, it will only emerge as the naive in relation to the sentimental and wherever the dividing line between the two falls, the drawing of it will engender a feeling of disquiet and estrangement. Winckelmann's approach to the Grecian norm through history becomes a path much traveled. The study of Greece advances along historical lines. The enormous expansion in knowledge of all aspects of the ancient world, the systematization of scholarly method, of the editorial principles of recension, the "Lachmannian" method — these gains in the nineteenth century only come at the expense of an increasingly tenuous connection with the animating zeal embodied in Winckelmann and, after him, in such as Goethe, Schiller, and Humboldt.

The importance of the Greeks to the Germans also rests on Winckelmann's equally astonishing claim that the imitation of nature may best be learnt through the imitation of the Greeks. The reason for this is that the beautiful one must emulate is not the beautiful of everyday perception, but the "Idealschöne." The "Idealschöne" is "eine bloß im Verstande entworfene geistige Natur" (*NGW*, 10). The accident of culture leading to the concentration of the sense of the beautiful among the Greeks presented artists with so frequent and varied encounters with individual examples of beauty that they eventually abstracted from them to arrive at the ideal, which they then represented in their artwork. The "Idealschöne" of art thus depicts the "schöne Natur." It is the completeness of this aesthetic ideal that Winckelmann proposes for modern imitation. His emphasis on nature and the "Idealschöne" brings his vision of the Greeks into the web of opinions around the state of nature and its artistic representation as idyllic nature. The idyll did not seek to emulate the everyday nature surrounding us. It sought rather through the adoption of a different perspective to gather the remembrances scattered in it of humanity's proper state and so present them in the artistic vision that it would awaken in the reader a sense of this prior condition. Winckelmann's vision facilitates Werther's adoption of Homer, especially the Odyssean Homer, as an emblem of idyllic, naive nature. To characterize the relationship of Greece and nature by paraphrase: from the mouth of nature, by the hand of Homer.

Likewise attractive to the German present of the eighteenth century is the more wholesale reordering of ancient history that it offers with the almost complete dismissal of Rome and concentration on Greece in its stead. The paradigmatic quality of the contrast between Greece and Rome only increases over time. A. W. Schlegel's dictum, "das Würdige und Große in der menschlichen Natur," is exemplified by the Greeks, whereas the Romans represent the deformation of humanity. When Winckelmann observes, "Eine Bildsäule von einer alten römischen Hand wird sich gegen ein griechisches Urbild allemal verhalten, wie Vergils Dido in ihrem Gefolge mit der Diana unter ihren Oreaden verglichen, sich gegen Homers Nausikaa verhält, welcher jener nachzuahmen gesucht hat" (*NGW*, 4), the comparison may have heuristic value for him.[103] He addresses an audience predisposed from the *Querelle* to regard the Greeks as the less polished, less refined, ruder versions of the Romans. Winckelmann, wishing to discover something new among the Greeks, must distinguish his Greeks from the Latins. And to counter the perception of their essential similarity he must insist on their radical difference. Further, since Winckelmann's vision of Greece is new, neither he nor his audience will be in possession of a well-recognized and defined set of ideas that habit might lead his reader to associate with Greece for the easy comprehension of this novelty. Precisely those ideas his audience is likely to have are largely not those Winckelmann wishes to conjure to mind. It thus behooves him to begin by making palpable what it is *not:* in this instance, that the Greek ideal is most definitely not that beautiful we find among the Latins, not even among the best of them, namely, Virgil. Winckelmann will employ the same technique to more lasting effect in his discussion of the Laocoon statue (see chap. 2). It is, however, more the vehemence of it that concerns us here.

It stems in part from the conception of historical time with which the Roman world comes to be associated. Winckelmann in his *Geschichte der Kunst des Altertums* recognizes the presence of art from other cultures, but deals with them in an abbreviated fashion.[104] He finds a place for art before Greece and thus for Egyptian, Phoenician, Persian, and Etruscan art. Yet for the art that comes after Greek art, namely Roman art, he denies that there is any such object to study.[105] The Romans failed to produce any art properly speaking as they were unable to develop an original style: ". . . ich [glaube] berechtigt zu sein, den Begriff eines römischen Stils in der Kunst, insoweit unsere jetzigen Kenntnisse gehen, für eine Einbildung zu halten" (*GKA*, 276–77). Roman artifacts as simply imitations of either Etruscan or Greek styles (*GKA*, 275) are non-art. Accordingly their place in a history of art is logically dubious. Winckelmann fixes his gaze almost exclusively on sculpture, yet in these few pages he prefigures the attitude to Roman culture that Herder will develop more fully and Friedrich Schlegel complete with his conclusion that Virgil is the poet who wrote no poems. They extend Winckelmann's judgment about Roman sculpture to the other areas of Roman culture and by use of the same argument, namely, the Romans have no aesthetic style truly their own, therefore their products, such as the poems of Virgil, are not really aesthetic objects in their own right.

"Geschmack," the aesthetic sense, first originates in Greece. It is the true starting point for the imagination of the eighteenth century, the origin from which it acknowledges its ultimate descent. Winckelmann patterns his study of Greek art on the stages of its development, of which he gives five, each with a historical period.¹⁰⁶ He discusses all of these except for the fifth and final stage, that of its dissolution, of which he cryptically notes: "da das Ende derselben außer der Grenzen der Kunst geht, so sind hier eigentlich nur vier Zeiten derselben zu betrachten" (*GKA*, 207). In part he is unable to discuss it because we know ourselves to be its descendants, thus in one sense it did not end, as the first sentence of the *Gedanken* proclaims: "Der gute Geschmack, welcher sich mehr und mehr durch die Welt ausbreitet, hat sich angefangen zuerst unter dem griechischen Himmel zu bilden" (*GKA*, 3). This sentiment runs counter to his presentation of Greek art as a historical unfolding according to an inner dynamic intrinsic to the culture and begs a more general statement on how culture or a particular form of culture, here the aesthetic sense, is deemed transmissible once it is removed from its historical setting. Winckelmann does not address the issue squarely. He remains adamant that the present must experience the Greek past directly; the youth of today must school its taste through the appreciation and study of the beautiful.¹⁰⁷ We thus return to the sentimental subject as the means of bridging the separation between past and present. This, however, results in a triadic sense of historical time. For the sentimental subject there is the present, the past with which it communes, and that which separates it from the desired past, a block of intermediary obtruding time that it knows stands between it, the present, and direct enjoyment of its treasured object. Increasingly the block of time separating kindred past and present comes to be associated with Rome.

The young Herder is much taken by Winckelmann's ideals and history, and claims to have read while still a young man his *Geschichte der Kunst* a total of seven times (*HW* 2:244). In a pair of two short texts from the Storm and Stress period, Herder puts down his vision of the dynamics of history.¹⁰⁸ In the first, *Auch eine Philosophie der Geschichte der Bildung der Menschen* (1774), he develops a vision of history patterned on the model of human life. Each people of antiquity makes a distinctive contribution to the general progress of humanity, runs its "natural" course before fading away as the next, having learnt the lessons of the "earlier" culture, steps forward to make its contribution. At first, in the dithyrambic sweep of *Auch eine Philosophie*, Rome appears as the culminating epoch of humanity in antiquity. After having passed through the stages of humanity's development, its earliest childhood among the patriarchs of Israel, boyhood in Egypt, youth in Greece, Herder finally hails Rome as "*Mannesalter menschlicher Kräfte und Bestrebungen*" (*HW* 4:30).¹⁰⁹ Its distinctive feature is to bring all of the other ancient cultures under its unifying dominion, for which task he cites the passage from Virgil always associated with the justification of Roman rule: *tu regere imperio populos* (*Aen.* 6:851; you have to guide the nations with your authority; 173). Yet apart from the capacity to govern and to make laws, the only cultural arts that maturity in Rome nurtures are rhetoric and history. The effect of Roman rule on ancient culture is to order it, to make it uniform, and to distribute it throughout its territories. Rome acts as a museum curator; it does not itself make contributions. As a whole, it represents the exhaustion of ancient culture and, after having prepared the way for the new religion of Christianity, it yields to the peoples of the north (*HW* 4:42). Eventually, after the long night of the Middle Ages, comes the morning of the Renaissance and Reformation.[110] Yet the humanists of the Renaissance in their search for antiquity find themselves compelled to turn to Rome: "Rom die *Mittelzeit* der *Härtung* des *Kerns* und seiner *Austeilung*" (*HW* 4:86). For those seeking access to the products of taste, Rome thus inevitably and regrettably remains the mediating stop along the way, through which one must pass on the journey back to Greece.[111]

In the second text, *Ursachen des gesunknen Geschmacks bei den verschiedenen Völkern, da er blühet* (1775), the Latin world appears less as the next element in a sequence and more as the inverse of Greece. Following Winckelmann, Herder views all facets of Greek culture as so imbued with the beautiful that art appears natural: "bei den Griechen war der Geschmack *Natur* gewesen" (*HW* 4:135). Among them taste or aesthetics is "*Nationalsache* und *Element der Bildung*" (*HW* 4:127). Among the Latins, however, such artistic activity is alien to the Roman temperament: "Den *Römern sind also die Produktionen des Geschmacks, . . . Kunst* und *Dichtkunst, nie würksame Triebfedern worden*" (*HW* 4:127). Consequently Rome's writers are technicians rather than creative poets, "und die besten Dichter waren Versifikateurs, d. i. Philosophen oder Redner, oder gar Schmeichler in Versen" *HW* 4:128). What little such innately unpoetic souls could achieve soon ended with the extinction of the republican spirit:

> *Da der Geist wich und das Republikanische Rom unter das Joch der Monarchie sank:* so hoch die Blumen und Kränze dieses Jochs gepriesen wurden, *so wenig* konnte doch ein zierlicher August und ein spielender Mäcenas mit allen ihren Geschenken *das ersetzen, woraus Römergeist worden war:* das sieht man stracks nach Augustus Tode. (*HW* 4:129)

For one not shy of naming names, Herder is here curiously reticent. He does not state explicitly from whom the dainty Augustus and the playful Maecenas purchase their flowers and garlands. Nonetheless, the shoe of flattering versifier seems best to fit Virgil; his *Eclogues*, by tradition, won back for him the lost family's estate, confiscated to reward Octavian's veterans, the *Georgics* he wrote at the behest of Maecenas in support of the new government's program, and the *Aeneid* pleased Augustus for its praise of the settlement after the battle of Actium and brought Virgil the adulation of Rome.

More than a decade later, in his *Ideen zur Philosophie der Geschichte der Menschheit* (1784–91), Herder's skepticism about Rome ripens to a now undisguised horror: to comprehend the history of Rome is to know a

"Dämongeschichte" (*HW* 6:595);[112] to reckon up the cultural accomplishments Rome gave to the world is to conclude that "in keiner nützlichen Kunst, in keinem Nahrungszweige der menschlichen Gesellschaft hat je ein Römer etwas erfunden" (*HW* 6:607); to draw the moral from the history of Rome's wars and empire is to judge that "nur Einmal standen jene alten Römer auf der Schaubühne und spielten meistens als Privatpersonen, das fürchterlich-große Spiel, dessen Wiederholung wir der Menschheit nie wünschen mögen" (*HW* 6:609–10); to feel it as human is to begin to curse it fervently — "Rom ist nicht mehr und auch bei seinem Leben mußte es jedem edlen Mann seine Empfindung sagen, daß Fluch und Verderben sich mit allen diesen ungeheuren, ehrsüchtigen Siegen auf sein Vaterland häufte" (*HW* 6:601). Rome has become less the last stage of ancient culture than its debasement, even negation. For the modern, it has become the historical barrier that has denied the modern world an easier, more direct continuity with the animating spirit of ancient Greece; it is that which the modern must sufficiently comprehend in order to overcome it if he wishes to understand the full scope of the task he has set himself in emulating through "Bildung" the "Idealschöne" more proper to the human spirit.

Rome's history gains added weight from the Janus-like position that it holds as the mediating term between the two. It casts its baleful glance not merely back toward the past but also perilously close to the present. Rome bequeathed its political talent for government and the necessary ruthlessness to maintain that rule to the bishops of Rome and they yoked it to their new religion: "Das meist sagt der Name *Rom* selbst" (*HW* 6:807). The spirit of old Rome transmitted itself to the new church so that the peoples arriving in the old empire would imbibe it: "die alte Königin der Welt, das Haupt und die Krone der Völker hauchte auch ihrem Bischofe den Geist ein, das Haupt der Völker auf *seine* Weise zu werden" (*HW* 6:807). As a people may only develop a voice of its own through the cultivation of its own language, Herder views the imposition of Latin as the language of all higher functions as a guaranty for arrested development: "Nur durch die Kultur der vaterländischen Sprache kann sich ein Volk aus der Barbarei heben; und Europa blieb auch deshalb so lange barbarisch, weil sich dem natürlichen Organ seiner Bewohner, fast ein Jahrtausend hin eine fremde Sprache vordrang" (*HW* 6:822). The continued effects of these bequests is present to Herder in the form of the Holy Roman Empire of the German nation when he notes that his country's political order is still constitutionally linked to Rome: "und noch jetzt ist Deutschland seiner Verfassung wegen ein Ruhekissen der römischen Krone" (*HW* 6:809). His choice of the crown of Rome as his metaphor for political sovereignty, though factually correct, underscores a sense of Germany as still a political ward, one that has not yet, in its own idiom, laid claim to its political maturity. The gradual widening of the sense of Roman history and its effects to include not merely the issue of culture but also that of the formation of national identity through it moves Rome into the sphere of powerful emotion. Rome is no longer simply a matter of the past; its lingering connection to the present makes it in a two-fold sense something to be overcome. It explains in part the vehemence of such language as "Dämongeschichte" in Herder and a generation later, Schlegel's insistence on Latin literature as a "warnendes Beispiel."

Axiomatic for this cultural view of history is its connection to freedom. Classical Greece with its many fiercely independent city states and Athenian democracy was by long tradition associated with freedom. Yet Winckelmann avails himself of this idea in support of his primary focus of Greece as the birthplace of the "Idealschöne" and thus of "Geschmack" in a fashion that yields a vision of Greece highly suitable to eighteenth-century Germany, and therefore appealing to it. Freedom most immediately is a concept from the political realm and this is the sense in which it will most easily and frequently occur. However, freedom, in keeping with Enlightenment philosophy, is also a more general animating principle of human nature, such as the right to self-determination, and one therefore reflected in all aspects of human society. Precisely what freedom means in the political realm for Winckelmann and others is of necessity nebulous since it must be a term of sufficient elasticity to encompass Greece from its earliest beginnings — the world of Agamemnon in the *Iliad* offers only a very restricted definition of the word freedom — up to more or less the introduction of Macedonian rule. The preference is naturally for some form of republican institutions, but it also means more loosely the right of individual states to self-determination, and, as a minimum, the freedom of the nation as a whole from rule imposed by what is perceived as a foreign power. The political realm merely offers the most easily accessible means of measuring the vigor of freedom in a given society. For Winckelmann, art, the beautiful, these too are expressions of humanity's essential freedom. He values political freedom for the boon it will give to art: it is "die vornehmste Ursache des Vorzugs der Kunst" (*GKA*, 130).[113] The importance of freedom to the aesthetic is that its presence is felt to guarantee an autonomous cultural development. Further, since for Winckelmann the chief claim of the Greeks to our attention is their art, their political circumstances are less of interest in their own right and more as a contributing factor to their supreme achievement, the representation of the beautiful. In the absence of a unified political state, art and culture become the sphere for the collective expression of the nation. Indeed, Winckelmann makes out of necessity, the division into many states, a virtue. It prevents any individual, either for good or for ill, from gaining ascendancy: "und die ganze Nation hat niemals ein einziges Oberhaupt erkannt. Daher ruhte nicht auf einer Person allein das Recht, groß in seinem Volke zu sein und sich mit Ausschließung anderer verewigen zu können" (*GKA*, 130). With the notion that the absence of a single ruler permits many talents to emerge and compete among themselves for the greater vigor of the nation's cultural life as a whole, Winckelmann presents an image of Greece of immediate appeal to educated Germans of the bourgeoisie in the eighteenth century. Winckelmann, when discussing some particular development among the Athenians in Athens, frequently refers to Greeks and Greece as if the Hellenes of the 450 B.C. thought of Athenians and Athens and Greeks and Greece as straightforward synonyms. Be that as it may, the usage does indicate that the Germans of the eighteenth century did incline to think of themselves not as producing Saxon, Prussian art, or the art of any of the other 350 odd states or statelets in the Germany of the day, but rather as contributing to a common undertaking, which was German. Winckelmann's Greece offers them a model for the highest cultural achievement and that, if achieved, must necessarily presuppose the possession of freedom of a sort for the nation that achieves it. They may make of taste or aesthetics the "Nationalsache und Element der Bildung," to use Herder's phrase.

For Greece, if we slip over the archaic age and accept Athenian freedoms as Greek freedoms, Winckelmann's model holds good. Only with Macedonian hegemony over the states of classical Greece under Philip and Alexander followed by the Hellenistic or Alexandrian age does freedom disappear and the cultural life of Greece go into long decline (*GKA*, 219 and 225). Rome, however, does not merely not fit the pattern: it actively contradicts it. The Roman Republic endured for centuries, without liberty producing an effusion of art. Its greatest literary flourishing comes not during the Republic, but after its *de facto* demise. This notion causes the interesting distortions in Herder touched on above. On the one hand, he feels compelled to regard Rome's best poets as merely flattering versifiers because they praise freedom's destroyer and, on the other hand, since they by rights should exist in the Republic and not in the Principate, he seems to entertain the notion that after the Republic's physical demise its spirit continued undiminished only to flower fully in the Augustan poets, inasmuch as an "ausländische Blume" can be said to flower in an alien and hostile climate, and only then definitively to pass away with the death of Augustus: "das sieht man stracks nach Augustus Tode" (*HW*, 4:129).

To alleviate the harshness of the exceptional status of this historical anomaly, a reconsideration of the obdurate facts of Latin literary history is advisable. The Roman canon stands in need of some deconstruction. Herder begins the process in an interesting fashion. By his own reckoning he considers Rome's "beste Zeiten" (*HW* 6:610) to have been the Republic, and its greatest soul Caesar. Caesar possessed a "große Seele" (*HW* 6:611), the embodiment of the best to be found within Roman culture. So high are Herder's expectations of the truly great soul's humane virtues that he imagines the temper of the Roman imperium would have been different had Caesar lived: "o hätte er [der höchste Thron der Erde] auch mit seiner [Cäsars] Seele schmücken können, daß Jahrtausende hin ihn der gütige, muntre umfassende Geist Cäsars hätte beleben mögen!" (*HW* 6:611).[114] To describe the character of the individual that disclosed itself in the *Gallic Wars* as "gütig" seems bizarre, and likewise, to anticipate that the ruthless conquering spirit exhibited in it would have resulted in an imperial rule quite different from what did eventually emerge under Augustus seems egregiously hopeful. But then that is the point: Caesar is not Augustus. Herder's animus is directed at Augustus: of his conduct after Actium he judges, "vergebens, daß der schwache, grausame August den friedsamen Gütigen spielte" (6:609). Herder proposes Caesar, and Scipio along with him, as the men of noble feeling alive at the time who would have cursed Rome. He places them in heaven, horrified at the outcome of what they have initiated and looking down "auf Rom, die Räuberhöhle und auf euer vollführtes Mörderhandwerk... Wie unrein mußte euch eure Ehre, wie blutig euer Lorbeer, wie niedrig und menschenfeindlich eure Würgekunst dünken!" (6:600–601). Herder views Caesar as *felix opportunitate mortis*.[115]

Herder stops well short of elevating Caesar to the model of successful literary achievement and carefully phrases most of his statements about Caesar in the subjunctive. The Romantics, in particular Friedrich Schlegel, are less diffident about pursuing the matter to its conclusion. Schlegel makes a similar connection between liberty and literary accomplishment. The thinness of Hellenistic poetry becomes self-evident with the decline of freedom: "so wie mit der Freiheit die öffentliche Sittlichkeit verschwand, so gab es auch in der Poesie eigentlich kein Pathos und Ethos mehr" (*KFS* 1:16). The same holds true for the course of Roman poetry, as becomes apparent in his lectures from 1812 on the history of literature. What greatness the Romans achieved in literature stems from their faithfulness to their grim, republican virtue. He laments greatly their failure to take up the early legends of heroic virtue for the sake of the Republic. Lucretius, although he had taken up the false form of didactic poetry and the equally mistaken sophistry of Epicurus (*KFS* 6:74), still possesses a "große Seele" that makes him "an Begeisterung und Erhabenheit der erste unter den römischen... Dichtern" (*KFS* 6:74). Schlegel also bestows considerable praise on Cicero but awards to Caesar the accolade of greatest writer: "Eine vollkommene Gleichmäßigkeit des Ausdrucks findet sich zuerst im Cäsar. Auch in der Schreibart zeigt sich, wie er im Handeln war" (*KFS* 6:78). The attribution of classical harmony to Caesar's actions and words marks his elevation to the sphere where the inner spirit is deemed to have found an aesthetic representation. What Herder suggested with his insistence on Caesar as the great soul among the Romans, Schlegel argues explicitly. In the slightly earlier *Geschichte der europäischen Literatur* from 1803–4, Caesar achieves what all other Romans failed to do; he combines literary sense with a Roman sensibility: "Caesar, der gar kein griechisches Muster nachahmte, ist von allen wohl der Eigentümlichste, römische Originellste" (*KFS* 11:133). He did so simply by remaining most truly Roman, by living entirely in the public sphere, by being orator, general, and statesman.

The limit on Caesar's rise in the literary canon is given by the fact that he is a prose writer, and verse remains the supreme achievement of a national literature. Thus outwardly, Schlegel retains the customary framework of Latin literary historiography, an earlier initial period, next the golden age of Augustus followed by the silver age of the first century. However, the golden age he only allows to stand as the "sogenannte" (*KFS* 11:135). It is characterized by the attempt to assimilate a Greek form and content to Roman letters, and its foremost proponent is Virgil. Yet the attempt "gelang aber nicht, wie Vergil auch selbst von seinen Gedichten eingesteht" (*KFS* 11:132). Since Schlegel is presumably referring to the story of Virgil's deathbed wish that the *Aeneid* be destroyed, the use of the more general "Gedichte" is slightly misleading and should rather read "Gesänge." However, the more general term "poems" is the more accurate for its reflection of Schlegel's final judgment that not merely Virgil, the putative leading poet of the golden age, but the entire history of Latin literature is a failure.

It remains relevant to the present not merely as cautionary tale but because it also, unhappily, served as the model to subsequent nations seeking to construct a national literature. Thus again the judgment on the Latin heritage, especially that of Virgil, comes also to be a means for Germans of the eighteenth century to articulate their own sense of national identity. The fashion in which Schlegel phrases this conclusion is noteworthy for the unique position he accords the Germans.

> Sie [die römische Literatur] ist ihm [dem philosophischen Beobachter] ein warnendes Beispiel, das sich auch bei den meisten neueren Literaturen, die deutsche ausgenommen, bewährt hat. Alle diese sind durch dasselbe Prinzip untergegangen, welches die römische Literatur verhinderte, etwas Großes zu werden: nämlich durch die strenge, ängstliche Nachahmung einer einzigen fremden Literatur. (*KFS* 11:136)

German literature escapes the fate of a failed literature through its attention to the originals themselves in Greek art and the imitation of them not as Greek, but as objects exemplifying the means for the aesthetic representation of the "Idealschöne." By discovering a "new" and "true" antiquity in Greece, preceding and underlying Latin antiquity with its false "beautiful" and false "nature," the Germans of the eighteenth century create a new authority for literary and cultural production, and by proclaiming their unique affinity to this new Greece they ensure the status of the German national culture they hope to produce. The view that other modern nations have chosen the wrong ancient nature to imitate is not unique to Schlegel. As an example we may take Schiller's comment in *Über naive und sentimentalische Dichtung* that the French are the nation that has at once succeeded in the greatest degree of "Unnatur" and of abstraction. It follows as a counter illustration to the success of the Greeks in reconciling culture to nature, "der Grieche [hatte] die Natur in der Menschheit nicht verloren."[116]

Though the quest for an antiquity in Greece suitable for imitation may owe its motivation to the habit of the modern world of assuring itself of the excellence of its own accomplishments by referring to the authority of the ancients, it does not account for the effort, ingenuity, and passion expended in making Rome and Virgil the opposite. The adamant insistence of Winckelmann, Herder, and Schlegel that Latin artistic culture represents the form of imitation that stifles the native voice so that only a banausic art — in spirit, not in execution, which is all the worse — may result, seems exaggerated. Neither the Herder of the 1770s, the Herder of the late 1780s, nor Schlegel of the 1790s and early 1800s could have seriously feared that German literature was on the brink of devoting itself either primarily or largely to the imitation of Latin literature, despite the dominance of Roman authors in the school curriculum.[117] Herder's animadversions against Latin and its deleterious effect on native cultures likewise seems overdone. It concerns events that occurred hundreds of years before his time, and the language had retreated from the literary field after the Baroque age and in his day was largely confined to the academy and the educational system. Yet, more importantly, in Herder's day Latin showed no signs of gaining new adherents or spreading its use to other areas; quite on the contrary, it showed every sign of further contraction. However, both of these circumstances do apply to German fears of French cultural models and the French language, not to mention French political power in the eighteenth century. Further, the French, if we follow such as Perrault and Voltaire, do proclaim Augustan Rome their great model, and one that they have surpassed. The attentions Herder and Schlegel lavish on Rome's failings gain an added edge not simply from their fears of what baneful influence it may exercise on Germans of the present, but from their anxieties about the cachet it may bestow on its modern avatar.

We may also find more direct traces of this anxiety in Herder. The notion of four golden ages that he works with in *Ursachen des gesunknen Geschmacks*, Periclean Athens, Augustan Rome, Medicean Florence, and the France of Louis XIV, is one most immediately familiar to him from Voltaire's *Siècle de Louis XIV*. The insistence on the connection between freedom and artistic excellence and the negation of freedom through the rule of a single individual also gains a new dimension. The language Herder uses to introduce his discussion of the Augustan age suggests the French parallel. In the passage cited previously he called the Principate "das Joch der Monarchie" (*HW* 4:129). The term "Monarchie," here etymologically accurate (single rule) as a description of the Principate, has the added benefit of also correctly designating, in the more modern sense of rule by a king, France's system of government. The vocabulary of the rest evokes more the atmosphere of the Rococo and of a modern court than it does of the Principate under Augustus. The use of flowers and garlands is a common trope of the era but most peculiar is the description of Augustus as "zierlich" and Maecenas as "spielend" as they are highly inappropriate and once again seem more appropriate to the courts of the eighteenth century.

The larger associations with antiquity first given currency by such as Winckelmann and Herder long remain valid. They both shape Nietzsche's view of the problem of antiquity and provide him with a quick and ready shorthand to frame his remarks on the downfall of Greek art in *Die Geburt der Tragödie*. Like Winckelmann, he identifies the classical period as the zenith of Greek art, but unlike Winckelmann he wishes to truncate this period so that it includes only the fifth century B.C. and not the fourth century B.C.[118] Winckelmann had allowed it to continue until Alexander the Great, after which Greek art went into decline with the imitative style of the Hellenistic period. Nietzsche famously has much to say about this decline. He, in contrast, makes of Socrates with his explicit rationality the decisive figure: "das Kunstwerk der griechischen Tragödie ging an ihm zu Grunde" (*NKS* 1:83). To indicate the gravity of the case, his argument moves in part by assimilating Socrates to the prevailing notion of the Hellenistic age and its deleterious effect so that Socrates becomes the next epoch's founding figure. By easing Socrates into the role of the "first Alexandrian," and so having at his disposal all the harmful effects that his readers have long been accustomed to associate with the period, Nietzsche makes his own task considerably easier. Socrates, according to Nietzsche, introduces critical reason into the consideration of art, " 'alles muss verständig sein, um schön zu sein' " (*NKS* 1:85). For Nietzsche too, modern man remains a creature of criticism so that he may write of him: "Er bleibt doch der ewig Hungernde, der 'Kritiker' ohne Lust und Kraft, der alexandrinische Mensch, der im Grunde Bibliothekar und Corrector ist und an Bücherstaub und Druckfehlern elend erblindet" (*NKS* 1:120). Nietzsche's Hellenistic age is more openly the site of trauma for modernity than previously. He likewise employs the further historical associations of the Hellenistic age. Like Herder, he considers the mark of alienation to be the pursuit of empire, "deren grossartigster, aber auch erschreklichster Ausdruck das römishe imperium ist" (*NKS* 1:133). It is the task of the present to free itself from the "Gängelband einer romanischen Civilisation" (*NKS* 1:129), the false antiquity recovered by the Renaissance, a task with relevance to the Franco-Prussian War in the present.[119]

Such connections are by no means commonplaces for Herder. Indeed he seems reluctant to follow where his arguments would seem to lead, as in his omission of Virgil's name when speaking of the flattering versifiers in the *Ursachen des gesunknen Geschmacks*. There one might merely attribute it to a coy reticence. In the *Ideen* his attitude grows more curious. Just as Herder did not carry the logic of his argument concerning Caesar to its conclusion, a task left to Schlegel, so too he refuses to draw the conclusion regarding Virgil that his position would seem to require. Again it will be left to Schlegel to argue that Virgil's works are "mit Recht" (*KFS* 5:38) denied the title of poems. In the *Ideen*, when it would seem to suit his argument, Herder makes no special mention of exactly the poet who not merely takes it as his task to sing of this "Dämongeschichte" but also prides himself on telling how, *tantae molis erat Romanam condere gentem* (*Aen.* 1: 33; such was the cost in heavy toil of beginning the life of Rome, 28). By rights he should receive particular attention. Surely such a poet cannot harbor a single human feeling within him, or, at the very least, he is not the noble individual whom Herder envisions alive at the time and cognizant of Rome's depravity. Indeed this poet must have a very limited conception of poetic creation for him to have put his art at the service of imperial Rome. Quite to the contrary, Herder's remarks about Virgil in the *Ideen* are more approving than previously. Poetry still remains an inherently "ausländische Blume" (*HW* 6:616) on Latin soil, although Herder now deems the cultivation of the "Wissenschaften ... und die Musen" to be "der einzig-unbefleckte Lorbeer in Augusts Krone" (*HW* 6:617). Among those Herder nominates to receive his thanks for this laurel, he singles out Augustus "daß er uns den halben Homer in der Aeneis seines Maro erhalten" (*HW* 6:617) and the monks of the scriptoria "daß ihr um Latein zu lernen, uns den Terenz, Horaz, Boethius, vor allen andern aber Euren Virgil als einen rechtgläubigen Dichter aufbewahrt" (*HW* 6:617). That he should cherish from the ruins of the "Dämongeschichte" the survival "vor allen andern" of the poet who is most "reichgläubig" — to put words in Herder's mouth — "vor allen andern," and further that he should prize him for his epic, though Virgil is in it only half a Homer, seems remarkable. To call the singer of a "Dämongeschichte" even half a Homer becomes thus a mark of approbation rather than of reprobation. It testifies not merely to the continued familiarity of the eighteenth century with Virgil but to the influence the Virgilian muse continues to exercise over the imagination, even if every argument militates against its acknowledgment. Herder, himself for instance is sufficiently enamored of a choice phrase that he uses a Virgilian epigraph for the fourth part of the *Ideen*, which traces the fortunes of the northern peoples after the fall of Rome: *Tantae molis erat, Germanias condere gentes* (*HW* 6:673; So great was the effort to found the German peoples). However, as Winckelmann provides the most striking example of the way in which Rome and a Virgilian muse may condition the possible view of Greece, we shall turn first to him.

Notes

[1] Cited according to Propertius, *Elegies I–IV*, ed. Lawrence Richardson (Norman: University of Oklahoma Press, 1976). On the dating of the poems see the introduction, 9.

[2] The standard study of Virgil in the Middle Ages remains Domenico Comparetti's *Vergil in the Middle Ages* from 1872, the English translation of which by E. F. M. Benecke from 1885 has recently been reissued with an introduction by Jan Ziolkowski (Princeton: Princeton UP, 1997). See also: Christopher Baswell, *Virgil in Medieval England* (Cambridge: Cambridge UP, 1995); Craig Kallendorf, *In Praise of Aeneas: Virgil and Epideictic Rhetoric in the Early Italian Renaissance* (Hanover and London: UP of New England, 1989). For a succinct presentation of Virgil's displacement of Homer see Antonie Wlosok, "Zur Geltung und Beurteilung Vergils und Homers in Spätantike und früher Neuzeit," in *Res humanae — res divinae*, ed. Eberhard Heck and Ernst A. Schmidt (Heidelberg: Winter, 1990), 476–98.

[3] Marco Girolamo Vida, *The "De arte poetica" of Marco Girolamo Vida*, trans. with commentary by Ralph G. Williams (New York: Columbia UP, 1976), 1:170–74. Williams reprints the text of the *editio princeps* from 1527 but also includes the unauthorized earlier version of ca. 1517; see introduction to the text of ca. 1517, 199–211.

[4] See the *vita Donatiana* from the fourth century but based on a second-century life by Suetonius for portents and auspicious signs attending Virgil's birth, in *Vitae Vergilianae antiquae*, ed. Giorgio Brugnoli and Fabio Stok (Romae: Typis Officinae Polygraphicae, 1997), 3–5, and for a discussion of it Nicholas Horsfall, "Virgil: His Life and Times," in *A Companion to the Study of Virgil*, ed. Nicholas Horsfall (Leiden: Brill, 1995), 1–25, and Werner Sauerbaum, "Vita Vergiliana — accessus Vergiliani — Zauberer Virgilius," in *Aufstieg und Niedergang der römischen Welt*, ed. Hildegard Temporini and Wolfgang Haase (Berlin: Walter de Gruyter, 1981), 31/2:1156–1262. On the popular Virgil see the second part of Comparetti, *Vergil in the Middle Ages*, as well as John Webster Spargo, *Virgil the Neocromancer* (Cambridge: Harvard UP, 1934), and also Suerbaum, "Vita Vergiliana," 1229–61.

[5] Johann Christoph Gottsched, *Ausgewählte Werke*, ed. Joachim Birke (Berlin: De Gruyter, 1968–95), 6/2:279.

[6] Adam Parry, "The Two Voices of Virgil's *Aeneid*," reprinted in *Virgil: A Collection of Critical Essays*, ed. Steele Commager (Englewood Cliffs, NJ: Prentice-Hall, 1966), 107–23.

[7] I have taken the term "Augustan reading" from Richard F. Thomas, *Virgil and the Augustan Reception* (Cambridge: Cambridge UP, 2001): "By 'Augustan reader' I mean a reader who sees the writings of Virgil as endorsements of the aims and achievements of Imperator Caesar Divi filius Augustus (as he would eventually be called), endorsements generated either by Virgil's own political and ideological conviction or by the application of external suggestion, chiefly from his 'patron' Maecenas; that is a reader who takes from Virgil what Augustus himself would presumably have wanted a contemporary reader to take" (xii).

[8] Servius, *Servii Grammatici qui ferunter in Vergilii carmina commentarii*, ed. Georg Thilo and Hermann Hagen, 3 vols. (1878–1902; Leipzig: Teubner, 1923–27), here 1:4.

[9] The full passage beginning the chapter is: *Primum igitur Graecos Latinosque inter se conferemus. Ac primum quidem primos, Homerum atque Vergilium, ex quorum comparatione cuiusmodi iudicium de aliis faciendum sit constabit facilius* in Julius Caesar Scaliger, *Poetices libri septem*, 5 vols., ed. Luc Deitz and Gregor Vogt-Spira (Stuttgart: Friedrich Frommann, 1994–98), 4:46.

[10] Luc Deitz, "Zur Wirkungsgeschichte," in Scaliger, *Poetices libri septem*, 1:xliii.

[11] Charles Perrault, "Le Siècle de Louis le Grand," in *Parallèle des anciens et des modernes* (repr. of 2nd ed.: Paris, 1692–97; repr.: Geneva: Slatkine Reprints, 1971), 79. The pagination refers to that of the reprint, not that of the 2nd edition itself.

[12] Perrault, "Le Siècle de Louis le Grand," 81.

[13] John Dryden, *The Works of John Dryden*, ed. Alan Roper (Berkeley: U of California P, 1987), 5:286.

[14] See Ronald Calinger, *Gottfried Wilhelm Leibniz* (Troy, NY: Renssaeler Polytechnic Institute, 1976), 16; and John Edwin Sandys, *A History of Classical Scholarship* (Cambridge: Cambridge UP, 1908), 3:2.

[15] Cited in Sigrid von der Schulenburg, *Leibniz als Sprachforscher*, Veröffentlichungen des Leibniz-Archivs 4 (Frankfurt am Main: Klostermann, 1973), 171.

[16] Douglas Lane Patey gives a summary of the *Querelle* and its main themes and effects in "Ancient and Moderns," in *The Cambridge History of Literary Criticism*, ed. H. B. Nisbett and Claude Rawson (Cambridge: Cambridge UP, 1997), 4:32–74. The standard accounts of the *Querelle* are by H. Rigault, *Histoire de la querelle des anciens et des modernes* (Paris: 1859; New York: Burt Franklin, 1965) and Hubert Gillot, *La Querelle des anciens et des modernes en France* (Paris: Édouard Champion, 1914). A more recent survey of the same ground, and more inclusive since it includes both the earlier Italian and Humanist contributions and also the later German responses in addition to the better known French and English parties in the *Querelle*, though with an "ancienist" bent, is by Marc de Fumaroli in "Les Abeilles et les araignées" (7–218), the introduction to the anthology of texts *La Querelle des anciens et des modernes*, ed. Anne-Marie Lecoq (n.p.: Gallimard, 2001). For a charming account of the poem's reading at the Academy based on Perrault's memoirs see Rigault, 150–57 as well as Hans Kortum, "Die Hintergründe einer Akademiesitzung im Jahre 1687," in *Antike und Moderne in der Literaturdiskussion des 18. Jahrhunderts*, ed. Werner Krauss and Hans Kortum (Berlin: Akademie Verlag, 1966), lxix–lxxi.

[17] Anne Madame de Dacier, *Des Causes de la Corruption du Goust* (1714; repr. Genève: Slatkine Reprints, 1970), 3.

[18] On the development of a historical sense see Werner Krauss, "Der Streit der Altertumsfreunde mit den Anhängern der Moderne und die Entstehung des geschichtlichen Weltbildes," in *Antike und Moderne in der Literaturdiskussion des 18. Jahrhunderts*, ix–lix and also Hans Robert Jauss, for particular attention to Perrault's sense of history and its implications, "Ästhetische Normen und geschichtliche

Reflexion in der 'Querelle des Anciens et des Modernes,'" in Charles Perrault, *Parallèle des anciens et des modernes en ce qui regarde les arts et les sciences*, ed. Max Imdahl, Wolfgang Iser, Hans Robert Jauss, Wolfgang Preisendanz and Jurij Striedter (Munich: Eidos Verlag, 1964), 8–65.

[19] *Grosses Vollständiges Universal Lexikon* (Leipzig und Halle: Zedler, 1735), 13: 737.

[20] See Michael Baridon, "Historiography," in *Cambridge History of Literary Criticism*, ed. H. B. Nisbet and Claude Rawson (Cambridge: Cambridge UP, 1997), 4:282–301, also Krauss, "Der Streit der Altertumsfreunde," xxii–xxviii, and for particular attention to the development of historical thought in Germany in the earlier German "Aufklärung" see Peter Hanns Reill, *The German Enlightenment and the Rise of Historicism* (Berkeley: U of California P, 1975).

[21] The connection between this historical attitude and the earlier French *Querelle* has been most forcefully argued by Hans Robert Jauss in "Schlegels und Schillers Replik auf die 'Querelle des Anciens et des Modernes,'" in *Literaturgeschichte als Provokation* (Frankfurt am Main: Suhrkamp, 1970), 67–106, which he argues (71) is the further development of many points he raised in his earlier "Ästhetische Normen." In this latter work he was influenced by Peter Szondi in his "Antike und Moderne in der Ästhetik der Goethezeit," in *Poetik und Geschichtsphilosophie 1*, ed. Senta Metz and Hans-Hagen Hildebrandt (Frankfurt am Main: Suhrkamp, 1974).

[22] Thomas, *Virgil and the Augustan Reception*.

[23] Heinze's importance is a point of agreement on all sides: "Am Anfang der neuen Vergilbetrachtung steht unbestritten R. Heinzes Buch über 'Vergils epische Technik' (1903, 1915)" (Antonie Wlosok, "Vergil in der neueren Forschung," in *Res humanae — res divinae*, ed. Eberhard Heck and Ernst A. Schmidt [Heidelberg: Winter, 1990], 281), and Duncan F. Kennedy, in the bibliographic note at the end of "Virgilian Epic," in *The Cambridge Companion to Virgil*, ed. Charles Martindale (Cambridge: Cambridge UP, 1997): "Richard Heinze's *Vergils epische Technik* underlies much of the scholarly work done on Virgilian epic during this century and is now belatedly available in an English translation" (153). See also: Charles Martindale, "Introduction: 'The Classic of All Europe,'" in *The Cambridge Companion to Virgil*, ed. Charles Martindale (Cambridge: Cambridge UP, 1997), 15 and Brooks Otis, *Virgil: A Study in Civilized Poetry* (Oxford: Clarendon Press, 1963), 3.

[24] See Theodore Ziolkowski, *Virgil and the Moderns* (Princeton: Princeton UP, 1993), especially chapter 1.

[25] The title of Haecker's book from 1931, which in full reads *Vergil: Vater des Abendlandes*. We might also mention here T. S. Eliot's 1945 essay "What is a Classic?" in which he defines the term in relation to Virgil, "the universal classic, like Virgil" (*What is a Classic?* [London: Faber & Faber, 1945], 10).

[26] On Haecker see Ziolkowski, *Virgil and the Moderns*, 48–52 and on Oppermann, Thomas, *Virgil and the Augustan Reception*, 241–46.

[27] Wendell Clausen, "An Interpretation of the *Aeneid*," in Commager, *Virgil: A Collection of Critical Essays*, 86.

[28] Thomas, *Virgil and the Augustan Reception*, 259.

[29] In Werner Suerbaum, *Vergils "Aeneis": Epos zwischen Geschichte und Gegenwart* (Stuttgart: Reclam, 1999), 396 about the Werner Suerbaum of *Vergils "Aeneis": Beiträge zu ihrer Rezeption in Gegenwart und Geschichte* (Bamberg: Buchner, 1981). The Suerbaum of 2002 seems to distance himself further from his earlier sympathies when he speaks in the article on Virgil in the *Neue Pauly* of a tendency to "enthistorisieren" the *Aeneid* and comments on newer approaches as "man könnte auch sagen: Subjektivität der Thesen" ("V. Maro, P.," in *Der neue Pauly: Enzyklopädie der Antike* [Stuttgart, Weimar: Metzler, 2002], 12/2: 52). For the pessimistic view of the omissions of the Augustan reading see W. R. Johnson, *Darkness Visible* (Berkeley: U of California P, 1976), 8–10, and for the Augustan view of pessimistic Virgil see Wlosok, "Vergil in der neueren Forschung." Wlosok finds it unhistorical and therefore defective scholarship: "Denn dieser neue Vergil ist eine Art Bastard, letzlich ist er unvergilisch. Er verdankt seine Existenz fundamentalen Mißverständnissen, die freilich symptomatisch sind für die zunehmende Vernachlässigung historischer Interpretation oder die verbreitete Unfähigkeit zu geschichtlichem Verstehen" (295; see also 299–300). For a more nuanced criticism along the same lines, see Viktor Pöschl, "Das befremdende in der Aeneis," in *2000 Jahre Vergil: Ein Symposium*, ed. Viktor Pöschl (Wiesbaden: in Kommission bei Otto Harrassowitz, 1983). He regards the tendency to use a work of the past as a "Vehikel eigener Aussage" (181) as common to the age, and not peculiar to Virgilian scholarship. For short presentations of twentieth-century approaches to Virgil, see Martindale, "Introduction," 1–18, and S. J. Harrison, "Some Views of the *Aeneid* in the Twentieth Century," in *Oxford Readings in Vergil's "Aeneid,"* ed S. J. Harrison (Oxford: Oxford UP, 1990), 1–20, which is slightly older, but since it focuses on the *Aeneid*, it also focuses more centrally on the two opposing views.

[30] Robert Graves, "The Virgil Cult," Virginia Quarterly Review, 38 (1962), 13. Graves writes in strong criticism of such as T. S. Eliot. More generally on trends for and against in English, see Charles Martindale's introduction to *Virgil and His Influence: Bimillenial Studies*, ed. Charles Martindale (Bristol: Bristol Classical Press, 1984), 11–13.

[31] Peta G. Fowler and Don P. Fowler, "Virgil," in *The Oxford Classical Dictionary*, ed. Simon Hornblower and Antony Spawforth, 3rd ed. (Oxford: Oxford UP, 1996), 1606.

[32] A. W. Schlegel, *Kritische Ausgabe der Vorlesungen*, ed. Ernst Behler (Paderborn: Schöningh, 1989), 623.

[33] A. W. Schlegel, *Vorlesungen*, 621.

[34] "Völlig beiseite gelassen habe ich Sprache und Vers der Aeneis: beides für die Wirkung des Gedichts von größter Bedeutung, nicht so für das Verständnis des Gedichts als epischen Kunstwerks" (Richard Heinze, "Vorwort zur ersten Auflage," in *Virgils epische Technik*, 3rd ed. [Leipzig: Teubner, 1915], v).

[35] Putnam notes that his work arise from Heinze's and characterizes the debt of Virgilian scholarship to Heinze as follows: "It is Heinze who first set as a specific goal the search for the original elements in the poetry of the *Aeneid*." See Michael C. J. Putnam, *The Poetry of the Aeneid* (Cambridge: Harvard UP, 1965), vii.

[36] Heinze, *Technik*, v.

[37] Heinze, *Technik*, vi.

[38] Johnson, *Darkness Visible*, 50.

[39] Gustav Seibt, "Die unnachahmlichen Nachahmer: Das seltsame Verhältnis der Deutschen zu den Griechen: Wie eine verspätete Nation den Zauber der Frühe suchte," *Die Zeit*, Zeitliteratur, Sonderbeilage, 4. Oct. 2001 (41): 55.

[40] Hans Oppermann, "Vergil," in *Wege zu Vergil: Drei Jahrzehnte Begegnungen in Dichtung und Wissenschaft*, ed. Hans Oppermann, Wege der Forschung 19 (Darmstadt: Wissenschaftliche Buchgesellschaft, 1963), 92.

[41] Rudolf Borchardt, "Vergil," in *Wege zu Vergil*, 199.

[42] Theodor Haecker, *Vergil, Vater des Abendlandes* (Leipzig: Hegner, 1931), 21.

[43] Haecker, *Vergil, Vater des Abendlandes*, 127.

[44] Friedrich Klingner, "Virgil: Wiederentdeckung eines Dichters," in *Römische Geisteswelt*, 5th enlarged ed. (Munich: Ellermann, 1965), 240 and 241.

[45] Klingner, "Virgil," 241.

[46] Immanuel Kant, *Gesammelte Schriften*, ed. Königliche Preußische Akademie der Wissenschaften (Berlin: Georg Reimer, 1905), 2:212.

[47] Works dealing with German Hellenism are numerous; those dealing with their response to the Latin tradition much less so. See the chapter on the eighteenth century in Volker Riedel, *Antikerezeption in der deutschen Literatur vom Renaissance-Humanismus bis zur Gegenwart* (Stuttgart: Metzler, 2000), 109–222. His treatment of the change from a Latin to a Greek model is laconic though telling: "Zugleich verlagerte sich der Schwerpunkt der Antike von Rom, das in der gesamten bisherigen Rezeptionstradition dominiert hatte, auf Griechenland. . . . Dieser Wandlungsprozeß — für den die Einstellung zu Homer und Vergil als paradigmatisch angesehen werden kann —. . ." (111–12).

[48] Voltaire, "Essai sur la poésie épique," in *The Complete Works of Voltaire*, ed. Ulla Köving (Oxford: Voltaire Foundation, 1968–), 3B:429. The "Essai" of 1733 is a revised version of the piece Voltaire first wrote and published in English in 1727 under the title, "An Essay on Epic Poetry." Voltaire's concern for the success of his epic *La Henriade* and his sense of the different bias between an English and a French audience led him to make changes between the English and French versions. For an account of the differences, their import, and other details see its introduction, 155–82. The line cited above is one of those differences; it does not occur in the English version.

[49] See John A. McCarthy, *Christoph Martin Wieland* (Boston: Twayne Publishers, 1979), 15.

[50] Karoline Schelling, *Caroline: Briefe aus der Frühromantik*, ed. Erich Schmidt (Leipzig: Insel, 1913), 2:170, from the letter of 12 June 1801 to A. W. Schlegel.

[51] Friedrich Schlegel, *Von den Schulen der griechischen Poesie*, 1794, in *Kritische Friedrich-Schlegel-Ausgabe*, ed. Ernst Behler et al. (Munich: F. Schöningh, 1958–), 1:16. Subsequent references to the collected works are cited in the text using the abbreviation *KFS* and the volume and page numbers.

[52] See John Chalker, *The English Georgic: A Study in the Development of a Form* (Baltimore: Johns Hopkins P, 1969).

53 From the letter of 16/9/1799 to Wilhelm von Humboldt, in *Goethes Werke*, commissioned by the Grand Duchess Sophia of Saxony (1893; repr. Tokyo: Sansyusya, 1975), ser. 4, 14:188.

54 A. W. Schlegel, *Vorlesungen*, 610.

55 C. S. Lewis, "Virgil and the Subject of Secondary Epic," in *Virgil: A Collection of Critical Essays*, ed. Steele Commager (Englewood Cliffs, NJ: Prentice-Hall, 1966), 63.

56 Taken from Friedrich Schlegel, *Geschichte der europäischen Literatur* (KFS 11:3–188); specifically on Latin literature, 126–37.

57 August Wilhelm Schlegel gives a detailed examination of the various ways in which, for a romantic, the circumstances opposed the poet in his "Vorlesungen über schöne Literatur und Kunst" (Berlin 1801–4), in *Vorlesungen*, 603–24.

58 Barthold Georg Niebuhr, *Vorträge über die römische Geschichte an der Universität zu Bonn gehalten*, ed. Myer Isler, 3 vols. (Berlin: Reimer, 1846–48), 3:130–32. Isler claims that he has made only slight use of the earlier lectures from 1826 that concluded with Sulla. An earlier, English version of these lectures was published with the cooperation of Isler in 1844, which must be regarded as testament to the avid English interest in Roman history and the authority of Niebuhr as a scholar familiar to them from the translation of his *History of Rome* (1828–42). It is very similar to the German edition although it ends with a judgment omitted from the German: ". . . it never occurs to me to place Virgil among the Roman poets of the first order, . . .," Barthold Georg Niebuhr, *Lectures of the History of Rome from the Earliest Times to the Fall of the Western Empire*, ed. Leonhard Schmitz, 4th ed. (London: Lockwood & Co., 1873), 663.

59 In English treatments of Virgil in England in the nineteenth century, the Germans are frequently mentioned as the source of the strongly unfavorable view of Virgil without, however, mention of names. W. Y. Sellar, the Victorian author of a popular general study of Virgil (1877), also wrote the entry for Virgil in the ninth edition of the *Encyclopaedia Britannica*, in which he dates the spread of the German view of Virgil to the first half of the nineteenth century without mentioning names: ". . . and during the first half of the present century, when English criticism first came under German influence, there was a strong reaction from the habitual deference paid to those writers who had moulded literary taste in the previous century. The estimation of Virgil, as the most consummate representative of Latin culture suffered most from this reaction" (24:248). And again, since Sellar cites in his general study of Virgil from French and Latin sources but not German ones, it is difficult to know whom precisely he is thinking of among the Germans. The exception to this is Niebuhr. Through his popularity in England he acted as a conduit for the German view with the result that he seems to become something of a *fons ab origine* for it in England. Matthew Arnold, for instance, makes an explicit reference to Niebuhr's views in his "The Modern Element in Literature," as is noted by Johnson in his consideration of nineteenth-century attitudes to Virgil in *Darkness Visible* (5), and also by Norman Vance in his essay, "Virgil and the Nineteenth Century," in *Virgil and His Influence*, 187. Vance discusses both the French (Victor Hugo and Sainte-Beuve) and the Germans as sources for the ingredients for the English view of Virgil. However, among the Germans, only the

historians Niebuhr and Theodor Mommsen are mentioned explicitly (171–72). Of Niebuhr's influence, he concludes: "This German view of Virgil, buttressed by formidable scholarship, was very influential in England, where Niebuhr's work attracted the interest of scholars such as the great Dr. Arnold of Rugby" (172).

[60] Charles Augustin Sainte-Beuve, *Étude sur Virgile*, ed. Calmann Lévy (Paris: Lévy Frères, 1891), 29.

[61] Sainte-Beuve, *Étude sur Virgile*, 30.

[62] Victor Hugo, "La préface de Cromwell," in *Oeuvres Complètes*, Centre National des Lettres, ed. Jacques Seebacher et al., 15 vols. (Paris: Robert Laffont, 1985), 12:22.

[63] Hugo, "A Virgile," in *Les voix intérieures* (*Oeuvres Complètes*, 4:845). Vance takes a different view of Hugo's attitude toward Virgil. He argues that from a youthful liking of Virgil he matures to the more romantic view of Virgil as a derivative poet (175 and 177).

[64] The English relation to Virgil is well documented. See Elizabeth Nitchie, *Vergil and the English Poets* (New York: Columbia UP, 1919), and a number of shorter, recent general treatments of the topic: R. D. Williams, *The Aeneid*, Unwin Critical Library, ed. Claude Rawson (London: Allen & Unwin, 1987), 155–61; Jasper Griffin, "Virgil," in *The Legacy of Rom: A New Appraisal*, ed. Richard Jenkyns (Oxford: Oxford UP, 1992), 125–50; and Martindale, "Introduction," 1–18. While English appreciation of Virgil in the nineteenth century may have been apologetic, it was nonetheless widespread and continuous. Frank M. Turner's statement, "The Victorian estimation of Virgil was not, however, simply critical; it was genuinely hostile" ("Why the Greeks and not the Romans?" in *Rediscovering Hellenism*, ed. G. W. Clarke [Cambridge: Cambridge UP, 1989], 71), should be balanced with the delightful romp through the nineteenth century by Jasper, and by Vance's more comprehensive treatment of the topic.

[65] See also Griffin, "Virgil," 139. The Aeneid is cited according to book and verse number from the text of Opera, ed. R. A. B. Mynors (Oxford: Oxford UP, 1969), and the translations are from W. F. Jackson Knight's translation (Baltimore: Penguin, 1958) unless otherwise noted.

[66] Samuel Taylor Coleridge, *The Collected Works*, ed. Kathleen Coburn et al. (London: Routledge and K. Paul; Princeton: Princeton UP, 1969–), 12/1:110.

[67] Samuel Taylor Coleridge, *Specimens of the Table Talk of the Late Samuel Taylor Coleridge*, ed. H. N. Coleridge (New York: Harper & Brothers, 1835), 1:57, 8 May 1824. See also his letter to Godwin from 8 July 1807, in which again he limits his estimation to Virgil's technical mastery (*Collected Letters of Samuel Taylor Coleridge*, ed. Earl Leslie Griggs [Oxford: Clarendon Press, 1956–71], 2:743).

[68] Publius Vergilius Maro, *Opera*, ed. John Conington and Henry Nettleship (London: Whitaker & Co., 1858–71). Conington judges the poetry of "external nature" to enjoy a verdant life in his day, yet the genre of pastoral and eclogue, that is the idyll, has become too distasteful to the English. "For this corruption probably no writer is so heavily chargeable as Virgil" (introduction to the *Eclogues*, 1:3). In his introduction to the *Georgics* he spends the first few pages detailing the excellences of Hesiod's *Works and Days*. His reason for this beginning: "I have thought it worth

while to give this sketch of Hesiod's poem, endeavouring to preserve something of its colour as well as its form, that it may be seen how far removed it stands in its rude simplicity from the pomp and circumstance of later didactic poetry, and how little Virgil understood of his author's genius or his own when he spoke of himself as singing the song of Ascra through the towns of Rome" (1:124). He also repeats the Enlightenment's judgment on the worth of the *Georgics*. "As enthusiasm is wanting, the reader's imagination will find no sustenance; but his taste will be gratified provided he considers only metre and diction" (1:133–34). Of the *Aeneid*, he begins, "In turning from the Eclogues and the Georgics to the Aeneid, we are no longer confronted by the opinion which insists on Virgil's claims as a strictly original poet" (2:2).

[69] W. Y. Sellar, *The Roman Poets of the Augustan Age: Virgil* (repr. 2nd ed. 1883; Oxford: Clarendon, 1897). Sellar accepts the theoretical categories of the Romantics. Of the three types of imagination, Greek, Italian, and Germanic, Sellar notes their divergence thus: "The genius of the ancient Latin race is further removed from that of the modern Germanic race, than either is from the genius of ancient Greece" (88). Were we to seek in Virgil "the original force of creative imagination which we find in Homer, Aeschylus, and Sophocles on the one hand, and in the greatest poets of modern times on the other, we shall fail to establish his equality with them" (87). He offers no insight into the bond between the "soul of man and the soul of Nature" (88). Within the narrow scope of objects that appeal to the Latin mind, Virgil, according to Sellar, achieves great imaginative clarity. Sellar, uncertain of the merits of these objects, does not push the claim very far. The strongest reason that he can find for the study of Virgil is historical; he was once important to Western culture: "Though the thoughts of the Latin poet may not help us to understand the spirit of our own era, they are a bond of union with the genius and culture of Europe in other times" (91). The English so relish this tepid endorsement that they require three editions of Sellar and numerous reprintings up to 1941.

[70] Alfred Tennyson, *The Poems of Tennyson*, ed. Christopher Ricks (Berkeley: U of California P, 1987), 3:102.

[71] W. Y. Sellar, *The Roman Poets*, 163–64.

[72] Williams, *The Aeneid*, 163.

[73] See also Griffin, "Virgil," 139.

[74] Ziolkowski, *Virgil and the Moderns*, 35–38.

[75] Friedrich Hölderlin, "Rousseau," in *Sämtliche Werke*, ed. Friedrich Beissner, Stuttgarter Ausgabe, im Auftrag des württembergischen Kultministeriums (Stuttgart: J. G. Cottasche Buchhandlung Nachfolger, 1944–85), 2/1:12.

[76] Johann Wolfgang von Goethe, *Sämtliche Werke nach Epochen seines Schaffens*, ed. Karl Richter et al., 21 vols. (Munich: Hanser, 1985–97), 2/2:351–52. All citations from Goethe's works, unless otherwise noted, are from this edition, known as the "Münchener Ausgabe," and reference will be made in the text citing the abbreviation *GSW*, the volume, and page number.

[77] See "Von deutscher Baukunst," *GSW* 1/2:835–37 for details on its composition and the "Stellenkommentar" for a note on the phrase "Bäume Gottes." Goethe uses the phrase again at greater length and more explicitly a few pages later to illustrate the inspiration in the Gothic treatment of columns to relieve the monotony

of rows of pillars: "Vermannigfaltige die ungeheure Mauer, die du gen Himmel führen sollst, daß sie aufsteige gleich einem hocherhabenen, weitverbreiteten Baume Gottes, der mit tausend Ästen, Millionen, Zweigen, und Blättern wie der Sand am Meer, rings um, der Gegend verkündet, die Herrlichkeit des Herrn, seines Meisters" (415). Goethe presumably intends us to call to mind the fine filigree-like work of Gothic vaulting.

[78] Tiberius Claudius Donatus, *Interpretationes Vergilianae*, ed. Heinrich Georg, Bibliotheca Scriptorum Graecorum et Romanorum Teubneriana (Stuttgart: B.G. Teubner, 1969), 2:240–49. Scaliger, *Poetices libri septem*, 1:95.

[79] Johann Gottfried Herder, *Werke*, ed. Martin Bollacher et al., 10 vols. (Frankfurt am Main: Deutscher Klassiker Verlag, 1985–2000), 1:734. Subsequent references to this work will be made using the abbreviation *HW*, and the volume and page numbers.

[80] Gottsched, *Ausgewählte Werke*, 6/2:76.

[81] The second passage is in the letter of March 15 (*GSW* 2/2:410). Voss achieves his great success as *the* translator of Homer with the *Odyssey* (1781); the *Iliad* only follows twelve years later. Schiller picks up on Werther's preference for Odysseus in the passage from *Über naive und sentimentale Dichtung* characterizing Greek nature as he leads to French "Unnatur" (see in *Schillers Werke*, ed. Julius Petersen and Gerhard Fricke, Nationalausgabe, im Auftrag des Goethe- und Schiller Archivs, des Schiller-Nationalmuseums und der Deutschen Akademie [Weimar: Böhlaus Nachfolger, 1934–], 20:431–32. Subsequent references to this work will be made by using the volume and page number). A. W. Schlegel, though he usually speaks of Homer in general language, also acknowledges that it is really the *Odyssey* that remains serviceable to the age: "Ein in unserm Zeitalter und unsern Sitten einheimisches Epos wird daher mehr eine Odysee als eine Ilias sein, sich mehr mit dem Privatleben als mit öffentlichen Taten und Verhältnissen beschäftigen müssen" (*Kritische Schriften*, ed. Emil Staiger [Zurich: Artemis, 1962]), 237). The success of the later eighteenth century in assimilating the Odyssean Homer to its benevolent view of a timeless humanity in nature lends both shock and vehemence to the second excursus of Horkheimer and Adorno's *Dialektik der Aufklärung* devoted to the *Odyssey*. Their use of such concepts as "das bürgerlich aufklärerische Element Homers" (58) and the insistence that epic is not a direct, unmediated conduit of myth (58–59) as well as the ubiquity of violence (*passim*) indicate that they aim at the Homer of the age of Goethe as they experience the hollowness of "Bildung" in the spirit of Greece during the Second World War. (Max Horkheimer, Theodor Adorno, *Dialektik der Aufklarung* [1944; Amsterdam: Querido, 1947]).

[82] A. W. Schlegel, "Hermann und Dorothea," in *Kritische Schriften*, 221.

[83] A. W. Schlegel, "Hermann und Dorothea," 221. Schlegel takes a number of runs at summing up in a phrase the quintessential characteristic of epic narrative (228, 230) but only later mints the phrase that encapsulates it: "als ruhige Darstellung des Fortschreitenden" (240). He repeats the phrase in his Berlin lectures of 1801–4 and other similar expressions to the same effect; of epic "Idealität," "wie eine höhere Intelligenz auf den nach ihren eignen Gesetzen umgestalteten Fortgang der Dinge herabschaut, den sie sich gleichmäßig und harmonisch abrollen

läßt" (*Vorlesungen*, 611). The prescription is of particularly sharp effect when made in the context of a consideration of the often dramatic passion of Virgil's characters and speeches. Heinze takes up the association when he turns to deal with the issue of peripeteia, a trait of drama, in Virgil. The section begins: "Dem rein epischen Stile entspricht die ruhig und stetig in einer Richtung ablaufende, wenn auch durch retardierende Momente zeitweise aufgehaltene Handlung, dem dramatischen der jähe Umschlag, die περιπέτεια" (*Technik* 323).

[84] A. W. Schlegel, *Vorlesungen*, 252.

[85] Manfred Fuhrmann expresses the same thought in "Die Querelle des Anciens et des Modernes, der Nationalismus und die deutsche Klassik," in *Brechungen: Wirkungsgeschichtliche Studien zur antik-europäischen Bildungstradition* (Stuttgart: Klett, 1982), 142. Fuhrmann desires to downplay the element of patriotic pride in the comparison between modern and ancient by emphasizing the more general scope the terms themselves imply (131). My desire is likewise not to argue that national myopia dictates the argument but that it sets some of its accents.

[86] Conrad Wiedemann places the issue of national identity within the context of an assimilation of and reaction to the French Enlightenment, "The Germans' Concern about their National Identity in the Pre-Romantic Era: An Answer to Montesquieu?" in *Concepts of National Identity: An Interdisciplinary Dialogue: Interdiisziplinäre Betrachtungen zur Frage der nationalen Identität*, ed. Peter Boerner (Baden-Baden: Nomos, 1986), 141–52. For the impact of the French Revolution on the sense of nation, see Otto Dann, "Deutsche Nationsbildung im Zeichen französischer Herausforderung," in *Die deutsche Nation: Gesichte — Probleme — Perspektiven*, ed. Otto Dann (Vierow bei Greifswald: SH-Verlag, 1994), 9–23.

[87] Walther Rehm also places the origins of German philhellenism in Winckelmann within the context of a Gallicized Rome. Of Winckelmann's response to the "Romgedanke," he argues, "Frankreich schenkte ihm neuen Auftrieb und führte ihn im 17. Jahrhundert großartig ins Wirkliche. 'Arma et Litterae' trugen den römisch untergründeten, romanisch-französischen Macht- und Kultureinfluß durch die gebildetet europäische Welt. Ein neuer 'Orbis Romanus' wurde tatsächlich sichtbar, und gegen ihn eröffnete Winckelmann den Kampf" (Rehm, *Griechentum und Goethezeit: Geschichte eines Glaubens* [Leipzig: Dieterich'sche Verlagsbuchhandlung, 1936], 26).

[88] In contrast to the earlier insistence on an autonomous German cultural development often measured by its supposed rejection of the intellectual and literary culture of the French Enlightenment, the decades after the Second World War have concentrated on the intimate connections between the two, a direction most notably taken by Werner Krauss, "Die französische Aufklärung und die deutsche Geisteswelt," in *Perspektiven und Probleme: Zur französischen und deutschen Aufklärung und andere Aufsätze* (Luchterhand: Berlin, 1965), 121–265.

[89] See Szondi, "Antike und Moderne," 57–58, and Fuhrmann, "Die Querelle des Anciens et des Modernes," 142.

[90] See Krauss, *Perspektiven*, 157.

[91] On the relation of "Germanistik" to the nationalist project in the nineteenth century, see Thomas Schmidt, "Deutsche National-Philologie oder Neuphilologie in Deutschland? Internationalität und Interdisziplinarität in der Frühgeschichte der

Germanistik," in *Internationalität nationaler Literaturen*, ed. Udo Schöning (Göttingen: Wallstein, 2000), 311–40, and Krauss, *Perspektiven*, 121–42. H. Cysarz in the article on "Klassik" in the *Reallexikon der deutschen Literaturgeschichte* (1926–28), argues it as the peak of national achievement with roots reaching back to the Carolingian age (2:94). The autochthonous nature of the development back to the age of Charlemagne denies or omits the role of many outside influences, in particular from France, against which modern critics argue: see Jauss, *Literaturgeschichte*, 68–106, and also Fuhrmann *passim*. It has also led to the questioning of the validity of the division between classical and romantic for German literary history; see the collection of essays edited by Jost Hermand und Reinhold Grimm, *Die Klassik-Legende* (Frankfurt am Main: Athenäum, 1971), a doubt also put forward earlier by Victor Klemperer in the article "Romanische Literaturen" in the *Reallexikon* (3: 100).

[92] Wulf Koepke illustrates the degree to which the reading of the term "Kulturnation" as simply the preceding stage for the emergence of the "Nationalstaat" results in a severely truncated view of the Protean concept of nation in Herder's thinking, "*Kulturnation* and its Authorization through Herder," in *Johann Gottfried Herder: Academic Disciplines and the Pursuit of Knowledge*, ed. Wulf Koepke (Columbia, SC: Camden House, 1996), 177–98.

[93] Friedrich Meinecke in his *Die Entstehung des Historicismus* (1936) develops his claims about German historicism in relation to Winckelmann's philhellenism; see *Die Entstehung des Historicismus*, ed. Carl Hinrichs (Munich: Oldenbourg, 1959), 299–301. The one-sidedness of his claims about German historicism has again led critics to argue for continuities in historical thought across the European Enlightenment. Reill concludes his study *The German Enlightenment and the Rise of Historicism* by paraphrasing Lukács against Meinecke: "the great achievements in late eighteenth- and nineteenth-century German thought were not achieved in opposition to the Enlightenment but flowed directly from it" (220).

[94] Recent scholarship, again in response to earlier claims of novelty and exceptionalism on Winckelmann's behalf, has investigated the ways in which many of the elements present in Winckelmann's thought are found in other, particularly French, sources, and his familiarity with them. The first to argue the point at some length was Martin Fontius, *Winckelmann und die französische Aufklärung* (Berlin: Akademie Verlag, 1968) and more recently and definitively Élisabeth Décultot, *Johann Joachim Winckelmann: Enquête sur la genèse de l'histoire de l'art* (Paris: Presses Universitaires de France, 2000). More briefly see Norbert Miller, "Winckelmann und der Griechenstreit: Überlegungen zur Historisierung der Antiken-Anschauung im 18. Jahrhundert," in *Johann Joachim Winckelmann 1717–1768*, ed. Thomas W. Gaehtgens (Hamburg: Felix Meiner, 1986).

[95] Johann Joachim Winckelmann, *Gedanken über die Nachahmung der griechischen Werke in der Malerei und Bildhauerkunst*, ed. Ludwig Uhlig (Stuttgart: Reclam, 1969), 4. For this sentence as a reading of La Bruyère see Décultot, 107. Subsequent references to this Winckelmann work will be made citing the abbreviation *NGW* and the page number.

[96] *Bibliothek der Kunstliteratur: Frühklassizismus*, ed. Helmut Pfotenhauer, Markus Bernauer, and Norbert Miller, with the assistance of Thomas Franke, Bibliothek der Kunstliteratur 2 (Frankfurt am Main: Deutscher Klassiker Verlag, 1995), 393.

[97] On Winckelmann's reception see Henry Hatfield, *Winckelmann and His German Critics* (Morningside Heights, NY: King's Crown Press, 1943) and also Max L. Baeumer, "Klassizität und republikanische Freiheit in der außerdeutschen Winckelmann-Rezeption des späten 18. Jahrhunderts," in Gaehtgens, *Johann Joachim Winckelmann*, 195–220.

[98] Goethe, "Skizzen zu einer Schilderung Winkelmanns," *GSW* 6/2:352.

[99] Henry Hatfield has explored one aspect of this under the rubric of "aesthetic paganism" in *Aesthetic Paganism in German Literature: From Winckelmann to the Death of Goethe* (Cambridge: Harvard UP, 1964).

[100] See Jauss, "Schlegel und Schillers Replik auf die 'Querelle des Anciens et des Modernes,'" 67–106. Jauss views the Winckelmann's *Gedanken* as an important "Bindeglied" (80) between the French *Querelle* and its German echo and argues for the "Widerspruch zwischen aufklärischem Historismus und klassizister Ästhetik" (82); similarly Szondi ("Antike und Moderne," 41). Baeumer responds to both by arguing that this contradiction was not understood as such at the time ("Klassizität," 195). For David Ferris, Winckelmann's yoking of nation and culture and their importation through historical investigation into the province of aesthetics is the introduction of ideology into aesthetics in a manner that fails to take account of this innovation within its own terms, which he views as definitive of modernity (Ferris, *Silent Urns: Romanticism, Hellenism, Modernity* [Stanford: Stanford UP, 2000], esp. introduction and chapter 1). For the curiously liberating and limiting effect of the Siamese-twin like joining of idealism to historicism at the inception of German philhellenism on the development of German classical scholarship in the nineteenth century, see Anthony Grafton, "Germany and the West, 1830–1900," in *Perceptions of the Ancient Greeks*, ed. K. J. Dover (Oxford: Blackwell, 1992), 225–455.

[101] For the role of such factors as climate, geography, and manners in German historical thought, see Reill, *The German Enlightenment*, 127–89.

[102] See Alex Potts, *Flesh and the Ideal: Winckelmann and the Origins of Art History* (New Haven: Yale UP, 1994), 11–46.

[103] Viktor Pöschl will revisit this comparison and devote a chapter to it in his *Die Dichtkunst Virgils: Bild und Symbol in der Äneis* (Innsbruck: Margarete Friedrich Verlag, 1950), 99–152. Although he draws no explicit connection to Winckelmann here, he earlier shows his awareness of Winckelmann's *Gedanken* when he mentions one of Winckelmann's favorable references to Virgil (34).

[104] In the first half of the *Geschichte der Kunst des Alterthums* (Darmstadt: Wissenschaftliche Buchgesellschaft, 1972), 80 pages suffice for the art of all the ancient world before Greece, to which some 140 pages are devoted, while Roman art is covered with extreme dismissiveness in a postscript of 15 pages. The second half of the book, another hundred pages, is entirely concerned with Greek art. Subsequent references to this work will be made using the abbreviation *GKA* and the page numbers.

[105] For the impact of Winckelmann's Graecomania on the subsequent course of archeology in Germany, see Suzanne L. Marchand, *Down from Olympus: Archaeology and Philhellenism in Germany, 1750–1970* (Princeton: Princeton UP, 1996).

[106] The five stages are beginning, development, maturity, decline, and end: "den Anfang, den Fortgang, den Stand, die Abnahme und das Ende" (207). Winckelmann also distinguishes between three or four styles of art, the older, which is emphatic even harsh (215), the second or alternatively final form of the older style, the high style (207) or the grand style (217). It begins with Phidias in the fifth century B.C. (and the artist charged by Pericles with decorating the Parthenon) and runs to Praxiteles in the fourth century B.C., who introduces the third (second) style, the beautiful style, characterized by gracefulness and agreeable sensuousness (Grazie und Gefälligkeit, 207), and ends not precisely with Alexander the Great though he sounds its death knell (219 and 225). Its decline is protracted but it eventually yields to the final style, the imitative style, which, from the failure to produce any further distinctive stylistic development, falls back onto the imitation of the earlier styles. The correlation between style and stage of development is somewhat unclear since if they are mapped simply the one onto the other, the older style corresponds to the beginning, the high or grand style to the development, the beautiful to maturity and the imitative to the decline. Yet Winckelmann regards the Periclean Republic as the acme of freedom and thus "die glückichsten Zeiten für die Kunst in Griechenland, sonderlich in Athen" (308).

[107] See Jeffery Morrison, *Winckelmann and the Notion of Aesthetic Education* (Oxford: Clarendon Press, 1996).

[108] Recent scholarship on Herder, like that on Winckelmann, places greater weight on his relationship to the French and the European Enlightenment more generally; see with respect to history Martin Bollacher, "Geschichte und Geschichtsschreibung in Herders 'Ideen zur Philosophie der Geschichte der Menschheit,'" in *Johann Gottfried Herder: Academic Disciplines and the Pursuit of Knowledge*, 168–77, and more generally, for the depth of Herder's intellectual engagement with the Enlightenment, Robert E. Norton, *Herder's Aesthetics and the European Enlightenment* (Ithaca, NY: Cornell UP, 1991).

[109] The use of italics in this and subsequent citations from Herder is his own.

[110] "Endlich folgte, wie wir sagen, die Auflösung, die Entwicklung: lange ewige Nacht klärte sich in *Morgen* auf: es ward *Reformation, Wiedergeburt* der Künste, Wissenschaften, Sitten! . . . *unser Denken! Kultur!*" (*HW* 4:56).

[111] The thought finds fuller expression in the *Ideen* of a decade later: "Also bliebe nichts übrig. als daß die Vorsehung den Römischen Staat und die lateinische Sprache als eine Brücke aufgestellt habe, auf welcher von den Schätzen der Vorwelt auch Etwas zu uns gelangen möchte. Die Brücke wäre die schlechtste, die gewählt werden konnte: denn eben ihre Errichtung hat uns das Meiste geraubet. Die Römer zerstörten und wurden zerstört; Zerstörer aber sind keine Erhalter der Welt" (*HW* 6:626).

[112] Slightly later, on the same theme of the animating spirit or *genius* of Rome: "Der Geist der Völkerfreiheit und Menschenfreundschaft war dieser Genius nicht; . . .: so wird man glauben müssen, ein gegen das Menschengeschlecht feindseliger Dämon habe Rom gegründet, um allen Irdischen die Spuren seiner dämonischen übermenschlichen Herrlichkeit zu zeigen" (*HW* 6:620). In the first instance, one may argue that Herder intends demon to be understood in the Greek sense of animating spirit; in the second instance, "demonic" as in maleficent seems the only reading possible.

[113] This proposition forms the basis for the historical part of the *Geschichte:* "Es war also nötig, die Umstände anzuzeigen in welchen sich die Griechen von Zeit zu Zeit befunden haben, welches kürzlich und bloß in Absicht auf unser Vorhaben geschehen wird; und aus dieser ganzen Geschichte erhellt, daß es die Freiheit gewesen, durch welche die Kunst emporgebracht wurde" (*GKA*, 295).

[114] Herder returns to similar sentiments a couple of times in these pages (*HW* 6:602 and 622).

[115] Herder also gives a slightly more jaundiced view of Caesar's fall, citing him as an example of the fallen angel (*HW* 6:652–53).

[116] The full passage concerning France is: "Diejenige Nation, welche es zugleich in der Unnatur und in der Reflexion darüber am weitesten gebracht hatte, mußte zuerst von dem Phänomen des *Naiven* am stärksten gerührt werden und demselben einen Namen geben. Diese Nation waren, die Franzosen" (*Schillers Werke*, 20:431–32). With respect to Herder, Szondi also points to the use of nature and the classification of poets of nature, both ancient and modern, to demote the poets of "Unnatur," that is, the literature of French classicism, but does not connect it to its historical correlative in Herder's conception of Roman history ("Antike und Moderne," 53 and 63).

[117] Admittedly, Herder in the third collection of the *Fragmente* does argue heatedly over the predominately Latin cast of early modern culture (*HW* 1:372) and argues against its dominance in the schools (see *HW* 1:387–92), yet he also notes that his compatriots, having once translated in very Latin fashion, have now set about translating in a French fashion.

[118] Friedrich Nietzsche, *Sämtliche Werke*, kritische Studienausgabe, ed. Giorgio Colli and Mazzino Montinari, 15 vols. (1967–77; Munich: Deutscher Taschenbuch Verlag; Berlin; New York: de Gruyter, 1980), 1:42. Subsequent references to this work will be made using the abbreviation *NKS*, and the volume and page numbers.

[119] Nietzsche considers the vitiation of myth through reason in the modern period as following from the humanists' over-great devotion to the too Roman, too Hellenistic, too Socratic antiquity: "Diesem Zustand haben wir uns seit der Wiedererweckung des alexandrinisch-römischen Alterthums im fünfzehnten Jahrhundert . . . in der auffälligsten Weise angenährt" (*NKS* 1:149). In underscoring the fact that the rebirth of myth in modernity must be an internal change, Nietzsche refers to the Franco-Prussian War: "Vielleicht wird Mancher meinen, jener Geist müsse seinen Kampf mit der Ausscheidung des Romanischen beginnen: wozu er, eine äusserliche Vorbereitung und Ermuthigung in der siegreichen Tapferkeit und blutigen Glorie des letzten Krieges erkennen dürfte, die innerliche Nöthigung aber in dem Wetteifer suchen muss, der erhabenen Vorkämpfer auf dieser Bahn, Luthers ebensowohl als unserer grossen Künstler und Dichter, stets werth zu sein" (*NKS* 1:149).

2: Virgil Both Read and Unread

"Edle Einfalt und stille Größe": Greek Art, Roman Eyes, German Vision

WINCKELMANN PUBLISHED THE TRACT *Gedanken über die Nachahmung der griechischen Werke in der Malerei und Bildhauerkunst* to great effect. In it he set down the arguments why the ancient Greeks, through a fortuitous coincidence of nature and culture, were unable to execute a work of art that was not beautiful, and so have remained the school for the cultivation of taste throughout the ages. The great example that he chose for his case was the Laocoon statue. It was in relation to this statue that, when attempting to sum up the essential attributes of Greek beauty, he hit upon the happy phrase "edle Einfalt und stille Größe." These few words served to establish the essential attributes of the classical conception of beauty or "das Schöne" of German aesthetics in the eighteenth century and, at the same time, to make that ideal of beauty the historical possession of a particular people and a particular time.

The combination of an enthusiasm for the beautiful and for the Greeks gave Winckelmann a good claim to be the spiritual progenitor of the intense Grecomania that so distinguished the generations of Germans immediately after him. The counterpart of this new enthusiasm was a disinclination towards all things Roman. In part Winckelmann's argument dictated the necessity for this corollary. In order for Winckelmann's Greece to emerge with a distinctive profile from under the shadow of Rome, he was compelled to reject the current notion that the Latin heritage assimilated the Greek world and brought it to completion. "Es ist die romanische Welt und ihre fast unumschränkte Herrschaft in Europa, gegen die Winckelmann seine neue ursprüngliche Sicht des Griechentums kraftvoll durchsetzt.... Mit einem gewaltsamen Ruck und aus innerer Leidenschaft stellt Winckelmann das Steuer um vom Römertum hin zum Griechentum.... Antike war seit der Renaissance schlechthin römische Antike."[1] Only by contrasting the one with the other could Winckelmann develop a sense of historical difference.

The Latin world entered Winckelmann's pamphlet in the figure of Virgil. He illustrated his point about the Greek beauty of the Laocoon statue by demonstrating the antithesis of that beauty. He cited incidentally the famous passage from the second book of the *Aeneid* that recounts the death of Laocoon and his sons.[2] He condemned the Virgilian passage for its lack of any true artistic feeling: namely, that Virgil should permit his Laocoon to issue "awful cries," *clamores horrendos* — a "schreckliches Geschrei" (*NGW* 20) in Winckelmann's words — betrayed the fact that he had no innate sense of the beautiful. Virgil had failed to grasp that the greater the physical tumult of the body, the greater the contrast with the steadfast composure of the soul: to shriek in protest is neither simple and great, nor serene and noble. At its very inception, the German enthusiasm for all things Greek was paralleled by its equally unique counterpart: the discovery of the Latin heritage as second-rate and derivative.[3]

Virgil may fairly be considered as representative of the "romanisch-abendländische Kulturidee" that Walter Rehm views Winckelmann as controverting in the citation above.[4] Arguably, on that account, Virgil remained intellectually and culturally closer to Winckelmann and the Germans of the eighteenth century than could a Greece, secure in a harmony of nature and culture, that they could not hope to possess, except vicariously in their imagination. Virgil as a poet and thinker represented a period of culture in antiquity that knew itself to be the heir of a long and rich tradition. It was a civilization acutely aware of its belated position not merely in the literary and intellectual world but also in the historical world. From that tradition it also possessed the habits of mind and philosophical categories to consider these matters with some power of insight. This was one basis of affinity between the Rome of Virgil and Germany of the eighteenth century, which likewise faced the difficulty of absorbing a tradition while staking out its own place within it.

Another affinity was the position of the modern national cultures in relation to antiquity. They were the offspring of the Latin West. They issued forth from the mixture of late pagan culture and Christianity during the Roman Empire. Virgil was in this world a figure of a stature so immense that he earned the title "Vater des Abendlandes." One need only think of Dante's Virgil to be reminded of this. Dante chose Virgil to be his guide up through the entrance of the earthly paradise, a symbol both of the distance natural reason, unaided by the Grace of Revelation, could carry the virtuous pagan and of the degree to which Christianity was the rightful heir to pagan antiquity.[5] Or alternatively one may recollect that Virgil's fourth eclogue gained the title of the "Messianic Eclogue," as it was viewed as a pagan prophecy of the birth of Christ.[6] Virgil was a Janus figure who belonged to the Christian future as much as he did to the pagan past.

The "romanisch-abendländische Kulturidee" found more pragmatic support in the privileged position of the Latin language in education and general culture as well as in the preeminence that the Humanists of the Renaissance conceded to classical authors. These advantages combined to elevate Virgil to a position rivaled, perhaps, only by Horace or Cicero.

Familiarity with his poetry formed so large a part of the educational curriculum that almost every scholar or poet of importance came into contact with him in the original. Even if the latter portion of the eighteenth century was reluctant to look with favor on his manner of composition or the subject matter of his works, this lack of overt interest did not prevent Virgil from remaining a living presence to the mind of the educated. He formed an inextricable part of the intellectual climate in which they were raised. The legacy of Latin culture remained a lens through which everyone had to look, even if he sought to examine a Greek object; and Winckelmann provided an example of this in the *Gedanken über die Nachahmung*.[7]

An observer beholding the statue for the first time would be struck by the impression of petrified motion, of the writhing serpents, the intertwined limbs, the contorted bodies, the anguished faces, and, above all, of immense suffering and outright pain. It is unlikely that the description of "serene grandeur" or "stille Größe" would spring to mind. Perhaps some intimation of nobility might suggest itself to him before such obvious suffering; but that such seething confusion would be "simple" seems an improbable response.[8] Why then should these attributes have impressed themselves on Winckelmann as he gazed upon a plaster copy in the Großer Garten at Dresden in the early 1750s? The discrepancy between the statue and Winckelmann's description perplexes E. M. Butler greatly, but she can find no answer to it beyond:

> Nothing accounts so satisfactorily for Winckelmann's extraordinary blindness as the natural explanation that, dazzled by the flash of a great revelation, he saw the distinctive qualities of Greek art as he looked at this supposedly genuine specimen. He was in fact in a trance; and like many another clairvoyant, he was uttering truths which did not apply to the object before him, but were associated with it in his mind.[9]

But why should that statue prove to have been the lightning rod for Winckelmann's "flash of a great revelation?" And why, or at least how, should revelation be deemed a "natural explanation?" In Dresden, he had other Greek statues in repose that would have offered a better illustration of his insight. Winckelmann saw Greek art, but looked with Roman eyes. He did not approach the statue without preconceptions, and these in turn came from an interpretative tradition. To answer Butler's query briefly: Virgil was the source of that tradition, and Winckelmann came by his inspiration in part from him. He took from Virgil the notion that the scene before his eyes was to be associated with a moment of supreme passion, a great pathos.[10] He also borrowed from Virgil the assumption that this pathos had something to do with Stoic steadfastness, even if he understood that Stoicism in relation to very different conceptions of greatness.[11]

But what of Winckelmann's knowledge of Virgil? As a child, Winckelmann was precocious and a voracious reader of the ancients. Carl Justi relates that at the small Latin school in Stendal that Winckelmann attended until the age of seventeen, he sang for his bread and tuition as one of the "Kurrendaner." At the same time he often contrived to memorize Greek and Latin vocabulary; or, when compelled to take part in the games of his peers by the need to be agreeable, he would slip a book into his pocket for something to read. What he read must have been very restricted, at least to judge by the inventory of the school library that Justi gives. It consisted of a handful of books, principally the works of Latin authors and included notably an incunabulum of Virgil.[12]

One need not rely on this as evidence of familiarity with the Virgilian text. Aware that nothing is more fatal to a reputation than silence and nothing attracts attention better than controversy, Winckelmann arranged for the second edition of his *Gedanken über die Nachahmung* in 1756 to appear with an anonymous piece strongly critical of his *Gedanken* and still another piece, a rebuttal of the criticism; both of which he wrote himself. In these three essays, Winckelmann adopted the practice common among the learned of adorning their efforts with *sententiae:* short, pithy quotations from the classical authors used to point the moral and display the erudition of the writer. The number he took from Horace was equal to that of all the rest taken together. Of those from Virgil, six are from the *Aeneid* — and only from books 1 and 6 — and one from the *Georgics*. Furthermore, in common with the age, they were as often as not slightly misquoted, a testament to the fact that they were frequently cited from memory.

This may sufficiently demonstrate Winckelmann's knowledge of Virgil, though it fails to argue any deeper debt. For evidence of that one must turn to Winckelmann's descriptions of the statue itself. During the course of his career, Winckelmann described the statue three times. The first, and the best known, description occurred in the *Gedanken über die Nachahmung*, the second in the *Florenzer Manuskript* (1757?), and the last in the *Geschichte der Kunst des Altertums* (1764).[13] In the first description, Winckelmann makes the Laocoon statue the example of "edle Einfalt und stille Größe." He stresses in the short description the pain of Laocoon, evident in the definition of the musculature and in the contortions of the body, in order to contrast the physical tumult with the resolute composure of the soul: hence his wish to interpret Virgil's awful cries, *clamores horrendos*, as mistaken. There is, however, no actual description of the statue. Winckelmann contents himself with indicating a few signs of the body that reflect physical suffering: "Schmerz . . . in allen Muskeln und Sehnen des Körpers" and "dem schmerzlich eingezogenen Unterleibe" (*NGW* 20–21).[14] The brevity of the description along with the suggestive use of "Schmerz" and "schmerzlich" has more the character of an assertion than a descriptive account. From his description one would not know that the statue is a group of three figures, as he fails even to mention the sons. The second description is much more detailed and includes all parts of the statue, the sons not exempted. The body is minutely detailed with the particulars of the hair, nose, nostrils, mouth, and other parts all meticulously recorded; yet this succession of details, lacking a connective interpretation, is disjointed. If the character of the first description is assertive, then that of the second is static.

The final description is a combination of the first two; each detail becomes the result of the external violence of nature and the internal resistance of the spirit. The "aufgetriebene[.] Stirn" expresses the "mit Stärke bewaffnete[n] Geist," and the chest is arched forward "durch den beklemmten Atem und durch Zurückhaltung des Ausbruches der Empfindung" (*GKA* 324). The result of the continual movement in the prose, from the inner condition to the outer effect and back again, is to make the description dramatic, to move from the immobility of the stone, through the interpretative review of the details, to the dramatic tension of the whole. In doing this Winckelmann moves much closer to Virgil.

Virgil's account of Laocoon's fate, at the same time as being dramatic, is also one calculated to heighten the pathos of the event. The point at which Winckelmann's debt to Virgil becomes clearest is in the passage:

> Sein eigenes Leiden aber scheint ihn weniger zu beängstigen als die Pein seiner Kinder, die ihr Angesicht zu ihrem Vater wenden und um Hilfe schreien: denn das väterliche Herz offenbart sich in den wehmütigen Augen, . . . (*GKA* 324–25)

when compared to the lines:

> *et primum parva duorum*
> *corpora natorum serpens amplexus uterque*
> *implicat et miseros morsu depascitur artus;*
> *post ipsum auxilio subeuntem ac tela ferentem. . . .*
> (*Aen.* 2. 213–16)

> [First each snake took one of his two little sons,
> twined round him, tightening, and bit, and devoured
> the tiny limbs. Next they seized Laocoon, who had armed
> himself and was hastening to the rescue . . . (57)]

In both passages the duties of the father are contrasted with the imperative of self-preservation. And in both, the word *auxillium*, "help" (rendered somewhat freely as "rescue" in Knight's English translation above), accentuates the drama of the moment; the one imagines cries of help from the mouths of the sons, the other tells us that it is rather the father rushing to their aid, *auxilio subeuntem*.[15] The change between Virgil's concept of the father who hurries unbidden to render futile assistance to his sons, and

Winckelmann's suggestion that the father responds to his children's cry for help is of great importance as a point of interpretation.

That Laocoon should, in Virgil's account, hasten to his sons' assistance heightens the pathos of the scene by emphasizing his selfless pursuit of his duty, even as the moment of his death is at hand. Indeed Virgil's composition of the entire episode is designed to accentuate the importance of Laocoon by drawing the attention of his audience to his figure. The narrative, at this juncture, has no other justification. If one tries to make sense of the sequence of the action as Virgil relates it, one stumbles on repeated inconsistencies. Laocoon had earlier offended the god to whom the wooden horse was dedicated with his attempt to warn the Trojans against accepting the horse into their city by throwing a spear into its side. In punishment two serpents rise up from the sea as Laocoon sacrifices a bull at Neptune's altar, and

> *illi agmine certo*
> *Laocoonta petunt; et primum parua duorum.* . . .
> (*Aen.* 2. 212–13)

[they forged on, straight at Laocoon. First each snake took one of his two little sons . . . (57)]

At the sight of these monstrous serpents, prudence prevails and all flee, abandoning Laocoon to his fate. Among the fleeing would presumably be the sons, who, we know, are at some distance from Laocoon since he must hasten to their aid. If that is the case, why should serpents, specifically *agmine certo Laocoonta petentes* (forging on, straight at Laocoon), be deflected from their divinely appointed task and make a detour to devour a pair of spectators?

The logic of the story is clearly not dictated by narrative requirements; rather it is necessitated by the needs of drama: by the wish to heighten the pathos of Laocoon's fate. The telling of the story should sweep, not lead, the listener along. Laocoon, the priest of Neptune, attempted to warn his fellow citizens of their danger, a warning that they ignored despite the fact that the side of the horse rang out hollowly under the impact of the spear's blow. Their failure was a sign that the gods had averted their eyes from the Trojans. Nonetheless, Laocoon continued to execute his duties, sacrificing to the gods, and attempting to rescue his children even though he knew the action to be futile. He died in the performance of a human being's three defining activities in antiquity: as a priest, he fulfilled the responsibilities of a mortal to the gods; as a citizen, those of the individual towards society; as a *paterfamilias*, those of the individual to the family. Laocoon's fault was not a personal one in the modern sense of the word, nor was his fate a personal one. That his children should be slaughtered before his eyes merely elevated the horror and pathos of the moment for the Romans, who felt it the gravest rupture of the natural order that children, the future representatives of the *gens*, should die before their parents. The punishment of Laocoon also foreshadowed the fate of Troy: as Laocoon and his family were extirpated root and branch, so too would Troy be destroyed. Finally, he presents a model of heroism that Aeneas repeatedly attempts to follow in the fall of Troy only to be thwarted by the gods. The power of the portrayal is such that greatness and nobility are not inappropriate words to describe the stature of Laocoon's heroism.

The sense of duty on which the tragedy hinges is very Roman. Likewise, the masterful evocation of the human cost of it is very Virgilian. The episodes of the *Aeneid* are replete with such examples, as is the entire conception of the epic. The understanding of it lies at the core of such words as *pius* and *grandanimus*. It is however a notion alien to the interests of the eighteenth century and contrary to its sensibility. Goethe, for example, is at loss to explain the presence of the Laocoon episode. In "Über Laokoon" (1797/98), he finds the comparison between the statue and the epic "ungerecht" (*GSW* 4/2:87). The statue is a masterpiece of the sculptor's art; the passage in the epic simply a plot device to explain how the horse gets into the city:

> und die Geschichte des Laokoons steht hier als ein rhetorisches Argument, bei dem eine Übertreibung, wenn sie nur zweckmäßig ist, gar wohl gebilligt werden kann. . . .
> So steht also die Geschichte Laokoons im Virgil bloß als Mittel zu einem höhern Zwecke, und es ist noch eine große Frage, ob die Begebenheit an sich ein poetischer Gegenstand sei? (*GSW* 4/2:87–88)

Formally Goethe's point is valid: Virgil must account for the fall of Troy. But then any writer must move his plot from A to B. That Goethe should fail utterly to understand its poetic justification indicates how incomprehensible its presuppositions have become both to him and to his age. In a letter to Schiller (23/12/1797), Goethe expresses even more categorically the same opinion, speaking this time of the whole episode of the fall of Troy: "Virgils rhetorisch sentimentale Behandlung kann hier nicht in Betracht kommen" (*GSW* 8/1:472). The point that does come across clearly to Goethe and his age is that the episode exudes a meretricious pathos, an indulgence in feeling that, bereft of any deeper justification, is empty, a purely rhetorical display of great technical virtuosity. It remains an affect unredeemed by any intimation of grandeur or nobility in Goethe's estimation; here was a great pathos in want of an explanation.[16]

Goethe's observation is identical to that of Winckelmann. He too felt the pathos of the Virgilian episode and transferred it to the statue while giving it a new justification. Winckelmann's lingering over the details of Laocoon's suffering, his dwelling on the children's cries "um Hülfe" and on the "väterliche Herz" revealed in "den wehmütigen Augen" seizes on the feeling of the Virgilian account for the same purpose: namely, for the sake of magnifying through emotion the importance of the moment. "Im Gesichte des Laocoons," there stands revealed the human spirit. Crucial to that spirit is that life should not force from it an admission of its own negation:

> So wie die Tiefe des Meers allezeit ruhig bleibt, die Oberfläche mag noch so wüten, ebenso zeiget der Ausdruck in den Figuren der Griechen bei allen Leidenschaften eine große und gesetzte Seele. (*NGW* 20)[17]

To demonstrate that the statue and, by extension, the Greeks, possessed a true greatness of spirit that others have misunderstood, he argued that a cry was tantamount to an admission of negation. Virgil permits Laocoon to emit a cry contrary to the dictates of the beautiful; the mouth of the statue, according to Winckelmann, does not admit the possibility of a cry. Winckelmann draws support for this contention from Jacopo Sadoleto (1477–1547), who is the only other candidate in this hermeneutic circle.[18]

Following the rediscovery of the statue in 1506, Sadoleto wrote in that same year a poem entitled *De Laocoontis statua*.[19] Winckelmann cites it as his source for the contention that Laocoon utters "ein ängstliches und beklemmtes Seufzen" (*NGW* 20). In point of fact Sadoleto mentions that Laocoon utters first a *gemitum ingentem* (a huge groan), then, as pain and exhaustion mount, a *murmur anhelum* (a panting rasp), neither of which can be easily construed as "ängstlich," "beklemmt" or a "Seufzen." Instead Sadoleto's imagination seems so fired by the Virgilian account that his enthusiasm presents things to his eyes not to be found in the statue. Perhaps thinking of the gore and black poison bespattering Virgil's Laocoon (poison is always black, a proleptic sign of corruption), he envisions that the snakes' constrictions with their pressure *liuentesque atro distendunt sanguine uenas* (gorge the veins until dark with blood) — but the statue is of white marble. Or again, when relating the fate of the younger son, he preserves the sequence of the action from Virgil: first the son, then the father. Virgil states that the father sees the serpent consuming (*depascitur*) the limbs of his sons; Sadoleto tells us that the serpent has shredded the boy's limbs, consumed his chest, and now supports the expiring body in its coils. He even repeats the Virgilian word *depasta*. Such a description bears only a loose relation to the statue that one can actually see with one's eyes. "Hievon sieht man nichts in der Gruppe," as Goethe sniffs in reference to this portion of Sadoleto's description.[20] Of equal interest, he attributes the source of the error to Sadoleto's misfortune of allowing himself to be influenced by Virgil. Goethe acknowledges here in the details the degree to which the Virgilian account prejudices the eyes of the observer, but not in the conception: namely that the suffering bears witness to a great pathos for a purpose.

Sadoleto assumes the drama of the story, but the explanation of that drama in relation to the statue does not interest him. Rather he elaborates at length on the magnitude of the body's suffering, even including some details of a struggle against the serpents. He does not, however, elevate it to an expression of the inner spirit. Of importance for Winckelmann, Sadoleto also states that the younger son, the one on the left, summons his father as he dies: *suprema genitorem voce cientis* (calling on his father with his last breath). The use of *cieo* not only intensifies the poignant drama of the situation, but also inverts the Virgilian account, which mentions no summoning shrieks from the children, only a father hastening to their aid without prompting. Of the other son, Sadoleto notes that he *horret ad adspectum miseri patris* (shudders at the sight of his wretched father), before dissolving into tears. It is the sons who weep for the father, not he for them; the adjective *miserus* is applied to the father, not the children as in Virgil's version, and there is no mention of any help, although the younger son does cry out in death to the father.[21]

Winckelmann takes the emphasis on the father's physical suffering and the sentimental portrayal of the sons by Sadoleto and combines it with the pathos of Virgil or, if one prefers, with the pathos of the interpretative tradition. He elevates the manifest suffering of the Laocoon group to a question of the fundamental attributes of the human spirit and of Greek art. Nonetheless, his use of the phrase "um Hülfe schreyen" attests the subtle persistence of the Virgilian hermeneutic. Sadoleto mentions only a last cry of the son to his father, Virgil mentions only a father hastening to the aid of his children (*auxilio subeuntem*): Winckelmann puts the help of the Virgilian father into the mouth of the son.[22]

Winckelmann's account transforms the older pathos associated with the statue. He discharges it from its ancient colors and presses it into modern service. What he borrows from the Virgilian Laocoon is his Stoic steadfastness, that is, the conception of a destructive confrontation between the individual and the world and the desirability of meeting that confrontation with resolve. No longer does the nobility and grandeur of Laocoon serve a Latin understanding of the world. Virtue is not measured by the degree to which one fulfills the obligations of the human community. Instead grandeur and nobility of spirit exemplify humanity in its "natural" state, or, in that odd synonym of the eighteenth century, in its Greek state.

That the suffering of Laocoon sits uneasily with a conception of the beautiful as a unity within difference, a harmonious whole composed of variegated parts, remains unobserved in the eighteenth century.[23] Only the differentiation of the beautiful through the development of the companion concept of the sublime permits the exploration of the tension between the visibly "baroque" statue and visual serenity, on the one hand, and, on the other hand, between the beautiful and the disfigurement of extreme suffering; between, on the one hand, Winckelmann's dictum "edle Einfalt und stille Größe" and the insistence "da, wohin der größte Schmerz gelegt ist, zeiget sich auch die größte Schönheit" (*GKA* 325), on the other hand — both of which statements are made in relation to the same statue. Lessing returns Laocoon's pathos and his suffering to its proper context by association when he considers it in relation to suffering in tragedy and takes Sophocles's *Philoctetes* as his example. The connection remains implicit until Schiller takes up the matter of pathos directly in relation to tragedy in *Über das Pathetische* (1793):

> Das erste Gesetz der tragischen Kunst war Darstellung der leidenden Natur. Das zweyte ist Darstellung des moralischen Widerstandes gegen das Leiden. (*SW* 20:199)

Oddly, in view of the stated interest in tragedy, Schiller gives as his most extensive example of this dynamic not some incident from drama but the Laocoon episode from Virgil. In doing so, he confirms the categories of analysis from Winckelmann and Lessing: he stresses that Laocoon depicts humanity as subject to nature, as "leidende Natur," and also humanity as having an ideal nature capable of opposing the physical impositions of the body. The starkness of the dichotomy in the Virgilian depiction obviously appeals to Schiller's Kantian predilection for the sharp separation of the noumenal and the phenomenal, since he bothers to introduce Laocoon into the same context in "Das Ideal und das Leben" (1795).[24] At the same time, Schiller's emphasis on the moral freedom of humanity assimilates the treatment of the Laocoon pathos to the sublime, an aesthetic category more appropriate to it.[25] Schiller moves the Laocoon incident, and thereby Virgil, closer to the interest of the late eighteenth century in the sublime as an experience that compels the individual to recognize the incommensurability of nature according to his subjective categories and to contemplate the isolation of humanity from nature. Schiller however fails to pursue his analysis beyond observing the ferocity of nature, on the one hand, and the freedom of spirit on the part of Laocoon on the other. He too does not go on to consider what is the moral purpose pursued by Laocoon, contenting himself with merely affirming its presence. Perhaps to have expected Schiller to ponder the motivation of the Laocoon scene within the context of the ancient epic is too much. Ultimately, Virgil does not conceive of the sublime as a moment of separation, nor is his solution of a fate realizing itself historically in the dominance of Rome as a universal community of any great appeal to Schiller. Instead, Schiller remains closely dependent on Winckelmann's idea of nature and humanity's relation to it as he exploits the Laocoon episode for his purposes. And Winckelmann's interpretation is in its presuppositions, though not in its conclusions, dependent on the Virgilian account.

Winckelmann's sharp turn from the Romans to the Greeks may owe its impetus to the necessity of distinguishing his vision of ancient Greece from the subsequent spread of ancient culture to Rome, but this ostensible rejection does not gainsay the fact that he had first to pass through

Rome both physically and intellectually to reach his beloved Greece. Precisely because the Greeks were so thoroughly enmeshed in a Roman embrace, Winckelmann had no well-defined set of analytical distinctions independent of that tradition with which to work as he began to extricate the Greeks from that oppressive presence. He found himself compelled unwittingly to work with those bequeathed to him. One may endorse Rehm's statement that "Winckelmann war tatsächlich der Grieche in Rom, derjenige, der von Rom aus Athen und den 'griechischen Geschmack' entdeckte und verkündete und damit das Römische in der Kunst und in der Menschenbildung bekämpfte" as an accurate summary of Winckelmann's intention and effect, but not of his means of accomplishing this end.[26] He may have fled to Greece but he took Rome with him. The Laocoon statue could become the catalyst for his "flash of revelation" because of its associations with the literary tradition definitively shaped by Virgil. The transposition of a literary tradition onto an art object accounts for the fruitful ambiguity of "edle Einfalt und stille Größe." If one considers the phrase in its aesthetic-literary context, then the notions of Stoicism, suffering, sublimity, pathos, and moral will, all inherent in the Virgilian text, come to the fore, as, for example, in Schiller. If one considers it in its art-historical context, then the insistence that the pose of the body reflect more directly the tranquillity of the soul comes to the fore; a condition that, for those of us who come after Winckelmann, seems best fulfilled by the sculpture of classical Greek antiquity, if of any period. As a result the Laocoon statue can only seem from this perspective increasingly "baroque" and a most puzzling, indeed inexplicable, example of serenity and grandeur. In this vein, one would concentrate on the physical pain manifest in the statue, as Goethe does, to cite but one example. Both of these positions may draw support from Winckelmann's contradictory statements, as first one side, first the literary text, and then the other, the artistic object itself, is uppermost in his mind.

The ultimate origin in the Virgilian text of the set of associations that Winckelmann brings to the statue remains opaque to him. The absence of any explicit acknowledgment of the ancient poet's presence compels careful attention to the means of transmission. The settings for the reading of the Virgilian texts rarely concern the text *in toto;* they rather approach them in the framework of a particular topic or tradition, the proper discussion of which includes mention of Virgil or, as is often the case, of a hallowed number of lines or passages. With the literary critical tradition of epic we have an instance of the first kind, while Winckelmann and the interpretative tradition surrounding the Laocoon statue offers an example of the second kind. In addition to Virgil's wording or a variation of it, these settings also perpetuate a constellation of expectations that over time obscures the Virgilian origin of the wording, while also through its amorphous nature incorporating new impulses reflecting the new age. Crucial therefore for examining the German reception of Virgil are the means of transmission and its various contexts, the first of which is the schoolroom.

Heyne's Virgil Edition: A Pedagogical Success for the Neo-Humanists, a Failure for Virgil

The almost exclusive aim of the school system in the eighteenth century was to instruct its pupils in the Latin language once they had mastered the catechism and acquired an ability to read the Psalms and the Bible in German.[27] The schools taught Latin; they did not teach literature. The Latin poets, if read, were read in excerpts and as rhetorical exercises to improve the pupil's own ability to write Latin. Once a pupil could read, write, and speak Latin, the schoolmasters had accomplished their appointed task. The pupil was now equipped to become a student. At the university the courses of study open to him depended on his ability to read and write Latin. The curriculum at the schools revolved around the first two elements of the trivium (grammar, rhetoric, and logic), a responsibility they shared with the university. Grammar was necessary for the learning of language and rhetorical training unavoidable for anyone wishing to acquire proficiency in the oral and written language. In addition to Latin, a good school might also equip its charges with some Greek and even a little Hebrew as both were necessary for the study of Scripture. In a bad school, however, the would-be student might depart with so faulty a command of Latin that he would have to work seriously to make good his deficiencies in the trivium. The divided responsibility for the curriculum and the unpredictable quality of the schools ensured that the boundary between the schools and the universities, as well as between teacher and professor, remained fluid throughout the century.

Only with the introduction in the Prussian lands of the "Abitur" in 1788 does the state begin to insist not only on its prerogative to regulate the educational system but also on a clearer distinction between the schools and the universities by imposing minimum qualifications, at least for the impoverished who hoped to apply for financial support ("Freitische," benefices, and scholarships). This reform represents but one instance of the century-long pedagogical ferment, which would result in the foundation of the university of Berlin in 1810 and the reform of the "Gymnasium" under Wilhelm von Humboldt's year-and-a-half directorship (1809–10) of the education section of the Prussian Home Office.

Grammar formed the backbone of instruction, and the grammar book was "Donatus." Aelius Donatus, famed as a grammarian and the tutor of St. Jerome in the fourth century A.D., wrote the *Ars grammatica*, the smaller version of which, the *Ars minor*, became a favorite school text in the Middle Ages and beyond. For Johann Wilhelm Ludwig Gleim

(1719–1803), the first task for a girl is to spin and for a boy to read "im Donat."[28] The method of instruction had the virtue of simplicity: memorization. "Er mußte," writes Karl Philipp Moritz (1757–93) in *Anton Reiser* (1785–90), "nun anfangen, den Donat auswendig zu lernen."[29] The child had to learn by heart the conjugations and declensions and later the rules of syntax, all the while learning vocabulary. Occasional texts were set for the purpose of construing as were German sentences for translation into Latin so that the pupil might learn to write easily and without error. As for the poets, they were read in excerpts or shorter pieces with an emphasis on construing them and noting their rhetorical devices: that is, they were read as elegant stylistic manuals.

This vast expenditure of precious years on Latin grammar and memorization seems calculated to crush the spirit of all those who did not learn with facility or lacked the motivation to learn the hallowed language at all costs. The twelve-year-old hero of *Anton Reiser*, wishing to become like the inspiring preachers he heard in church and wanting to escape his apparently ineluctable fate as an apprentice in a trade, recognizes the necessity to learn Latin. He eventually succeeds in attending the Latin "Privatstunde" given by the schoolmaster of the local school. The precise expertise of the four pupils to whom the schoolmaster awards the accolade "Veteraner" could not credibly have been Latin, as Anton Reiser memorized enough of Donatus to advance to their table within the space of the two short months.[30]

The position of Latin in the curriculum was well fortified by the respect in which a good Latin style was still, unthinkingly, held by the wider educated public. Not a few possessed an inordinate admiration for a man of good Latinity, so much so that such a man might seem to be in need of no other accomplishment to secure advancement. Heyne's own early career offers two examples of this prejudice, and in the latter instance it contributed decisively to his subsequent good fortune. At the age of twelve, once a week, hardly master of the rudiments of Latin, Heyne had to recite Latin verse to his godfather to prove that the school fees paid by the godfather was money well spent. Soon afterwards he had also to compose the verses himself, which task he accomplished after having read only Erasmus's *De civilitate morum*. He achieved notoriety amongst his classmates at the age of thirteen by successfully answering the school inspector's request for an anagram on *Austria*. He not only knew, to the discomfort of his teacher, what an anagram was but could also supply one (*uastari*). This effort did not fail to please the inspector as it was then the middle of the War of Austrian Succession.

The young Heyne seems to have rested on the laurels of his Latin composition and left the school without having read any one author in his entirety, and often only short excerpts: "von keinem Autor besaß ich eine vollständige Kenntniß, noch weniger von dem Umfang der ganzen

Litteratur; nichts von den Hülfekenntnissen, Erdkunde, Geschichte u.s.w."[31] Only while attending the university at Leipzig was Heyne exposed to a new approach. His ambition first led him to imitate Scaliger and attempt to read all of the ancients in order. He soon, however, discovered, or perhaps more accurately since he was penniless, somehow contrived to take part in one of Johann August Ernesti's "Privatissima." From him he learnt a new method of reading and interpretation: "Allein die zweckmäßige Kürze, die Gründlichkeit und gute Ordnung im Vortrage des Professors Ernesti hefteten mich mehr und fester an sich. In meinen andern Collegien war kein Plan."[32] Nor was it his learning that eventually secured Heyne advancement in the world. He wrote a Latin elegy on the death of the Calvinist preacher Lacoste that came to the notice of Duke Brühl, then Prime Minister of Saxony. After fobbing off the impecunious young Heyne, whom he had summoned, with a summer of promises, he eventually granted him a modest position in his library. With the library at his disposal and disturbed only by the frequent requests of the young Winckelmann, he published an edition of Tibullus in 1755 and in the succeeding year one of Epictetus. He owed his appointment to the vacant chair in Göttingen in 1763 to these two publications.

Initially, at the beginning of the century, all varieties of reformers found common cause in the desperate situation confronting them: for some, any reform was better than none.[33] Increasingly during the course of the century the different and ultimately competing presuppositions led to dissension, which the neo-humanists would settle in their favor with Humboldt's reforms. Convinced that the general progress of humanity would benefit from universal education, reformers of all stripes wished for a curriculum devoted neither to religion nor to the few destined to attend university. The early neo-humanists, in common with other reformers, wished to moderate the older preoccupation with the speaking and writing of Latin. They favored rather the acquisition of the language for the sake of reading and understanding. The texts of poets and prose writers should become an object of study, not a model of emulation in the older humanist style. The epoch-making nature of this rather prosaic change comes largely from its later effects. The classical authors require a new justification for their place in the curriculum. The belief in the timeless beauty of the ancient writers provides content, figures such as Winckelmann provide the stirring examples, while the neo-humanists supplied the methods for grasping this new content. They together usher in so radical a transformation that Rudolf Pfeiffer suggests for the eighteenth century the name "the age of the humanistic revolution."[34] The changes in the treatment of the ancient texts that the early neo-humanists champion bear within them the seeds of what Friedrich August Wolf will first define and elevate to the dignity of an academic discipline under the name of "Alterthumswissenschaft" in 1807.

For Heyne, the youngest of the triumvirate of early neo-humanists most responsible for the revival of classical learning in the eighteenth century, the pursuit of the new style of reading and interpretation was not separate from the concern for pedagogical reform.[35] Heyne's predecessor at Göttingen had established a "philological seminar" that aimed at training teachers for the schools by instructing them in the reading and interpretation of the ancients through the encouragement of individual study and interests, an establishment that represents the genesis of the modern university's seminar method of instruction.[36] From the time of his arrival in Göttingen in 1763 until his retirement in 1812, Heyne's nearly fifty-year long tenure of the philological seminar gradually won him great influence: "doch [wurde] viele Jahre hindurch kaum eine öffentliche Lehrstelle in Deutschland besetzt ohne daß man Heyne deshalb um Rath gefragt hätte."[37]

While Heyne may owe his influence to the seminar, he owes his fame to his Virgil edition (1767–75). He undertook the task because Virgil was the school text *par excellence* on which to demonstrate the utility of the new method; scholarly interest and pedagogical interest went hand in hand. His Virgil's success soon brought Göttingen to the notice of the young. In *Dichtung und Wahrheit* Goethe reflects on his first choice of university, "Bei diesen Gesinnungen hatte ich immer Göttingen im Auge. Auf Männern, wie *Heyne, Michaelis* und so manchem Anderen ruhte mein ganzes Vertrauen; mein sehnlichster Wunsch war, zu ihren Füßen zu sitzen und auf ihre Lehren zu merken."[38] During the course of his lengthy career Heyne taught and influenced numerous scholars and writers, among whom the more famous are: Voss, Wolf, the Schlegel brothers, Wilhelm von Humboldt, and Karl Lachmann, the founder of modern textual criticism.

Any assessment of Heyne's edition of Virgil must take into account its larger pedagogical and interpretative ambitions rather than its purely scholarly merit if its true impact is to emerge. Although the Greek poets and philosophers benefited most from the new "Wissenschaft" of philology, Virgil, as well as other Latin poets, retained a central role in this larger change because of Latin's dominance in the schools. The measure of that dominance is as much apparent in Heyne's selection of the Virgilian corpus to serve as the example of the new method of philology as it is in the international renown that the success of the edition brought him. Gibbon, who published an anonymous essay in 1770 entitled *Critical Observations on the Sixth Book of the Aeneid*, comforts himself in his autobiography with Heyne's praise: "but the public coldness was overbalanced to my feelings by the weighty approbation of the last and best editor of Virgil, Professor Heyne of Göttingen, who acquiesces in my confutation, and styles the unknown author, *doctus . . . et elegantissimus Britannus* (a learned and most tasteful Englishman)."[39]

Dominance in the schools, however, is no guarantee of true affection for a poet. Heyne already adopts the new attitude toward the Greeks. It is he who first begins to articulate the consequences of it for Virgil. His "last, best editor" writes in a prefatory essay:

> *Iliadis argumentum feliciorem materiam et epicae gravitatis haud paullo plus habere si quis dixerit, me habet assentientem; et delector ipse multo magis Homeri lectione quam Virgilii; regnat in Homericis heroibus naturalis affectus, animi impetus, iniurae acceptae sensus, qualem et ipse habeo, desiderium reditus ad Lares, quale ipse sentiam; in Aeneide sunt consilia de novis sedibus in terra ignota parandis; nihil quod magnopere animum impellat et percutiat.* (*O* 2: xlviii–xlix)[40]

[If someone had said that the *Iliad* has the more fortunate subject matter for its narrative and no small measure of epic gravity, he would find me in agreement. I myself take much greater delight in reading Homer than in reading Virgil. There dominates in the Homeric heroes a natural feeling, a passion of the spirit, a sense of injustice suffered such as I too have, and a desire to return home, such as I also feel; in the *Aeneid* we have deliberations concerning the founding of settlements in unknown lands, nothing which greatly stirs my soul and transfixes it.]

Nonetheless, despite these misgivings, Heyne devotes eight years to the publication of the first edition (1767–75) and then, just twelve years later, oversees the revisions for the second edition (1787–89), with the assistance of A.W. Schlegel. These he followed with the third and final edition in 1803, while the fourth edition by Heyne's student Georg Philipp Eberhard Wagner after his death appeared from 1830 to 1833. It secured Heyne the attention of all subsequent editors in the nineteenth and twentieth centuries.

Heyne set out to inform his readers what precisely was excellent or beautiful about the Virgilian texts not merely because, *difficile est Virgilium et sine interprete recte legere, et cum interprete* (*O* 1:iii; it is difficult both with and without a commentator to read Virgil properly), but also *cum Virgilius is sit, in quo legendo magna iuuenilium studiorum pars consumi soleat* (*O* 1:viii; because it is Virgil, in the reading of Virgil that a large portion of the curriculum for the young is customarily spent). So many of the young find themselves subjected to Virgil because of the expectation *vt ad adolescentum ingenia polienda, ad sensum et gustum pulchritudinis acuendum, ad iuducium de omnibus iis, quae ab arte et ingenio elaborata et expressa oculorum animique sensui subiici possunt, informandum valere illa lectio et vim habere debeat* (*O* 1:viii; that this reading should be able to give shape and form and have the power to refine the imagination of the young, to sharpen their sense and taste of beauty and their discernment of all those things that skill and talent can bring to the perception of the eyes and the soul). The study of Virgil promises the cultivation of all those attributes that the Enlightenment valued so highly in an individual: the refinement of the imagination, the exercise of the faculty of taste, the training of judgment in the products of art and talent, in short, nothing that Kant did not himself likewise hope from an acquaintance of the classics.

Were that all that Heyne set himself, he would be little different from other poetic preceptors of his era, such as Gottsched or the Swiss critics. Yet he continues:

> *feci id, quod in alio poeta, qui non ita omnium manibus teritur, aut non nisi a callentioribus et doctioribus legitur, non mihi faciendum esse putarem, vt non modo ad ea, quae difficilia ad intelligendum et obscura sunt, verum ad illa etiam legentium animos aduerterem, quae pulchra in poeta et praeclara insignique aliqua venustate nobilitata sunt vt iisdem, in aliis poetis, siue observandis ac deprehendis siue diiudicandis, adsuescerent. Quam interpretum siue sollertiam siue industriam cum saepe in puerili lectione desiderarim, aliorum votis similibus satis facere hoc instituto volui.* (*O* 1:viii)

> [I have done what I should not have imagined needed to be done by me for an author whom everyone pages through and who is read by the more experienced and learned, and I have done it in order to direct readers' attention not only to passages difficult to understand or unclear but also to those beautiful, remarkable, or famous for some particular charm so that readers might grow accustomed to noting, understanding, and judging these same matters in other poets. I want to demonstrate in this endeavor sufficient of the interpreter's skill and diligence to satisfy a similar wish on the part of others because I have often found it lacking in the texts set the young.]

Heyne intends not merely to clear up difficult passages but also to provide arguments that demonstrate why a particular passage is said to be beautiful: to take the general and vague statement that something is beautiful and give textual reasons for its accuracy. Furthermore, he intends to do this so frequently that little by little the reader will insensibly acquire the ability to exercise such judgment for himself. The basis for this is the change in reading practices entailed by the shift from the older *lectio stataria* or "statarisch" to the newer *lectio cursoria* or "cursorisch." The former involves the reading of passage for the purposes of grammatical and rhetorical analysis, using it as a model for stylistic and grammatical exercises and also the explanation of references, often detailed to the point that one cannot see the forest for the trees. It also meant that very little of an author might in fact be read: "daher es kommt, daß über ein paar Capiteln aus einem Auctore gantze Monate zugebracht werden, und Jahre hingehn, ehe ein Buch aus den Episteln Ciceronis oder Virgilio erkläret werden."[41] The latter, *lectio cursoria*, means the relatively swift and repeated reading of a piece without stopping to label and explicate the finer points of the grammatical construction, but rather paying attention to the "Sachen" or "Realien" that facilitate comprehension. The object is to gain a sense of the whole by paying attention to the development and order of the argument or story.[42] Heyne aims ultimately to teach a method of reading, of literary analysis: learning marshaled by judicious argument to display insight.

The singular success of his edition, even its charm, stems from the boldness with which he executes his plan. He allows his judgment on aesthetic matters to be influenced by the newer directions of his time represented by Winckelmann and Lessing.[43] In practice he banishes pedantic compilations from his notes at the foot of the page and keeps only what is needed to aid the reader's understanding. Since Virgil is a learned writer, students must resort to a commentary to read him; yet commentaries notoriously offer copious explanation where the sense is clear yet pass over the problematic passages. And, when they do have an explanation, it is often a learned compilation devoid of the concise discernment essential for making a useful point. Furthermore, the bulk of such an inappropriate note means that the flow of the story is interrupted while the reader pores through a note that leaves his question unanswered in return for having robbed him of the pleasure of being swept up by the text. For Heyne a useful note means closer attention to "Sachen" rather than to "Wörter," more explanations of ritual, mythology, and history, and fewer of grammatical, philological, or metrical questions. Heyne's strength lies not in textual criticism, but in explanation. Any more detailed discussion on a given point he reserves for the *excursus* at the end of each book; they range from as many as twenty-six on book 1 of the *Aeneid* to a scant two on such books as 10 and 11. The great appeal of the edition lies in Heyne's willingness to exercise his critical judgment in lively and strong language that leaves the reader in little doubt where he stands on a point of interpretation.

The new expectations brought new methods in their train and will soon, with the re-evaluation of the Greeks, also bring new authors and new texts. For the period of this transition, Heyne's Virgil edition succeeds because it responds so brilliantly to its needs; he gauges his audience well. He knows that many struggle with Virgil at school, plagued by grammatical and stylistic exercises and without the aid of useful commentary. He may well surmise that this situation in the schools leads to a poet more mangled than read. Georg Brandes, Heyne's future father-in-law, makes an admission in a letter to Heyne typical for the age:

> Ich habe es bisher nicht gewagt zu bekennen, daß mich dieser letztere [d.h. Vergil] nur an wenig Orten gerührt habe. Ich las ihn vor ein paar Jahren vielleicht zum zehnten Male, um mich zu prüfen, ob mich nicht etwa der Ekel von den Schulstunden her gegen ihn kaltsinnig gemacht hätte ... Ich fand zwar hie und da, was ich vorher nicht empfunden; doch war ich froh daß ich zu Ende kam.[44]

Heyne wishes not merely to plead the utility of the new learning by explaining a difficult author but also to make a case for the neo-humanist reforms. His edition must also demonstrate the value of the new reading; it must provide a concrete example of the advantages promised. He first provides a comprehensive consideration of the poems that he intends to use as a model of instruction in how to read and then adds a commentary that displays an aesthetic judgment that, combined with a lucid exposition, allows him to make the best use of his considerable erudition.

He promises his readers the benefits commonly expected from a humanistic education; the self is cultivated in order to make it aware of the range of human emotion and thought and to foster its ability to appreciate the entire span of human activity. Readers should imbibe from his work the philological principles that they in turn need in order to disentangle textual problems for themselves. He grounds them in the critical principles that will allow them to form their own aesthetic judgments. His programmatic aim is thus twofold. He wishes to teach by example the elements of textual criticism and then to show how this is the basis for arriving at an aesthetic valuation of the part as well as the whole.

The notes and *excursus* that surround the text cannot but help by their clarity and learning to contribute a great deal to the understanding of the Virgilian poems. Wolf-Hartmut Friedrich puzzles over the oddity that "Heyne hat die Besonnenheit eingehend gewürdigt, mit der Virgil sein schwieriges Unternehmen zu Ziel führte, ohne doch die Entfremdung der Deutschen von der Aeneis aufhalten zu können."[45] Yet the prefaces and introductory essays make it clear that Heyne does not aim to check the German alienation from the *Aeneid;* if anything he gives it a significant push. His ability to sense the heady enthusiasm of Winckelmann and Lessing for Homer and the Greeks gives his prefatory material much of its verve and conviction. At the same time it also sets the tone for the body of the work to follow. In it the programmatic and neo-humanist aims that underlie the project emerge clearly, and they do not favor a new appreciation of the Virgilian texts.

Heyne expends his greatest effort on the two volumes devoted to the *Aeneid* (vols. 2 and 3). In addition to the notes, the poem comes decked out with 109 *excursus*, two prefaces (one for each volume), and two lengthy essays. The first *disquisitio* is entitled "On Virgil's Epic Poem" (*De carmine epico Virgiliano*), and the second "On the Invention shown in the Matters dealt with in the *Aeneid*" (*De rerum in Aeneide tractatarum inventione*). In them, Heyne begins from the position that Virgil, unlike Homer, exhibits no insight into the emotions and wants that move humans. Homer is also the genius who creates directly from nature without need of the rules of art (*O* 2:xxvi). The absence of these things defines the sense in which Virgil is a learned poet. Heyne devotes these essays to the redefinition of the term *poeta doctus* in relation not to a Greek uncouthness but to a natural simplicity. In doing so, Heyne essentially inverts the approbation of style so familiar from the classroom; it becomes the mark of a derivative poet to whom, once character, plot, invention, and every deeper insight into the human condition has been stripped away, only a residual verbal brilliance remains. Friedrich sums up Heyne's accomplishment thus: "Wichtiger ist aber, daß er mit der Einsicht ernst macht, das virgilische Epos könne sich nur als Sprachwunder gegen das in unverbrauchten Glanze erstrahlende homerische behaupten."[46] As appealing as that accomplishment may be to the age of Goethe, it does not account for all of Virgil's poems.

Despite the attention he lavishes on the *Aeneid*, Heyne does not consider it Virgil's greatest work; this accolade he reserves for the *Georgics*. Both his introductions for the *Eclogues* and the *Aeneid* begin not so much with an investigation of the respective poems but rather a statement of first principle, namely what a bucolic is and what an epic. The first essay on the *Aeneid* does bear the title *De carmine epico Virgiliano* but its first sentence reads: *De carmine epico vniuerse multa disputare* (*O* 2:xv; many things in epic are widely considered to be a matter of debate). It then turns on the definition of epic for which Homer provides the authoritative model. Heyne does not bother to disguise the starting point of his introduction to the *Eclogues*, simply writing "On Pastoral," *De carmine bucolico*, and not "On Virgil's Pastoral," *De carmine bucolico Virgiliano* or the more specific "On Virgil's Pastoral Poems," *De carminibus bucolicis Virgilianis*.[47] With the *Georgics* he sets off on a different tack; his introduction he calls simply "An Introduction to the *Georgics*," *Proemium in Georgica*. And in truth, it differs markedly in content and argumentation from the introductory material to the other two poems; it lacks the normative declaration that the Virgilian work is then pruned to fit.

Heyne's preference for the *Georgics* seems to be of long standing as it antedates his Virgil edition, and is one he shares with the more advanced opinion of his age. His biographer Arnold Hermann Ludwig Heeren (1760–1842) reports that during his first few years at Göttingen Heyne lectured on the major authors of antiquity and their works: Horace, Virgil's *Georgics*, some of the tragedians, and the *Iliad* (for the first time in 1766). Nonetheless, in his edition Heyne can only bring himself to write a scant dozen pages on the work of which he says: *Magnificam autem et praeclaram esse illam Virgiliani carminis praedicationem, quis non videt? Est scilicet summa laus, quae in id carminis genus cadere possit, quod* **didactum** *appellare solemus* (*O* 1:177–78; Who doesn't know of this praise of Virgil's poem as splendid and excellent? This is doubtless the highest praise that can be bestowed on the type of poetry we commonly call *didactic*); or again, yet more extravagantly: *Itaque hoc in genere Virgilium, poetarum Ciceronem appellare nonnunquam lubet. Illa autem ingenii Maroniani propria uenustas in nullo eius opere magis cognoscitur, quam in Georgicis*

(*O* 1:184; And so it sometimes pleases to call Virgil the Cicero of poets in this genre. Indeed, the distinctive beauty of Virgil's genius is more easily studied in the *Georgics* than in any other of his works). Yet for the *Aeneid* and the *Eclogues*, that is for the poems that belong by his own reckoning less properly to the genius or talent of Virgil he can write two long essays for the epic, and even a whole seventeen pages for the bucolics.

In part Heyne's difficulty has already been noted above. His strength is to begin with a general definition of genre and, by relating it to the deeper mysteries of poetry and the beautiful, to discuss the several ways in which the Virgilian style fails completely or partially to embody the indispensable traits of the true artwork. Didactic poetry, however, forbids such an approach since it is not thought to be true art: it is not a fiction or, to use the language of the time, it is not an invented imitation. Gottsched states the matter most simply:

> Das fragt sich nur, ob man diese und dergleichen Schriften Gedichte nennen könne? Nach der oben fest gestellten Beschreibung der Poesie überhaupt, kann man ihnen diesen Namen nicht einräumen. Alle diese großen und weitläufigen Werke sind zwar in Versen geschrieben; in der That aber keine Gedichte: weil sie nichts gedichtetes, das ist, keine Fabeln sind.[48]

Although Gottsched does continue with a "but," it is purely an empirical one; poets have written poetical treatises, even if the thinker cannot imagine this in his theory.

Heyne finds himself constrained to begin where he usually likes to conclude only after having shown that the Virgilian beauty does not derive from nature, nor simplicity, nor genius, but from linguistic adroitness and artistic technique. Thus he must begin: *Ad Georgica **facetum** illud ac **molle**, quod peculiari aliquo Musarum munere Virgilio concessum esse Horatius memorat, proprio quodam modo spectare uidetur* (*O* 1:177; it seems proper to consider in what particular way the *Georgics* have that tenderness and grace which Horace remarks is the particular gift of the Muses bestowed on Virgil). Virgil can achieve such a pitch of technical perfection because he led a life shaped by Greek letters, the urbanity of Rome, social interaction with the most cultivated and elegant of men, and a talent for ever more exquisite song; as a result, *ex Alexandrinis imprimis poetis Virgilium nostrum profecisse; his eum naturalem illam et parum operosam, cum tanto tamen cultu, ornatu, et dignitate coniunctam, uenustatem debere arbitramur* (*O* 1:182; our Virgil has most of all drawn on the Alexandrian poets; and we judge him to owe to them that natural beauty so effortlessly harnessed to such refinement, embellishment, and dignity). As a work of description really has no point beyond the display of its own artistry, diversions are needed to relieve tedium, and Virgil excels in this. Virgil makes his own the two virtues of description: embellishment and digression: *Digressionum itaque ad ornandum huiusmodi carmen* *imprimis magna laus habenda. In iis autem Virgilii ingenium inprimis commendat hoc* (*O* 1:180; Digressions are especially to be praised for their decorative role in this kind of poetry. Virgil's genius exhibits itself especially in digressions).

Lest, however, the reader should gain a false impression of Virgil's accomplishments, Heyne quickly moves to point out the limitations of these poetic virtues. Virgil has lifted many of his poetic embellishments from other poets in an attempt to invigorate his verse: *annon multo plura irrigati fontibus alienis ingenii uestigia essemus deprehensuri?* (*O* 1:182; Must we not indeed observe the many and numerous traces of a genius watered by others' springs?). Heyne also notes of his capacity for invention: *si animi sensa libere eloqui fas est, non maiorem in Georgicis quam in reliquis eius carminibus deprehendimus* (*O* 1:181; we consider it no greater in the *Georgics* than in the rest of his poems, if it is proper to express one's sentiments freely). Virgil has plundered his material from a comprehensive list of ancient authors (*O* 1:181–82). And finally, as for a comparison with Hesiod, Heyne denies flat out that it is possible except in three or four instances:

> *Hesiodus non Georgica, h.e. de re rustica, scripsit aut scribere uoluit, sed totius uitae domesticae, qualis tum erat, coniunctae scilicet illius uel maxime cum agricolatione, rationes tradere, prudentiae etiam et morum praecepta proponere. Quod autem Ascraeum carmen appellat suum opus Virgilius, id eo pertinet, quod in simili fere genere uersatur, non quod ex Hesiodeo petitum aut transcriptum aut ad eius formam est compositum.* (*O* 1:186)

> [Hesiod neither wrote nor wished to write a Georgic, that is, about life in the country, but rather about all of domestic life, obviously at that time very closely connected with agriculture, to catalogue its methods, and to expound its way of life and wisdom. Virgil however calls his piece a Hesiodic poem because it shares in a very similar genre and therefore it is related to it, and not because it was taken from Hesiod's work, nor copied it, nor was composed according to its model.]

Hesiod wished to sing of life, domestic life as it really was, of agriculture and ethical habits; Virgil did not. This introduces Heyne's discussion of the poem's content, which covers two pages and manages by speaking of Hesiod to avoid any mention of the golden age, nature, the Praises of Italy, and others passages for which the poem enjoyed such popularity in the eighteenth century.

Heyne concludes his survey with the confident expectation that: *Ita demum eos (i.e. adulescentes) intellecturos esse speramus, qua in re poeticae imprimisque Virgilianae orationis pulchritudo ac praestantia quaerenda sit* (*O* 1:188; Thus we hope that the young will at length understand how beauty and excellence are to be sought in poetic language, especially

Virgil's). Arguably his treatment of the *Georgics* is the weakest point in his edition. In comparison to Heyne's editions of other poets, Conrad Bursian judges "so müssen wir die Ausgabe des Virgil (abgesehen von der in Hinsicht der Sacherklärung sehr mangelhaften Bearbeitung der *Georgica*) als die bedeutendste . . . bezeichnen."[49] Whatever the quality of Heyne's commentary on the *Georgics*, it is nevertheless striking that they should be deemed weak and that his introduction would leave any one praying not to be nominated as the "poetic Cicero," as both introduction and commentary are ostensibly offered up in support of his belief that Virgil displays his genius at its best in this work.

The paradox simply points to the degree to which Heyne's interest in the poets stems purely from his programmatic aim to demonstrate the new learning advocated by the neo-humanists: to explain the cultural context of the poems, to judge their aesthetic merit, to teach others to do the same, and, most of all, to shape the soul of the modern through the beauty of the ancient. When Friedrich argues that despite Heyne's assiduous labors he could not hinder the German estrangement from the Latin poet, it would perhaps be more accurate to say that he did not intended to stay any encroaching alienation — indeed he already shared it himself, having imbibed the new philhellenic spirit from Lessing and Winckelmann.

In one sense Heyne is consistent and remains true to his principles: he has the least to say exactly where poetics and the newer aesthetic thinking provide him with the least fodder. Neo-humanism was driven from the outset by an ever-deepening reflection on the meaning of reading a text, by the need to devise new methods of approaching the ancient text that it might draw nearer to the spirit dwelling within it and assimilate it. This hope, this promise, motivates Heyne even if he possesses neither the creative fervor of a Winckelmann nor the rigorously systematic and synthetic imagination of a Wolf. Heyne grounds his exegesis on beautiful passages that need an explanation of their mythological, religious, geographical, or other allusions and contexts for their further interpretation. The *Aeneid* naturally attracts his attention for its wealth of compressed references. The *Georgics*, on the other hand, are exactly those poems that Addison cherished for their artistry, their style, not their things; it is the poem Lessing feared to translate and Goethe criticized Voss for failing to translate well enough. Style also lay at the core of the old humanist training in the schools. It was the method that the earlier neo-humanists fought against with the new method: the teaching of the ancient languages and texts must not be reduced simply to stylistic exercises of composition. In failing to warm to the Georgic style Heyne merely remains true to his life-long endeavors — of a work with only its style to recommend it, nothing really can be said.

An irony can be observed in Heyne's commentary on Virgil: like the enormous old oak that sends forth a superabundant and verdant foliage while inwardly the trunk dies, Heyne's edition spurs outwardly a luxurious growth in interest while inwardly it gnaws at the last tap-root, that of style. Many new translations using his text sprout up in the last three decades of the century, everyone reads his edition, Lessing finds volume two of great interest, Wieland purchases the school edition of it, Novalis studies it in school, the English request he touch up the second edition for a special printing in London, and Goethe wishes to come to Göttingen to sit at the great man's feet.

Soon, however, Herder will present a more synthetic conception of Greek culture, Werther will take up the reading of Homer, Voss will make him speak German, and the full energy of neo-humanist philhellenism will break forth. Nonetheless, the success of Heyne's edition probably ensures that Virgil is better studied and more widely read than at any other time previously in Germany.

It falls to two of Heyne's students to draw out the full implications of his edition for the Latin poet. August Wilhelm Schlegel attended the university at Göttingen from 1786 until 1791, during which time he helped prepare the index in the fourth volume that covered the entire second edition (1789) and attended Heyne's seminar for the interpretation of ancient texts. In the spring of 1790 his younger brother, Friedrich Schlegel, joined him both in Göttingen and in Heyne's seminar until he went to the university of Leipzig at Easter 1791.[50] Friedrich Schlegel absorbs the points established by Heyne and reevaluates them from a different perspective, one influenced by Winckelmann and Herder. Heyne contented himself with the *uenustas*, "the beauty," the *nitor*, "the elegance," the *sollertia*, the "artistry," the *verecundia*, the "modesty," the *mollitudo*, the "gentleness," of a particular passage. He carefully pointed out that Virgil had borrowed here and how he had artistically arranged it and he showed how this belonged to the learned style acquired from the Alexandrians.

As early as 1794, in his *Von den Schulen der griechischen Poesie*, Friedrich Schlegel concludes that "der Stil Ovids, Properzens, Virgil ist im ganzen Alexandrinisch" (*KFS* 1:15). And as Heyne had argued for a certain appreciation of the elegance and artistry of Virgil's learned style in his introduction to the *Georgics*, so too does Friedrich Schlegel grant a certain measure of beauty to it in his *Über das Studium der Griechischen Poesie* (1795–97):

> Dieser gelehrte Künstler [Vergil] . . . Zwar fehlt ihm die letzte Rundung und Feinheit der Alexandriner, aber durch die frische Römerkraft seines Dichtertalents übertrifft er die kraftlosen Griechen jenes Zeitalters in ihrem eignen Stil sehr weit. Er ist in diesem an sich unvollkommen Stil zwar nicht schlechthin vollkommen, aber doch der trefflichste. (*KFS* 1:349)

As has already been mentioned, it is a matter of some puzzlement why Schlegel should strain so, first to remark so paltry a thing (a certain borrowed style) and then to engage in such contortions to assign it some measure of excellence. If it is supposed that he has before his mind the problem as Heyne left it, then his diffidence becomes easily intelligible.

It also sheds some light on his view of the *Georgics*. In common with the entire eighteenth century, including Heyne, he judges Virgil's Georgic poem to be the artist's supreme achievement. In the *Geschichte der alten und neuen Literatur* (1812) Schlegel speaks of this work as his "vollendetstes Gedicht" and laments, "Hätte er nur diese herrliche, für das jetzige, endlich beruhigte Rom so wohltätige, in Italien dem Geiste und dem Inhalte nach wahrhaft einheimische Poesie, nicht in der fremden und ausländischen Kunstform des alexandrinischen Lehrgedichts niedergelegt" (*KFS* 6:80). Earlier on, two lectures previously, he had defined the didactic poem, "daß diese Form des sogenannten Lehrgedichts, welche wir von den Alexandrinern überkommen haben, eine verfehlte Form falscher Kunst und Künstelei ist, bedarf wohl eigentlich keines ausführlichen Beweises" (*KFS* 6:61). Schlegel, in addition to his more general inversion of Virgil's reputation, now takes the one poem the eighteenth century judged Virgil to have least put a foot astray in and upends its praise by turning around the traits Heyne so tepidly, yet exactly, lauded. At that point when Virgil had a subject native to his Italy and suitable to his talent he took up the learned style and the false poetic form of the Alexandrians. In this fashion Schlegel arrives by easy stages at the idea of the Latin poet as a "warnendes Beispiel" to the ages.

The influence of Herder emerges in Friedrich Schlegel's ability to weigh Virgil's feeling for nature; Heyne had been oblivious of it. Schlegel considers "Virgils Liebe zur Natur und zum Landleben" (*KFS* 6:81) to be Virgil's true δαίμων. The belated recognition that, from the perspective of the end of the eighteenth century, a sense for nature joins the *Eclogues* and the *Georgics* represents the acknowledgment of the condition for their continued appeal to the entire eighteenth century. While nature constitutes an idea, a sentiment of immense variety and fascination for the eighteenth century, the first two Virgilian poems, being the least fixed by a tradition of theoretical criticism stretching back to antiquity, have the fewest barriers to overcome. The theory of the didactic poem is an embarrassment confronted by many examples it cannot readily explain. Nor does the theory of the bucolic have any roots in antiquity; Aristotle is silent and Horace keeps quiet. The way is clear for modern theorists of the pastoral.

However, the epic must be the first object of study as the *Aeneid* remains the more widely known text even if the tight embrace of tradition keeps it more remote. The epitome of the highest genre, it is apparently securely entrenched as an object of emulation. The fashion in which it serves this purpose varies both according to Virgil's displacement by

Homer as *the* rhapsode and also according to the generic conundrum of grand epic in the eighteenth century. The formal prescriptions of grand epic are more obdurate, less amenable to the cultural and literary interests of poets and critics than either eclogue or Georgic is in theory and practice to the concerns of nature and sentiment.

Notes

[1] Rehm, *Griechentum*, 24.

[2] "Incidentally" because the remark has the character of an aside in the *Gedanken*, and Winckelmann does not make any mention of Virgil in either the *Florenzer Manuskript* (1757?) or the *Geschichte der Kunst des Altherthums* (1764). The omission of Virgil from his later descriptions and the meagerness of the original reference notwithstanding, the Virgilian association echoes strongly. Lessing, ostensibly writing his *Laokoon oder über die Grenzen der Mahlerei und Poesie* (1766) in response to Winckelmann's *Geschichte der Kunst*, nonetheless begins with exactly this point of difference between Virgil's account and the statue. One might even sense some of the daring of Winckelmann's comment in the outraged shock contained in Lessing's admission: "Ich bekenne, daß der mißbilligende Seitenblick, welchen er auf den Virgil wirft, mich zuerst stutzig gemacht hat, . . ." Gotthold Ephraim Lessing, *Werke und Briefe*, ed. Wilfried Barner et al. (Frankfurt am Main: Deutscher Klassiker, 1985–), 5/2:18.

[3] Rehm, *Griechentum*, 24–9; see also Conrad Wiedemann, "Römische Staatsnation und griechische Kulturnation: Zum Paradigmawechsel zwischen Gottsched und Winckelmann," *Akten des VII. Internationallen-Germanisten-Kongresses*, Göttingen (1985), v. 9, 173–78.

[4] Rehm, *Griechentum*, 22.

[5] See Comparetti, *Vergil in the Middle Ages*, 195–231, and also Ernst Robert Curtius, *Europäische Literatur und lateinisches Mittelalter* (Bern: Francke, 1948), 25–27 and 352–83.

[6] See Eduard Norden, *Die Geburt des Kindes: Die Geschichte einer religiösen Idee* (Leipzig: Teubner, 1924).

[7] In recent years scholars have shown renewed interest in the provenance and interpretation of the Laocoon statue. Foremost among them is Bernard Andreae, with two books on the subject: *Laokoon und die Gründung Roms*, Kulturgeschichte der antiken Welt 39 (Mainz: Zabern, 1988) and *Laokoon und die Kunst von Pergamum: Die Hybris der Giganten* (Frankfurt am Main: Fischer, 1991). He argues that the Vatican statue is a copy of a bronze original from Pergamum. German Hafner takes a wholly different position in *Die Laokoon-Gruppen: Ein gordischer Knoten*, Akademie der Wissenschaften und der Literatur 5 (Stuttgart: Steiner, 1992). He argues that the statue referred to by Pliny's famous comment (*Naturalis Historiae*, bk. 36, chap. 37) is not the Vatican statue, but rather refers to a lost statue that antedates the *Aeneid*. The Vatican statue, on the other hand, was sculpted in response to the Virgilian epic. Bettina Preiß gives a detailed account

of the art-historical and aesthetic-literary reception of the statue since its rediscovery in 1506, along with reproductions of much of the source material: see Bettina Preiß, *Die wissenschaftliche Beschäftigung mit der Laokoongruppe* (Bonn: VDG, 1992). Slightly before these, yet offering a readable and concise account of the statue and the vicissitudes since its rediscovery is Georg Daltrop, *Die Laokoongruppe im Vatikan: Ein Kapitel aus der römischen Museumsgeschichte und der Antiken-Erkundung*, Xenia: Konstanzer Althistorische Vorträge und Forschungen 5 (Constance: Universitätsverlag Konstanz, 1982).

[8] Hafner argues for the aptness of "edle Einfalt und stille Größe," *Die Laokoon-Gruppen*, 39–41.

[9] E. M. Butler, *The Tyranny of Greece over Germany* (New York: Macmillan, 1935), 47. Hatfield also notes its inappropriateness, calling the Laocoon "that painfully effective product of Hellenistic baroque" (*Aesthetic Paganism*, 9). He points to a likely origin in Winckelmann's familiarity with Greek literature: "To put it crudely, he read into the Laocoön and other renowned statues ideals derived from Sophocles, Homer and Plato, his favorite authors" (9). Hatfield's comment reflects the tendency to accept Winckelmann's phrase as essentially accurate but transfer it to the classical period of the fifth and fourth centuries: in less fulsome form he earlier voiced the same opinion; see Hatfield, *Winckelmann*, 19–20.

[10] This point does not prejudice the question of the wording. For various earlier occurrences of elements in the phrase see the "Stellenkommentar" by Pfotenhauer to the *Gedanken* in *Frühklassizimus*, 444 and 363. For a reading of it in the context of Winckelmann's text see Reinhard Brandt, ". . . ist endlich eine edle Einfalt, und eine stille Größe," in *Johann Joachim Winckelmann 1717–1768*, ed. Thomas W. Gaehtgens (Hamburg: Felix Meiner, 1986), 41–54. One such earlier association of the phrase "edle Einfalt" with ancient Greece and an urgent need for the muse to return to the purer springs of that Grecian nature may be found in the *Lyrische Gedichte* of Johann Peter Uz. In the preface to the edition of 1749, he speaks of "der edlen Einfalt, dem ungekünstelten Ausdrucke, oder der schönen Natur der Alten" and repeats the phrase in the opening stanza of *Lobgesang des Frühlings:*

> Wie lang hat meine Muse schon,
> Die Witz und edle Einfalt ehret,
> Am blumenvollen Helikon,
> Den Musen Griechenlands begierig zugehöret!

Winckelmann replaces "Witz" with "stille Größe" and opposes Greek to Roman antiquity, unlike Uz, who regards them as part of a seamless whole. Both the preface and the poem are cited according to Johann Peter Uz, *Sämtliche poetische Werke*, ed. A. Sauer, Deutsche Litteraturdenkmale des 18. und 19. Jahrhunderts in Neudrucken 33 (Stuttgart: Göschen, 1890), 5 and 7 respectively.

[11] Stoicism neither exhausts the scope of the ideals and ideas that animate Winckelmann's writings nor is clearly separated from them; rather one must keep in mind the interdependence of his conception of history, his style, his vision of humanity, the beautiful, and freedom, on which various points see: Horst Rüdiger,

"Winckelmanns Geschichtsauffassung: Ein Dresdner Entwurf als Keimzelle seines historischen Denkens," *Euphorion*, 62/2 (1968): 99–116; Bernd Bräutigam, "Poetizität und der Ursprung literarischer Ästhetik im 18. Jahrhundert," in *Neuere Studien zur Aphoristik und Essayistik*, ed. Giulia Cantarutti and Hans Schumacher, Berliner Beiträge zur neueren deutschen Literaturgeschichte (Frankfurt am Main: Lang, 1986), 9:223–49; and Eberhard Wilhelm Schulz, "Winckelmanns Schreibart," in *Studien zur Goethezeit: Erich Trunz zum 75. Geburtstag*, ed. Hans-Joachim Mähl and Eberhard Mannack (Heidelberg: Carl Winter, 1981), 233–55.

[12] See Carl Justi, *Winckelmann und seine Zeitgenossen*, ed. Walter Rehm, 5th ed. (Cologne: Phaidon Verlag, 1956), 1:29.

[13] Carl Justi discovered a miscellany of writings by Winckelmann in Florence that included among the letters and rough sketches a description of the statues in the Belvedere. He published a selection of them in "Ein Manuscript über die Statuen im Belvedere" (*Preussische Jahrbücher* 28 [1871], 581–609) together with some notes on their composition and place within Winckelmann's writings. He dates the descriptions to the year 1757. For the description of the Laocoon statue, see 586–88. All three descriptions are now more easily accessible and printed together in the *Frühklassizimus*, 186–91.

[14] In addition to claiming that the Laocoon statue represents the principle of noble simplicity and quiet tranquillity *par excellence*, Winckelmann also maintains that it is the perfect instance of the technical standard of the ideal proportions of the human body established by Polyclitus, and that it was also historically acknowledged as such by the Romans (*NGW* 4).

[15] If one holds that the statue antedates the epic, and that Virgil may reasonably be supposed to have seen it in Rome (see Bernard Andreae, *Laokoon und die Kunst*, 82–85), then one may well object, why should it surprise that from the same powerful statue two different viewers should arrive at similar understandings of it? This is anachronistic on two accounts. First, in Winckelmann's day the matter of priority was no more settled than it is today. To Winckelmann's assertion in *Geschichte der Kunst* that the statue came before the epic, Lessing devotes two sections of his *Laokoon* treatise (*Werke und Briefe*, sections 26–27; 5/2:183–96) to proving the contrary and Virgil's originality. Second, Virgil's text was the artifact first known and the one in relation to which the statue was measured when it was rediscovered in 1506. It therefore forms the basis for the reception of the statue.

[16] The prominence of the Laocoon episode in Winckelmann, and then in almost all writers of note for the rest of century, explains Heinze's choice of the passage to begin his detailed examination of exactly how Virgil constructed his narrative. On exactly this point, the older criticism was declared obsolete: "Damit werden die klassischen Deutungen (Lessing, *Laokoon;* Schiller, *Über das Pathetische;* Goethe, *Über Laokoon;* Herder, *Kritische Wälder*) hinfällig," in Karl Büchner, *P. Vergilius Maro. Der Dichter der Römer* (Stuttgart: Druckenmüller, 1957), 327.

[17] Recent criticism focuses on the dynamism, be it contradictory or not, of this metaphor to counter the later association of neo-classical ideals with a cold lifelessness, see Alex Potts, *Flesh and the Ideal: Winckelmann and the Origins of Art History* (New Haven: Yale UP, 1994), 1–2, but also Szondi where his desire to do this leads him to

argue that Laocoon's face is calm, his spirit turbulent: "Obwohl die Oberfläche wütet, bleibt die Tiefe ruhig; obwohl das Gesicht ruhig ist, wüten hinter ihm Leidenschaften. Und ebenso gilt die Umkehrung: Zwar wüten die Leidenschaften, aber ihr Ausdruck, das Gesicht, ist ruhig" (Szondi, "Antike und Moderne," 44–45). Brandt takes the simile in the more customary sense of the face and body of Laocoon as the surface, his spirit as the depths (". . . ist endlich eine edle Einfalt," 45).

[18] The texts most important for the interpretation of the Laocoon statue are Pliny's comment, the episode from Virgil, and a poem by Jacopo Sadoleto, which, according to Andreae, ushers in, after the initial phase of wonderment, "die zweite Phase . . . im Zeitalter der deutschen Klassik" (Andreae, *Laokoon und die Gründung*, 14). Preiß provides an extensive analysis of the innumerable references before Winckelmann to the statue, found mostly, though by no means exclusively, in travel guides and letters (*Die wissenschaftliche Beschäftigung*). Hafner gives the most easily accessible and clearest account of the discovery of the Laocoon and the initial reaction to it, complete with copies of the above-mentioned texts and translations of them (*Die Laokoon-Gruppen*, 9–20). See also Daltrop, *Die Laokoongruppe*. For the remnants of other ancient portrayals of Laocoon before Virgil's see Andreae, *Laokoon und die Gründung*, 149–51.

[19] Lessing prints the poem in its entirety in a footnote to *Laokoon* (*Werke und Briefe* 5/2:61–63), from which note all citations of the poem are taken. The poem is also reprinted by Hafner, *Die Laokoon-Gruppen*, 15–17.

[20] From Johann Wolfgang Goethe, "Propyläen: Eine periodische Schrift" (1799; more commonly "Anzeige der Propyläen"), *GSW* 6/2:134.

[21] The suggestive power of the Virgilian phrase *Laocoonta auxilio subeuntem* continues undiminished. The translation offered next to the poem in the "Stellenkommentar" of Lessing's *Laokoon* gives for the Latin:

> *iamque alterius depasta <serpens> cruentum*
> *Pectus suprema genitorem voce cientis . . .*

the German:

> . . . Und schon ist die blutiger Brust des einen zerfressen, der, indem er mit versagender Stimme den Vater zu Hilfe ruft. . . . (*Werke und Briefe*, 5/2:769).

Cieo means to cause to move, and then by degrees: to stir, stimulate, call, summon. There is no reason, looking at the statue, why the boy should wish either to stimulate his father or to summon him. His father, inches away, does not need summoning, nor does it seem possible that he should be stimulated to still greater exertion. The same is true of the translation offered in the notes to *Laokoon* in Gotthold Ephraim Lessing, *Gesammelte Werke*, ed. Wolfgang Stammler (Munich: Hanser, 1959): "schon zerbeißt sie die Brust des einen, der mit letzter Stimme den Erzeuger zu Hilfe ruft . . ." (2:827). Hafner's translation of the last portion of the lines in question, "der den Vater ruft mit ersterbender Stimme" (*Die Laokoon-Gruppen*, 17), while more accurate, still does not resolve the problem of *cieo* as it ignores the causative sense of the verb. To make sense of *cieo* one requires the Virgilian gloss, and the translations reflect this.

22 The question of the expression on the faces of the figures is of interest. They are all in essence identical, with the exception of Laocoon's being larger and more carefully executed. Each head is tilted in relation to the shoulders, the eyebrows are canted upwards and inward causing the forehead to wrinkle, the hair is tousled and matted, and the mouth is open slightly, allowing for sound and interpretation. The common treatment of expression suggests that one is dealing with an established artistic convention (Andreae, *Laokoon und die Kunst*, 5–35). Winckelmann would seem to have taken the notion of the children crying out from Sadoleto but the notion of help and the father's distress from Virgil, both of which elements serve to heighten the pathos and, in Winckelmann, to underline the magnanimity of Laocoon. It is also ironic to note that Winckelmann is prepared to call the sound the dying child utters a "Schrei" when his mouth is no more open than that of Laocoon.

23 Simon Richter makes this observation the starting point for his book, *Laocoon's Body and the Aesthetics of Pain: Winckelmann, Lessing, Herder, Moritz, Goethe* (Detroit: Wayne State UP, 1992). He rejects Butler's notion of the accidental association of Winckelmann's insight with the statue by noting that if it were merely an idiosyncrasy of Winckelmann then it would hardly have led to such prolonged controversy on the part of others (11). He argues that the association is not accidental, since the discourse of pain decenters the classical aesthetical concept of the beautiful. If, however, the dynamic of the Laocoon description stems from Virgil's dramatic pathos, and does not belong to the concept of harmonious beauty, then suffering is a moral instance, and less a subtext of mutilation. Richter mentions that pain forms a part of the concept of tragedy from the time of Aristotle but does not explore the connection, preferring instead to regard pain as a marginalized subtext (33 and 61) and search for unconscious motivations: "The discourse from outside, that is, the historical and the biographical, is theory's body" (43). It is of interest that he omits Schiller in the list of authors he considers in his title. A similar process of discursive othering is pursued by Kevin Parker, "Winckelmann, Historical Difference, and the Problem of the Boy," *Eighteenth Century Studies* 25,4 (1992): 523–44, and Potts, 113–44.

24 For an examination of Schiller's relation to Winckelmann, see Ludwig Uhlig, "Schiller und Winckelmann," *Jahrbuch für internationale Germanistik* 17/1 (1985): 131–46; and more generally of Schiller's "Griechentum," see Rehm, *Griechentum*, 199–239.

25 The final paragraph in the section on the "Pathetischerhabene" in Schiller's treatise *Vom Erhabenen* (1793) is almost identical in its formulation to the sentence cited above from *Über das Pathetische*: "Aus diesem Grundsatz fließen die beiden Fundamentalgesetze aller tragischen Kunst. Diese sind *erstlich:* Darstellung der leidenden Natur; *zweytens:* Darstellung der moralischen Selbstständigkeit im Leiden" (*Schillers Werke* 20:195).

26 Rehm, *Griechentum*, 27.

27 For information on the condition of education in the eighteenth century see: Friedrich Paulsen, *Geschichte des gelehrten Unterrichts auf den deutschen Schulen und Universitäten vom Ausgang des Mittelalters bis zur Gegenwart*, ed. Rudolf Lehman, 3rd enlarged ed. (Berlin and Leipzig: Walter de Gruyter, 1921), vol. 2; and also Karl

Adolf Schmid, *Geschichte der Erziehung vom Anfang an bis auf unsere Zeit* (Stuttgart: J.G. Cotta'sche Buchhandlung, 1884–1902), 4/2 and 5/1. For specific information on the methodology of Latin instruction, with copious examples, see Julius Lattmann, *Geschichte der Methodik des lateinischen Elementarunterrichts seit der Reformation* (Göttingen: Vandenhoek und Ruprecht, 1896).

[28] Johann Wilhelm Ludwig Gleim, *Sämmtliche Schriften* (Amsterdam: n.p., 1770), 1:105.

[29] Karl Philipp Moritz, *Anton Reiser*, in *Werke*, ed. Jürgen Hahn, Bibliothek deutscher Klassiker (Berlin und Weimar: Aufbau, 1973), 2:41.

[30] Moritz, *Anton Reiser*, 42–43.

[31] Arnold Hermann Ludwig Heeren, *Christian Gottlob Heyne* (Göttingen: Johann Friedrich Röwer, 1813), 18. Much of the biography consists of excerpts from Heyne's correspondence and other writings, among which is one under the title "Heyne's Nachricht von seiner Jugendgeschichte" (5–28).

[32] Heeren, *Heyne*, 26–27. Ernesti would later prove instrumental in securing Heyne the post in Göttingen left vacant following Gesner's death (see Heeren, *Heyne*, 72ff.).

[33] For an account of classical studies in Germany during the eighteenth century see Conrad Bursian, *Die Geschichte der classischen Philologie in Deutschland von den Anfängen bis zur Gegenwart*, 2 vols. (Munich and Leipzig: Oldenbourg, 1883). Bursian provides a catalog-like list of German scholars and their works for which Paulsen, *Geschichte des gelehrten Unterrichts*, provides the more interpretative framework and commentary. John Edwin Sandys provides a service similar to Bursian without the concentration on one country, in his *History of Classical Scholarship*, 3 vols. The third volume contains the eighteenth century, for which the relevant pages are 1–87. Rudolf Pfeiffer provides a more interpretative narrative, *History of Classical Scholarship: From 1300 to 1850* (Oxford: Oxford UP, 1976). He judges German scholarship at the start of this period as follows: "The study of classics has never been extinct in Germany, but it lived on in a quiet and modest way throughout the seventeenth century" (167).

[34] Pfeiffer, *Classical Scholarship*, 167.

[35] The other two are Johann August Ernesti (1708–81) and Johann Matthias Gesner (1691–1761), Heyne's predecessor at Göttingen. On Gesner see Ulrich Schindel, "Johann Matthias Gesner, Professor der Poesie und Beredsamkeit 1734–1761," in *Die Klassische Altertumswissenschaft an der Georg-August-Universität Göttingen*, ed. Carl Joachim Classen (Göttingen: Vandenhoeck & Ruprecht, 1989), 9–27. Alfred Rach in his *Biographien zur deutschen Erziehungsgeschichte* (Weinheim and Berlin: Beltz, 1968) characterizes the relationship of the three scholars to neo-humanism as "*Wegbereiter* des Neuhumanismus," "*Vorläufer des Neuhumanismus*" and the "*Begründer[.]* des Neuhumanismus in Deutschland," respectively (157, 158, and 162).

[36] Pfeiffer is inclined to reserve this distinction for Wolf's seminar: "Wolf was not only an influential writer, but also an effective organizer. His favorite creation was his philological 'seminar,' intended specially for the training of classical teachers. Göttingen and Leipzig also had classes as well as lectures, but since they

were occasional and temporary they are not to be compared with Wolf's permanent and methodical creation at Halle" (*Classical Scholarship*, 176). What Gesner created at Göttingen for the training of classical teachers and called a "philological seminar" and his successor continued can scarcely be accurately labeled a lecture, a class, or temporary and occasional. Robert S. Leventhal considers Heyne one of the founding figures of hermeneutics and his seminar as both the origin of the modern seminar and the site for the institutionalization of the hermeneutic method; see *The Disciplines of Interpretation: Lessing, Herder, Schlegel and Hermeneutics in Germany, 1750–1800* (Berlin: De Gruyter, 1994), 13, 33–34, and 240–41.

[37] Bursian, *Geschichte der classischen Philologie*, 1:478. For a brief introduction to Heyne with a good bibliography see Ulrich Schindel, "C. G. Heyne," in *Classical Scholarship: A Biographical Encyclopedia*, ed. Ward W. Briggs and William M. Calder III, Garland Reference Library of the Humanities 928 (New York: Garland, 1990), 176–82, a shorter version of which in German may be found in *Neue Deutsche Biographie* 9:93–95. No study exists that places the various aspects of Heyne's diverse undertakings in their context.

[38] *GSW* 16:264. At the beginning of book 9 Goethe cites a passage from a review by Heyne that begins with "das Herz," and passes through "Kenntnis," "die alten Dichter," a "gütiger Schöpfer," the "Seelenkräfte," "das Schöne" and "Natur," among other things, within the space of one paragraph. "Sie machten," notes Goethe, "auf uns rege Jünglinge sehr großen Eindruck" (382).

[39] Edward Gibbon, *The Memoirs of The Life of Edward Gibbon with Various Observations and Excursions by Himself*, ed. George Birkbeck Hill (London: Methuen, 1900), 179–80.

[40] Christian Gottlob Heyne, ed., *Opera: Virgilius Publius Maro*, 2nd ed. (Leipzig: Caspar Fritsch, 1787–89). The 2nd edition of Heyne's work is used for most purposes since it is the consolidated and revised version of the 1st edition. In it Heyne reprints the all-important prefaces and the introductory essays from the earlier edition and adds a new brief foreword. All subsequent references to this work will be made using the abbreviation *O*, and the volume and page numbers. All translations from Heyne are my own.

[41] The citation is from the *Kurfürstliche Braunschweig-Lüneburgische Schulordnung* of 1737 written by Rector Buttstedt, revised by Gesner, and printed in *Evangelische Schulordnungen*, ed. Reinhold Vormbaum (Gütersloh: Bertelsmann, 1864), 3:386. In the *Geschichte der Erziehung*, Hermann Bender characterizes the "statarisch" manner of exposition thus: "von sachlicher Erklärung ist keine Rede" (5/1:134).

[42] Later Gesner gives an example of the speed he envisages. A play of Terence can in: "4 oder 5 Stunden geendigt werden" (Vormbaum, *Evangelische Schulordnungen*, 3:389).

[43] Heyne, having a different approach to archaeology and art history, disappointed many who expected him to continue the work of Winckelmann after his unexpected death in 1768. A number of contributions on his relationship to Winckelmann appeared in *Winckelmanns Wirkung auf seine Zeit: Lessing, Herder, Heyne*, ed. Johannes Irmscher (Stendal: Winckelmann Gesellschaft, 1988).

[44] Heeren, *Heyne*, 155. These two enjoyed a correspondence over 26 years until Brandes's death in 1791. Heeren reports that only one side of the correspondence was preserved, the more than 2000 letters from Brandes; Brandes destroyed those he received from Heyne (Heeren, *Heyne*, 146).

[45] Wolf-Hartmut Friedrich, "Heyne als Philologe," in *Der Vormann der Georgia Augusta: Christian Gottlob Heyne zum 250. Geburtstag; Sechs akademische Reden* (Göttingen: Vandenhoeck & Ruprecht, 1980), 25.

[46] Friedrich, "Heyne als Philologe," 25.

[47] For an analysis of this introduction see chapter 4.

[48] Gottsched, *Ausgewählte Werke*, 6/2:242.

[49] Conrad Bursian, *Die Geschichte der classischen Philologie*, 1:480–81. Sandys concurs with Bursian in thought and wording: "Of the above editions the most important, as a whole, is the Virgil, the least successful part being the treatment of the subject-matter of the *Georgics* (Sandys, *History* 3:40).

[50] For Schlegel's relation to Heyne see Werner Mettler, *Der junge Friedrich Schlegel und die griechische Literatur* (Zurich: Atlantis, 1955), 46–97. Mettler gives a general presentation of Heyne's views of nature, mythology, and philology.

3: Virgil the Rhapsode

The *Aeneid* and the Problematic Prestige of Epic

LITERARY TRADITION STRETCHING BACK to antiquity ensures that for a national literature of any pretension a great national epic remains imperative. Virgil owes much of his preeminence to his accomplishment of this feat. Yet by the seventeenth and eighteenth centuries the genre is deeply problematic. The imperative and Virgil's accomplishment are undiminished, yet precisely how to compose a poem according to the definition that will do more than simply illustrate adherence to the definition remains a standing challenge; and one that many attempt, confident that epic represents the supreme achievement of culture. In this vein Dryden will begin his "Dedication of the Aeneis" with the sentence, "A heroick poem, truly such, is undoubedly (sic) the greatest Work which the Soul of Man is capable to perform."[1] Boileau too continues the preferment of epic to drama, accomplishing in his *L'Art poetique* the transition from tragedy to epic with the understatement that epic is "d'un air plus grand encore."[2] Gottsched, as noted previously, repeats and propagates this truism of criticism for German readers in his *Critische Dichtkunst;* epic is "das rechte Hauptwerk und Meisterstück der ganzen Poesie."[3]

This same tradition has also with equal dogmatism fixed the subject matter of epic in a manner that makes it impossible for the modern poet to produce a work that will hold a place in the vernacular similar to that achieved by Homer among the Greeks and Virgil among the Latins. Gottsched's definition gives the canonical elements of an epic's contents: "Ein Heldengedicht überhaupt beschreibt man: Es sey die poetische Nachahmung einer berühmten Handlung, die so wichtig ist, daß sie ein ganzes Volk, ja wo möglich mehr als eins angeht."[4] The tales of kings and wars, *arma uirumque cano*, must have a universal, that is, a national appeal, a criterion that entails bestowing on the life of the state some purpose larger than the mere aggrandizement of one nation or dynasty. The *prima facie* impossibility of this demand for more modern times is evident if one attempts to recollect the titles of epics written according to this formula; the list is likely to be short as they are usually only known to the literary historian.

Nonetheless, since poetics insisted on the supremacy of epic, no nation would willingly own itself unable to match the triumphs of Greece and Rome. Yet every poet who nourishes this *caecus ignis* (*Aen*. 4. 2; invisible fire; 97) in his veins sets his work on the royal road of oblivion. Pierre de Ronsard's *Le Franciade* (1572) is remembered for its failure. Nonetheless others follow and fare no better, for example George de Scudéry's *Alaric* (1654), Jean Chapelain's *La Pucelle d'Orleans ou la France délivrée* (1656), Voltaire's *Henriade* (1723), Richard Blackmore's *King Arthur* (1697), Richard Glover's *Leonidas* (1737); and among the Germans, Wolf Helmhardt von Hohberg's *Ottobert* (1663–64), Christian Heinrich Postel's *Der große Wittekind* (1724), Johann Valentin Pietsch's *Carl des Sechsten Sieg über die Türken* (1725); all of which, as the common currency of the age, find mention in Gottsched's *Critische Dichtkunst*.[5] As representative of the success of these epics one may read Klopstock's epigram *Malezieux Meynung* on Voltaire's *Henriade*:

> Wir Franzosen, sagt der zweyte Partü zu Voltäre,
> Haben keinen epischen Kopf.
> Der Tropf!
> Denkt Arouet, und geht, und schreibt die Henriade.
> O Jammerschade
> Um diese gutgereimte Henriade;
> Wenn Patrü nicht, allein Voltäre
> Der Tropf
> Gewesen wäre![6]

Nonetheless, Germany in these middle decades was no more immune to the *furor epicus* than other nations had been. In 1734 Gottsched's Swiss opponent, Johann Jakob Bodmer (1698–1783), surveying German literature in *Character der teutschen Gedichte* from its earliest unknown prehistory down to his own times, had concluded with a fervent call for the great German epic in wholly conventional language reminiscent of Virgil's *arma uirumque cano*, "Erscheine, grosser Geist, und singe Ding' und Thaten."[7] Despite having no poems of the ancient Teutons by which to judge their quality, Bodmer does not let this deficiency stop him from savoring Tacitus's approving depiction of the Teutons opposing the Romans (35) as enjoying a golden age of moral purity and heroism, with bards to sing of their deeds. In the slightly later *Versuch einer Critik über die deutschen Dichter* (1737), Bodmer is more direct, at once more despairing of present circumstances and less hesitant on ancient Germanic bards. Every nation boasts an epic: Greece (Homer), Rome (Virgil), Italy (Tasso), France (Voltaire), England (Addison), even so slight a land as Belgium (Catzen),

> Nur Deutschland muß allein, wenn andre pralen, schweigen;
> Und kann nicht einen Geist, wie diese Geister, zeugen? (15–16)[8]

Herman's feats for the preservation of Germany's freedom he attributes to the inspiration of the ancient bards' song (76–94). Not only does this speculation confirm Bodmer's fond belief in the social efficacy of poetry as the true guardian of virtue and also of freedom, but it also directs literary attention towards the patriotic Herman theme. This last suggestion was more in keeping with the times than the earlier recommendation at the end of the *Character der deutschen Gedichte* of Columbus as a suitable subject for epic treatment (in the manner of Camões's *Lusiads* [1572], chronicling Vasco de Gama's discovery of a sea passage to India). Christoph Otto Freiherr von Schönaich wrote a "Hermanniade" (*Hermann, das befreite Deutschland*, 1751). And Klopstock too toyed with the idea of an epic on the subject of Herman, before moving on to Henry the Fowler, until finally giving up the idea of a national epic altogether. Only then did he turn to the notion of a sacred poem.[9] To judge by the later series of his Herman dramas, the fascination seems to have left its mark. The same period of the late forties and early fifties also witnessed a floodlet of "epiades": Franz Christoph von Scheyb's Theresiade (1746), Ludwig Friedrich Hudemann's Friedrichiade (*Der großmüthige Friedrich der Dritte*, 1750), Christian Nicolaus Naumann's Nimrodiade (*Nimrod, ein Heldengedicht in vierundzwanzig Büchern*, 1752), not to mention Bodmer's own *Colombona* (1753), which are now no better remembered, though more numerous, than those of earlier decades.

To modern readers the universal importance to a people of battles and kings is more apparent than real; a concentration on dynastic wars, even among peoples of strong national feeling, is incapable of achieving the epic totality so cherished. Epic totality, or the capacity of an epic to capture compellingly a people's sense of itself, must include the emotional and intellectual attachments at the core of a person's existence, both as an individual and as a member of society. This involves some relation to the set of religious and mythical beliefs with which a people articulates its primary views about the order of the world and its place in it. The two ancient epics from which the prescription of heroes and wars derive, the *Iliad* and the *Aeneid*, are examples of this. Homer, with the aid of Hesiod, gave to the Greeks their gods; and Virgil, to reconcile the Romans to their history, drew heavily on the religious feeling of the Romans. To this end he did not, as Ennius or Naevius did, pick a war within historical memory; rather he chose the moment that commanded the greatest reverence, the mythical foundation of the Roman race. His war he then invented for himself. In other words, the heroes and their deeds in these epics retain their interest for their respective peoples as an embodiment of their beliefs and convictions about themselves, not because of their martial exploits.

The connection between state and religion was not of the poet's invention; each merely made use of it. In each case there is no meaningful separation of sacred and secular; the city-state of antiquity can, with as much justification, be called the church-state. For the Christian, who is in, but not of, this world, no such position is tenable. For the modern period this dichotomy becomes only more transparent with the idea of religious toleration and the preoccupation of the Enlightenment with the separation of church and state. Kings and their "Kabinettskriege" can lay claim to no special reverence; their wars are not the reflection of disturbances in heaven.

In view of the challenges confronting epic during the eighteenth century, it does not come as a matter of surprise that the *Aeneid* (or even the *Iliad* for that matter) leaves no readily discernable imprint. Reverence before the "Meisterstück der ganzen Poesie" is not of itself strong enough to revive the older themes of epic, although it can and does prove equal to the less arduous task of enforcing some of its formal elements. Wieland, in the final, more familiar version of *Oberon*, reduced the poem from fourteen to twelve cantos in an attempt to place his work in the minds of his readers in the tradition of grand epic. They were supposed to remind themselves that Virgil had divided his epic into twelve books.

As no eighteenth-century epic of the *arma uirumque cano* variety has survived, tracing the *Aeneid*'s impact on German epic in the eighteenth century is rather a matter of tracing the different attempts to grapple with the genre. It is in these various approaches to the matter that elements of *Aeneid* lend themselves to the interests of the eighteenth century. One solution to the difficulty of epic in the early modern period was to concentrate not on epic's national appeal but on its other component, its spiritual or religious inspiration. Tasso famously makes the conquest of Jerusalem by the First Crusade the subject of his epic, *Gerusalemme liberata* (1581). Tasso's solution, however, was not without theoretical hazards. In France, in the seventeenth century, Chapelain and Jean Desmarets de Saint-Sorlin also championed the Christian epic, provoking the *Querelle du merveilleux*. It is one of the forerunners to the better-known *Querelle des anciens et des modernes*, because it also touches on the question of whether moderns can create works worthy to be placed alongside the ancients. More immediately, it poses the problem of whether sacred Christian Revelation may be used for the profane purpose of poetry; and if so, whether it is permissible to deck it out in the devices, forms, and even images of heathen poets.

In this context Milton's epic *Paradise Lost* (1667) provides a corroborative example, with much appeal to the German poets in the middle decades of the eighteenth century. As a young man, during his days at Cambridge Milton contemplated writing an epic, for a long time thinking in terms of a national epic about a great hero. The legend of King Arthur occupied his ambition before he turned instead to the idea of a religious theme. The eventual epic owes its success to the sincerity of the religious feeling that animates it. Despite the cosmic geography, the transcendent figures, and the hosts, the human interest of the epic devolves onto a single couple. Implicitly, *Paradise Lost* elevates the individual's private life to a matter of high importance. Domestic life, to which any mortal may aspire, not merely kings, becomes a fit object for the highest of genres. Further, Milton depicts the Garden and life in it in strongly idyllic or pastoral colors. *Paradise Lost* promotes a religious topic, yet it also contains elements in its representation of domestic life and nature that will have as much as appeal as religion to the bourgeois intelligentsia of the eighteenth century.

The difficulties of reconciling a religious epic increasingly focused on the private self and nature to the older concern for nations and their conflicts became acute in poetological contemplations. Pyra, filled as a young poet of twenty-two with the ambition of heralding a new German poetry grounded in religion, sets himself this task in a didactic poem. The attempt is ultimately a failure as it illustrates succinctly the limits of the poetological desire to secure the prestige and prescriptions of ancient epic for the interests of the eighteenth century. In accordance with the notion that to consider epic is to discuss Virgil, the *Aeneid* is the source for Pyra's epic principles, and for his problems. His poem is thus representative of the *Aeneid*'s presence in theoretical reflections on the topic, and this is the first context in which I shall consider Virgil's epic.

The second context is that of epic style. The measure of an epic's high and lofty themes was its matching high and lofty style. More practically, this meant that reading the *Aeneid* in school devolved into the detailed examination and practice of its rhetorical devices according to the humanist tradition. Goethe's assertion, mentioned above, that Virgil's treatment of the Laocoon episode is merely rhetorical confirms this habit, for that, often enough, is what reading Virgil in the schools degenerated into.

The other side of the matter, however, is that this Virgil becomes *the* epic style, a fact that emerges most clearly in Klopstock's *Messias* (1748–73). To gain a better sense of what the rhetorical approach entailed calls for an admittedly dry analysis of Klopstock's diction. It is, however, warranted not merely on the grounds that his *Messias* is the most successful of the religious epics in the grand style inspired by Milton but also because it is through the refinement of the German language that Klopstock had his greatest effect, even if his epic rapidly came to seem labored and did not long survive. Indeed as a religious epic, the *Messias* is more an example of the aesthetic use of religion rather than a sacred poem; what is at issue seems often to be more the quality of feeling in the religion than the quality of religion in the feeling. To make this feeling tangible to his readers, Klopstock relies primarily on a refined poetic diction. The effect and fame of the *Messias* rest on the first three cantos in 1748, and less on those that follow with persistence till 1773 and the publication of the twentieth and final canto. In 1803, upon hearing the news of Klopstock's death, Herder had Klopstock assess his poem in the lively mixture of what would be Herder's own final work, the periodical *Adrastea:*

> Ich zählte und maß nicht nur, ich wägte die Sylben im Fluge des Wohllauts; auf eine vorher ungeahnte Weise machte ich Euch Eure ganze Sprache *melodisch.* Was kümmerte mich, wofür Ihr meinen *Meßias* haltet? Was er wirken sollte, hat er gewirkt und wird es wirken; *nächst Luthers Bibelübersetzung* bleibt er Euch das erste klassische Buch Eurer Sprache. (*HW* 10:763)

Lyrical intensity, linguistic innovation, involved syntax, and metrical novelty raised at first great hopes for German epic, but technical, poetic excellence proved insufficient to sustain the weight of the poem.

The tendency to concentrate on the smaller, private side of life in increasingly idyllic colors — and the third context for the consideration of the *Aeneid* — undergoes a vast sentimental expansion in the course of the century. Though it runs counter to the desire for epic grandeur, it nonetheless becomes an expectation sufficiently well associated with the genre for August Wilhelm Schlegel to espy plausibly in Goethe's rendition of a young love in an idyllic setting in *Hermann und Dorothea* the true epic form of the age.

The desire to harness the pastoral "grüne Stille" to the dignity of epic had vexed and frustrated Pyra in the earlier part of the century, and at the century's midpoint it spurred on Gessner's ambition after the triumph of his *Idyllen* (1756). He claims the status of epic for his idyllic prose tale on a biblical subject, *Der Tod Abels* (1758), when he sets the quotation *paulo maiora canamus* (*Ec.* 4. 1) opposite his introduction, which begins: "Ich habe an einen hoehern Gegenstand gewaget." He changes the "I would sing of things a little greater" of his original to "I have dared it." He insists that he writes epic, but in truth he unwittingly expands the notion of idyllic to include a range of modes and genres previously distributed among the pastoral at the low end to epic at the highest. Although for Gessner the solemnity of a biblical tale seems sufficient to justify the belief in an elevated tone in his epic, for the reader it seems rather the tragic, sentimental counterpart to his earlier comic, sentimental pieces in the *Idyllen.* The proemium frames the scope of Gessner's undertaking within the Virgilian context of a change from bucolic/Georgic (the two are conflated in Gessner's conception) to epic:

> Ein erhabnes Lied moecht' ich izt singen, die Haushaltung der Erstgeschaffenen nach dem traurigen Fall, und den ersten, der seinen Staub der Erde wieder gab, der durch die Wuth seines Bruders fiel. Ruhe du izt, sanfte laendliche Flöt', auf der ich sonst die gefaellige Einfalt und die Sitten des Landmanns sang.[10]

The passage grafts the bucolic line *paulo maiora canamus* onto a proemium that is itself a would-be *imitatio* of the pseudo-beginning of the *Aeneid*. Compare:

> *Ille, ego qui quondam gracili modulatus auena*
> *carmen, et egressus siluis uicina coegi*
> *ut quamuis auido parerent arua colono,*
> *gratum opus agricolis; at nunc horrentia Martis*
> *arma uirumque cano. . . .*[11]

[I am the poet who in times past made the light melody of pastoral poetry. In my next poem I left the woods for the adjacent farmlands, teaching them to obey even the most exacting tillers of the soil; and the farmers liked my work. But now I turn to the terrible strife of Mars. (27)]

Gessner probably intends no irony in the use of *paulo maiora canamus*, but succeeds despite himself. With these words, he does not, as he hopes, truly break free of the pastoral for the epic genre. Instead willy-nilly they demonstrate the opposite. They introduce a domestic scene, a "Haushaltung," that, after a mishap, is no more than "traurig"; the whole affair ends in a family spat.

Even if Gessner's elevation tips over into inadvertent farce, it shows the manner in which a religious subject matter and an idyllic mode combine in drawing together two formerly distinct genres. The culmination of this tendency in the idyllic epic of Voss and Goethe is thus attributable not merely to the ramification of the idyll, but also to a development internal to the epic itself. On this trajectory the religious epic of the middle decades of the century represents the form in which the two genres begin to mix. It displays at once many of the traits of high epic mediated by Milton, while, in tone and subject matter, it approaches the niche soon to be filled by Gessner's *Idyllen* and later the idyllic epic.

In the development of the "domestic" theme of the genre, with strong idyllic overtones, but this time dispensing with the attempt at high earnestness in favor of humor, the Virgilian epic retains some vitality; or rather, some episodes do, since it is a question of parts rather than of the whole. Wieland with his *Oberon* (1780) is here the great exemplar. His poem represents the wish of the newest subspecies of epic, the comic, or mock heroic epic, for the status of grand epic or at least its penumbra. Alexander Pope's (1688–1740) *Rape of the Lock* (1712), following in the tradition of Boileau's *Le Lutrin* (1674–83), initiates this subspecies of epic in Germany. The German Rococo avidly follows Pope's lead, seizing on the scope for wit and elegance the ironic distance unlocks. The shorter length also suits the Rococo's "Zug zum Kleinen."[12] Although the inexact sense of the word "mock" — whether it is comic, satiric, parodic, or fantastic, whether it is mere entertainment or mocks with a reproving yet benevolent indulgence for human weakness (as in *Musarion*, 1768) — makes the heterogeneous mass of works gathered under the rubric of mock-heroic unwieldy, Wieland nonetheless stands out as the genre's great practitioner.[13] In his *Oberon*, Wieland makes relatively extensive use of the Dido and Aeneas tragedy in order to inject his "Scherz" with some "Ernst." The parallels to the Dido story act as elevating echoes in the second half of Wieland's epic and assist his hero's predicament in emerging more clearly, that is less comically, as part of the universal human condition. They also uplift his epic to the vicinity of grand epic. He too continues the tendency of drawing the high theme of epic closer to pastoral by the role he gives to a more idyllic nature; his personages may be high, the situation bathetic, but his tale is of a young couple and their love.

The fourth and final context, and the one in which we find the direct and instantly identifiable imprint of the *Aeneid*, is parody. The very success of Alois Blumauer's *Virgils Aeneis travestiert* (1784–88) ensures that the now cumbrous machinery of traditional epic and its undisputed champion Virgil readily tip over into farce in the more common and popular imagination. Still, to achieve its effect, literary parody presumes that all have read a work, or are at least so familiar with it by reputation that they know enough about it to enjoy the parody, without having read it or needing to do so. This Virgil is once again the Virgil of the schoolroom, where, as is often the case, authors frequently used to make the young miserable can seldom count on their favor or fairness in later years. Translators, produced roughly a hundred translations of partial or complete Virgilian works for those not privileged to have spent their younger years in this way. The images and associations the satirist employs tell much about the more common impression an age may harbor about a given poem and author outside of the official pieties proffered on behalf of a staple of the curriculum. Blumauer closely ties his travesty to Virgil's apron strings in phrasing, structure, and episode so that his reader may easily perceive the Latin original and so flatter his learning while enjoying the parody. Nor does Blumauer neglect to appeal to the reader less well-versed in Latin. The Austrian ex-Jesuit novitiate, by selecting the Vatican as his Rome in the age of Josephinian reforms and giving his characters French airs and graces, picks two contemporary topics for satire appealing to his audience. The popularity of Blumauer's parody notwithstanding, it is the first three contexts that will be of concern here.

Pyra and the Poetological Quandary of Epic

Pyra's *Der Tempel der wahren Dichtkunst* (1737) shows the tension between the desire for a religious epic and the constraining hand of poetics with its dogma of heroes and great deeds as the essence of epic. Insofar as one gains a sense of Pyra's desired religious epic, it is to concern itself with a nature very idyllic in tone. In this instance, traditional poetics with its schema of genres culminating in a martial epic runs counter to Pyra's "modern" interest in a more idyllic nature. Pyra's poem is insufficiently unified to yield a convincing whole; one critic speaks of the poem's "*formal* adherence to the doctrines of neoclassicism while revolting against its *spirit*."[14] Formally, *Der Tempel der wahren Dichtkunst* is a didactic poem. The teaching point, as the title states, is poetry or "die Dichtkunst," and in accordance with the precepts of poetics, Pyra lavishes great attention on epic. As such his poem stands in the tradition of Horace's *epistola ad Pisonem* and Boileau's *L'Art poétique*, while the poetics espoused are those of Gottsched's *Critische Dichtkunst*. Equally, from the other half of the title, it also belongs to the tradition of temple poems, of which Pope's *Temple of Fame* (1715) is the most important here.

A further source, and a deeper affinity, lies in Haller's *Die Alpen* (1732) and its strong idyllic strain. The strongest image of idyllic life, tranquil detachment, and the muse occurs at the very conclusion of Pyra's poem with a faint echo of the Georgic *o fortunatos* (*Ge.* 2. 458), the apostrophe that introduces the "Praises of the Country Life":

> O! glücklich! Wer also dem höchsten spielen kan.
> Was wünscht ein Dichter mehr? Nichts, als ein wenig Acker,
> Wobey ein klarer Quell in einem Garten rauscht,
> Und einen Wald dabey. Hier solte meine Leyer
> Stets mein Gefehrte seyn. Hier wolte ich vergnügt
> In grüner Still auch wohl von Mann und Waffen spielen.
> Hier solte endlich mich des Lebens blasser Feind
> Mit seinem kalten Arm im Singen noch umschließen.[15]

The affinity is not accidental, as the interest in nature and in its description elsewhere also shows Haller's influence.[16] What makes this idyllic passage so unusual is its position at the end and the company it keeps. Pyra boldly proposes to reconcile the Virgilian epic, "Mann und Waffen" to the pastoral "grüner Still."

The combination of leisure and poetry in an idyllic setting is not an unusual association; nor particularly is the appeal to the divinity. Its presence represents Pyra's strong Pietistic leaning. The entire argument of the poem rests on the premise that all true poetry reflects a sincere religious conviction: no heathen poet will secure a niche within the precincts of Pyra's temple for new poetry. If poets do not possess "ein himmlisch hoher Geist" (5. 70), if their hearts are not pure and full of God's spirit, then they bear "unverdient der frommen Dichter Namen" (5. 74). The intensity of Pyra's desire to subordinate poetry to religious ends, though characteristic of him, clashes neither with the wider associations of the idyllic nor with the bourgeois transformation of it. The intrusion of epic into this world does, however, and, in a number of ways, all indicative of why the poem fails to cohere into a whole.

His choice of words to invoke epic, "von Mann und Waffen spielen," harks back to the first words of the *Aeneid: arma uirumque cano*. First, it is a pagan reference where a Christian reference might be expected to drive home the point made throughout and accentuate the novelty of Poetry's new temple. Milton, for instance, offers himself with such a phrase as, "to sing of the ways of God to man," the same Milton whom Pyra had already introduced to the holy of holies with the highest of praise:

> Mit majestätischen Schritten
> Trat Milton nun einher. Er hat die Poesie
> Vom heydnischen Parnaß ins Paradies geführet. (5. 28–30)

Second, the content of the words "Mann und Waffen" themselves is inappropriate. They suggest national epics written about kings and wars, topics that do not lend themselves to a divine epic. In them, as in Milton's *Paradise Lost*, there may well be fights and struggles, but these heavenly ructions can scarcely be reduced to the level of one nation vying against another. Pyra thus touches upon one of the difficulties that bedeviled the genre, the distinction between a sacred and a secular mode. Third, and most significant, the formal poetics of tradition is an inadequate vehicle for the elucidation of the enthusiasms embodied in the constellation of nature, poetry, and religious feeling. The emphasis in the poetics on genre, and epic as the highest, explains Pyra's selection of epic to represent the acme of the poet's ambition. Yet the conclusion Pyra reaches, though arrived at through the language of poetic tradition, in fact contradicts it.[17] It is antithetical to the "grüne Stille" that it should be the site for epic.

While Pyra's use of Virgil is thus symptomatic of the way in which old and new are present in the poem, it should also be borne in mind that the presence of Virgil is due not simply to received poetics but also represents, on the part of Pyra, a genuine poetic attachment to the Virgilian epic. He was also a translator of Virgil. In his *Aeneid* translation he used a line of eight iambs unrhymed; in the *Tempel* he shortens the line to six iambs and incorporates a polemic against meretricious rhyme into the body of the poem (1. 5–16 and 162–69). In short, both personal inclination and traditional poetics conspire to ensure Virgil a prominent place in Pyra's poem. Conversely, the difficulties inspired by this prominence only underscore the increasingly problematic nature of the epic genre and of the understanding of Virgil limited to that older poetics. The two, Virgil and the epic genre, in theory separable, are treated in practice by the weight of tradition as synonymous.

Several, though by no means all, of the odder passages in the poem are attributable to Pyra's attempt to incorporate elements of the *Aeneid* into his new temple of poetry. *Der Tempel der wahren Dichtkunst*, first published in 1737, consists of five cantos varying in length from 150 to 350 lines. Composed ostensibly to honor the ordination of his friend Samuel Lange (1711–81), the poem relates the ascent of the aspiring young poet Pyra under the guidance of "die heilige Poesie" to the top of the mountain on which Poetry's new temple sits. In the first canto, Poetry appears to the fervid young poet late one night in his rooms and transports him to the site of her new temple. Before the mountain proper, Pyra and his guide survey the paths of true and false poetry. A chasm separates the way of true poetry from the mountain before which Pyra falls unconscious. On regaining consciousness (canto 2), he finds himself transported to an Elysian Paradise at the foot of the mountain, in which he encounters the virtues, the arts, and the realm of dreams, both good and bad. As they begin to move up the mountain, they come across the abode of the ancient poets, meet Lange, and pass over Lethe where they doff all tokens of mere worldly ambition (crown and scepter) to arrive finally at the summit before the temple complex. The next two cantos are devoted to a description of the temple's various sections and their contents: canto 3 to the "Vorhof" and its buildings, and the courtyard of the temple itself; canto 4 to the temple proper, both its exterior and interior. In the final canto, Poetry, on her throne beneath the Cross surrounded by her daughters, Eclogue, Elegy, Ode, Tragedy, and Epic, summons before her all the poets (Christians only) to receive her instructions and witness the induction of Lange into their high office with veil and garland.

At the level of language the poem contains many a casual allusion and evocation of Virgilian phrasing. The first appearance of Poetry, in the main more reminiscent of Philosophy's appearance to Boethius, offers a number of such examples. Pyra uses the verb "abfliessen" to describe the way Poetry's dress hangs down from her shoulder as Virgil used *defluere* to describe Venus's garments; compare: Ein perlenweisses Kleid floß von den Schultern ab (1. 87) and *pedes uestis defluxit ad imos* (*Aen.* 1. 404; her gown trailed down to her feet (40). Or again compare: "Um ihren Scheitel brennt ein Kranz von lichten Sternen" (1. 82) and *ecce leuis summo de uertice uisus Iuli/ fundere lumen apex* (*Aen.* 2. 682–83; a bright flame, . . ., licked his soft hair, and played about his forehead; 71). And Pyra sets off following his guide "mit nicht gleichem Schritt" (1. 82), that is as Iulus followed his father Aeneis: *sequitur patrem non passibus aequis* (*Aen.* 2. 724; kept beside his father with his short steps [more literally, "with unequal steps"; 72). Finally the description of the abode of the "grausen Träume" repeats Virgil's description of Aeolus's cave (2. 165ff and *Aen.* 1. 52–59). All of these examples attest the pervasive impression left on Pyra's poetic imagination by his reading and translation of the *Aeneid*.

At the level of technique Pyra also makes extensive use of the epic catalogue and ekphrasis, a device of description much favored by Virgil, made renowned as painterly description by Haller's gentian description, and soon to be brought into disrepute by Lessing. Cantos 3 and 4 are one lengthy ekphrasis of the temple, within which Pyra sets many smaller examples. The seasons of the year decorate the massive cupola of the temple while the story of David and Saul is engraved on its door.[18] The Hall of History in the "Vorhof" dominates the description of it. All of the other halls to the other arts and sciences are passed over in seventy-four lines, but history occupies ninety-five. It contains an ekphrasis of the door on which one sees the Creation story laid out in six panels. Within the hall there are first scenes from ancient history (featuring Xerxes, Alexander, Hannibal, Augustus — and here the heroes on the walls of Dido's temple come to mind) and then, at considerable length, after a brief mention of Charlemagne and Prince Eugene, a survey of the house of Hohenzollern. The passage concludes with the poet's exclamation — would that he had but the "Geist und Kraft" to sing of Prussia (3. 114). Like Virgil before him, who had voiced the ambition his earlier poems to write epic about great men (*Ecs.* 6. 1–12; 8. 6–12; and *Ge.* 3. 16–39), Pyra in imitation also expresses his desire to sing in the epic strain and on a thoroughly conventional, that is Virgilian, subject.

The elaboration and length of the passage on history, as well as its content, are out of proportion to its position within the poem.[19] Again the incongruity is to be explained with reference to the status of epic and to Virgil's place within the genre. History in the form of the chronicle given here relates the events that epic is to make its subject. Clio is the muse of history and therefore, according to Gottsched, uniquely suitable for epic invocation.[20] Since epic is the highest genre, its learned discipline, history, should and does receive careful attention. The proper epic poet is still a learned poet.

Yet the attention Pyra lavishes on it only underscores the larger theoretical and formal difficulties of the genre and of Virgil's place within that epic tradition. The two divisions of history are modeled on Anchises' speech to Aeneas in the underworld (*Aen.* 6. 724–853). The brief return to the third person narrative in the middle of it (*Aen.* 6. 752–55) punctuates Anchises' oration and so causes it to fall into two parts externally. Virgil fits the thematic division to parallel the narrative division. The first, smaller, portion deals with cosmology and the transmigration of souls; the second, larger, portion presents Aeneas with a review of Roman heroes that culminates not with a person (namely Augustus, as one might expect) but with an ethos or ideal:

> *tu regere imperio populos, Romane, memento*
> *(hae tibi erunt artes), pacique imponere morem,*
> *parcere subiectis et debellare superbos.* (*Aen.* 6. 851–53)
>
> [But you, Roman, must remember that you have to guide the nations by your authority, for this is to be your skill, to graft tradition onto peace, to shew mercy to the conquered, and to wage war until the haughty are brought low. (173)]

(He reserves the embodiment of this ideal in a person for the shield description with the battle of Actium and Augustus at its center.) The placing of a human history next to the cosmological history aids Virgil in bestowing a teleological dignity to the rise of Roman might to dominance. The gloss provided at the end by stating a principle as opposed to nominating an individual only emphasizes the teleological claim for Roman history as the purposeful design of fate.

Pyra's Hall of History lacks exactly this implication, although he has spared little to give himself the opportunity. We are within the precinct of the true temple, our guide is the new, chaste muse, the doors of the Hall present us with the Christian cosmology, and the walls illustrate human history. The entrance of great figures from ancient history precedes that of the Hohenzollerns. The history, a universal history up to the appearance of the Hohenzollerns, fails to become a teleological one; no providential plan is realized in it. It sinks to the level of a particular history. The story of Prussia is merely a human history, not the human history. Prince Eugene of Savoy, a near-contemporary, appears with no explanation of his relation to the house of Hohenzollern. But an explanation would only be needed if it were supposed that Pyra envisioned some deeper purpose to an epic about Prussia than the simple glorification of his native land, a supposition for which there is no evidence. His use here therefore of a tradition fails through his inability to incorporate it fully into his own vision. Further, that the Christian poet should cherish an overly fond desire to sing of such things argues that he did not drink deeply of Lethe at the start of the climb to Poetry's temple. For at the bottom of the river Pyra and Lange could see rolling there "Purpur, Kron und Zepter" (2. 310). It also ignores the question of how this desire conforms to the world of "grüne Stille."

The same objections made above to "Mann und Waffen" bear repetition. One would expect some Christian theme to replace the purely factional history of the Hohenzollerns, a strategy that would gain for the epic the mantle of totality. In *Paradise Lost* Milton again points the way Pyra's purer muse would ostensibly have her poets travel.

> Not sedulous by Nature to indite
> Wars, hitherto the only Argument
> Heroic deem'd,
> . . .
> The skill of Artifice or Office mean,
> not that which justly gives Heroic
> To Person or to Poem. Mee of these
> Nor skill'd nor studious, higher Argument
> Remains, sufficient of itself to raise
> That name, unless an age too late, . . . (9. 27–44)[21]

Taking as granted that the *Aeneid* and the *Iliad* prescribe war for heroic poetry, Milton does not think to equal them on that ground, but instead proposes an alternative definition of heroic. His "Celestial Patroness" (9. 21) inspires the elevated theme of Revelation; it uplifts his "deprest" wing (9. 46). In effect, the totality that Milton senses is missing for him from tales of war he derives instead from religion. His Titanomachia and cosmology, both related to Adam by Raphael (books 5–7) are followed after the Fall and its immediate aftermath (books 9–10) by human history, by the history of salvation from the Fall through the Flood to the Incarnation and Resurrection, that is, the covenants of the Old and the New Testaments (books 11–12).

The only place where Pyra addresses this matter is in the fourth canto in the allegorical descriptions of the five genres that surround Poetry's throne beneath the cross. Epic appears as a figure fully caparisoned for war, with helm, breastplate, and a shield on which battles can be seen. She holds a spear and trumpet. Among the spoils at her feet are two banners on which can be seen Milton's epic, although he is not mentioned by name; of the mountains used as weapons in Milton's Titanomachia in place of the traditional *arma*, Pyra states explicitly that they appear "statt Pfeil und Spieß" (4. 190). Without pause or explanation he continues on to the second banner with the scene of Eve and the serpent in the Garden. Unlike the weapons of the Titanomachia there is no interpretative "statt" to establish the correspondence to the epic tradition. In fact it stands in marked contrast to the earlier insistence on the military splendor of epic. Milton had painted the Garden of Eden in strongly bucolic terms, about which Pyra would have to reach a decision, were he to repeat the "statt." Instead Pyra simply juxtaposes Christian and pagan, epic and bucolic in a fashion that does more to indicate the contradictory impulses at work in the genres than to address the question of their relation.

That for Pyra the true, if perhaps unacknowledged, rival to epic, as it were, is the bucolic becomes apparent not merely from the incongruous juxtapositions of epic and eclogue in these two banners, nor from the *arma uirumque* in the "grüne Stille," but from their relative weight in the succession of eclogue, elegy, ode, tragedy, and epic. Epic, the poet's highest aspiration, occupies twelve lines; the eclogue, the meanest, most elementary branch, receives fourteen verses on its charms (the rest receive 7, 6, and 10 respectively).

All of the tensions inherent in the received understanding of the genre manifest themselves in Pyra's *Tempel der wahren Dichtkunst*. Virgil defines that tradition and his epic is defined by *arma uirumque cano*. The gloss for this is heroic deeds by great heroes with national importance. Yet this understanding of epic finds little echo in the eighteenth century. Instead the understanding of the bucolic inclines "upwards" as that of epic declines "downwards." Christianity, in its enlightened moral guise beneath the retelling of biblical episodes, is infused in an effort to uplift the genre. But this infusion has the unintended effect of intensifying the shift towards the smaller world of the bucolic. Again Milton points the way: love emerges as the prime reason for Adam's transgression, and the setting for love's tragedy is a garden. Following Adam's decision to eat of the apple, the narrator observes:

> So saying, she embrac'd him, and for joy
> Tenderly wept, much won that he his Love
> Had so ennobl'd, as of choice to incur
> Divine displeasure for her sake, or Death. (9. 990–93)

In a conscious inversion of the Dido and Aeneas episode, love triumphs over duty. Adam, finding his sense of self integrally related to the satisfaction of his private, earthly self, discovers within himself the resolve to insist on it, come what may. Milton's conception of love here, hardly an inward and romantic one, does possess all the elements needed to develop in a more private, bourgeois, and sentimental direction.

Klopstock and Epic Style

If, then, the traditional conception of a martial, national epic seems implausible and the desire in the middle decades of the eighteenth century for a more explicitly Christian poetry has little use for an epic overly pagan in its associations, the cachet of epic still remains a prize much sought after. The assumption of the grand style of epic becomes a means of signaling one's entrance into the lists. Klopstock's successful importation of the epic hexameter into German in his *Messias* satisfies this requirement. Now, as then, it was taken as throwing down the gauntlet before Homer: "Klopstock ruft die deutschen Dichter mit seinem Hexameter-Epos in den Wettstreit mit Homer."[22] The statement, though correct, omits the question of the hexameter's transmission. Klopstock, in his treatment of the hexameter and matters of diction, reflects the humanist approach to metrics and rhetoric, that is, the methods the schools used for the reading of the Virgilian texts. In addition, Klopstock's own approach to his artistry and his unceasing efforts to ensure that his poetic diction is not prose set to meter predispose him to the Latin of the Augustan poets. They too labored unceasingly on the language at their disposal in an effort to forge a tool suitable both for poetry and for competition with the Greeks. Virgil's epic diction becomes one of the ingredients in Klopstock's search for a unique German epic idiom at once sublime and moving.

The scope of Klopstock's humanist and rhetorical education so convincingly argued by Kevin Hilliard has not yet led to a reexamination of his practices in the *Messias*. Karl Ludwig Schneider's 1960 study of Klopstock's contribution to the linguistic renovation of German, which marks the beginning of modern research into Klopstock's critical views, surveys the resources available to Klopstock.[23] He mentions especially the poets Pyra and Haller, in addition to the theoretical writings of the Swiss critics Bodmer and Johann Jakob Breitinger (1701–76), and, behind them, the English, above all Milton. Homer again figures prominently as the inspiration for the German hexameter. However, he neglects to include any more than a passing reference to Virgil. In his discussion of the *Messias*, Gerhard Kaiser, the author of the other principal study of Klopstock (1963), concentrates his attention almost entirely on the degree to which Klopstock responds to Milton as his model and competitor in the use of the ancient pagan genre as the vehicle for Christian revelation.[24] Since then the concentration on Homer and Milton has undergone only limited modification.[25]

As a result, obvious instances of a dynamic relation to the Virgilian epic pass unnoticed. Kaiser, for instance, when discussing Klopstock's striving to find a language and imagery neither too specific nor corporeal, but one that leaves the imagination with vivid, though immaterial and somewhat mysterious impressions, comments on Klopstock's editorial changes from the 1748 version to the final version in 1799 only with regard to Milton (210–11). The passage in question, however, about the archangel Gabriel's preparations for a journey to earth,

>   Ein festliches niederwallendes Glänzen
> Floß, da er gieng, den Fuß des Unsterblichen prächtig herunter.
>   (1. 689–90, 1748)

and in 1799,

>   Der Feyer
> Festlicher Glanz floß über den Fuß des Unsterblichen nieder.
>   (1. 705–6)

also indicates Klopstock's close attention to the same lines of the *Aeneid* that Pyra before him found attractive, namely, the description of how Venus's divinity, despite her disguise, betrayed itself at the end of her conversation with Aeneas:

> *Dixit et auertens rosea ceruice refulsit,*
> *ambrosiaeque comae diuinun uertice odorem*
> *spirauere; pedes uestis defluxit ad imos,*
> *et uera incessu patuit dea.* (*Aen.* 1. 402–5)

[So Venus spoke, and as she turned away her loveliness shone, a tint of rose glowed on her neck and a scent of Heaven breathed from the divine hair of her head. Her grown trailed down to her feet; her gait alone proved her a goddess. (40)]

It seems not improbable that Virgil's use of a highly poetic and deliberately unproselike language as well as his treatment of the hexameter should have had as great an effect on one of Klopstock's temperament as it did on

Milton. Both were the recipients of a humanist rhetorical training; both strain the sense and grammar of their respective languages to achieve a suitably epic style: similarities are to be expected.[26]

The young Klopstock met Milton through Bodmer, to whose critical writing he paid great attention. More important, Klopstock was unable to read English until 1752, that is, after he had published to great effect the first three cantos of the *Messias* in 1748 and up through canto 5 in 1750. Klopstock only knew of Milton from Bodmer's prose translation of *Paradise Lost* (1st ed. 1732, 2nd ed. 1742), of which experience he writes in his first, famous letter to Bodmer: *Miltonus vero . . . ignes ex Homero haustos excitavit penitus, animumque, ad caelum et religionis poesin, extulit* (Milton indeed . . . nourished within himself the sparks drawn from Homer and bore his soul aloft to heaven and the poetry of religion).[27] Similarly Klopstock formed his opinions very much in the spirit and under the tutelage of the Swiss critics Bodmer and Breitinger. In the same letter he singles out Bodmer's *imaginem poetae epici, quam in critico Tuo poematis duxisti* (image of the epic poet laid out in your critical poem, [by which he presumably means *Charakter der deutschen Gedichte*]). More germane to Klopstock is the pointer contained in Bodmer's comparison of the diction of Lucretius and Virgil in favor of Virgil, who is "beständig, lauter, rein und sanft."[28]

Any early linguistic influence of Milton upon Klopstock thus depends on these translations and, as important, the accompanying poetological pronouncements made by Bodmer to give support to his and Breitinger's strenuous efforts to resuscitate a poetic diction in German that would be distinct from prose.[29] This includes, among other things, the extended use of participles, ellipsis, composite adjectives, and a freer word order. Such a poetic diction is not "ungrammatical" in the sense that it renders the German incomprehensible, but rather it contravenes established grammatical understanding and appeals directly to the reader's linguistic intuitions for its comprehensibility. Though these sources on which Klopstock drew for linguistic and artistic direction show no marked slighting of the Roman poet, a possible Virgilian role has not been pursued. Schneider, for example, in support of the importance to the Swiss critics of composite adjectives, cites the passage from the *Critische Dichtkunst* that deals with the use of compound adjectives to impart vividly sound and motion to the reader's imagination. This device originates in Greek, and Breitinger praises Homer for diligently seeking out such adjectives to separate his diction from prose. He then gives two examples from Homer before commenting:

> Und ob die lateinische Sprache gleich dergleichen zusammengesezte Beywörter nicht wohl vertragen kan, so hat dennoch Virgil um seine Hochachtung für die Homerische Kunst in diesem Stücke an den Tag zu legen, einige nachzumachen nicht unglücklich gewaget; als *Malesuada*

fames; Auricomi rami; Fumigera nox; Sylvicolae Fauni; Caprigenum pecus; Velivolum mare.[30]

Yet Schneider's comment on it reads: "In beiden Fällen haben ihm [Klopstock] die Schweizer den Anstoß gegeben, sich einzelne Ausdrucksformen der griechischen Dichtung anzueignen und mit Zügen der Sprache Miltons im Feuer einer neuen künstlerischen Erlebnisweise zu verschmelzen."[31] No mention is made of Virgil, although Breitinger recommended him with hardly less approbation to the receptive reader. Indeed the number of examples taken from Virgil far exceed the two taken from Homer. Schneider similarly stresses the English influence in the poetic accomplishments of Pyra and Haller while failing to consider the creative role played by the Virgilian texts in their fermentation and final form. The Latin influence is thus scarcely less present in the poems and critical texts favored by the young Klopstock than is an English influence, particularly if one recollects that Klopstock possessed Latin enough to sense and judge for himself the Latinate qualities of these texts while he could form only a secondhand opinion of poetic excellences derived from English.

The scope of Klopstock's linguistic and metrical fecundity is too vast to be adequately considered here. Nor is an argument being made for a preponderant Virgilian influence on him; but rather that Klopstock's knowledge of Virgil did not remain without effect on his poetic development. Klopstock's hexameter may owe its inspiration to the thought that he is writing in the same meter as the poet of the *Iliad* and *Odyssey;* yet his manner of using it — in the matter of word order, ellipsis, and the length of the periods — is much more strongly reminiscent of Virgil than of Homer. The use of such techniques in aid of the prized "gedrängte Kürze" is typical of Klopstock, and in Virgil's epic diction he had a familiar example of such "Kürze," which was recommended to him by Breitinger in his *Critische Dichtkunst* as the special trait of Virgil in contrast to Homer:

> Hingegen ist Virgil viel kürzer, und sucht seinen besten Vortheil in Beywörtern, so die Gestalten und Beschaffenheiten der Dinge erklären; die Begriffe liegen bey ihm viel enger zusammengepresset; und seine Gemählde haben ein kunstreicheres Aussehen, da in den Homerischen Schildereyen die Kunst mehr in der Wahl der Gedancken und vortheilhaftigsten Umstände, als in der Höhe und dem Glantz der Farben bestehet, und unter einem einfaltigen und natürlichen Ansehen verstecket lieget. (1.41)[32]

To Virgil there belong brevity, adjectives, the *colores*, and artistry: to Homer, nature, simplicity, and content. Although a poet wishes to aspire to the Homeric virtues, the means offered are frequently at cross-purposes to that end. Breitinger remains bound to the earlier poetics insofar as he seeks to promote nature and simplicity largely through an examination of style. As a result there occurs a disjunction between the judgment passed on Virgil the poet and the use made of his works. Breitinger can and does draw frequently on examples from the Virgilian texts to support his argument without wishing to recommend Virgil the poet as a model of nature. In short, he uses Virgil to teach how one can become like Homer.

He would find fertile ground in Klopstock for this method, as Klopstock shares an artistic temperament similar to Virgil's. Klopstock's theoretical treatises invariably turn on technical points of metrical and linguistic usage in poetic diction, and he worked on the *Messias* with a meticulousness equal to that of Virgil and, in time, for a much longer period than Virgil. Virgil spent eleven years on the *Aeneid* and would have liked to have spent a few more polishing; Klopstock conceived of the *Messias* while at Schulpforta, published the first three cantos in 1748, cantos 1–5 in 1750, the whole up to canto 10 in 1755, a revised edition of the first ten cantos in 1760, while the next volume with cantos 11–15 only appeared in 1768, and the final five cantos, 16–20, in 1773. He carefully polished the epic for publication in 1780 and also one last time in 1799 for the "Ausgabe letzter Hand." In these successive editions Klopstock devotes his attention to revisions that promote his views on poetic diction at the same time as they result in a highly mannered style, closer to that of Virgil than that of Homer; which is to say a metrical period that is shaped by the rhetorical and syntactical relation of its parts rather than by parataxis.[33]

Though the young Klopstock, to judge by his letter to Bodmer, did not shy from giving strong opinions, he did not possess the linguistic wherewithal to make such judgments fully his own. Of the three foreign languages that he could read with any ease (Greek, Latin, and French), Latin was the one he knew best as a young man. At the Schulpforta, which he attended from the ages of fifteen to twenty-one (1739–45), Latin was the language of instruction as well as that appointed for casual conversation among the pupils outside of class. The widespread use of Latin at the school also entailed the ability to write it fluently, of which Klopstock's valedictorian speech *Poetae epopoeiae auctores* and the Latin letters among his early correspondence are sufficient proof.[34]

The young poet of the *Messias* had already worked out the plan of the entire poem at Schulpforta and written out portions of it in prose. His valedictorian speech given on 21 September 1745 is an interesting historical document for the picture it gives of his thinking about epic poetry. His opinions, culled from Bodmer, Gottsched, Pyra, and Voltaire, are displayed in a manner remarkable not for the acumen of judgment but for the fervency of conviction. He generally presents a poet in a string of encomiastic adjectives too general to do more than give the reader a strong sense of his approval. The framework for his hierarchy does, however, emerge with great clarity. The premise of his entire argument appears on the first page; the noblest impulse of the human mind is the imitation of nature, an imitation in which poetry is understood not as a disinterested representation of nature but as an ordered presentation in which the beauty and perfection of creation are made visible. This poetical power of divination bespeaks the hand of God who *saepius hanc* (that is, poetry) *divinis illis vatibus inspiravit, quibus arduum ac sublime negotium dederat, ut remoto velo, se atque adoranda religionis mysteria hominibus aperirent* (had often enough breathed this poetry into those bardic prophets and given them the difficult and lofty task of disclosing God himself and the holy mysteries of religion to mankind once the veil was drawn aside).[35] Taking his cue from Pyra, he then follows this up with a brief characterization of the biblical "poets" such as Moses, Job, and David. The exuberance of this initial section only makes the leap to the pagan poets of epic all the more odd since the assimilation of the prophets to the status of poets implies a concomitant assimilation of the epic poets to the rank of "prophet." Nevertheless, once the transition is accomplished, the remainder of the oration, by far the larger part, concerns itself exclusively with the traditional epic canon and, at the end, with Germany's lack of an epic.[36]

The relative position of Virgil and Homer reflects the judgment of the Swiss critics and Pope; Klopstock merely uses more effusive language with a boldness that foretells the imminent inversion of their positions. Pope wrote, "*Homer* was the greater Genius, *Virgil* the better Artist"[37] and discussed this in relation to the categories of invention and judgment; Breitinger had repeated the phrase in the superlative without attribution as "Homer war der gröste Genius, Virgil der beste Künstler,"[38] and discussed the matter in terms of natural simplicity and technical expression; and Klopstock enthuses without qualification: *Natura erat Homerus, et Homerus natura!* (nature was Homer, and Homer nature).[39] Virgil he judges in no way less than Homer, *quam imitatione* (59; except in imitation, that is, in the imitation of nature). He places both in the embraces of Poetry as the objects of emulous veneration.[40] The only blemish on their perfection that he acknowledges is their ignorance of the Christian religion. Nor does this veneration seem to have changed much up to 1748 if one is to credit the claim in his letter to Bodmer that he kept Breitinger's *Critische Dichtkunst* next to him, "at [his] left hand while Homer and Virgil were of course at [his] right hand," *cum ad dextram Homerus essent Virgiliusque, ad sinistram deinde.*[41]

While it is almost, but not absolutely, certain that Klopstock had already read Homer in the original, it is indisputable that he was very familiar with Virgil as he was part of the curriculum at Pforta.[42] A testament to the lifelong impression of Latin verse on Klopstock's poetic sensibility may be found in the *Grammatische Gespräche* (1794–95). In the "Zwischengespräche," the characters conduct translation competitions.

The almost exclusive choices are the poets Homer, Virgil, Ovid, and Horace. The point of the competition is to translate with brevity, that is, to produce a German rendering that is shorter than the original. It is a condition that is better suited to the translation of Virgil than it is of Homer. Virgil makes full use of the conciseness innate in the Latin language as well as the entire repertoire of Neoteric techniques (such as rhetorical devices, ellipsis, new or unusual meanings of the words, strained or unconventional syntax) to heighten this effect. In short he indulges in that liberty with the Latin language that Klopstock himself takes with German. Compare, for example, the last sentence of the Laocoon passage:

> *ille simul manibus tendit diuellere nodos*
> *perfusus sanie uittas atroque ueneno,*
> *clamores simul horrendos ad sidera tollit:*
> *qualis mugitus, fugit cum saucius aram*
> *taurus et incertam excussit ceruice securim.* (*Aen.* 2, 220–24)

> [His hands strove frantically to wrench the knots apart. Filth and black venom drenched his priestly hands. His shrieks were horrible and filled the sky, like a bull's bellow when an axe has struck awry, and he flings his neck and gallops wounded from the altar. (57–58)]

and,

> Und er strebt mit den Händen, daß er den Knoten entreiße, So wie Eiter die Stirn und schwarzes Gift ihn beströmen; Und erhebet zugleich zu dem Himmel jammernden Notschrei, Gleich dem Gebrülle des Stiers, so verwundet geflohn vom Altar ist, Und dem Nacken das irrende Beil entschüttelt hat.[43]

Virgil uses the plain *simul . . . simul . . .* in an infrequent conjunctival construction with a participial phrase, hendiadys, and a Greek accusative to interrupt the flow of the sentence. In a novel expression he also uses *tendere* with an infinitive. Klopstock retains the parallel structure using "und . . . und zugleich . . ." and the *tendere* plus infinitive he translates with a "daß" plus the subjunctive in a final clause instead of the simpler and neater "um . . . zu. . . ." In both instances each poet has chosen in his respective language a construction that saves words at the same time as it stretches the grammatical conventions of his time. Both attain Klopstock's cherished goals of "Kürze" and estrangement from the prose language of their age. Furthermore, by echoing *ut* plus the subjunctive Klopstock gives a very literary and Latinate effect to the German. He also adds to this effect through the ellipsis of "sich" from the verb "entreißen." The intervening participial phrase (*perfusus . . .*, with a Greek accusative) presents Klopstock with greater problems that he solves by turning it into a clause introduced by "so wie" but complicated by the double use of "beströmen," perhaps suggested to him by *sanie uittas atroque ueneno*. While such changes and substitutions may not preserve the exact sense of the Latin words, they do retain their general import as well as their poetic diction and effect. Klopstock reproduces the linguistic texture of the Latin, not by imitating the exact devices used by Virgil, but through his approach to language and its poetic use; both seek, in a highly conscious fashion, a mannered and artistic style.

So ingrained in Klopstock is the sense of an elevated poetic diction that he is not shy of outstripping his original. The second half of Virgil's sentence, *qualis...*, unfolds smoothly in comparison to the first half. Klopstock, on the other hand, selects the grammatically odd expression "so verwundet geflohn vom Altar ist" for the temporal *cum* with the indicative. If it is supposed that "so" is a conjunction then, first, the subject is omitted, and second, since the conditional conjunction of anteriority seems most likely, a suppressed "-wie" must be assumed.[44] Alternatively it may be construed by inserting the relative pronoun "der" and taking "so" as a particle equivalent to "sehr."

Or again when translating Homer, Klopstock favors a style of translation that would do a Neoteric poet proud. The Homeric diction is more straightforward and less contrived than the Virgilian, yet Klopstock feels compelled to add complication where none is called for. Odysseus relates in a grammatically very simple passage how they were sacrificing a hecatomb to the gods at sacred altars beneath a plane tree around a clear spring when there appeared a great sign, a dragon. To construe these lines is a simple task. Yet Klopstock translates the last three lines of this passage from book 2, 308–10, of the *Iliad*,

> ἔνθ' ἐφάνη μέγα σῆμα· δράκων ἐπὶ νῶτα δαφοινὸς,
> σμερδαλέος, τόν ῥ' αὐτὸς Ὀλύμπιος ἧκε φόωσδε
> βωμοῦ ὑπαΐξας πρός ῥα πλατάνιστον ὄρουσεν.[45]

[There appeared a great sign: a terrible dragon blood-red along his back — whom the Olympian himself had sent to the light — and having burst from under the altar, it rushed to the plane tree (my translation).]

as:

> ..., da erschien uns ein Zeichen.
> Unter dem Altar hervor kam, eilte zum Ahorn ein grauser
> Drache, den Rücken besprengt wie mit Blut; der Olympier sandt ihn.

Out of one syntactically simple sentence Klopstock has made two, the second of which is awkward and, in the first line, metrically very rough. Homer joined two main clauses with a colon. The second reads easily: a noun phrase followed by a relative clause, then a participle phrase and finally the predicate. Klopstock's translation is first of all shorter through the omission of the preposition phrase "to the plane tree" in accordance with his general goal of brevity. He has unpacked the aorist participle to give himself two verbs that he joins with asyndeton (in this instance "und"). However the word order of the first clause suggests initially a subordinate clause because of its dependence, although it is an inversion likely due to metrical exigencies. He has also inserted what appears to be the Latin construction of the Greek accusative, which neither exists in German nor is called for by the simple use of ἐπί with the accusative to indicate extension of time or place.[46]

The Greek accusative is, however, a particular favorite of Virgil and one that Klopstock was conscious of. Again from the Laocoon passage, Virgil has another example of it when describing the serpents, *ardentisque oculos suffecti sanguine et igni* (*Aen.* 2. 210; literally, "suffused as to their eyes with blood and fire," or in better English, "with blazing and blood-shot eyes"; 57). Klopstock translates this as "Jetzt im Gefilde, durchströmt die funkelnden Augen von Blute/Und von Feuer, beleckten sie."[47] His version is an exact translation preserving, apparently, both the Greek accusative and the hendiadys. The natural reflex of the German reader will be to insert the appropriate part of the verb "sein" so that the phrase is intelligible without further ado. However this can only be done by rendering the sentence ungrammatical, as the more momentous instance below illustrates.

The same preference for an epic diction in German that suggests his familiarity with the Virgilian model also appears in the *Messias*. As an example, the same passage that Schneider uses — it has since become something of a proof text[48] — can be selected to illustrate the combined effect of all the linguistic and syntactical devices. It is from the passage relating the Crucifixion:

Starr, mit tiefgesunkenem Haupt, die heilige Schläfe
Mit der Krone der Schmach bedeckt, im Blute, das auch starr
Stillstand, jetzo nicht mehr um Gnade zum Richtenden rufte,
In die Himmel der Himmel hinauf, um die Gnade des Vaters!
Hing dein Leichnam, o hätt' ich Namen, dich würdig zu nennen,
Hing dein Leichnam, nicht Thränen, und nicht des bebenden Stimme
Nennet dich! hing an dem hohen Kreuz dein Leichnam herunter.
(11. 720–26)[49]

The main clause of the sentence is, "Starr hing dein Leichnam an dem hohen Kreuz herunter."[50] Everything that intervenes between the adverb "starr" and the rest of the clause suggests Klopstock's attention to the way in which Virgil structures his periods to extend over several hexameters. This is not to argue that all of the various devices used stem from Virgil, merely that the syntactical arrangement of the parts echo in structure and rhetorical effect the Virgilian period. Klopstock's use of the perfect participle to expand rhetorically the length of his sentence is also a trait of Virgil's epic diction. The sentence can be construed as follows: lines 720–24 depend on "mit tiefgesunkenem Haupt," at which juncture Klopstock returns to the main clause, only to twice interrupt its completion with two parenthetical interjections of the narrator before completing the thought. In order to make the lines depending on "mit tiefgesunkenem Haupt" cohere grammatically, it is assumed that "die heilige Schläfe" functions as a Greek accusative after "bedeckt" and that the coordinating conjunction "und" is omitted in line 722 by asyndeton. The use of interjections is a trait of Virgil's style, though hardly with the rhetorical repetition with which Klopstock employs it in the latter portion of the period. Virgil inserts such interjections to heighten the pathos of a moment, perhaps most famously from the Laocoon passage, *horresco referens* (*Aen.* 2. 204; and I sicken to recall it; 57). The parenthetic interjections, asyndeton, the rhetorical repetition of "hing dein Leichnam," all correspond to Virgilian usages. Indeed so redolent is Klopstock's diction of Virgil's that a student wishing to gain a sense of the difficulties that await him in the *Aeneid* and of the frame of mind needed for their comprehension could not prepare himself better than by reading the *Messias* and wrestling with its peculiarities.

Wieland and Idyllic Episodes

Wieland's mock epics represent the third avenue of approach to the genre in the eighteenth century. When seeking to elevate the comic verse epic, Wieland takes the tack in his *Oberon* (1780) suggested by Pyra in his wish to join the "grüne Stille" to epic. This naturally entails that he dispense with the martial and national themes of *arma uirumque cano* in a serious vein. He thus does not deal with the *Aeneid* as a whole but settles rather on a part or episode. The theme that the *Aeneid* shares with the green cabinet is love, and Wieland turns his attention to a proven and perennial favorite no less of the classroom than of the general public, to the Dido and Aeneas story. It also leads an independent existence in drama and opera, largely disassociated from the epic. Largely, but not quite in this instance, because it is for its epic pedigree and the status it might confer that Wieland cherishes it.

Low epic forsakes a direct claim to high epic's gravity and monumentality. The reader is immediately aware of the change as it affects all aspects of the poem: meter, plot, character, diction, and the narrator. The attempt, however, to define the sense in which the new epic is comic or mock is inevitably fraught with difficulty, as the critic must set up a straw figure of high epic in relation to which to weigh and judge the ironic element of the low. Is it pure parody, literary satire, or satire of a social class, attitude, or party? Or is it merely frivolous wit with no greater aim than its own brilliance or an ironic detachment with, nonetheless, a core of seriousness?

Critics generally agree that Wieland falls into the last category, but differ in the interpretation of this irony. With regard to his *Oberon* a consideration of the question involves forming an opinion first on the plot and then on the style of its narration. The second of these is the more important of the two. The Oberon of the title is not the hero of the epic, but the agent of the divine machinery in the epic. He is a king of the little people. The hero of the tale is Hüon, a young knight from Guyenne at the time of Charlemagne. Banned from France by Charlemagne until he steals the Sultan of Baghdad's daughter and brings back to the Emperor some hairs from the Sultan's beard and four of his molars, Hüon undergoes a series of adventures. During the course of these adventures Hüon proves his true merit, gains the favor of Oberon, loses it, and after great and fabulous trials of love regains it (along with the Sultan's daughter whom he likewise wins, loses, and wins again). The plot itself is of little interest. It consists of a sequence of wild and fantastic episodes strung together by implausible coincidences or a cavalier treatment of epic convention. For example, when, for reasons of plot, Wieland needs to convey Hüon, who is stranded on an island in the Mediterranean, to Tunis where all the other major figures are now gathered for the final trial, he simply has Oberon spirit him away to Tunis in a bare-faced exploitation of epic machinery (*Ob.* 10. 13–21).[51]

Of greater interest is the theme of love around which Wieland spins the events of the plot. In the attempt to sketch the conception of feeling and human character explored through this theme, the critic is compelled to state in what sense he takes its representation to be humorous or ironic. This ensnares him in a discussion of such matters as its Rococo tincture, its literary precedents, its relation to epic, its meter, its language, and so on: namely, all of those things that give it its texture. Wieland intends his reader to situate his epic if not within the tradition of high epic, then in relation to it. In the first edition of *Oberon* in 1780 he published the poem divided into fourteen cantos.[52] The second edition of 1781 likewise retained the fourteen cantos. However, with the edition of 1785, Wieland rearranged the work into twelve cantos, like Milton before him, deliberately placing it in the Virgilian epic tradition.[53] It is this feature most of all that is cited as evidence for a dawning classicism in Wieland. For Friedrich Sengle (1949) in the aftermath of the Second World War, *Oberon* becomes "Ausdruck der humanen deutschen Bürgerklassik"[54] and so moves into the orbit of Weimar Classicism. However, as Weimar Classicism stands under the aegis of Homer and Greece, the effect of the discussion is once again to arrive at Greece without acknowledging the intermediate stop in Rome.[55] The interest here is to consider this stop, to consider what the role of the Virgilian texts is in shaping such considerations, that is, what role Virgil plays in shaping the structure of *Oberon* and in the manner of its telling.

The change from fourteen to twelve cantos does not affect the balance of the poem, which still falls neatly into two halves: the first six cantos of the new epic contain the same material as the first seven of the old epic and the same for the latter half.[56] The new division does, however, strengthen the resemblance to the Virgilian poem, which can likewise be divided into two symmetrical halves of six books each, the first an Odyssean, the second an Iliadic half. Or, alternatively, the first half bringing Aeneas up to the threshold of Latium represents the education of Aeneas to his mission. It covers all of his adventures and presents both us, the readers, and Aeneas with the scope of the task before him. The second half brings Aeneas into Latium and the time of his testing in the Iliadic war there that results in the fusion of Trojan and Latin, of East and West into a new people.

Wieland follows this pattern by dividing the action of his epic into an "Odyssean" first half and an "Iliadic" second. As this is a mock-heroic epic, the themes taken up in the two halves do not parallel those of the Virgilian original. Nor by the use of the word "Odyssean" is it suggested that there should be no travel in the second half of *Oberon*, which would be manifest nonsense as our hero moves from his desert island to Tunis to the court of the Emperor Charlemagne in France. The parallel consists rather in Wieland's treatment of his hero's character. In the first half of *Oberon* everything happens *to* Hüon; nothing happens *within* him. Numerous fantastic and untoward obstacles are placed in his way, and each time, as soon as he simply acts according to that virtue innate within him, they melt away before him. He passes from triumph to triumph in a placid, spotless progression. This half corresponds to the largely knight-errant tale that Wieland mentions in his preface as one of his three stories in the poem.

The first six cantos also introduce all of the characters and set up the problem that the latter half must resolve. This is largely a question of introducing the fairy-tale element with Titania and Oberon, which is the second tale Wieland mentions in his preface. As the realm of the fairy tale also doubles as Wieland's divine apparatus in his epic, its presence does not slacken in the second half as the knight-errant associations do. The problem that the fairy-tale world poses for the epic is that in his quarrel with his queen Titania about love, Oberon, with ill-considered anger, said words and made vows that, once made, he cannot undo. He swore that they should remain from that day onward separated "*Bis ein getreues Paar*, vom Schicksal selbst erkoren, / *Durch keusche Lieb in Eins zusammen fließt*, . . ." (Wieland's emphasis, *Ob.* 6. 101). The last three stanzas of the canto, 105–7, make it clear that this couple is Hüon and his princess, now christened "Amanda," that is, one who is or must be loved.

The second half presents the tale of this testing, a story of "Iliadic" conflict and the third tale that Wieland mentions in his preface. It is, of course, not a conflict of arms but rather a conflict in which the true measure of character is revealed. For the first time there is an inner division within Hüon between the dictates of virtue and his own desire. In parting from the young couple, Oberon had enjoined them with dire threats to remain chaste until their arrival in Rome where the pope would join them in matrimony. Being young, they naturally fail. The rest of the epic concerns how they make good this first disobedience. Thus the change of plot from the end of the sixth canto to the beginning of the seventh injects the "Ernst" into Wieland's "Scherz." This change also corresponds to other equally important changes.

Since each tale had its own dominant mood, its own narrative idiom — Hüon and his escapades that of the knight-errant, Titania and Oberon that of the fairy tale — Wieland introduces a third idiom for his tale of love, that of the elevated idyll. The love of the young couple takes place within an idyllic island setting, in which we find both references to Virgil's fourth eclogue, used here loosely by Wieland for its prophetic promise, and a more extended parallel to the Dido and Aeneas tragedy from the *Aeneid*. The grander register of high epic assists the elevation of the entire work to a level of gravity. Wieland is so successful in this that Schiller will later feel Wieland's verse measure to be sufficiently dignified for him to use it in his own translations from the *Aeneid*.

When Hüon and Amanda succumb to human weakness, a storm arises on the sea; the sailors pacify it by throwing Hüon into the waves, where Amanda joins him of her own accord. Cast up on the shores of a desolate island, they eventually discover a hermit and a paradisial garden sealed away behind high cliffs. There they live happily, rearing their son, until the old hermit dies and the garden disappears, a mirage sustained for the benefit of the good hermit. Hüon and Amanda inhabited it by right of nature; they had not earned it. The scene now moves to the harem in Tunis, where Hüon, pursued by the Sultana, and Amanda, by the Sultan, find themselves placed on a common pyre for their resolute refusal to yield. The moment the fire is lit, thunder roars, the earth shakes, Hüon is restored to Oberon's good graces, and the favored couple returns home to health and happiness.

By placing the heart of his epic within an idyllic context, Wieland promotes the continued reduction of epic to the pastoral. In addition to tapping into such literary resources as the Robinsonade, he again places his comic work in the context of high modern epic. His island garden behind its cliffs harks back to Bodmer's paradisial mountain in his *Noah*, and behind him to Milton's Garden of Eden, and through Milton, to the Dido and Aeneas episode of the *Aeneid*. As Milton corrected the error in that Virgilian episode by rewriting the outcome of the conflict between obligation and love in a Christian register, Wieland in turn rewrites the expulsion from Paradise in an Enlightened, secular register — the biblical resonance of thunder and earthquake at the moment of death for adherence to virtue is unlikely to be accidental. In the last two books of *Paradise Lost*, the angel Gabriel comforts Adam for his loss of Eden with the Christian prospect of the history of salvation. In Wieland's *Oberon* human nature receives its due on earth within the span of the individual's life. The compensatory comic twist of this blissful end is that the sting is taken from the Fall; it becomes the moment of an individual's loss of innocence without any necessary connection to the divine.

Beginning from such a position one would expect therefore to find in Wieland's poem some allusion to the *Aeneid*. This brings us to the second point; namely, how does Virgil influence the style of the narration? As one might surmise, most of the references to Virgil revolve around the Dido and Aeneas episode. Wieland also makes explicit reference to the *Eclogues*, which belong to the pastoral canon. The eclogue in question is the famous fourth with the smiling child. Virgil, adopting the lofty tone of prophecy, tells of the return of a golden age inaugurated with the birth of a wondrous child and gradually strengthening as the child grows to maturity and takes up the reins of government. The eclogue concludes with the admonishment of the precocious newborn to smile at its parent (*Ec.* 4. 60–63). It is this element Wieland picks up on. Shortly before her son's birth, Amanda sits in the "Schattengänge des Tempels der Natur" (*Ob.* 8. 51) and imagines that she holds the infant in her arms:

> Ein lieblich Kind, das ihre Mutterliebe
> Mit jedem süssen Reitz verschwenderisch begabt,
> Sich schon voraus an jedem zarten Triebe,
> Der ihm entkeimt, sich schon am ersten Lächeln labt,
> Womit es ihr die Leiden alle danket
> Die sie so gern um seinetwillen trug,
> Sich labt an jedem schönen Zug
> Worin des Vaters Bild sanft zwischen ihrem schwanket. (*Ob.* 8. 54)

Wieland intends considerable mischief with so subtle a reference. The presiding numen is that of Nature. Gone is any mention of prophetic sibyls, new ages, and empire from the fourth eclogue. Nonetheless by evoking that eclogue Wieland suggests a strong association with the golden age. It is not a political golden age, nor one of universal cultural renewal, but rather a personal and private one, open to all who, within the bosom of the family, live close to nature. It is furthermore one that does not exist within the world of fact; it exists by the power of inner apprehension, in the imagination. By removing the golden age to the inner world of the self, Wieland leaves open the question of its validity.

The more extended use of the Dido and Aeneas tale is also present in this passage in the words and context of the phrase "des Vaters Bild." Dido had stoked her passion for Aeneas with his little son Ascanius's likeness to his father (*genitoris imagine capta*, 4. 85; under the spell of his resemblance to his father; 99) and, when she knew of his resolve to depart, she begged of him a child, a tiny Aeneas for her consolation (*qui te tamen ore referret*, 4. 329; bring you back to me if only in his likeness; 107). Wieland gains grandeur for his low epic by the contrast; the elevated tragedy of Dido upstairs accompanies the low farce of Hüon and Amanda in the harem downstairs. His rewriting of the original in a more intimate, personal vein opens up the ironic distance between model and imitation. A comic ghost haunts the modern rhapsode behind his curtain. Another side of this ironic distance occurs when Wieland does not intend farce, but still brings the two accounts sufficiently close together for the difference in epic love between his account and Virgil's to emerge clearly. In Wieland's epic the sense of self and the demand for its gratification in feeling lead to the fulfillment of love as an essential necessity of the self, and not, as in Virgil, to the renunciation of the demands of sentiment when they conflict with the divine order.

Wieland opens his remodeling of the Dido and Aeneas episode by characterizing the ineluctable suasion of love, just before the heroic couple yields to set the catastrophe in motion, in language that recalls Dido's predicament at the beginning of book 4.

> Die armen Seelen büssen
> Der Liebe süsses Gift. Wie wühlt sein heißer Brand
> in ihrem Blut! (*Ob.* 7. 11)

Virgil's Dido nourished a quiescent wound within her veins, a hidden fire (*Aen.* 4. 1–2) that soon broke into open flame with Aeneas's continual presence,

> *est mollis flamma medullas*
> *interea et tacitum uiuit sub pectore uulnus.*
> *uritur infelix Dido* (*Aen.* 4. 66–68)

> [for all the time the flame ate into her melting marrow, and deep in her heart the wound was silently alive. Poor Dido was afire (99)]

Aeneas came to Carthage by the agency of a storm on the Tyrrhenian Sea that drove Aeneas onto the coast of Libya (*Aen.* 1. 34–156). Wieland adopts this device. Virgil's storm was heaven sent as is also Wieland's, though in Wieland's case it follows the lovers' lapse. The approach of Wieland's storm vaguely echoes that of Virgil's (*Ob.* 7. 17 and *Aen.* 1. 81–89). In the one, clouds extinguish the stars, "Stracks schwärzt der Himmel sich" (*Ob.* 7. 17); in the other, the clouds remove day from the sky: *ponto nox incubat atra* (*Aen.* 1. 89; a blackness as of night fell on the ocean; 30). In the one, the storm hits: "Des Erdballs Axe kracht; der Wolken schwarzer Schooss/Gießt Feuerströme aus" (*Ob.* 7. 18); in the other: *intonuere poli et crebris micat ignibus aether* (*Aen.* 1. 90; the thunder cracked in heaven's height, and in the air above a continuous lightning flared; 30). In both, water piles up into mountains as the ships broach (*Ob.* 7. 18 and *Aen.* 1. 104–5); and then, according to Wieland, his one ship,

Das wechselweis' bald von der tiefsten Flut
Verschlungen scheint, bald, himmelan getrieben,
Auf Wogenspitzen schwebt, die unter ihm zerstieben: (*Ob.* 7. 19)

while Virgil, having a whole fleet to dispose of, writes:

*hi summo in fluctu pendent; his unda dehiscens
terram inter fluctus aperit, furit aestus harenis.* (*Aen.* 1. 106–7)

[some . . . hung poised on wave-crests; others saw the waves sink beneath them to disclose, below seething water and sand, the very bottom of the sea (30)][57]

In the face of the storm, Wieland's captain decides to consult the will of heaven to discover the reason for its anger. After the drawing of lots leaves Hüon marked for death, the hero gives a speech in which he surveys his predicament and admits his guilt. In this speech Hüon speaks essentially out of character, with an insight and pathos hitherto unremarked in him. Yet by introducing in a short space the thick repetition of the notions of fate and noble suffering common to serious epic, Wieland signals the appearance of a grander, soberer note in his own work, and one he takes advantage of to express most directly his doctrine of *humanitas*. In the manner of Hüon's speech, Wieland also seems to be paralleling his hero to Dido.

In the soliloquies leading up to her suicide Dido speaks of her dying as *ut merita es* (*Aen.* 4. 547; you have deserved your death; 114) because she has broken her promise of celibacy to the shade of her first husband, her *fides non servata promissa* (*Aen.* 4. 552; and also 4. 15–29; the vow which I have made . . . is broken; 114). This she labels a crime or something not allowed, *non licuit thalami expertem sine crimine uitam* (*Aen.* 4. 550; if only I could have been allowed to pass my life . . ., without any wedding; 114). The status of this admission is however ambiguous. Dido does not deny the guilt incurred by breaking her oath, but that is a legalistic guilt, not necessarily a moral guilt. Dido says of herself a short while later:

*uixi et quem dederat cursum Fortuna peregi,
et nunc magna mei sub terras ibit imago.* (*Aen.* 4. 653–54)

[I have lived my life and finished the course Fortune allotted me. Now my wraith shall pass in state to the world below (117)]

She deems herself to have acquitted herself sufficiently well in that lot that fortune apportioned to her for her now to die with a *magna imago*. The narrator states that Juno hastens the end of her suffering as she lay dying,

*nam quia nec fato, merita nec morte peribat,
sed misera ante diem subitoque accensa furore.* (*Aen.* 4. 696–97)

[For since she perished neither by destiny nor by a death deserved but tragically, before her day, in the mad heat of a great passion (118)]

Virgil again harps on the troubling horror of her death when, after the meeting of Dido and Aeneas in the underworld, he writes of his hero: *nec minus Aeneas casu percussus iniquo* (*Aen.* 6. 475; Aeneas was shocked by her unjust fate; 161).

Wieland seizes on exactly this ambiguity and dresses it up in similar portentous language in Hüon's speech, to come, however, to a very different conclusion.

> "Ihr, die mein Tod erhält, schenkt eine fromme Zähre
> Dem Jüngling, den der Sterne Missgunst trifft!
> Nicht schuldlos sterb' ich zwar, doch lebt' ich stets mit Ehre;
> Ein Augenblick, wo ich, berauscht von süssem Gift,
> Des Worts vergass, das ich zu rasch geschworen,
> Der Warnung, die zu spät in meinen bangen Ohren
> Itzt widerhallt — das allgemeine Los
> Der Menschheit, schwach zu sein — ist mein Verbrechen bloss!
> Schwer büss' ich's nun, doch klaglos! denn, gereuen
> Des liebenswürdigen Verbrechens soll mich's nicht!
> Ist *Lieben* Schuld so mag der Himmel mir verzeihen!
> Mein sterbend Herz, erkennt nun keine andre Pflicht.
> Was kann ich sonst als Liebe dir erstatten,
> O du, die mir aus Liebe alles gab?
> Nein! diese heil'ge Glut erstickt kein Wellengrab!
> Unsterblich lebt sie fort in deines *Hüons* schatten."
>
> Hier ward das Herz ihm gross; er hält die blasse Hand
> Vors Aug, und schweigt. . . .
> Und da der Himmel selbst zum Opfer ihn ersehn,
> Wer dürfte, sagen sie, dem Himmel widerstehn? (*Ob.* 7. 25–27)

The language and situation echo those of Dido. Both dramas turn on the role of love in human affairs. Each hero breaks a pledge of chastity, each admits to a "Verbrechen" or *crimen*, and each without complaint submits her- or himself to punishment. Likewise, each lessens the moral blame, each harps on the cruel role of heaven or fate, each promises immortality to his or her shade for the manner of his or her fall, and finally neither expects the confession to sway the will of heaven.

However the two accounts are also very different. Wieland sweeps away the disquieting ambiguity of the Virgilian account. Virgil does not speak of love and the rights of subjective human feeling. Yet there is hardly a line in Wieland's stanzas in which there is not either a direct mention of love or an allusion to it. Wieland makes Hüon's predicament not merely a statement of the universal and fundamental human condition of the conflict between morality and desire — "Das allgemeine Los der Menschheit, schwach zu sein" — but also the quintessence of being human. Hüon knows there is no way for him to renounce his love and live. Virgil makes no such claims for Dido's predicament, although a palpable unease at it hovers over the account. Virgil speaks of love as a *caecus ignis* (a hidden fire), repeatedly as a *furor*, as insanity, and finally as an all-consuming conflagration: *amor magnoque irarum fluctuat aestu* (*Aen.* 4. 532; her [Dido's] love . . . heaved in ocean-tides of rage; 113). For Wieland it is a "süsses Gift" and a "heil'ge Glut," the stuff of which we yearn to burn, not that of which we fear the burning. In neither instance do these considerations avert the impending calamity. The sacrifice of Hüon to the sea calms it as quickly as Neptune did the storm besetting Aeneas. Hüon, however, does not die, as Dido did, rather, Aeneas-like, he survives the storm.

The echoes of the Dido tragedy do not recur until the other moment of would-be high and sounding passion, namely, the temptation of Hüon and Amanda in the seraglio. In this instance the echoes are much more openly parodistic even as they lend a certain elevation to the style. One of the numerous hints Wieland employs to signal that the epic is moving to its climax is again reminiscent of Virgil. Wieland has Titania whisk Amanda and Hüon's child the little Hüonet to safety out of harm's way as Venus before her had removed little Ascanius from the grasp of the Dido.

At the very beginning of book 4 Dido lies, her sleep disturbed, already in the grip of her fatal fever, and again on the eve of her last day she is unable to sleep: *rursusque resurgens/ saeuit amor magnoque irarum fluctuat aestu* (*Aen.* 4. 531–32; her love came back again and again, and heaved in ocean-tides of rage; 113). Thwarted of immediate revenge, she ends with a magnificent curse on the Romans. There is not now, nor ever to be, peace between the Romans and the Carthaginians (*nunc, olim, quocumque dabunt se tempore uires, Aen.* 4. 627). Wieland's thwarted Sultana assumes a similar pose,

> Indessen sucht auf Polstern von Damast
> *Almansaris*, mit Amors wildestem Feuer
> In ihrer Brust, umsonst nur eine Stunde Rast. (*Ob.* 12. 1)

What vexes her is "das schnöde Abenteuer" and the thought "ein Mann verachtet dich" (*Ob.* 12. 1). Nonetheless the magnitude of the offense drives her too to thoughts of limitless revenge:

> Zur Wut treibt der Gedanke sie;
> Sie schwört sich grenzlose Rache
> Wie häßlich wird er ihr! (*Ob.* 12. 2)

Lest we should think that she is not in the grip of some great passion we learn, "*Almansaris*, in deren warmen Blut/ Schon ein *Verführer* schleicht" (*Ob.* 12, 7), an image that reverberates with the lines,

> *At regina graui iamdudum saucia cura*
> *uulnus alit uenis et caeco carpitur igni.* (*Aen.* 4. 1–2)

[But meanwhile Queen Dido, gnawed by love's invisible fire, had long suffered from the deep wound draining her lifeblood. (97)]

and,

> *et mollis flamma medullas*
> *interea et tacitum uiuit sub pectore uulnus.* (*Aen.* 4. 66–67)

[For all the time the flame ate into her melting marrow, and deep in her heart the wound was silently alive. (99)]

The more ironic and witty intent is immediately apparent in the language, which is bathetic in relation to its original context. Wieland speaks not of love, "Liebe," as earlier in Hüon's speech but of the rascal Amor; Almansaris's indignation expresses itself in the somewhat frivolous condemnation "häßlich," Dido's madness becomes in her blood "ein Verführer." Almansaris does not despair of her infatuation, even when Hüon sits in the dungeon at night awaiting his death in the morning, but visits him there to offer him the kingdom if he should marry her, as Dido once offered kingship to Aeneas in return for marriage (*Ob.* 12. 32–38). Hüon replies that he must reject her in favor of his "Ehre" and "Treu"; however in this instance honor and faith are to a person, Amanda, not to some mission of the gods. Similarly, as Dido once raged through Carthage with love of Aeneas, *qualis coniecta cerua sagitta* (*Aen.* 4. 69; like a doe . . . pierced by an arrow; 99), the Sultan afflicted by his love of Amanda wanders about the harem's garden, "gleich einem angeschossnen Wild" (*Ob.* 12. 21). And finally, the pyre and stake at which Hüon and Amanda are to be burnt to death are reminiscent both of Dido's funeral pyre and of a martyr's death, neither of which association would Wieland, presumably, object to.

Wieland's ambiguous attitude toward both epic and Virgil harbors within itself many strands that either were already discernable in Germany or would later be unraveled elsewhere in German literature. In view of its length (Wieland's longest epic), *Oberon* can ill conceal itself behind the label "Kleinepos." The sincere plea for a humane love within the bounds of bourgeois domesticity places it at the outer limit of the "mock-heroic" epic. Equally, the ironic invocation of the Muses, the continual rupture of "epic objectivity" and the narrative fiction, the witty language, the light and flowing verse, the literary burlesque, all live up to the designation "mock-heroic." Both of these approaches repeat themselves in his use of Virgil; on the one hand, a rewriting of the Dido and Aeneas episode in a mood of idyllic or more innocent love, a transposition from the tragic to the comic register that does not by this transfer dispense with every intimation of gravity, and on the other hand, a refined, parodic play with literary convention.

If one pursues the idyllic golden age strand of domestic love, purging it of Wieland's ironic frame, then one moves easily to the world of *Luise* and *Hermann und Dorothea*, and to the reciprocal assimilation of epic and idyll.

If one chooses instead to pursue the burlesque of Virgil, then one moves easily into a choice and as yet unexploited field in German literature. If one pursues the Dido parallel, then one adds to the long line of literary works that make the Dido and Aeneas episode a separate study.[58] It is however Wieland's handling of the Dido episode to bring out its more idyllic and sentimental elements that corresponds to the more creative response to Virgil's other two poems in the pastoral theory and literature during the century.

Notes

[1] John Dryden, *The Works of John Dryden*, 5:276.

[2] Nicolas Boileau-Despreaux, *Oeuvres Complètes*, ed. Francoise Escal, Bibliothèque de la Pléiade 188 (Paris: Gallimard, 1966), 1:172 (Canto 3).

[3] Gottsched, *Ausgewählte Werke*, 6/2:279.

[4] Gottsched, *Ausgewählte Werke*, 6/2:292.

[5] Dieter Martin has produced the only detailed study of German grand epic in the eighteenth century, which usefully includes lengthy appendices on the scope and number of verse epics, *Das deutsche Versepos im 18. Jahrhundert* (Berlin: de Gruyter, 1993).

[6] Friedrich Gottlieb Klopstock, *Werke und Briefe*, ed. Adolf Beck et al., Hamburger Klopstock-Ausgabe (Berlin: Walter de Gruyter, 1982), ser. 1, 2:37. All citations from Klopstock are from this edition unless otherwise noted. Voltaire's *Henriade* excites Klopstock's particular scorn. He returns to it again in the epigrams "Die Henriade" (# 52), "Vorlesung der Henriade" (# 203) and "An die Franzosen" (# 218). The English receive more favorable treatment in "An die Engländer" (# 219).

[7] Johann Jacob Bodmer, *Vier kritische Gedichte*, ed. Jakob Baechtold, Deutsche Litteraturdenkmale des 18. Jahrhunderts in Neudrucken 12 (Stuttgart: Göschen, 1883), 859. The number refers to the verse number, not the pagination. Subsequent references in the following text are by verse number only.

[8] Why Bodmer should choose the name of Addison over Milton is not entirely clear as Addison did not write an epic. Bodmer may have had *The Campaign* (1704) in mind. A panegyric to Marlborough on the Allied victory at Blenheim, the poem, though written in heroic couplets, is well short of epic length. Its national and martial theme may have recommended it to Bodmer to follow Homer, Virgil, Tasso, and Voltaire just as the lack of national theme in Milton and so lack of conformity to the definition may have excluded him.

[9] Friedrich Gottlieb Klopstock, *Ausgewählte Werke*, ed. Karl August Schleiden, afterword, Friedrich Georg Jünger (Munich: Hanser, 1962), 1264.

[10] Salomon Gessner, *Sämtliche Schriften*, ed. Martin Bircher (1762; repr. Zurich: Füssli, 1972), 1:1.

[11] Cited from Servius, *Commentarii*, 1:2.

[12] Alfred Anger, *Literarisches Rokoko*, Sammlung Metzler 25 (Stuttgart: Metzler, 1962), 54.

[13] For a general discussion of the gradations of the word "mock-heroic" and the Rococo epyllion see Anger, *Rokoko*, 88–96. For particular attention to Wieland see Emil Staiger, "Wielands 'Musarion,'" in *Christoph Martin Wieland*, ed. Hansjörg Schelle, Wege der Forschung 421 (Darmstadt: Wissenschaftliche Buchgesellschaft, 1981), 93–108, who argues that the lightness and airiness of *Musarion* is an apology for an urbane sociability and happiness. Friedrich Sengle conceives of the change from *Der neue Amadis* (1771) to *Oberon* as a change from "dem spielerischen Rokoko-Leichtsinn" to something "humaner, zugleich bürgerlicher, ein deutlicher Schritt in Richtung auf 'Hermann und Dorothea"; see "Von Wielands Epenfragmenten zum 'Oberon,'" in *Christoph Martin Wieland*, ed. Hansjörg Schelle, Wege der Forschung 421 (Darmstadt: Wissenschaftliche Buchgesellschaft, 1981), 64. Hans Mayer concentrates on the sense in which *Oberon* is humorous and argues that the effect depends not on the subject matter but on the "humoristisch-distanziertes Spiel des Autors mit einer als grundsätzlich ernst verstandenen Gattung"; see "Wielands 'Oberon,'" in Schelle, *Christoph Martin Wieland*, 194. An ironic attitude towards one's cultural heritage betokens the "Spätzeit" of that culture, see Mayer, "Wieland's "Oberon,"" *passim*. Friedrich Beißner argues the dangers of contenting oneself with the term Rococo in relation to Wieland's epics by focusing on the tension between "Ernst und Scherz"; see afterword, Christoph Martin Wieland, *Ausgewählte Werke in drei Bänden*, ed. Friedrich Beißner (Munich: Winkler, 1964), 1: 913–39.

[14] Robert Browning, *German Poetry in the Age of the Enlightenment* (University Park and London: Pennsylvania State UP, 1978), 187; Browning's italics.

[15] Immanuel Jacob Pyra and Samuel Gotthold Lange, *Freundschaftliche Lieder*, ed. August Sauer, deutsche Litteraturdenkmale des 18. und 19. Jahrhunderts in Neudrucken 22 (Stuttgart: Göschen, 1885), 5. 151–58. The edition of the *Freundschaftliche Lieder* contains as a hundred-page appendix with continuous pagination the poems Pyra wrote himself. Quotations from the *Tempel der wahren Dichtkunst* in the next several paragraphs are given, as above, according to canto and line number.

[16] Gustav Waniek, in his book *Immanuel Pyra und sein Einfluß auf die deutsche Litteratur des achtzehnten Jahrhunderts* (Leipzig: Breitkopf & Härtel, 1882), presses the point that diction and manner of nature description argue for the influence of Haller (38); to which one may add in general confirmation of Waniek and of the above point with respect to its inspiration, though not with respect to its technique, that as Pyra, Lange, and their guide, Poetry, stand on the temple's threshold looking down at the prospect of the world and its vanities, the effect is described by a simile in the epic style taken from Haller's *Die Alpen*. Haller's shepherd stands at the peak of the Alps and surveys the panorama at his feet: "Er siehet Berg und Thäler,/Und schwindelt, wenn sein Blick von dem erhabnen Fels,/Der schrecklich überhängt, in grause Tiefen sincket./So ging es uns auch hier" (Albrecht von Haller, *Die Alpen und andere Gedichte*, selected with an afterword by Adalbert Elschenbroich [Stuttgart: Reclam, 1965], 14).

[17] See Robert Browning, *German Poetry in the Age of the Enlightenment*, 187.

[18] Among the possible sources for this, Sauer lists the description of the pictures from the siege of Troy that decorate the Dido's temple to Juno (introduction to Pyra and Lange, *Lieder*, xxxiv).

[19] Sauer, introduction to Pyra and Lange's *Lieder*, xxxii, gives two further examples where the desire to imitate the *Aeneid* causes an awkwardness in the poem. One is the imitation of the Aeolus episode (*Aen.* 1. 52–59) in the description of the Realm of Dreams (2. 130–200). Sauer objects to it neither for its content nor its mood, but simply for its disproportionate length. The second, noted by Seuffert and related by Sauer, occurs at the end of canto 1 when Pyra faints at the chasm. Seuffert objects that the dark mood of the passage, out of keeping with the light and airy atmosphere of the poem as a whole, is attributable to its dependence on book 6 of the *Aeneid*.

[20] Gottsched, *Ausgewählte Werke*, 6/1:231.

[21] All quotations from Milton's *Paradise Lost* are taken from John Milton, *Paradise Lost: A Poem in Twelve Books*, ed. Merritt Y. Hughes (Indianapolis: The Odyssey Press, 1962). Although the first edition of *Paradise Lost* was published in 1667, the more familiar second edition published in 1674 (with twelve books instead of the original ten) has become the established text; see Hughes, preface to Milton's *Paradise Lost*, vii.

[22] Katrin Kohl, *Friedrich Gottlieb Klopstock*, Sammlung Metzler, vol. 325 (Stuttgart: Metzler, 2000), 19.

[23] Kevin Hilliard, *Philosophy, Letters, and the Fine Arts in Klopstock's Thought* (London: Institute of Germanic Studies, University of London, 1987), 11. He is discussing Karl Ludwig Schneider's book, *Klopstock und die Erneuerung der deutschen Dichtersprache im 18. Jahrhundert* (Heidelberg: Winter, 1960). Schneider's careful presentation and classification with abundant examples of Klopstock's innovations, particularly in chapters 3–5, is a most comprehensive and concise exposition of the issue.

[24] Typical concerns framing Gerhard Kaiser's interest emerge in his summary of Freivogel's judgment of Klopstock: "Klopstocks Anspruch auf die Würde des heiligen Dichters gilt Freivogel als blasphemisch, da Klopstock über die Addition homerischer Form und christlichen Inhalts nicht hinwegkomme. . . . Im übrigen habe Klopstock ungebuhrlich aus Milton entlehnt" (Kaiser, *Klopstock: Religion und Dichtung* [Gütersloh: Mohn, 1963], 19–20). In the section on the *Messias*, Kaiser shows how Klopstock's response to Milton is not merely creative but also quite different in purpose and effect from Milton (204–58).

[25] Katrin Kohl, the author of the Sammlung Metzler volume on Klopstock, places the epic squarely on the side of Homer and Milton: "Während Gottsched auf den deutschen Vergil hoffte, führte Klopstock die Deutschen unter Berufung auch auf die von Bodmer zum Vorbild erhobene englische Tradition in einen Wettstreit mit Homer" (*Klopstock*, 70). Equally, Martin in his often detailed and precise comment on Klopstock's epic technique and style moves entirely within the Miltonic and Homeric reference (*Das deutsche Versepos*, 85–139); and Kevin Hilliard, in his *Philosophy, Letters, and the Fine Arts in Klopstock's Thought*, whose object is Klopstock's more general relation to the humanist rhetorical tradition rather than an examination of specific works, makes no more than occasional reference to Virgil.

[26] Milton, for example, strained the English language to shape a native epic diction for which Virgil was the model. He transports many Virgilian devices into English. As Virgil used Graecisms in both syntax and vocabulary so does Milton Latinisms in his English syntax and vocabulary. In addition to giving words derived from Latin

their Latin meaning, he imitates a host of devices. He repeatedly uses "or . . . or . . ." in imitation of *aut . . . aut . . .* and "nor . . . nor . . ." for *neque . . . neque . . .* instead of "either . . . or . . ." and "neither . . . nor. . . ." For "he, who . . ." a simple "who," like the Latin *qui,* suffices. He also uses impersonal verbal constructions foreign to English. He makes extensive use of ellipsis, omitting the verb "to be," again in imitation of the Latin. He drops the accustomed preposition in many positions: when it is prefixed to the verb, when it occurs in the phrasal verb or alternatively in the prepositional object. Or again he uses the conjunction "that" without the "so" in a purpose/final clause for the Latin *ut.* Finally the syntax of his sentence is highly Latinate, leading to long and involved periods.

[27] From 10th August 1748, Klopstock, *Werke und Briefe,* ser. 2, 1:14.

[28] Bodmer, *Versuch,* in *Vier kritische Gedichte,* verse 64.

[29] See Wolfgang Bender, "Johann Jacob Bodmer und Johann Miltons 'Verlohrnes Paradies,'" *Jahrbuch der deutschen Schillergesellschaft,* 11 (1967): 225–67, for a consideration of the poetological implications of Bodmer's stylistic change between the first two editions.

[30] Johann Jakob Breitinger, *Critische Dichtkunst,* afterword, Wolfgang Bender (1740; repr. Stuttgart: Metzler, 1966), 2:271–72. Again Breitinger borrows silently from Pope, who selects exactly these examples from Homer to support his contention that Homer was greater in invention:

> To throw his Language more out of Prose, *Homer* seems to have affected the *Compound-Epithets.* . . . We see the Motion of *Hector's* Plume in the Epithet κορυθαίολος, the Landscape of Mount *Neritus* in that of εἰνοσίφυλλος, and so others; which particular Images could not have been insisted upon so long as to express them in Description (tho' but of a single Line) without diverting the Reader too much from the principal Action or Figure. As a Metaphor is a short Simile, one of these Epithets is a short Description.

(Alexander Pope, "Preface to the *Iliad,*" *The Poems of Alexander Pope,* gen. ed. John Butt [London: Methuen, 1951–69], 11 vols.; here 7:10. Subsequent references to Pope's works are to this edition.)

Breitinger also derives his comment on their function from the same source. The examples from Virgil, however, are his own addition.

[31] Schneider, *Klopstock,* 19.

[32] See Schneider, *Klopstock, passim,* esp. chapter 5, "Das Stilprinzip der Kürze."

[33] This by no means argues that the Homeric diction is "simple" or devoid of rhetorical adornment, but merely that it is so in relation to Virgilian verse.

[34] Franz Muncker gives an evaluation of Klopstock's linguistic training and his ability in Latin in *Friedrich Gottlieb Klopstock: Geschichte seines Lebens und seiner Schriften* (Berlin: Behr, 1893), 16–18.

[35] Friedrich Gottlieb Klopstock, *Declamatio qua poetas epopoeiae auctores recenset Frideric Gottlieb Klopstock,* in *Sämmtliche Werke,* ed. A. L. Back and A. R. C. Spindler (Leipzig: Fleischer, 1830), 16:52.

⁳⁶ His attentiveness to Bodmer's opinions on this point may be judged from the mention of Belgium's fortune to highlight by contrast the magnitude of Germany's shame: *Ita vero et Belgium poetae epici gloria illustre nunc conspicitur. Semper igitur hic honor, ad nostros finos, o Germani, magis magisque appropinquat, nunquam ingreditur* (Klopstock, *Declamatio*, 16:72; Indeed the epic poet's shining glory even gazes upon Belgium. To our borders, o Germans, this honor always draws closer and closer, and never enters).

³⁷ Pope, preface to the *Iliad*, 7:12.

³⁸ Breitinger, *Critische Dichtkunst* 1:43.

³⁹ Klopstock, *Declamatio*, 16:58.

⁴⁰ Muncker, although he does not cite Klopstock's valedictorian speech, argues that from his time in the Schulpforta Klopstock conceived for Homer "einen leisen Vorzug vor Virgil" (*Klopstock*, 19). However in his essay "Über einige Vorbilder für Klopstocks Dichtungen," he expresses himself more circumspectly: "Aus ähnlichen Quellen floß dem Jüngling der Gedanke zu, daß Homer als Erfinder des heroischen Epos den Vorzug vor Virgil, seinem Nachahmer verdiene" (in *Sitzungsberichte der philisophisch-philologischen und der historischen Klasse der königlichen bayerischen Akademie* 6 [1908], 3–33; here, 8). A preference for a poet conceived simply on the distinction of his having been first does not argue either for a close acquaintance of that poet, nor for a nuanced conception of the original. Muncker recognizes that the conventional nature of Klopstock's utterances makes it difficult to know how genuine an expression of informed opinion they are. It is impossible to ascertain whether Klopstock had already read Homer in the original, in whole or in part, as he was not on the curriculum at Schulpforta, although it is unlikely that he had not.

⁴¹ Klopstock, *Werke und Briefe*, ser. 2, 1:14.

⁴² Muncker, "Einige Vorbilder," 6.

⁴³ Klopstock, *Sämmtliche Werke*, 17:18. The translation is not from the *Grammatische Gespräche* but Klopstock's translations from Horace, Virgil, Homer, and Xenophon. They are sufficiently numerous for the editors to collect them together in their own section.

⁴⁴ A supposition that is in no way unconventional for Klopstock who is particularly keen on asyndeton, see. Schneider, *Klopstock*, 74.

⁴⁵ Homer, *Opera Iliadis*, ed. David B. Monro and Thomas W. Allen, 3rd ed. (Oxford: Oxford UP, 1920).

⁴⁶ The accusative designated by the name Greek Accusative identifies a Latin use of that case according to its origin, that is, a construction developed under the influence of Greek. Its other name of Accusative of Respect or Specification identifies the same construction according to its function, which is the occurrence of the accusative after an adjective or a passive or intransitive verb. The accusative denotes or limits what the adjectival or verbal statement effects, or that "with respect to" which it applies. For example, *Silenum . . . inflatum hesterno uenas, ut semper, Iaccho* (*Ec.* 6. 15) translates literally as "[him] Silenus swollen as to his veins with yesterday's wine, as always." The participle *inflatum* is acc. masc. sing. and so does not agree with *uenas*, which is acc. fem. plu.; however, to turn it into good English and make the "natural" sense accord with the grammar, one reverses

the grammatical order and makes "swollen" depend upon "veins": "his veins swollen with yesterday's wine, as always." It is a construction of which Virgil was very fond.

The point at issue is not whether the German is comprehensible — it is immediately intelligible — but how to account for it grammatically. The participial phrase presents the simplest and most immediate solution; e.g. Da lag sie, *die plumpen, geschmückten Hände von sich gestreckt*, unfähig, sich zu regen," *Duden: Grammatik der Gegenwartssprache*, 4th ed. (Mannheim: Dudenverlag, 1984), 4:§1253, 3. Such an example can be rewritten "Da lag sie, die die Hände von sich gestreckt hatte, unfähig, sich zu bewegen," without detriment to its content though not to its style. However, one cannot, as a test, do the same for Klopstock's phrase (i.e. "der Drachen, der den Rücken wie mit Blut besprengt hatte"), unless one wishes to accuse him of a license with the Greek tantamount to a misunderstanding of it. As a second solution, German also recognizes an accusative absolute such as, "Neben ihm saß der dünnhaarige Pianist, *den Kopf* im Nacken, und lauschte" (*Duden* 4:§1044), in which one supposes that the grammatical relation to the main clause is given by the omitted present participle "haltend" or "habend." Otto Behagel, *Deutsche Syntax: Eine geschichtliche Darstellung* (Heidelberg: Winter, 1923), 1:§503, specifically excludes the accusative with the perfect participle from the accusative absolute in the note to paragraph 503. Thus he argues the sentence "er stand da, den Kopf gesenkt," is the equivalent, at most, of "den Kopf senkend." Furthermore, even if one does alter Klopstock's phrase to match the Duden example (den wie mit Blut besprengten Rücken [habend]), it does not correspond to that example since it is not a noun phrase followed by a prepositional phrase, and it also, in this modified form, lacks an easy sense. Nor does it help to consider it a pure absolute — e.g. "Seinen üblichen Eifer vorausgesetzt, wird er sicher Erfolg haben," A. E. Hammer, *German Grammar and Usage* (Baltimore: Arnold, 1983), §59 — as the absolute modifies the verbal predicate of the main clause: not a possible reading here.

[47] Klopstock, *Sämmtliche Werke*, 17:17.

[48] Kaiser also uses it, although for him it is one among many. More recently, Kohl too chooses it, aware of its previous appearances (*Klopstock*, 80).

[49] Klopstock, *Werke und Briefe*, ser. 1, 4/2:20. This is only the concluding sentence from the longer passage (IX, 709–26) that Schneider cites (*Klopstock*, 82).

[50] Schneider's comment on these lines is as follows: "Der mit Zeile 720 abermals aufkommende Eindruck der Länge geht primär von dem zunächst noch nicht zu überblickend Satz aus, der tatsächlich auch erst mit Vers 726 zum Abschluß kommt. Mit nur einer Durchbrechung in Vers 725 läßt die durchgängige asyndetische Bauform an strenger Zusammenschließung nichts zu wünschen übrig. Das stark akzentuierte Wort 'nennen' ist als Simplex von 'benennen' zu deuten. Im substantivierten Partizip Zeile 725 und seiner Voranstellung wiederholt sich die den Artikel eliminierende Kurzform" (*Klopstock*, 83).

[51] Christoph Martin Wieland, "Oberon: Ein romantisches Heldengedicht in zwölf Gesängen," in *Ausgewählte Werke* (Munich: Winkler, 1964), 1:5–225. All citations from the poem, listed according to the abbreviation *Ob*. and the canto and stanza, are from this edition.

[52] Sengle takes him up on this offer and generally considers Wieland's relation to the idea of the national epic, although he does so without recourse to Virgil; see Sengle, "Von Wielands Epenfragmenten," *passim* and on *Oberon*, 62–65. In this progression he regards *Oberon* as Wielands "größtes Kleinepos," and continues, "Der in dieser Dichtung erreichte Ausgleich von Ironie und Ernst, von Leichtigkeit und Gewicht, von Märchenhaftigkeit und Menschlichkeit war ihm vorher und nachher unerreichbar" (62). Mayer accepts the invitation directly. He considers that the attempt to place *Oberon* in the succession of the epic tradition proves empty. Wieland's poem leads neither back to Homer and Virgil nor forward to Goethe's *Hermann und Dorothea:* "Der 'Oberon' ist daher in aller Bewußtheit als ein Abschied vom Epos gedacht ("Wielands 'Oberon,'" 197).

[53] Mayer points in a parenthetical aside to the donning of a Virgilian costume — "um der bewunderten 'Aeneis' auch darin zu gleichen" ("Wielands 'Oberon,'" 189) — but takes the matter no further. John A. McCarthy also mentions the parallel to Virgil but goes no further; see John A. McCarthy, *Christoph Martin Wieland*, Twayne World Author Series 528 (Boston: Twayne, 1979), 129.

[54] Friedrich Sengle, *Wieland* (Stuttgart: Metzler, 1949), 363.

[55] More recently Michael Hoffmann takes issue with Sengle's interpretation; see *Reine Seelen und komische Ritter: Aspekte literarischer Aufklärung in Christoph Martin Wielands Versepik* (Stuttgart: Metzler, 1998), 281–85. Hoffmann, while acknowledging a certain classicism in form (337), argues for the distancing effect of the narrative style and against any view of the plot as embodying "ein[.] normative[s] Bild griechischen Menschentums (299).

[56] Apart from the alteration of some words and phrases and the shortening of stanzas 38 and 39 in canto 2 into one stanza in the new canto 2, the most important change is the disposition of the 372 stanzas of the six cantos (5 to 10) into the four new cantos (5 to 8).

[57] *Hi . . . his* are more commonly read as referring to the several ships and not to crew of the one ship. I have therefore taken the liberty of omitting the words "of the crew" from Jackson Knight's translation.

[58] See Eberhard Semrau, *Dido in der deutschen Dichtung*, Stoff- und Motivgeschichte der deutschen Literatur 9, ed. Paul Merker and Gerhard Lüdtke (Berlin: De Gruyter, 1930).

4: Theorizing Genre: From Pastoral to Idyll

Defining the Pastoral: From Idyll to Eclogue, from Theocritus to Virgil

THE GERMAN IDYLL OF THE eighteenth century represents the final efflorescence of the European pastoral tradition. In contrast to the enormous vitality pastoral displayed in the previous four centuries, the success of the German idyll with Gessner is much more modest. The list of pastoral writers from the earlier period represents a virtual honor role of figures instrumental to the development of European literary culture.[1] The allegorical tradition, sanctioned by the range and variety of the Virgilian bucolic, allowed the imagination of the humanist scholars and poets and their successors in the seventeenth century ample scope to pursue their own interests. The modern pastoral soon spread to include significant works in all genres: lyric, drama, and the novel.

The scholarly consequence of this enormous pastoral output has rightly been to focus on this period for a sense of generic definition, with of course some qualification for the link to the ancient bucolic.[2] However, this scholarship frequently does so by adopting a critical overlay that stems from the eighteenth century and Schiller. In his busy essay *Über naive und sentimentale Dichtung* Schiller develops a concept of the idyllic (as the pastoral had become in his day) that is no longer based on genre but instead represents a mode.[3] The idyllic embodies a particular configuration of the sentimental in relation to the naive. While retaining a close proximity to nature and nature scenes, it is largely independent of the older pastoral's specific traits, as they seem optional props, not essential attributes. The idyllic becomes a generalized attitude or perspective, capable of insertion as a moment or episode into larger works.[4] Schiller's concept of the idyllic, for instance, appears, reinscribed into a different, still more expansive register in William Empson's dictum about the pastoral as the placing of "the complex into the simple."[5]

Pastoral scholarship inherited from the eighteenth century its largely successful reformulation of the pastoral around the sentimental subject's belief in a state of nature and the gratification of this belief in the idyllic vision. This reformulation draws on elements long part of the pastoral mix in the modern era, such as Arcadia, the golden age, the multifaceted contrast between town and country, or nature and civilization, and the satisfaction of love. However by making them the determining, if not exclusive, criteria of the pastoral, it pushes to the margins the degree to which the pastoral throughout its long tradition was also, if not more so, a site for programmatic poetological statements, mixed with veiled social and political commentary. These became obscured, even alien traits. The pastoral of the eighteenth century expresses the longing of the worldly weary for a dreamlike land where the sun always shines and we are always happy, and does it in a fashion that convinces us this vision is real, that it has psychological veracity and is not a figment of the imagination. Theocritus, according to the eighteenth century, sanctions this form of pastoral. In the image of the naive poet of the lesser epic form (which endures as a shibboleth of criticism until well into the twentieth century), Theocritus is scarcely recognizable as an Alexandrian poet. He is instead the serendipitous conduit of the last lingering vestiges of the historical age of pastoralism among the Greeks. He is the poet of realism, the writer who records the rough joyful life of Sicilian shepherds. For Herder, Theocritus writes directly "aus dem Leben" (*HW* 1:357) with the barest minimum of art.

In twentieth-century Virgilian scholarship, this view of the pastoral appears in such classical scholars as Pöschl and Klingner. Belief in a beneficent nature pervades pastoral poetry. It is comforting play, a glimpse among the wonders of the landscape and beauty that proclaims humanity's proper home in the world of this numinous nature, even though the present may contradict the claim.[6] Virgil creates Arcadia as a homeland for this pastoral. It is his imaginative response to the horrors of civil war as the Republic collapses[7] and is perhaps best known through Bruno Snell's influential 1946 essay, "Arkadien, die Entdeckung einer geistigen Landschaft."[8] This Arcadia is no less attractive to other scholars and forms the starting point for Renato Poggioli's "The Oaten Flute" (1957), a general reflection on the pastoral impulse in the Western tradition.[9] However, for later scholars, the increasing recognition of the distortion it introduces into the concept of the pastoral causes a partial shift in focus and a variety of attempts to reconsider the question of genre. Thomas Rosenmeyer (1969), among others, begins this process by arguing for a critical engagement with the Theocritean bucolic idyll in order to bring it within the purview of pastoral scholarship where formerly the Virgilian eclogue was preponderant.[10] David Halperin (1983) tackles the issue in a much more radical fashion by pointing out that the incorporation of Theocritus into a concept of pastoral is likely to be a dubious enterprise, if it means measuring by the standards of the subsequent genre an author who wrote without consciousness of such a fixed generic profile.[11] Rather, all assumptions about what pastoral is, and especially where such notions come from, must be reexamined and the attempt made to read Theocritus in his own context.

In Virgilian criticism, the qualification or problematization of the strong Arcadian reading of pastoral takes place within the larger context of the European, German pro-Augustan reading and the more pessimistic, "Harvard" view in America. For both, the *Eclogues* are a reflection on the role of the imagination and the artist in society according to the Neoteric reading of Greek literature. The two approaches share their concentration on the constructed nature of the Virgilian texts, but differ on the judgment figured in them of the new order taking shape under Augustus. The more positive reading sees an expression of a longing for an untroubled pastoral life, first envisioned in response to the upheavals in society and then discarded in favor of the more constructive engagement that appears in the *Georgics* and the *Aeneid*. For the other, attention focuses much less on the dream world of Arcadia than on the sensitive and often dark reflection within the pastoral. For Putnam, Virgil is not primarily to be identified, as is done by long tradition, with the fortunate shepherd Tityrus in *Eclogue* 1, but is more vitally (because more sympathetically) involved with the banished shepherd, Meliboeus.[12]

Whatever the meaning attributed to pastoral in antiquity, interpretations such as these take as their starting point exactly those elements the eighteenth century succeeded in removing from its idyll.

> Interpreters have gradually moved from the emphasis on the mimetic realism of a genre whose principal trait is simplicity to acknowledging the complexity of works informed by the subtleties of late Hellenistic poetics. In ancient pastoral both sides exist. The resultant tension between the simple and the complex, between nature and artifice, is an essential part of the meaning of these works and should not be prematurely resolved on one side or the other.[13]

Perhaps the most radical concentration on the constructed nature of the pastoral to date is Thomas Hubbard's recent reading (1998) of pastoral as programmatic intertextuality.[14] In his consideration of the Virgilian bucolics, his focus on the intertext, primarily the Theocritean, is so complete that the teeming social and political elements scarcely appear, even at the margins.[15]

The gradual overcoming in the twentieth century of the eighteenth century's understanding of pastoral simplicity is not matched by a corresponding interest in the origins of the eighteenth century's reformulation of the pastoral. Its end result is taken as a starting point, and Schiller, loosely, as its spokesman.[16] The start of this process, however, occurs not in Germany but in French neoclassicism, with René Rapin and Fontenelle, as part of the *Querelle*. In their theoretical reflections, they initiate a radical reforming and pruning of the early modern pastoral tradition from a desire to produce a normative definition of a genre. The German tradition continues this undertaking but gradually enlarges the scope of pastoral through its insistent recourse to the general Enlightenment preoccupation with nature.[17]

This process reaches its conclusion with Schiller, in two senses. In the first more general sense, he articulates the notion that what is at issue in a pastoral, an eclogue, or an idyll is not the definition of its proper attributes but the attitude toward nature embodied in it. In other words, the theoretical treatment of the pastoral is not a question of defining a genre, a type of poem, that is an idyll, but of defining a mode, an overarching attribute, a mood, that is the idyllic.

In the second, more circumscribed sense, Schiller's transformation represents the theoretical acknowledgment of pastoral theory's release from the leading reins of the ancient bucolic. Both Rapin and Fontenelle, by explicitly and narrowly basing their conceptions on the ancient bucolic of Theocritus and Virgil, succeed in binding the understanding of the newly reformed French eclogue, and later the new German idyll, to the ancient bucolic. Following this pattern, German pastoral theory develops by continually referring back to Theocritus and Virgil, and in the process greatly transforming both. Theocritus emerges as the great exemplar of the proper representation of idyllic nature; he becomes the great "realist," the artist of the naive. He becomes a writer so struck by the charm and freshness of the countryside, encountered as he strolled about among the country folk in the vicinity of his native Syracuse, that he was driven to portray, and to portray realistically, the attractions of the shepherd's life for his fellow-citizens at home in Syracuse. Any coarseness or moral infractions in his idylls are merely the proofs of his shepherds' authenticity, their naive ignorance of better standards. Virgil, in contrast, becomes the repository of all those devices and allegorical concerns that the modern idyll under the influence of sentimental nature can no longer accept. As a result the process of transmuting the pastoral genre into the idyllic mode has as a corollary the removal of Virgil from the bucolic canon and, as the late medieval and early modern pastoral tradition stands so squarely in the Virgilian sphere, a farewell to it as a viable option for the literary imagination.

If we may assert that the ancient bucolic in almost every way contradicts the prevailing eighteenth-century opinions about the pastoral, we should also recognize that it does contain much that the eighteenth century can and does make use of. For the sake of clarity some remarks on the poems of Theocritus and Virgil are advisable. It is not my intention in any way to do justice to these poems, but to characterize them in a way that gives some sense of their complex nature as well as of those features that are most attractive to the eighteenth century, and by the same token most problematic for it.

Stripped to its most basic generic features, pastoral consists of songs sung by shepherds, either individually or in a contest, called amœbean because one song responds to the previous one and, by bettering it, wins the competition and the prize. The topic of the songs is most often love, but not happy, requited love. Love in the ancient pastoral is not merely unrequited but a disorder of the passions and harmful to the balance of one's mind. Another common topic is the dirge or lament for a dead shepherd, who is frequently hailed as a great singer. This is somewhat misleadingly called in English the pastoral elegy. The greatest legendary shepherd singer is Daphnis and the tutelary god is Pan, for his invention of the syrinx or Pan pipe, the shepherd's instrument. Very frequently the singing shepherds are introduced by a frame device, which offers the poet enormous scope for subtle and sophisticated commentary. The distancing device of the frame greatly increases the depth and complexity of the pastoral. The eighteenth century directs its animus against it if the poet indulges himself and introduces a comment or tone that does anything more than introduce the pastoral's characters in a straightforward fashion.

The precise origins of the pastoral are obscure, and what moved the refined Alexandrian poet Theocritus to adopt the shepherd as his mouthpiece is unknown. Shepherds do play music and sing songs, but the Theocritean shepherd stands for the office of the poet, and his inset song, as well as the idyll itself, incorporates a vast amount of recherché literary allusion. The pleasure for the reader lies in having the wit to recognize it and to relish its cleverness. The bucolic idyll also provides Theocritus with an opportunity for serious comment on the literary issues of his day, yet it does so in a situation that is inherently comic or ironic. One source of the idyll's piquancy stems from the transposition of the urban literary elite's preoccupations into the countryside, the home of the bumpkin. The scope for spoof and satire, not just of the literary sort but also of the social variety, is considerable, and Theocritus is not slow to take advantage of it. The realism of the *Idylls* partially results from this comic intent.[18] For something to be found amusing, it must incorporate a strong element from everyday life. Theocritus does not however directly take as his theme within the bucolic idyll the split between town and country so much as he draws on his readers' expectations about this divide. It allows him to flatter their expectations of the crude, credulous, and sexually undisciplined ignoramus, but also to puncture their sophistication by transferring to the mouths of the rustics behaviors and attitudes that the sophisticated urbanite will recognize as his own. Very often within the scope of one bucolic idyll, Theocritus with consummate skill presents a medley of these different features, with the result that his poems become highly literate and demanding works. They are meant to be read and reread — or rather recited and recited again — in order to appreciate their various levels.

What precisely was associated with the name of Theocritus in antiquity is as unclear as is what was meant by bucolic. Nonetheless, when Virgil invokes the "Sicilian muses" in the proemium of the fourth eclogue, he voices the common belief that bucolics were first cultivated on that island and that Theocritus was the first to raise this pastoral song to the level of poetry. Theocritus was a native of Sicily; his *Idyll* 17, a panegyric to Ptolemy Philadelphus, the ruler of Egypt, places him in the first third of the third century B.C.[19] The corpus of the works attributed to Theocritus consists of thirty idylls, a few fragments, twenty-seven epigrams, and one stunt poem written in the shape of the Pan pipe and therefore called "Syrinx." His fame rests on his idylls, which Virgil most likely knew from the edition of bucolic works that Artimedorous is thought to have collected around the time of Virgil's birth.[20] The volume apparently did not contain only the bucolic idylls of Theocritus but also those of other Greek poets. Which poems of Theocritus found their way into this volume is unclear as one cannot now tell what the first century B.C. attributed to him. Virgil himself produced a book of ten eclogues, and Servius's dictum about Theocritus's idylls confirms it as the canonical number: *eclogae merae rusticae decem* (there are ten purely rustic eclogues). The difficulty with this is that Theocritus wrote more than ten idylls. If one adheres rigorously to *Epigram* 26, which is thought to have served as an introduction to Artimedorous's volume, which states that only the bucolic muses are to be gathered into the "flock," then to fill the measure one must include some poems that are thought to be spurious as well as one that is nonbucolic, though rural. To complicate the matter further: Virgil shows no knowledge of the rural tenth idyll but he does show knowledge in *Eclogue* 8 of Theocritus's non-bucolic second idyll. In short, the collection of poems Virgil took for his model was not narrowly bucolic in character.

Apart from the charm of the pastoral subject matter itself, the reader's enjoyment of the poems will in larger part depend upon his recognition of the manner in which Theocritus plays with his literary expectations.[21] Theocritus writes his idylls in dactylic hexameter, the meter of epic, and readily familiar to the Hellenistic reader from the poems of Homer and Hesiod. Yet he handles his meter so that it is dactylic hexameter, but nonepic. His hexameter also uses not the customary Ionic dialect, but the nonliterary Doric dialect.[22] He attempts to encompass in it the rhythm of song, for which task a lyric meter might be expected.[23] He even stretches it to include mime, a subspecies of drama and a further tweaking of his audience's expectations. And finally, the hexameter is the meter for recounting the deeds of mythical heroes, men better than those of today, a class into which herdsman and slaves do not easily fit. Nonetheless, Theocritus's poets-shepherds, if not themselves of heroic status, "know their Homer," as Dover puts it.[24] The gap between the literary oughtto-be of epic convention and the often all too non-heroic characters of the bucolic idylls with their trivial concerns is comic or ironic in origin. It also, if it is to be appreciated to the full, depends on an audience well versed in the literary tradition so gently and variously deployed.

Theocritus's language is of a piece with his metrical complexity. Doric, in particular the dialects from western Greater Greece, is not a literary dialect. Although the Spartan Alcman wrote some lyric poetry in the sixth century B.C., Doric ceases to be a literary idiom with the retirement of Sparta from the field of the arts. It comes to be regarded as provincial and unrefined (an attitude Theocritus calls attention to in *Id*. 15.) Theocritus's Doric, however, is not the language of the street, nor for that matter of the pasture. It is not in fact spoken anywhere at any time. He fashions an amalgam of Doric forms from various localities and times, with an admixture of epic language, recondite words, and even Aeolic.[25] Theocritus creates his own artificial speech, intended to be appreciated as such by an audience aware of these facts and of his daring. In his use of Doric, Theocritus conforms to the norms of Hellenistic poetics; he strives for novel words, twists of expression: in short, a highly literate language.

We may look more closely at two idylls, the first, the lament for Daphnis, and the eleventh, the Plaints of Polyphemus the Cyclops, for some sense of how Theocritus handles his themes. The Polyphemus idyll is of particular relevance because of its later appearance in Goethe's idyll, "Alexis und Dora." The first idyll opens by setting the scene, a *locus amoenus:* two herdsmen meet in the noonday heat, seek out shade from the heat, a bit of water to refresh themselves, and one, unnamed, asks the other, Thyrsis, for a song; all very bucolic. He pleads with Thyrsis to sing the tale of the legendary Daphnis's last suffering, in return for which he promises to give him a cup, whose elaborate decoration he describes at length. It could be anywhere, but to judge from Thyrsis's song, the idyll seems to be set in Sicily. Thrysis announces at the beginning of his song that he is Thyrsis of Etna (*Id*. 1. 65), and with local patriotism admonishes the nymphs for being absent in far-off Greece while Daphnis, the local pastoral hero of Sicily, lay dying. Yet just previously in praising his cup the goatherd mentioned that he bought it from the ferryman from Calydna (*Id*. 1. 57). Calydna refers, most likely, to the island in the Aegean just off Cos (where, it is concluded from remarks such as these, Theocritus must have been living when he wrote many of the bucolic idylls). What a simple goatherd from Cos should be doing in the westernmost part of Greece, or alternatively, if he is in Cos, what Thyrsis of Etna should be doing so far from Sicily are matters of some speculative difficulty. This is particularly so if one insists that "authenticity" is the aim of Theocritus. Such details as these do not allow the reader to suppose that the idyll is intended solely to furnish him with a sample of a shepherd's pastime. Rather the details of the setting summon to mind the image of a general pastoral scene with sufficient local color to seem plausibly somewhere but, nevertheless, nowhere exactly.

And similarly the display on the part of each herdsman of greater learning than is customary in an untutored rustic leaves their status as simple herdsmen somewhat suspect. Thyrsis refers to Mount Pindus in Thessaly and even, with a circumlocution, to the poetic vale of Tempe, in addition to the more expected localities in Sicily (*Id.* 1. 67). Thyrsis also demonstrates considerable mythical learning to complement his unusual geographic knowledge. He alludes to Aphrodite's wounding at the hand of Diomedes in Homer, when he has his Daphnis taunt Aphrodite by telling her to go and challenge Diomedes to a second bout and to be sure to announce herself with the boast that she is the victor over Daphnis (*Id.* 1. 112–13). The goatherd too makes literary allusions, though in his case he may be unaware of them himself. In addition to establishing ekphrasis as an obligatory part of the bucolic repertory, his lengthy description of the cup (*Id.* 1. 27–61) is also reminiscent of the ekphrasis of Achilles shield in the *Iliad*, of the shield of Hercules in the Homeric hymn of the same name, while Theocritus's word for the cup (*Id.* 1. 27) itself comes from the *Odyssey*.[26] The three individual scenes on the cup add a further level to the idyll. They may be interpreted both by their implication in the themes of the idyll and also by their comment on the literary tradition.[27] Once again Theocritus does not suppose these inconsistencies will escape the listener. In fact to refer to them as inconsistencies misleads, since they only become inconsistencies on the assumption that the bucolic genre is simple and naive. The deliberate incongruities of setting and character, while foiling any wish to conceive of the place or person as "real" through the introduction of lyrical and mythical aspects, do not have the effect of transposing the bucolic from some approximate here and now to the dream landscape of the imagination, as does the curious mixture of historical and mythical, familiar and unfamiliar in Virgil.[28] Theocritus's bucolic idyll does not offer an idealized or sentimental account of the pastoral life of shepherds. It is essentially a literary construct, which seeks to please on account of, not despite of, its literariness. Its appeal rests on the discrepancy between the figures who appear in the idylls and the complex of literary and social motifs, forms, and conventions that Theocritus uses in the poems. The bucolic element in them — the *locus amoenus*, the singing contests, the pursuit of love — is only the foil for the literary taste of the audience. A largely ironic or comic mood dominates the mood of their composition, that is to say, a temperament that delights in drawing attention to the discrepancy between appearances and expectations.

Equally refined and sophisticated is Theocritus's treatment of love. In Thyrsis's song about Daphnis, the shepherd begins in a grand manner by using an extended example of pathetic fallacy; all nature grieves at Daphnis's impending death: the wild animals in their lairs, the beasts of the herds, as well as such un-Sicilian and unpastoral animals as jackals and lions. Even the gods themselves visit him, as do other shepherds and goatherds. Theocritus succeeds in elevating Daphnis's pining and injecting some noble pathos into it, which he then immediately punctures in a good example of sinking poetry. The urgency of Daphnis's pining is said to be like the desire of the goatherd engendered by watching the promiscuous behavior of his goats. The source of Daphnis's affliction appears only elliptically, as if the audience should already be familiar with it. It is a favorite tactic of the Alexandrian poet, though deeply annoying to the readers of a later age. Still if one follows Priapus's suggestion that he may at any time end his suffering simply by yielding to any of the many woman who favor him (*Id*. 1. 81–83), we can conclude that his pining is self-imposed. It seems that chastity, not love, is the ideal of Daphnis.[29] Cypris arrives smiling fondly and departs miffed, rightly angered when Daphnis scorns her honor by holding to his pledge, even though he is beaten. They spend their time trading insults, at the end of which exchange Daphnis bids the world adieu and calls on Pan himself to take note and all of nature to invert its natural order. This concluding example of the pathetic fallacy has the opposite effect of the initial one. It is bathetic rather than sublime, the delusion of the proud fool who refuses to acknowledge love's ineluctable power.

One might suppose the fate of those who do yield to love's power to be more appealing; it is not. In *Idyll* 11, the frame opens with one Nikias, a most unpastoral doctor, who is informed that, if the physic's medicine will not remedy love's afflictions, poetry will. However, the kind of consolation to be gleaned from the idyll's tale about the love-sick cyclops is rather cold comfort. Polyphemus has been so smitten by the Nereid Galateia that he neglects his flocks and moons after her. She remains resolutely deaf to his pleas. In his song Polyphemus enumerates his charms. He has a nice bushy eyebrow that runs from one side of his face to the other and beneath it one large saucer-like eye, and, if a silly young girl should be impervious to these delights, he can also offer her his great wealth in flocks and such like. His song might not move Galateia, but Polyphemus persists in singing it until at least he is moved by it.

In view of the importance of physical beauty and youth to the Greeks — Achilles was not merely the greatest hero to go to Troy, he was also the fairest hero — there could hardly be a more inappropriate lover than a cyclops. Polyphemus is a hapless and comical figure. If we strip him of his mythical character, then we have any individual for whom indulgence in the hopes of love are vain, even inappropriate, but who nonetheless is helpless before love's power. It may be one physically ill-favored or, if we pursue the suggestion of purchasing the love of a young woman with wealth and status, then perhaps it is a middle-aged lover, whose youth is past and whose chest time and gravity have moved down a foot or two, but who nonetheless flatters himself that he is attractive to the young and, perhaps with more acumen, also woos with the promise of wealth. Polyphemus's tale and his remedy, to persist in singing a song that simply gratifies his self-delusion, are unlikely to give much comfort to Nikias. He will learn that love will strike the most unlikely individuals, that they will succumb to its delusions, and that the best palliative is to flatter them. Theocritus's depiction of love is consistent with Virgil's. The power of Eros is unavoidable. Eros afflicts and disorders the passions and unbalances the mind.

Many of the points made about Theocritus's bucolic *Idylls* also apply to the *Eclogues* of Virgil. The aim here, however, must be to point out their differences, to stress the innovations Virgil introduces that later come to define the genre and, consequently, the thinking of later ages. Virgil turned to the pastoral some two centuries after Theocritus and was the first Latin poet to do so. The ten eclogues Virgil wrote between 42 B.C., and 37 B.C. and published together as a book all contain references, borrowings, and reworkings of Theocritus, with the proviso: the later the eclogue, the freer and more daring Virgil's treatment of his predecessor.[30] Many of the changes Virgil introduces are cumulative. They come about as the result of seizing on a trait in Theocritus's *Idylls*, enlarging it, and investing it with such significance that it becomes something new with a different purpose in his poems. Good examples of this are the transformation of the pastoral landscape into Arcadia, the explicit juxtaposition of town and country within the poems, and the extension of the bucolic masque or metaphor. Other changes are more readily apparent, and easily totted up, such as the explicitly political nature of the eclogues known as Roman in recognition of this trait, *Eclogues* 1, 4, and 9. The addition of the prophetic voice in *Eclogue* 4 also adds an entirely new register to the bucolic genre, a voice that corresponds to the new theme of the golden age, which it likewise introduces to the bucolic. These changes become distinctive of the genre and retain their appeal to writers and thinkers in the eighteenth century. To these eclogues we should also add the sixth. It contains a creation story and a medley of myths about pathological love. It and the previous three are the problematic eclogues. Problematic because Virgil appears not merely to bend the rules of the genre but so to overstep their limits that he explodes them. These poems return time and again in comment and imitation. They are at once deeply attractive and highly repugnant. The features on which this ambivalent reaction most often focuses are Arcadia and love, the golden age and nature, the pastoral style, and the use of the bucolic masque or metaphor to introduce historical personages as well as topical social and political themes.

Virgil, no less than Theocritus, confuses place and time, past and present, mythic and real, poet and shepherd. The difference is that Virgil recognized this confusion, bundled up the various strands and gave his creation a name, Arcadia.[31] The giving of a name facilitates the process by which the impulse at work in the genre becomes an idea. The motifs of town and country, the bucolic metaphor, and the golden age, they all, though firmly rooted in the bucolic soil, come increasingly to revolve around different aspects of the social and political order. The imaginative realm of Arcadia aids this transformation by allowing a starker delineation of a poetic landscape whose clarity becomes more perceptible to one who senses his own world to be in conflict with it. For Theocritus, an "Arcadian" illusion does not exist; the pastoral setting serves as the backdrop that throws into relief his literary and satiric concerns. For Virgil, Arcadia gains a limited independence through the tension with historical and political circumstances; it becomes a distinct and recognizable space in and for the poetic imagination. Nature figures strongly in it, but it has no independence from the human and divine community. Nor does Arcadia obtain a vicarious independence through the private individual's emotion since he is a social being who acquires character and individuality in the Virgilian world only through his other social relations. Nonetheless, the very suggestive looseness and complexity of the Virgilian bucolic will allow the early modern poets to turn the pastoral to various ends and develop elements of its thematic mixture. Arcadia gradually becomes more defined and crystallizes, taking on a recognizable form. Equally, as something fixed, it gains in familiarity and settles more easily into tropes.

Surprisingly, for a land of such immense power in modern times, Arcadia's presence in the *Eclogues* is very modest.[32] It appears as a passing or incidental detail in three eclogues (4. 58–59; 7. 4, and 8. 21–61) but only takes a more central role in the last eclogue, the tenth, in which Virgil bids explicit farewell to the pastoral world: *Extremum hunc, Arethusa, mihi concede laborem* (*Ec.* 10. 1; One task, my last, I pray you to favour me in, Arethusa; 44).[33] Only in this eclogue does Arcadia emerge unmistakably as an imaginary and poetic space, yoked to the pursuit of love. The setting of the eclogue in Arcadia adds materially to the pathos of the love of its main figure, C. Cornelius Gallus. Gallus, a historical figure, an elegiac poet and soldier, wanders about Arcadia, seeking to find there an antidote to his mad love for a mistress who has jilted him. All the resources of Arcadia are called upon to soothe him: as in Theocritus's *Idyll* 1, the land weeps at the hero's plight, the animals take note of it, the shepherds inquire of him, as do the gods (Apollo, Silvanus, and Pan, the *deus Arcadiae, Ec.* 10. 26; the "god of Arcady"; 44). Gallus's wishes make explicit the ideal character the Arcadian life has assumed. He wishes he were a simple shepherd that he might enjoy the untroubled rhythm of pastoral labor and love. At the same time he also recognizes that he does not and cannot inhabit this world, and so bids it farewell to return to the Roman present.

Central to Arcadia is the complicated reflection on emotion conducted in the eclogue. It contains the famous phrase, *Amor uincit omnia* (*Ec.* 10. 69; Love conquers all), the leitmotif of the *Eclogues*. The attributes of this love, in keeping with the ancient notion of love as a disease of the emotions, are *crudelis* (*Ec.* 10. 29; "cruelty"), *insanus* (*Ec.* 10. 44; "madness"), unconcern for the affliction it causes (*Ec.* 10. 28), and of course omnipotence; all must succumb to it (*Ec.* 10. 69). Emotional need, *Amor*, creates the space of Arcadia and Gallus's yearning to inhabit that land. It also puts Arcadia safely elsewhere and elsewhen, in a time and a place where gods, men, and nature mingle together. It creates a world desirable exactly because it is not subject to the pressures of life as we experience it. The expression of this need is thus elegiac and contains the knowledge that by voicing the emotion, by raising it from the level of immediate feeling to an object of reflection, it tempers love's consuming madness and prepares the lover for his failure to gain the undisturbed enjoyment of his love, the same notion more jocularly employed by Theocritus in *Idyll* 11. The feeling, though not expurgated through its expression, is rendered less fervid, more bearable. Arcadia remains the land to which the lover would return. The poetic reflection indulges and soothes it. Love remains *crudelis Amor* and still conquers all, making fools of its victims in the process. The eclogue recognizes and presents with some sympathy the power of this emotional longing, but there is neither the sense nor expectation that its gratification is essential to the individual. Virgil will later repeat his Arcadian farewell much more severely in the Dido and Aeneas episode of his epic. One may readily be inclined to characterize this mode of feeling as "romantic" or "sentimental" in the modern sense of those words. Such a designation is not inaccurate insofar as it accentuates the proximity of the Virgilian mode of feeling to a modern one. To the degree that it obscures the distance between the two, it misleads. The core of the Virgilian individual does not lie within the individual's emotional life and the subjective perspective it affords.[34] In the *Eclogues* questions of order in the human and poetic world look to the political sphere. Without this order neither rural peace nor poetic pursuits seem feasible to the poet of the *Eclogues*.[35] Human sentiment may entertain a deep desire for a more direct satisfaction, but it can only mature and find expression within the larger human community, which for Virgil is always political, even if this community is a problematic one. There is no conception of a world of nature, constructed according to the desires of the heart, that exists in opposition to the political order of civilization. Virgil's Gallus must leave Arcadia.[36]

This is the side of the eclogue capable of sentimental expansion; the side, however, that disturbs, and is therefore often neglected, is the self-conscious artificiality of the eclogue.[37] The premise of the poem is comic and absurd: that Gallus, a man of the world, himself a poet of love elegies, should become so besotted not with some coy young shepherd lass, but with a lady accustomed to entertaining Roman gentlemen, that he pursues her to the ends of the earth. Although inherently ironic, the eclogue escapes being purely so through the poignancy of the evocation. The details of the poem — the imitation of *Idyll* 1, the introduction of mythic and historical figures — make the irony clear. They make the mythic quality of Arcadia a transparent fiction even as Gallus in his song points out and takes leave from, perhaps, the most appealing feature of this land, its echoing woods. They are the symbol of the pastoral Arcadia familiar from the first eclogue: *resonare doces Amaryllida siluas* (*Ec.* 1. 5; you can . . . teach the woods to repeat "Fair Amaryllis"; 9). There nature seems most congenial to the fortunate shepherd: he is at home in it, and both are united in the song of poetry. In the tenth eclogue the *siluae* make repeated appeals on Arcadia's behalf. They suck up the song of the bucolic poet, *non canimus surdis, respondent omnia siluae* (*Ec.* 10. 8; Not to deaf ears I sing, for the woods echo my song; 44). Briefly Gallus allows himself to think he passes among the *lucos sonantis* (*Ec.* 10. 58; the sounding groves), but soon bids these woods depart: *ipsae rursus concedite siluae* (*Ec.* 10. 63; Again be gone, you woods).[38] By doing so he acknowledges the emotional need to imagine an idyllic world corresponding to the aspirations of the heart at the same time as he also denies that it has more than poetic truth. In the end, Arcadia is neither a geographical nor a historical place, but an emotional one that dwells in the poetic imagination, and one that is deliberately pointed out as such within the eclogue itself.

The golden age, the *aurea aetas*, is the second theme closely connected to the pastoral, and it too has a far from unambiguous presence in the *Eclogues*. It appears in the problematic fourth eclogue and is announced by the phrase, *paulo maiora canamus* (*Ec.* 4. 1; I would now try a somewhat grander theme; 23), an admission that recognizes an outer limit to the bucolic, yet one that remains visible within the pastoral horizon. Exactly how far the horizon extends for Virgil remains unclear, though it does include the majestic prophecy of the golden age. The golden age will be a return of the *Saturnia regna* (*Ec.* 4. 6; the Saturnian Age)[39] and of Virgo, the embodiment of justice. Its advent will begin with the birth of a child, whose progression through infancy to manhood will match the progressive strengthening of the golden age's hold over the world. At first nature will only be slightly more amenable to the wants of man; the virtue of heroes will still find employment, as will labor itself. In the end the necessity for these endeavors will vanish as will even the need for commerce and agriculture. The initial relation of this world to the state is indicated in v. 17, *pacatumque rege patriis uirtutibus orbem* (and rule a world made peaceful by his father's virtuous acts; 23). The golden age does not arise in opposition to civilization but derives from it as its highest accomplishment and, more particularly, from the exercise of those arts for which Rome was famed: the art of making war and the art of governing. The relation of the state, however, to the full-fledged golden age is less clearly ascertainable. The absence of the necessity of work, of the need for defense, or of any reason compelling one individual to associate himself with another, points to the withering and dissolution of civilization. All these blessings will accrue as the golden child grows up. The poem ends with a return to the beginning of the process with the auspicious image of mother and her smiling infant.

The notion of the golden age is one that will have immense resonance in the later bucolic tradition, but it is not one that Virgil either develops fully here or associates particularly firmly with Arcadia.[40] Nonetheless, to give some sense to the notion of an "Arcadian" golden age it is helpful to combine it with Gallus's Arcadia. It is a world in which nature is amenable to human wants, where the pursuit of love and song are the main employments, and one that derives from political action, not the solitary undertaking of the individual. The eighteenth century finds this golden age less than entirely appealing: the love it advocates cannot even by euphemism be called virtuous, nor can what is secured by the state possibly be the birthright of the individual. Much more to the eighteenth century's liking is the golden age contained in Virgil's second set of poems, the *Georgics*. The Georgic golden age has a much more marked moral character, which appeals in a number of ways. The golden age of the eighteenth century contains elements of the pastoral golden age and the Georgic golden age, a conflation that eventually results in poems that exhibit features of both.

The leitmotif of the *Georgics* is *labor omnia uincit* (*Ge.* 1. 145; work conquers all). The set of four didactic poems deals with the role of work in human society, of hard toil and bitter want, of *labor improbus et urgens egestas* (*Ge.* 1. 146). These are the means by which humans participate in the divine order of the cosmos. The reason for the introduction of want and work and the end of Saturn's benign reign is not given, only that Jove so willed it (*Ge.* 1. 121–22). It is not this labor, nor the nature of the present that all too often fails to reward the farmer's backbreaking toil that find later acceptance. Accordingly the *Georgics* are only really read in excerpts with the passages that tell of a benign, smiling nature finding a wide audience. These are concentrated in book 2, which contains the three celebrated Praises: of Italy, Spring, and the Country Life. The idea of the golden age is finally made more precise, moving from the indeterminacy of a general, preceding age to the history, albeit mythic history, of a particular people, who may on that account be presumed to retain an affinity, if not responsibility, for it. Italy, we learn, was the last refuge of Saturn after his deposition by Jove (*Ge.* 2. 173 and 538). And here, among these people, we must look for the last traces of Justitia, Saturn's companion. Not the city dweller, but the country man, the rustic, retains by virtue of the rhythm of labor, ritual, and leisure a natural habit of virtue lost to the inhabitant of the city. The restraints this life imposes upon him keep him from desiring the luxury of the city, and make him delight in the simple pleasures of his life, such as the lowing of the cattle, repose beneath a tree, the rituals of the deities, and the *sancti patres* (*Ge.* 2. 473; reverend age; 322).[41] Honest labor, not base cupidity, has its reward: the possession of tangible wealth (herds, not gold) and provision for his little ones, the *parui nepotes*

(*Ge.* 2. 514; the little grandchildren; 322) and for the community, the *patria* (*Ge.* 2. 515; the native land; 322). In this hymn to the Georgic life, the earlier Saturnian Age is contaminated by the need for work. Yet the individual still enjoys a serene life, within the institutions of the family and *patria* that make communal and individual life possible.

This view of the Georgic life does not oppose the impositions of civilization against a life free of those cares, as was so notably the case in the golden age of the fourth eclogue. Now the comparison is the two modes of communal life, one urban and one rural. And further, both with a concrete history represented in the history of the Latin people and Rome. The city is a nest of rapacity, ambition, ostentation, mindless folly, and ultimately of those who *gaudent perfusi sanguine fratum* (*Ge.* 2. 510; "joyfully . . . steep themselves in the blood of their brethren; 322). Knowledge of urban life, however, forms the prerequisite for the disaffected who wish to discern the worth of rural existence. Therefore Virgil's view of the country from the city is an idealized, perhaps sentimental one, in Schiller's sense of the word, and one that lends itself to a "bürgerlich" turn — provided, of course, that much else can be ignored:

> *interea dulces pendent circum oscula nati,*
> *casta pudicitiam seruat domus, ubera uaccae*
> *lactae demittunt.* (*Ge.* 2. 523–25)

[Meanwhile sweet children cling round his kisses, the home abides in sacred purity, the kine droop their milky udders. (322)]

The reverse side of this coin, which Virgil also mentions, is that only harsh experience engenders in the urbanite the recognition of the country's merit, just as only ignorance of the urban life succors the rustic: *O fortunatos nimium, sua si bona norint, agricolas!* (*Ge.* 2, 458–59; Ah too fortunate the husbandmen, did they know their own felicity! 320). To point the contrast: the rustic must be "naive" to preserve virtue, but the wise urbanite must exercise profound self-knowledge to regain it. However, the two forms of communal life turn out to be related because they are capable of reconciliation. Happiness is attainable for both the reformed city dweller, who is the philosopher, and the countryman. Virgil calls the one *felix* (*Ge.* 2. 490; happy; 321) and the other *fortunatus* (*Ge.* 2. 494; blessed; 321) a parity insisted on by the following *et ille* (*Ge.* 2. 494; yet he no less; 321). The two are not ultimately opposed as they come to be for such as Werther, in whom sentimental awareness cannot bridge the gap to the naive.

The Georgic elements that appeal to the writers and thinkers of the eighteenth century are the idea of a love, monogamous, chaste, and resulting in the family and in the smaller human community of the village; a nature that invites and rewards work; and also very much the moralizing effect of work in establishing and sustaining the relation to nature and the rhythms of daily, social life. The notion of the establishment of a harmony between the individual and nature, between the individual and the family through work also carries strong religious overtones for the Enlightenment. We may recollect that Robinson Crusoe transforms the wild island on which he is cast into a garden through labor, while he rescues the fallen Adam — who is then redeemed through educative work — Friday, that is, on the day of the death of the second Adam.

The final aspect of the *Eclogues*, a source of delight to the early modern period, but one of vexation to the theorists of the Enlightenment, is Virgil's use of the bucolic masque or metaphor. With the notable exception of the seventh idyll, Theocritus kept the contrast between town and country implicit. Virgil on the other hand delights rather in making it explicit, by presenting it as a theme directly within the pastoral in many ways. The most important of these is the simple broadening of the significance of the town to the city. The city, the polis, is the site of the cults that sustain the community, the seat of government, and, through metonymy, the state. This aspect is grafted onto the bucolic in *Eclogue* 1. Virgil uses the rustic Tityrus's ignorant wonder at the city to introduce the subject of Rome and the youthful Augustus as the young "god," whose majesty restores order and tranquillity to Tityrus's pastoral world. While remaining within the bucolic sphere, the order of the pastoral life is shown to exist within a larger framework on which it is dependent. The partiality of this order also becomes clear; the other shepherd in the eclogue, Meliboeus, deprived of his land, must continue his uncertain trek to a foreign country. Friedrich Klingner describes the result of this shift thus: "So wandelt sich eine hellenistische Gattung in etwas sehr Römisches um, indem die an sich geschichtslose Welt ihre Verbindung mit der geschichtlichen Wirklichkeit Roms findet."[42] The novelty was not the presence of the larger society; that was always implicit in the division town/country. The novelty is the tone and the bluntness of the intrusion. The distance between town and country no longer furnishes a source of amusement. It has become a serious topic of reflection within the bucolic horizon. However we may view the introduction of the political order into the *Eclogues* — whether as a foreign intrusion into the pastoral sphere by fate from without, or the coincidence of Virgil's expansion of the bucolic's loose structure and his own misfortune — a further source for the association of literature and politics can be found in the historical personages Virgil includes in his poems.

The habit so prevalent in Virgil of inserting historical figures directly into the pastoral is again one traceable to Theocritus: for instance the physician Nikias of *Idyll* 11, or the poets thinly disguised beneath shepherds' garb in *Idyll* 7. Who these people are and how widespread the use of allusion and mask are in the bucolic *Idylls* cannot now be determined, although Gow's remark on *Idyll* 7 — "One has the impression that in more than one place some point is made to which the clue is lost, and that as a whole the Idyll had more meaning for T.'s contemporaries than it has for us" — is one that applies equally to other idylls.[43] In Virgil, the examples of this simply grow more numerous, or rather, we have many more of the clues and are able to decipher many more of the allusions. In addition to mentioning or addressing many poets, Virgil's figures are often also political figures, which again has the effect of reinforcing and complicating the relation of the pastoral to the larger world of the state. It makes little difference whether such figures occur as merely the addressees in the frame, such as Pollio in the fourth and Varus in the sixth, or whether they become actors in the eclogue more directly, such as Gallus in the tenth.

Virgil will often overlay many such elements at once so that they seem too openly to burst the bounds of the pastoral. Particularly egregious in this regard is the sixth eclogue, one of the problematic eclogues. It has two frames. In the first, the poet inserts himself directly into the figure of the shepherd to say that, though he would rather sing of battles and kings, that is of epic, the poet's divine patron Apollo commands him to sing of shepherds as befits a shepherd singer. This he offers to the consul Varus as an explanation of why he cannot sing of Varus's triumphs, presenting him instead with a bucolic. No comment is offered on the incongruity of a shepherd familiar both with a figure from the highest level of the state and with the literary distinctions between his song and epic, yet both are presented within the pastoral song. The poet then proceeds to offer an eclogue filled initially with Epicurean doctrines about the creation of the world and then a medley of mythological stories, related with incredible brevity. And to complete the matter he also introduces Gallus into this landscape.[44] Whether the frame was in fact written to placate a demanding patron, or but a clever device to insist on the poem's bucolic credentials (or some combination of both), the mood of the creation story is of such elevation that it would be easy to mistake the poem for something other than a pastoral. The Varus frame openly points to pastoral as a literary construct and places the small world in relation to the large world of epic. The poet complicates matters still further by inserting yet another frame in which the drunken satyr Silenus, caught and bound while he slept, must sing a song for his release. It is from his vulgar mouth that such high sentiments about creation come. More in keeping with his character as a satyr are the mythological tales since, although they all revolve around love, they do so around a distempered love (particularly the story of Pasiphae's desire for a steer). The open and multilayered reflections on what the bucolic is and contains forbid the assumption of a naive, simple existence in nature. The golden age, Arcadia, and love are merely some of the pastoral's themes rather than *the* themes of the pastoral.

The highly reflective nature of the poems, their extremely literary character, the open and playful conceit of the pastoral fiction, the often ironic and comic tone, the layering of multiple themes and allusion, are all traits that make Virgil the Neoteric poet the student of the Hellenistic artist Theocritus. To argue that the conception of artistry differs radically between the two does not seem tenable. These are also the features that ensure that the pastoral remains a vibrant, even exuberant, genre in the modern period up to the Enlightenment. They give it a dynamic capable of adapting to the interests of later writers and readers. They are, however, precisely the features that Werther cannot abide in his idyll. The sentimental subject requires that feeling in its undisturbed state offer proof of its veracity through its consonance with nature. For this purpose the idyll must offer an artistic representation that insists on the reality of this feeling and this nature, and not on its possibly fictional character, nor on any distance of the sentimental subject from it. A Werther, however, is not produced in a day; and he, so far as his lineage can be traced in the pastoral, is rather the product of a century-long deliberation on the pastoral. It is in the theoretical debates in neo-classical France and then in Germany that the ground is laid for the transformation of the ancient bucolic and the early modern pastoral into the sentimental idyll. These debates naturally do not proceed in a straightforward fashion, but they result in the removal from the pastoral of the devices for reflection. In doing so they cut the genre's taproot, render it insipid, and, soon thereafter, defunct.

This is not all that the theoretical deliberations accomplish. To purge the pastoral of its objectionable elements these deliberations must, of course, discuss them; for this reason the debate about the pastoral is often more interesting than the poems themselves. It proceeds through the use of recurrent topics, such as allegory, the problematic eclogues, the proper pastoral style, the status of love and of nature, and the golden age. Allegory is an elastic term that can stretch to include social and political concerns and events in addition to contemporary individuals, all of which disrupt the pleasure in the idyllic representation by pressing the question of its relation to the present, of who the idyll's proper inhabitants are, and the question of the reader's relation to it. The problematic eclogues present numerous difficulties, but especially those of too literary, too elevated a style and poetological, epic reflections that make too transparent the representation's constructed character. They also inevitably bring in their train the question of Arcadia's relation to the larger world and to the present. Love in the ancient bucolic of Theocritus and Virgil is unrequited. It is also very often lusty and on a fair number of occasions homosexual in character. The repeated discussion of love, Arcadia, and the golden age flesh out the new evolving view of nature and life in it while also acting as the measure with which to weigh and remove elements of the pastoral found wanting. What begins with Rapin and Fontenelle in France and passes into Germany with Gottsched and Johann Adolf Schlegel (1721–93), and from there to Heyne and Herder, acquires such a depth, nuance, and intellectual solidity that it would be wrong to say that it misreads the ancient bucolic; rather it retains specific tropes or fragments as talismanic points of reference at the same time as it reshapes them around more contemporary concerns. Throughout the period under consideration here these changes are expressed in the critical judgments rendered on the ancient bucoliasts Virgil and Theocritus. The two poets, who seem to have so many traits in common, become diametrically opposed. Theocritus becomes the champion for the new emerging Greece and, by association, simple, natural, and authentic; Virgil, on the other hand becomes mannered, inept, unpastoral; that is, Latin.

It is the concern for nature and the development of the sentimental subject in relation to it that so radically and progressively alters the sense of the pastoral. In broad strokes we may note three general changes effected with regard to the pastoral. Erwin Panofsky famously observed that in the eighteenth century the understanding of *Et in Arcadia ego* underwent a great change.[45] He traces the phrase's origin to the pictorial tradition, where it appears in the depiction of death in Arcadia, a topic present in the bucolic since antiquity with the laments for dead shepherds (for example, *Idyll* 1 and *Eclogue* 5).[46] It is however somewhat limiting for the sentimental subject wishing to indulge his feeling for a closeness to nature if he translates the *Et in Arcadia ego* as, "I, Death, am here in Arcadia as well," as King George III correctly does.[47] It is much more gratifying for the conviction that one's inward emotional condition still recollects an intimation of humanity's true estate in nature if the phrase is translated as Dr. Johnson translates it, "I too am/was once in that fair state of Arcadia."

The second and allied change is in the treatment of love. Virgil's Amor, indeed that of Theocritus as well, is *crudelis* (*Ec.* 10. 29) or *insanus* (*Ec.* 10. 44) and it is the love that conquers all. The adjectives "cruel" and "mad" are increasingly suppressed in the understanding of love so that what remains is love fulfilled. The difference on this score between the modern and the ancient pastoral is quite striking. In Virgil there is not one instance of an unequivocal success.[48] While shepherds complaining of obdurate lovers bulk large in the modern pastoral (for instance the pair of poems, "The Passionate Shepherd to His Love" by Marlowe and the reply by Raleigh, "The Nymph's Reply to the Shepherd"), the concern for requited love is also present, as in Guarini's *Il Pastor fido*. This tendency becomes the almost exclusive bias of the German idyll in the eighteenth century. Dalliance and coquetry recede to become, if present, cloyingly cute. Love is increasingly a chaste courtship, followed by the inevitable marriage. Voss's *Luise* and Goethe's *Hermann und Dorothea* end in marriage and betrothal respectively. The desire of the sentimental heart to have its fondest occupation at home in nature leaves little room for love of any other sort.

The final change comes from the joining together of the state of nature as a historical age of humanity's development and the psychological present of the sentimental individual. The pastoral as the first form of poetry is regarded both as the nearest historical record of the age when humanity was deemed either still to have lived in or just to have emerged from the state of nature and also as a vehicle for the contemporary individual to confirm that in his feeling before nature there is still a vestige of that original golden era. The need to draw the past into the present promotes the conflation of the mythic Arcadian golden age with the more real Georgic golden age, with the emphasis increasingly on the latter. The shepherd no longer appears as a solitary individual but is increasingly placed within the fold of the family and of work. The smallest human community, the village, takes up more space in the pastoral world. Arcadia loses its obviously dream-like unreality in favor of approaching the here and now of the village. The realism the pastoral world acquires, such as it is, is a psychological realism. It is the work of such as Werther, who insist on finding in the world about them reminiscences of humanity's original condition and, through the demonstration of their own sensitivity to it, its continued existence in themselves.

"Ancients" and "Moderns": Binding the Pastoral to Theocritus and Virgil

In 1659, Rapin attached a long theoretical treatise to his sacred eclogues, to which Fontenelle responded with a short elegant essay in 1688. These two texts pruned the previously luxurious growth of the pastoral in prose and verse, in drama and the novel, by making the discussion of the bucolic almost exclusively an examination of Theocritus and Virgil.[49] They helped to promote the vogue for short refined pastoral poems with their own offerings, to which their respective theoretical statements were meant as an introduction. Both were less successful with their poems than with their theories. Much better regarded were the slightly earlier eclogues (1653) of Jean Renaud de Segrais (1624–1701), Virgil's French translator, and Madame Deshoulières's (1638–94) later ones (periodically after 1672).

The opposing views of Rapin and Fontenelle also involve the pastoral in the *Querelle des anciens et des modernes*. "Le moderne" Fontenelle pens a light and airy treatise to confound the fustian learning of his classicizing predecessor. It expresses a strong and original opinion on the subject and excites greater furor among critics. Knightly Chetwood, the author of the preface for the *Eclogues* in Dryden's translation (1697), writes explicitly against Fontenelle: his title reads *Preface to the Pastorals, With a short Defence of Virgil, Against some of the Reflections of Monsieur Fontanelle (sic)*. Likewise Pope is familiar with him in England, and in Germany Gottsched refers to him repeatedly in the section of the *Critische Dichtkunst* devoted to the pastoral. Gottsched's fondness for Fontenelle is ironic since his own views on the eclogue agree on important points not with Fontenelle but with Rapin. Nonetheless, he also translates Fontenelle's essay in 1730, ensuring for his opinions a wide currency in Germany.

Rapin's work, *Eclogae sacrae cum dissertatione de carmine pastorali* has a less direct influence on German pastoral deliberations. Rapin is not only Fontenelle's foil; his views are widely canvassed in England. Chetwood in his refutation of Fontenelle silently makes use of many of Rapin's arguments, only bothering to mention at one point that Rapin has collected many fine specimens from Theocritus and Virgil. Thomas Creech had already translated most of Rapin's treatise into English in 1684. Dryden knew of him in another context, and Pope refers to him in his writings on the pastoral, which he affixes as a preface to his own pastoral poems. From the imprint of Rapin on the English, his ideas came to shape German thinking on the subject, in particular Gottsched's insistence on the pastoral as an imitation of a historically true golden age.[50]

Rapin's treatise presents two main arguments about the pastoral: the first is its relation to the earliest age, the golden age, and the second the relation of poetic style to simplicity. In neither of these arguments is he original; he is merely drawing on elements of the earlier humanist position.[51] Scaliger in his *Poetices libri septem* had proposed that poetry may be considered either according to the "nobility" of its subject matter or according to the antiquity of its origins. He settles on the latter method since in imitation the complex proceeds from the simple. The earliest times are the *mollissimum et simplicissimum et ineptissimum* (the tenderest, simplest, and coarsest).[52] There is nothing of the golden age in Scaliger's historical view of these earliest products of the imagination. Quite the contrary; pastorals do not directly depict this earliest condition. In fact, the greater their proximity to the earliest age, the less worthy they are of critical attention. They require refinement. From the general mass of unwritten bucolic songs, the first winnowing produced with Theocritus a few small pieces called *idullia* on account of their brevity or perhaps also their *modestia* and *humilitas*.[53] The Virgilian eclogue results from a further process of refinement and polishing, hence their name, which means selections.[54] Virgil's poems are at one further remove from the coarse original song than are those of Theocritus, which is to his advantage. Later when Scaliger turns to consider the poems of Virgil and Theocritus in the fifth chapter of book 5, the *Criticus*, the entire comparison will revolve around the question of *decorum*, that is, the correct poetic style. Virgil is everywhere praised as the more learned and elegant, and his poetry esteemed for not being uncouth or low. Stylistic decorum recommends the *poeta doctus*, as moral decorum does the more chaste poem. Time and again one reads that Virgil possesses these desirable traits of decorum so lacking in Theocritus: *argutius et suavius adeo noster, ut nihil supra* (*supra* refers to a citation from

Theocritus that introduces this remark;[55] our poet is so much finer and more delightful, unlike anything above). This process of refinement also permits an easy broadening of the themes of the pastoral beyond the supposedly purely amorous concerns of the original bucolic song. Scaliger even singles out the problematic *Eclogues* 6, 1, 4, and 9 and makes them the final argument for preferring Virgil to Theocritus:

> *Silenum vero et Tityrum, et Pollionem, et Moerim, totas illius esse constat, ita ut nullis locis ad eum Theocritus aspirare posse videatur. Quare pauci, corruptique iudicii, infelicissimae eruditionis Grammatici exuant perditam illam temeritatem, qua professi sunt a Theocrito Maronem superatum.*[56]
>
> [It is agreed that the Silenus, Tityrus, Pollio, and Moeris [*Ecs.* 6, 1, 4, and 9] are wholly his own, so much so that Theocritus seems unable to reach up to him at any point. Let therefore the few critics, defective in their judgment and of a most dismal learning, put aside that mad rashness with which they have avowed Theocritus surpassed Virgil.]

Scaliger does not really offer any arguments for the inclusion of these eclogues in the canon; nor need he, since he does not attempt to develop an idea of the pastoral in relation to which pastorals may be judged. The fact of their existence and the reputation of their author are sufficient grounds for their inclusion as pastorals, an argument that amounts to an appeal to authority.

What is novel in Rapin's criticism is the consistency with which he attempts to apply the historical notion of the earliest age to the pastoral and that of pastoral simplicity to style. It exemplifies the rationalist demand that individual, poetic phenomena adhere to an abstract norm. It allows Rapin to give free reign to systematic and normative impulses. In this regard the pastoral presents a delightful prospect to any theorist of neoclassical or rationalist bent. In the *Eclogues* of the prestigious Virgil, and to a lesser extent the *Idylls* of Theocritus, the critic has poetic examples with an impeccable ancient pedigree. However the canonical poetic arbiters of antiquity, Aristotle and Horace, neglected to lay down the rules for the genre and so left the field open to the modern theorist.[57] Rapin will however follow their model. He derives his premise from Aristotle's dictum that art is an imitation of an action, in this instance the imitation of the shepherd's life. This premise will not however supply him with a method for extrapolating the rules for its composition. This he takes from the Horatian precepts, which he will apply to the canonical materials of Virgil and Theocritus: "So I will gather from *Theocritus* and *Virgil*, those Fathers of *Pastoral*, what I shall deliver on this account" (52; 1:lxxv). For the generation of his normative poetic system Rapin requires only three assumptions: first, the materials to be analyzed, the poems of Theocritus and Virgil; second, the Aristotelian doctrine of the mimesis of an action; and third, a method of analysis that relates the principle to the phenomena, the Horatian concept of decorum.

Rapin finds the life of the shepherd the pastoral imitates to be in the earliest historical age, which he also insists is the golden age. Such an association with the pastoral was not absent from the modern pastoral as, for example, the praise of the golden age from Tasso's *Aminta* shows. Rapin, however, makes it the cornerstone of his conception of the shepherd's life that the pastoral imitates. The golden age becomes a general era of humanity with a strongly moral character and a Christian accent.[58] Rapin cites both pagan myths in which heroes appeared as shepherds and the tales of the patriarchs from the Bible in support of his conclusion that the pastoral as the product of the most ancient and perfect age is to be preferred to the products of all subsequent ages.[59] The pastoral is now so firmly a reflection of the golden age, an age equated with a biblical, nearly prelapsarian state, that pastoral song even takes precedence over epic. As the golden age is to be preferred over the heroic age, so pastorals are to be preferred over epics. Rapin does not dispute the primacy of epic in majesty and loftiness, though he does introduce a but:

> But if the unaffected neatness, elegant, graceful smartness of the expression, or the polite dress of a Poem be considered (*si <spectetur> sermonis ingenuitas, mundities, elegantia, venustas, lepores et quidquid cultus est politioris*), then they fall short of *Pastorals:* for this sort flows with Sweet, Elegant, neat and pleasing fancies; as is too evident to every one that hath tasted the sweeter muses, to need a farther explanation: for 'tis not probable that *Asinius Pollio, Cinna, Varius, Cornelius Gallus,* men of the neatest Wit, and that lived in the most polite Age, or that *August Caesar* the Prince of the *Roman* elegance, as well as of the common Wealth, should be so extreamly taken with *Virgils Bucolicks,* or that *Virgil* himself a man of such singular prudence, and so correct a judgment, should dedicate his Eclogues to those great Persons; unless he had known that there is somewhat more than ordinary Elegance in those sort of Composures, which the wise perceive, tho far above the understanding of the Crowd. (6; 1:xxv)

Though the pastoral age may be the earliest age, the excellence of the pastoral poem rests, on the evidence of this passage, on its capacity to speak the best Horace; Rapin and Scaliger are in agreement on this.

The lack of historical feeling evident to a more modern sensibility in supposing that the most refined of a refined age are on that account best suited to represent the simplest age is a juxtaposition that does not disturb Rapin. The juxtaposition becomes all the more pointed if read in relation to his vision of that simplicity that immediately precedes the passage quoted above:

> For what is that ["the lowly simplicity of a Sheapards Life"] but a perfect image of the state of Innocence, of that golden Age, that blessed time, when Sincerity and Innocence, Peace, Ease, and Plenty inhabited the Plains? Take the Poets description. (5)[60]

Of more interest for the view of Virgil is the fact that of the two quotations Rapin now gives to support his view of the golden age, the first, significantly, is from the *Georgics* (2. 467–71), not the *Eclogues*, while the second is from Horace. It points to the tendency to conflate the *Georgics* and the *Eclogues* through their common interest in a happier age. It illustrates first the increasing Georgic aspect of the golden age, reshaping the more visionary pastoral conception by imparting to it a moral tincture.[61] The only distinction holding them apart is the predominance of *otium*, "leisure," in the one and of *labor*, "work," in the other, a somewhat external distinction if the Georgic concern for the golden age forms the basis for the pastoral. At any rate the representation of the golden age is now firmly *the* task of the bucolic.

The second point about the use of the *Georgics* is that it is introduced to buttress an argument about the historical veracity of the golden age, although this comes to be of secondary importance to the moral quality of the golden age it substantiates. It is axiomatic that the first way of life is shepherding. The importance to Rapin of the notion of the golden age and hence of pastoral poetry as the "true" relic and record of it in fallen times may be judged by the conclusion he draws from his lengthy and learned survey of the origins of pastoral poetry, which is: *In quo assentior Lucretio accuratissimo naturae pervestigatori, qui jam tum ab illa innocentissima, qua florebat aurea aetas, tempestate docet carmen pastorale fuisse in usu* (1:xxxv; And indeed I cannot but agree with *Lucretius* that accurate Searcher into Nature, who delivers that from that state of Innocence the Golden Age, Pastorals continued down to his time; 14). It is not the ostensible origin that is important, but the proximity of pastoral to the age of *simplicitas* and *innocentia*. The historical argument is subordinated to the moral concern, even though the entire issue is cast in the terms of a historical argument. For Rapin, the dogma of the golden age, and of pastoral poetry as its witness, remains a primarily historical argument, inseparably intertwined with his moral and poetological convictions.

The citation of the *Georgics* and of the *Eclogues* involves Rapin's overall undertaking in a further difficulty, as it makes his entire argument somewhat circular. Greek myths and the Bible may substantiate the existence of pastoralists, but they are not themselves pastoral song. To give as examples of such song the products known to be from a much later time, and then to cite evidence from them (if we leave aside for the moment the objection that the *Georgics* are not pastorals) as proof of their authentic ancient character, is flawed. It is a weakness Fontenelle will exploit to the fullest but one that after him the eighteenth century will overlook, although it will prefer to call on Theocritus for proof rather than Virgil. However, exchanging the court of Alexandria for the court of Rome does little to address the logical fallacy.

Rapin's wish to derive his rules for the pastoral from the Virgilian bucolic compels him to argue for their unspotted pastoral authenticity. It allows him to define the pastoral as follows: "From all which we may gather this definition of Pastoral: *It is the imitation of the Action of a Sheapard, or of one taken under that Character*" (19). Having argued so strenuously for the pastoral as the witness of a historical golden age, Rapin now lets the matter drop and concentrates on the second portion of his definition after the "or," when he turns to consider what the style of the pastoral should be. Two points in his remarks on style are of interest for the subsequent tradition: the first concerns his view of the problematic eclogues and the question of allegory, the second more generally the relation of art to nature in the refined style of the pastoral.

The qualification *ad modum pastoralis* (1:xl; in the manner of the shepherd) grants the poet the license to present something other than the life of the golden-age shepherd. He can present something entirely different, provided only that he dresses it up as the action of a shepherd. Rapin's most immediate motive for introducing this precept stems from his wish to allow for the "problematic" Eclogues 1, 6, 9, and 10 (though not 4), as they will sanction his own bucolics, in which shepherds give voice to Christian revelation. The tenth, sixth, first, and ninth can in Rapin's view all be embraced under the concept of the proper insertion of *res arduae* (lofty matters) in the dress of the shepherd. He balks at the fourth: "to declare my opinion freely, I cannot think [it] to be [a] fit Subject for *Bucolick*" (26). Its subject matter is simply too lofty and not sufficiently in the character of the shepherd.[62] Rapin is not interested in the content of the lofty matters, but only in the use of the technique for their insertion. As the sense of what constitutes a lofty topic is undefined it becomes a matter for the discretion of the individual reader. Further, by placing the focus on the poet's skill in having his rustics speak of most unrustic topics, he turns the whole enterprise into essentially one of wit. It also reduces the scope of allegory in the genre as Rapin leaves no theoretical means for the recognition and exploration of the openly fictive and self-reflexive nature of the ancient bucolic. Such matters must be judged by the quality of their concealment. Devices and motifs that too explicitly highlight the literary nature of the ancient bucolic become implicitly infractions, infractions that will appear more grievous the more the reader insists that his shepherds stay in character as true representatives of the golden age.

Rapin's reliance on the Virgilian bucolic for the insertion of lofty matters into the pastoral makes of Virgil the artful bucoliast above all else. Should the reader seek the representation of the simple and "real" shepherd, then Virgil will not likely be the first association that springs to mind. Theocritus will soon be nominated as the poet of this other, more "realistic" shepherd. So long as the authority of the tradition remains uncontested and the norms of rationalistic, neoclassical poetics retain their currency, the position of Virgil is assured, as is his standing relative to Theocritus. Once these conditions no longer obtain — once critics expect to discover a more Georgic shepherd in the pastoral, and once the judgment on how art can be simple changes — then their greatest model, the text of Virgil, loses its currency.

Despite his concern for lofty matters, Rapin once again resorts to a golden age simplicity for the more general derivation of normative stylistic rules for pastorals. He subsumes all formal and thematic diversity under the heading of a golden age style. As the Virgilian bucolic remains for him the definitive expression of this style, his unfailing use of Virgil to illustrate his every point once again succeeds in binding the Virgilian eclogue to questions of simplicity, of the golden age, and of the proper mode of expression. He elevates the pastoral from the low style to a middle style, in which art and nature are deemed to be joined in simplicity, and, through reference to the moral quality of the golden age, he also establishes virtue as an important feature of this simplicity.

Rapin's premise in approaching this problem is that the greatest simplicity comes from the finest polish. In the first two parts of his treatise, he broached the matter above and used such descriptive terms as, "unaffected neatness, elegant, graceful smartness" or "sweet, elegant, neat and pleasing Fancies." These he now explicates at length in the third part. He holds that true simplicity and true artfulness are complementary, not mutually exclusive. Nature without art cannot please, although nature is the source: "But that every Part may be suitable to a Shepherd, we must consult unstain'd, uncorrupted Nature; so that the manners might not be too Clownish nor too Caurtly" (33). The model of style that he wishes to promote is the mean, a middle style between excessive rusticity and affected urbanity. When Creech translates these two contraries of *agrestis* and *exquisitus* as "clownish" and "caurtly," they are not inappropriate within the terms of the culture of the seventeenth-century court. They adequately catch Rapin's censure of the comic element within the bucolic on the one hand and his rejection of a mannered refinement on the other.[63]

Rapin only tentatively approaches this stylistic middle ground. Normally when attempting to articulate bucolic decorum as a harmonious unity of opposites, which pleases by virtue of the interplay between the two, he uses prolix paraphrase, saying it is at once this and this, but not this and this, with copious examples. He does, however, twice use the oxymoronic phrase *ingenua simplicitas* (ingenuous simplicity) to catch the synthesis of polish and unaffectedness that he envisions.[64]

As with the lofty matters discussed above, Rapin's stylistic prescriptions lessen the sense of the ancient pastorals as literary constructs. The details of the poem must be understood as the necessary consequence of the specific principle. Theocritus's artful language becomes purely a question of a rustic dialect embodying pastoral simplicity and on this account possessing "sweetness."[65] No consideration of its literary character is possible where rustic simplicity must be asserted. The same is true for the literary play involved in ekphrasis. Theocritus's cup from *Idyll* 1 argues for his proximity to the countryside, but his lack of refinement causes him to err; his garrulity escapes him and the description is as a consequence "too extravagant and prolix" (1:lxxxix). Virgil, as he makes twelve verses in *Eclogue* 3 out of Theocritus's thirty-four, shows us the proper manner of pastoral description. Once gain the stylistic imperative of modest simplicity checks any possible understanding of the genre's literary character.

More important is the consequence of this golden age simplicity for the pastoral's chief preoccupation, love. The passions suitable for depiction in the pastoral are moderate, in keeping with the style. All extreme emotions are excluded, only the lovelorn have a place within it since they are not deemed to be too strongly agitated: "Despairing Love is not attended with those frightful and horrible consequences, but looks more like *grief to be pittied*, and a *pleasing madness*, than *rage* and *fury, Eclogue* is so far from refusing, that it rather loves, and passionately requires them" (61; 1:lxxxiij).[66] The immediate simplicity in which the lovers dwell does not allow for either a satiric or scurrilous treatment, as in Theocritus, or for a more reflective, longing view of it, as in Virgil. Rapin's only concession to the ancient texts is that love, contrary to the expectations the idea of an golden age of contentment and happiness may create, is a despairing state, an unfulfilled passion.

The parameters Rapin sets for the genre remain valid for the next century. Many will simply undergo further development, while in other instances the judgment Rapin passed will be overturned without the criteria undergoing alteration. The premise of a virtuous, more Georgic golden age only grows more dominant. Love will continue to be an emotion without danger in the pastoral, and find increasingly not frustration but virtuous fulfillment. The sense of the degree to which nature stands in need of art shifts in favor of less obvious art so that Rapin's judgment on the relative merit of Virgil and Theocritus seems faulty. Virgil becomes the failed bucoliast and Theocritus the successful one. Georg Christoph Lichtenberg's (1742–99) aphorism illustrates the complaint of the eighteenth century, "Die Linien der Humanität und der Urbanität fallen nicht zusammen."[67] Virgil nestles too close to the refinement of the court.

In his reply to Rapin in his *Discours sur la nature de l'eglogue*, Fontenelle picks up the weakest point of Rapin's argument, the insistence on the golden age, and dismantles it. The story of civilization that begins with the shepherd is, he admits, a good and likely story, yet plausibility has no bearing on any shepherd of today or long ago, or his supposed song; "ainsi, et la vie de la campagne et la Poesie des Pasteurs, ont toujours dû être fort grossières" (and so both life in the country and the poetry of shepherds must always have been very coarse).[68] The shepherd of old may well have enjoyed "une assez grande abondance" (a sufficiently large abundance), but "le monde n'avoit pas encore eu le loisir de se polir" (2:385; the world had not yet had the leisure to refine itself); his modern successor is "trop misérable" (2:385; too wretched), too oppressed by the struggle of survival to serve as a model for bucolic poetry. Fontenelle's lack of historical preconceptions about the genre affords him a sharpened perception of Theocritus's poems. He is able to recognize the fictive, non-imitative character of the Theocritean shepherd. Citing *Idylls* 1 and 4, he concludes: "Je crois que l'on trouvera dans tout cela, et plus de beauté et plus de délicatesse d'imagination, que n'en ont de vrais Bergers" (2:386; I think one will find in them more of beauty and delicacy of imagination than true shepherds possess).

As Fontenelle rejects the notion of pastoral as the song of shepherds, he needs another explanation for the pastoral, a search that leads him to make his most significant contribution to pastoral theory. He recognizes that the genre stems from the sentiment of its readers, although he restricts the pastoral purely to the gratification of this urge and does not include its explicit examination within the literary work. He also defines the psychological need expressed in the pastoral universally: "Car les hommes veulent être heureux, et ils voudroient l'être à peu de frais. Le plaisir, et le plaisir tranquille, est l'objet commun de toutes leurs passions, et ils sont tous dominés par une certaine paresse" (2:390; since men wish to be happy, and wish to be so at little cost to themselves. Pleasure, a quiet pleasure, is the common object of all their passions, and these are all dominated by a certain sluggishness). Since an unspecific longing, a wish only for indolent contentment, produces the pastoral, no necessary connection exists between it and the shepherd. He has no special bucolic stature in his capacity as shepherd, as a person concerned with flocks, cheese, and other details of daily life in the country; rather he claims our attention because of the mood we can associate with such a life: "ce qui plaît, c'est l'idée de tranquillité attachée à la vie de ceux qui prennent soin des brebis et des chèvres" (2:389; what pleases is the idea of tranquillity connected to those who tend sheep and goats).[69] As a result bucolics that deal, not with dalliance, but with too many details "purement rustiques" (2:388; purely rustic), are wide of the mark, in particular *Idylls* 4 (2:386–87) and 10 (2:392). Fontenelle's most immediate interest here is to distinguish the impulse from the objects that are confused with it.

His second interest is to criticize an ancient. Fontenelle does not challenge Virgil's claim to urbane polish and takes only occasional swipes at Virgil's eminence. He instead singles out the less favored Theocritus for the charge of rusticity. However, by selecting Theocritus as his example to show that rural details are not in themselves uniquely pastoral, he forges for his successors the identity of Theocritus with the "purely rustic" countryside, and so performs for Theocritus much the same service as Rapin did for Virgil. Thus, when the concept of unadorned nature and of its proper imitation in art takes hold, Theocritus unfailingly appears as the "realist." For Fontenelle, however, "realist" hardly constitutes a term of praise since he favors the representation of a dream and, together with Rapin, one that is all polish and elegance.

His recognition of the relation between an inner aspiration and the bucolic genre makes Fontenelle more strikingly modern than Rapin. His psychological explanation is subjective and individual in a way that Rapin's historicist appeal to the golden age is not. Fontenelle draws the consequences from his position much more quickly. If the bucolic is an acknowledged illusion, a pleasant dream that is unimportant; important is the strength of its appeal for the emotions, that is, how well it evokes the feeling of a leisured love enjoyed in tranquillity. Fontenelle measures this success by its intensity, by whether it "me transporte dans la condition de Berger, je suis Berger" (2:395; transports me into the condition of the shepherd, I am a shepherd) — a rapture Herder will later insist on for the bucolic. The reader judges the illusion by its emotional effect on himself, not by any comparison with a supposed pastoral age, nor with contemporary rural life. The very delicacy of the pastoral's constitution as a "demi-vrai" (2:394; a half-truth) is only further grounds for reproaching any suggestion of "la misère" (misery) and "la bassesse" (2:393; lowliness); nothing Georgic or oafish may impede the preoccupation with love.

At first glance Fontenelle seems diametrically opposed to Rapin: the pastoral rests on a psychological state, not on any historical age; love, not some chaste moralizing, is its object; and rusticity has no place in it. Yet in many respects, the similarities they share are as great as their differences. To a large degree, Fontenelle's demolition of a quasi-historical golden age merely secularizes Rapin's position. In place of a historical, religious golden age, Fontenelle substitutes "a golden mood," a subjective, psychological conception framed in the language of the Enlightenment, in the language of happiness and pleasure. They both agree on the essential qualities of this state: the pastoral state or charm is one of simplicity, tranquillity, and innocence. Fontenelle voices openly the idealizing tendency only implicit in Rapin's historical-religious argument by grounding it in a normative view of subjective longing.[70] He also shares with Rapin the all-embracing concern for polish.

It is in the application of this concern that he differs from Rapin: a matter of degree, not of kind. Burdened neither by a dependence on the authority of an earlier example nor by a belief in its imitative truth, Fontenelle is able, much more consistently than Rapin, to impose the normative dictates of a "simple" style on the amorphous matter of the genre. This leads primarily, at the one extreme, to the simultaneous recognition and condemnation of the low and comic elements in Theocritus's poems, and, at the other extreme, to the outright rejection of all matters external to the pursuit of idleness and romance as simply the incomprehensible, wayward willfulness of the poet. Thus the comparison of Daphnis's love to that of rutting goats in *Idyll* 1 (2:386), the harvester's mocking song in *Idyll* 10 (2:392), the grotesque Polyphemus's passion for the fair Galateia *Idyll* 11 (2:408), and most especially the scurrilous and lewd *Idyll* 5 (2:386–87) are noted often with the accompanying remark: "Mais je ne sais pourquoi Théocrite, ayant quelquefois élevé ses Bergers d'une manière si agréable au-dessus de leur génie naturel, les y a laissé retomber très-souvent. Je ne sais comment il n'a pas senti . . ." (2:286; but I do not understand why Theocritus, having on occasion raised his shepherds in such an agreeable fashion above their natural condition, let them relapse so often. I don't know how he could not have sensed . . .). Intriguingly, Fontenelle exactly senses the intended comic effect, but is wholly incapable of accounting for it. Fontenelle's condemnation of Theocritus represents the nadir of his reputation. It is so incomprehensible to him that he lays the blame for what little fame Theocritus may hitherto have enjoyed at Virgil's door: the Latin poet's reverence for the Theocritean muse set a bad example for posterity.

When Fontenelle turns his attention to the Virgilian poems, he is equally blunt. By the simple arrangement of his remarks on the problematic *Eclogues*, Fontenelle adds a new point not present in Rapin. He treats only *Eclogues* 4 and 6 (19–21) under the heading of "loftiness"; the rest, presumably *Eclogues* 1, 9 and 10, are considered as examples of "les louanges" (2:399; encomiastic praise). He singles out *Eclogues* 4 and 6 as particularly egregious examples of disregard for the proper bucolic sphere. The prophetic tone offends in the one — "leur voix [*musae sicelides*] ne va point jusqu'à ce ton-là" (2:396; their [the muses'] voice does not extend to that key); in the other, the medley of myths stitched together elicits from him the following aside on Phoebus Apollo's advice to poet at the beginning of the eclogue that shepherd singers should keep to pastoral topics: "je ne comprends pas comment Virgile s'en souvient si peu" (2:397; I do not understand how Virgil pays it such little heed). And more generally he declares "allegory," with direct reference to Rapin's adroit defense of *ad modum pastoralis* (though without mention of his name), to be the blatant "Stilbruch" that Rapin had striven by circumlocution to avoid naming (2:399).[71] Since no poet would willingly disrupt the fragility of the pastoral dream by introducing foreign elements into it, these intrusions must be false. Furthermore, adopting the voice of a shepherd neither disguises an alien origin nor changes its character: a panegyric uttered by the shepherd has recourse to the same flattering language as any courtier might.

On many other stylistic points Fontenelle agrees with Rapin, more or less repeating his maxims: the censure of Theocritus's description of the cup in *Idyll* 1; the rule that eclogues contain action or narratives, not reflection; the precept that simplicity of diction does not mean too dull nor too witty. Fontenelle does not speak of an "ingenuous simplicity," but the effect is the same: "On est étonné de voir quelque chose de fin et de délicat sous des termes communs et qui n'ont point été affectés" (2:403; one is surprised to see beneath ordinary terms something of such delicacy and subtlety, which are in no way affected). Corresponding to the niceness of the diction, the reader experiences "de surprise douce et une petite admiration" (2:403; a gentle surprise and a modest admiration).

The diminution of Virgil's reputation is relatively minor, since Rapin's defense revolved largely around the question of style, on which point Fontenelle concurs with Rapin. Throughout, Fontenelle exhibits a cavalier attitude towards the ancients, as befits one on the side of the moderns.[72] Generally he turns to the ancients in his discourse to find examples in order to criticize, and not to praise. This tactic, however, only confirms the centrality of Virgil and Theocritus for his thinking and the lack of a suitable modern model. Fontenelle's delight in his tossing of stones, in his "sacrilège" (2:409; sacrilege), and saucy daring in preferring the later Greek bucoliasts Bion and Moschus to Theocritus, and the Latin Calpurnius to his predecessor Virgil, do not affect the prominence given to a simple style and, through Rapin's example, to the estimation of Virgil.

The combination of the dream principle and the insistence on happiness does lead Fontenelle to dispense with Rapin's diffidence on the subject of love. Fontenelle moves it to the center of the bucolic and makes it very much a question of requited love. Fontenelle's descriptions of it do not include the word "despairing." Instead they call to mind images of dalliance and coquetry, conducted with a youthful insouciance, half-knowing but without predatory cynicism. It is a simple love because its spirit is not dangerously refined; more concentrated because no other passion competes with it; more unassuming because vanity is largely unknown, more faithful because its imagination is not jaded, less subject to anxiety and to caprice: "c'est-a-dire, en un mot, l'amour purgé de tout ce que les excès de fantaisies humaines y ont mêlé d'étranger et de mauvais" (2:391–92; in a word a love purged of everything vile and foreign that the excesses of human fantasies have mixed in). The words "tendre, simple, délicat, fidèle" (2:391; tender, simple, delicate, faithful) exhaust the proper range for the sentiments and the language of this "purged" love.

Not only does Fontenelle reduce the legitimate themes of the bucolic to love alone, but he also transforms the character of that pastoral love on three counts. First, Rapin managed to retain the unrequited lover because the languor of his grief was not felt to be a violent emotion. But Fontenelle can not accommodate it, since he has a place neither for the ironic worldly view that underlies it in Theocritus, nor for the more sorrowful view of it in Virgil's later eclogues. And thus, second, it is much clearer to Fontenelle that the pastoral should focus on the pursuit of love and its happiness.

And third, as part of Fontenelle's reconstitution of the pastoral around love, he, like Rapin, not only excludes the range of strong passions but also explicitly prohibits "ambition," before all the others are mentioned: "parce qu'elle est trop contraire à cette paresse naturelle, n'est ni une passion générale, ni une passion fort délicieuse" (2:390; because it is too contrary to this natural indolence, it is neither a general passion nor an especially delightful one). Ambition does not merely distract from the business of love; it is inimical to it, as it compels an involvement in the larger social and political world. Pastoral love, which was in tension with the larger world, now necessarily entails the rejection of this world. The emphasis shifts from comparing the two worlds explicitly to imagining life in the pastoral world, in the language of Fontenelle, to picturing oneself vividly as the contented shepherd.

The German pastoral theorists will in essence combine Rapin with Fontenelle. The golden age will remain a historical age and pastoral song its surviving witness, while the psychological affinity to it will become the innate and indelible trace of the state of nature in the human psyche. In this fashion the German idyll will combine both ancient and modern, a historical and a normative, ideal side, just as the more general German philhellenism does. As the concern for the state of nature in the pastoral grows, the last refuge of conscious artistry permitted by both Fontenelle and Rapin, namely style, becomes dubious. The only manner in which they allowed the poet to intrude consciously into the poem was in the question of style. For its effect, whether as "ingenuous simplicity" or as "gentle surprise," it relied on the poet's conscious intention to play with his reader's expectations of rustic simplicity and the reader's recognition of this intent. In all other instances the aim is not to encourage the contrast between the reader's conceptions and the pastoral, and certainly not to make it a constitutive thematic element within the poems. The literary reflective character of the poems so prominent in the ancient bucolic has no place in the new pastoral. However, this will come to be Virgil's particular fault, while Theocritus will become the great master of pastoral simplicity. Questions of how expectation relates to the poetic work become the preserve of the theorist; they may not become a theme within the work itself.[73]

The German Enlightenment: Releasing the Idyll from Theocritus und Virgil

As is true for German poetics as whole, the German pastoral theorists of the earlier Enlightenment largely work out their positions in relation to French opinions on the genre and its canon. The same sets of themes and topics recur again and again, no less than the canonical references to the ancient poets when the need arises to substantiate a point. These continual reformulations and restatements progressively reshape the sense of the genre around a sentimental view of nature. The pastoral becomes the imaginative representation of the state of nature. In it humans enjoy the closest possible life led in accordance with this ideal condition, before, that is, the collective reflective enterprise of civilization causes its increasingly injurious separation from nature. The inhabitants become simple and virtuous, leading lives circumscribed by the immediate concerns of family and village life, which appear to the reader as a trenchant criticism of his own existence and also sweetly, if unattainably, appealing. As this sense of the pastoral grows, the Virgilian eclogue will rightly be seen as not so much irrelevant but in flat contradiction to the pastoral. By the other side of the same theoretical coin, the Theocritean idyll will be compelled to take up the role of champion for the new pastoral, even though an overly close perusal of his works is not recommended.

The positions elaborated by Gottsched in his *Critische Dichtkunst* and Johann Adolf Schlegel in the treatise affixed to his translation of Charles Batteux's (1713–80) *Les Beaux-Arts réduits à un même principe* (The Fine Arts Reduced to a Single Principle; 2nd ed. 1759) represent the initial stage of this process. The need to refer to Virgil and Theocritus persists, while many of the arguments and comments made either by Fontenelle or Rapin reappear. A more independent development occurs with Wieland (1753?), Heyne, and Herder, the latter pair both in 1767. Collectively they overturn the need to ground pastoral theory in the practice of the ancient poets. As this was more a question of the Virgilian bucolic, the rejection of the ancient model is expressed with regard to Virgil's poems and also to Virgil the poet. Theocritus conversely gains in popularity, although not so much on the basis of an examination of his poems but as further confirmation of the general Greek attitude toward nature. Subsequently, in such as Schiller or Jean Paul (1763–1825), pastoral theory is better able to conform to the shift in interest that has occurred from a specific type of poetic work, the idyll, to a more diffuse idyllic mode or attitude.

In France, Fontenelle's open admission of the illusion of the imaginary pastoral carried the day.[74] The pastoral as golden age and primeval song found no defenders. The neoclassical ideal of Rapin found vigorous champions in England. Pope restated it and effortlessly grafted nature as the object of imitation onto the notion of the golden age:

> If we would copy Nature, it may be useful to take this Idea along with us, that pastoral is an image of what they call the Golden age. So that we are not to describe our shepherds as shepherds at this day really are, but as they may be conceiv'd then to have been; when the best of men follow'd that employment.[75]

He does not elaborate on the "Nature" to be copied. Pope's championing of an ideal, bygone shepherd existence does not win out in England, where a greater interest in a more contemporary country existence with a pronounced Georgic flavor dominates.[76] The English understanding of the Georgic pastoral may often have a less obvious cultural critique and therefore also a less fraught relation to the contemporary reader than the German pastoral comes to have. Dr Johnson (1750), for instance, sees little problem for any contemporary in stepping into the pastoral world because it is accessible to "all ranks of persons, because persons of all ranks inhabit the country."[77]

In Germany, Gottsched firmly restates the pastoral's dependence on the golden age within the context of his neoclassical poetics. The nature that so recommends itself for imitation in the golden age is strongly moral in character.

> Will man wissen, worinn das rechte Wesen eines guten Schäfergedichtes besteht; so kann ich kürzlich sagen: in der Nachahmung des unschuldigen und ungekünstelten Schäferlebens, welches vorzeiten in der Welt geführet worden. Poetisch würde ich sagen, es sey eine Abschilderung des güldenen Weltalters; auf christliche Art zu reden aber: eine Vorstellung des Standes der Unschuld, oder doch wenigstens der patriarchalischen Zeit, vor und nach der Sündfluth.[78]

Many of the particular opinions Gottsched voices here are not new. They are familiar either from the French debate or from the earlier German Baroque tradition, such as in the golden age moralism of the seventeenth-century critic and poet Georg Philipp Harsdörffer's (1607–58) capacious concept of the pastoral.[79] Gottsched's depiction of the golden age strongly emphasizes its moral independence; that is, he makes of it a past age that is strongly critical of the failings of the present. It sharpens the bourgeois criticism of the excess of the princely court from the familiar trope of "Hütte und Palast" that he incorporates into his vision of the golden age.[80] He also turns the underlying historical notion of a progression from pastoral through agricultural to urban ages into a more general cultural critique. His interests are those that dominate in the subsequent theoretical debates.

Gottsched enumerates the life and customs of the golden age's inhabitants in a fashion that casts Arcadia in a Georgic hue. Apart from the insistence on a shepherd's dress and the golden age as a past era, nothing separates the themes of the bucolic from those of the Georgic "Landgedicht." The Georgic interest in the pastoral and the lack of an easy division between a pastoral and a "Landgedicht" only add to the larger muddle of definition. The hopeless confusion on this point so common to these decades — whether one catalogs such poems by genre as epic, dramatic, or even lyric, or by the subject matter deemed appropriate to each genre, or by the numerous poetic forms and meters, not to mention prose — is made no less convoluted by the appeal to the ancient bucolic, as it too presents an amorphous generic profile.[81]

Gottsched's golden age shepherd, like Fontenelle's shepherd, is ignorant of ambition, not because it disturbs his amorous indolence, but because he is morally innocent of the vices afflicting the larger society "Der Geiz und Ehrgeiz verleitet sie [die Hirten] zu keiner Ungerechtigkeit" (6/2:87); or, lest the reader should fail to be certain of the benefits to be had from shunning greed and ambition, he concludes: "Endlich sind sie auch mäßig und nüchtern und mit einem Worte, ganz tugendhaft und allezeit vergnügt" (6/2:78). The *crudelis Amor* of the ancient bucolic has no place here: "Kurz, die unschuldige Schäferliebe muß von allen Lastern frey seyn, die durch die Bosheit der Menschen allmählich eingeschlichen haben" (6/2:79). Its transformation into a modern sentimental version is in theory complete. Rapin could recommend a "disappointed love," Fontenelle, dalliance, but Gottsched calls for only a little "Unbeständigkeit."

In addition to this nearly prelapsarian innocence, Gottsched establishes his pastoral world as one explicitly parallel to the larger civilized one through the use of an extended political simile:

> Man stelle sich die Welt in ihrer ersten Unschuld vor. Ein freyes Volk, welches von keinen Königen und Fürsten weis, wohnet in einem warmen und fetten Lande, welches an allem einen Ueberfluß hat, . . . Von schwerer Arbeit weis man daselbst eben so wenig, als von Drangsalen und Kriegen. Ein jeder Hausvater ist sein eigener König und Herr. (6/2:77)

By drawing a firm connection between moral innocence and a pre-political habit of association, Gottsched makes of the pastoral age a more general criticism of civilization. The pre-political aspect of pastoral life excludes all forms of larger association, whether "von einem solchen republikanischen oder monarchischen Zustand" (6/2:94). Nonetheless he often returns to the criticism of the current political order, as, for example, in the opinion that shepherds "ihre güldene Freyheit allem Pracht der Städte vorziehen" (6/2:94), or in his criticism of Fontenelle's rustics as "scharfsinnige Pariser" dressed in "seidenen Kleidern" (6/2:83).

However, Gottsched does not use his view of the pastoral age in his consideration of the literary tradition. He relies rather on the French critics, with the result that the substance of his comments on Virgil remain unchanged, as well as Virgil's standing. He goes only marginally further than his predecessors. His criticism of *Eclogues* 4 and 6 agrees on all points with that of Fontenelle: in *Eclogue* 4, Virgil misguidedly attempts something sublime, "denn sie [die Musen] können auf ihre Flöte keinen Trompetenklang erzwingen" (6/2:80), and engages in prophecy; in the sixth, the cosmology of the Epicureans and the presence of Gallus seem improper, not to mention that the eclogue is an impossible confusion of erotic tales. (Only at the end of this section does he mention Fontenelle.)

Gottsched is silent, like Fontenelle, on the more direct appearances of "Drangsale und Kriege" and Rome in *Eclogues* 1 and 9. Although

Gottsched had earlier asserted that "die Schäfer nichts von Königen und Fürsten wissen sollen" (6/2:93), he finds himself compelled by tradition to admit their presence in "allegorischen Eklogen" (6/2:93). He adds the stipulation reminiscent of Rapin's *ad modum pastoralium* that shepherds should speak of "Könige und Fürsten von benachbarten Ländern" (6/2:93) as things beyond their ken. The example he gives is Virgil's first eclogue in which Augustus appears in the guise of a god. Gottsched praises the recognition of the need for a disguise, but criticizes its manner as "hochgetriebene Schmeicheley" (6/2:94).

On the question of style, Gottsched makes one notable change. He repeats the notion of a middle style, neither base nor refined, neither "niederträchtig" nor "scharfsinning." It ought rather to be "niedrig und zärtlich" (6/2:95).[82] The formulation lessens what recognition remained of the bucolic's artificial style in Rapin's "ingenuous simplicity" or Fontenelle's "gentle surprise" by directing attention elsewhere. Although Gottsched's terms do suggest a form of contrast, the style's purpose is not to draw attention to itself, not to clash with the reader's expectations and cause as marked a reaction as a "gentle surprise." Nonetheless, Gottsched retains the canonical status of the ancient poets, recommending them to modern bucoliasts: "Folge, wenn du sie [die Mittelstraße] finden willst, dem Theokrit und Virgil" (6/2:96).

Johann Adolf Schlegel argues strongly against the new style of pastoral that arose in response to Gottsched's *Critische Dichtkunst*. He first satirized it in 1746 and returned to the subject with the first version of his theoretical treatise "Vom eigentlichen Gegenstande der Schäferpoesie" in 1751, which he revised in 1759 to take account of Gessner's appearance on the pastoral scene.[83] Like Fontenelle before him with Rapin, Schlegel takes aim at the weakness of Gottsched's position within his, Gottsched's, own theoretical system. Schlegel does not disagree with Gottsched's overall idealist position. Yet the pastoral, he points out, does not follow Gottsched's principle of imitating nature. The eclogue cannot be a "Nachahmung" in the customary sense of that word since it has no object of imitation in nature; it is "kein Ausdruck der wahren Natur."[84] Gottsched had specifically denied that the contemporary peasant could be the pastoral shepherd; it was an imitation of an age that had existed "vorzeiten." If that it is so, how can the poet confirm for himself its appearance in nature?

It must have a different basis of imitation. Schlegel argues that the nature so represented has only the status of a "Wahrscheinliches." Although a word from the vocabulary of Gottsched, this corresponds in meaning more to Bodmer and Breitinger's term "das Mögliche." He does not reject Gottsched's notion of the golden age but instead elevates it to the level of an ideal, purging it of its dependence on a historical age and restoring, at least to theory, its more problematic and reflective character.

It also becomes subjective because it, like Fontenelle's "demi-vrai," appeals to the sphere of the imagination and allows for a freer play of Rococo feeling in that imaginary world.[85]

It does not lose entirely the moral severity of Gottsched. "Sie [die Ekloge] führet die erste Gleichheit wieder unter die Menschen ein; sie bringt uns zu dem Stande der Natur zurücke" (129). The political aspect of Gottsched's golden age is more than preserved in "die erste Gleichheit," and nature, the "Stand der Natur," now assumes the position formerly filled by the idea of the golden age as a historical era. "Stand" indicates that the pastoral condition in nature is a passing, not a permanent one. Any history of it is purely an ideal, logical one. Appropriately the eclogue belongs to the class of the "Historienmalerei der Poesie" (119) and the golden age is the timeless world of the ideal imagination.

This distinction leads Schlegel to argue for another type of poem that takes account of nature as it presents itself to the contemporary viewer. The portraiture of landscape and of the contemporary rustic is the task of the "Landgedicht": "es *schildert Gegenstände;* Gegenstände die schon in der Natur an und für sich gefallen" (119). Because of this imitative restriction to "das Wahre" (119), the Georgic poem belongs to the category of the "Lehrgedicht." Such a poem may be rounded out by "Bilder des Stadtlebens" to provide the contrast to "das Landleben." His example of this sort of poem is Gessner's "Der Wunsch" and its task is "den wirklichen Bauer nachzukopieren, seinen Stand und Sitten nicht umzubilden" (117). Schlegel's attempt to consign the pastoral to the past and to make a generic distinction between it and a Georgic "Landgedicht" of the present, meets with no great success.

For Schlegel, the state of nature is part both of an ideal history and also of the present to the sentimental observer. With the notion that it is not nature but rather culture that changes over time, Schlegel's thought is more intriguing, as it leads to a new, more explicit, historical consciousness with respect to the pastoral. He is, however, no more successful with it than he is in his attempt at separating the bucolic past from the Georgic present. He explores it under the dual heading of "Wahrscheinlichkeit" and style, which is here the expression of naivety. To fail to allow for the fictive character of the eclogue would, he argues, be tantamount to denying the title of bucolic author to Fontenelle, Gessner, "und nicht weniger Virgil, ja vielleicht selbst Theokritus" (122). The eclogue that Schlegel chooses to discuss is the sixth. Both Fontenelle and Gottsched objected to the wide scope of the myths incorporated into the poem, a point on which Schlegel is silent. He concentrates on the question of style: on the question of whether the French poet Jean Baptiste Gresset (1709–77) in his 1730s translation of Virgil bucolics was right to omit as offensive to good taste the line *sanguineis frontem moris et tempora pinget* (rougeing his brow and temples with mulberry juice; 30).[86] Bodmer strongly censored Gresset in the pages of his journal *Neue Critische Briefe* for his omission as proof that French elegance could not acknowledge true rustic simplicity; German taste naturally could and was on this account more flexible. With considerable historical acuity, Schlegel argues that Gresset was justified in doing so on the grounds that he made Virgil speak as a Frenchman of Gresset's day. The taste then prevalent in France required such a change from the Latin taste of Virgil's day for the poem to have the same effect in the French on a contemporary French audience (125–26). German taste, however, is able to appreciate the naivety of the scene without offense at its phrasing in the Latin, and any additions that German translators may introduce to their versions only heighten "für uns" the "Anmut" (126) of it.

Taste functions as a historical principle for Schlegel. Each nation's poetry is distinguished by a taste peculiar both to it and to its time. It does not, however, grant sympathy for these changes, merely an explanation of why they offend subsequent ages. He prefers not to talk about Theocritus and excuses himself with the comment that the "Entlegenheit der Zeit" leaves us "in allzuvieler Dunkelheit" (136). The French, he judges, and in particular Fontenelle, moved the standard of taste from "vom Stadtleben zum Hofleben" (137). Since it is not to be denied that a court may imagine a pastoral according to its taste that has for it the quality of "Wahrscheinlichkeit," no one may object in principle to Fontenelle's eclogues. Their details are another matter. Schlegel uses the same insight to account for Virgil's problematic eclogues. It accounts for the incomprehension of the "Weltbürger" (136) in Schlegel's day of many of the eclogues, "wie besonders die erste, die vierte, die zehnte ganz offenbar beweisen" (136–37). Schlegel's explanation may account to his readers why their reaction is one of incomprehension, yet it does not bring the poems closer to them and to the present. Style is not explicated in relation to the details of the poem but as a more general question of taste susceptible to change over time. Recognizing the "bon goût" of an earlier age and culture becomes a critical enterprise, and less an activity of connoisseurship, less the cultivation of certain beautiful "Empfindungen" in oneself and their confirmation through the appreciation of a work of art.

Only in one instance does Schlegel try to make his historical insight productive for the interpretation of the *Eclogues*. He attempts to construct the poems' historical context. Schlegel explains that changes of taste correspond to the shifts of history. This he conceives of in conventional terms as the development of civilization away from the golden age. First farming came to be added to the original occupation of shepherding, after which the other institutions of the larger polis gradually accumulated:

> Auch *Virgil* schrieb in einer Republik, wo das Landleben, wo überhaupt alles, was zum Ackerbaue, und zur Landwirthschaft gehört, in weit

größerm Ansehen stund, als unter uns, weil man sich der alten Zeiten erinnerte, in denen die größten Staatsmänner und Helden ihren Acker mit eigner Hand geflüget, . . .; weil man sich dieser Zeiten, da sie zur Größe Roms den ersten Grund gelegt . . . erinnerte. (123)

Not only does the language here ("Landleben," "Ackerbau," "Landwirthschaft," and so on) better describes a Georgic than it does an eclogue, but Schlegel's presentation of the relation of the work to its historical circumstances is strained. Rome's success reflects its moral stature: the simple virtue of a community of farmers united in a republic. Implicit is also the notion that Virgil shares this view: "Virgil schrieb in einer Republic." Schlegel does not go on to express an opinion on whether the *Eclogues* argue for the Republic or for Octavian. Since the reigning view is that the Virgil of the *Eclogues* at the very least intends to ingratiate himself with Octavian, Schlegel's argument that the tenor of the times is one of rustic republicanism suggests that Virgil is neither in step with his times nor with his nation, a charge that will become explicit after Heyne. Further, Schlegel's characterization of the historical circumstances better suits a work such as the *Georgics*, not a pastoral work. Explicitly Schlegel argues that changes in taste, historically conditioned, lead to the disappearance of the feeling that makes plausible such bucolics as *Eclogues* 1, 4, 9, and 10. Implicitly the increasing emphasis on the political aspect of the golden age renders the Roman eclogues not merely opaque but contrary to the bucolic illusion; the state of nature includes an original equality. Schlegel does not draw the consequences for Virgil from his natural primitivism, nor from his consideration of taste. Feeling, the object of taste, is still a matter of style and its appreciation. His defense of the sixth eclogue is limited to a consideration of style measured by the feeling it inspires. Taste as an instrument of historical distance serves to prove the status of eclogues as naive, or in Schlegel's terminology "anmuthig." It measures the distance of a culture from nature; it is not a tool for exploring a culture's artificiality.

Schlegel's historical view of taste, and thus of the pastorals each age and nation produces, finds no echo. The preference is rather for an original nature speaking directly through the genius of the poet. As the concentration on rural domesticity strengthens, the explicit contrast with the city fades, while the pastoral world of the golden age fills out and gains a Georgic solidity. More representative of this are Johann Georg Sulzer (1709–79), professor, theoretician, and the author of the much read encyclopedia *Allgemeine Theorie der schönen Künste* (1771–74, 1787), and Carl Wilhelm Ramler (1725–98), well known for his odes and the popular *Einleitung in die schönen Wissenschaften* (1756–58), yet another translation of Batteux. For both of them, the household, as a world complete within itself, forms the starting point without further ado.

Ramler defines a pastoral as "eine Nachahmung des Landlebens," and for Sulzer it is the direct expression of an entire "Volk" or "Hirtenvolk" that lives in a primitive pastoralism.[87] The young Wieland, thought to be the author of the passage inserted into Sulzer's article on "Hirtengedichte," also begins with the solidity of the pastoral world; the Muses always loved "die ländlichen Szenen und das kunstlose freie und anmutige Landleben."[88]

In the same article the young Wieland also states more forthrightly and categorically the enthusiasms of the Rococo vogue for the pastoral. He points to the reevaluation of Theocritus in connection with the pastoral household at home in nature. Certainly Schlegel and Ramler had evinced little enthusiasm for Theocritus. In the 1751 edition of his Batteux translation, Schlegel mentioned only Virgil as an ancient model for the bucolic, omitting Theocritus entirely.[89] Although Sulzer did not publish the first part of *Allgemeine Theorie der schönen Künste* until 1771, the small piece by Wieland was most likely written in the 1750s.[90] In this piece, Wieland had already proceeded to make tighter the connection between the household, innocent feeling, nature, and Theocritus. Originally these earliest pastoral songs were those in which "die Menschen die Rührungen ausdruckten, welche die Natur, die Freiheit und die Liebe in ihnen hervorbrachten" (1:721). This nature is the "schöne Natur," nature uncontaminated by human culture, "die nackte Natur ohne alle Kunst, Verstellung, Zwang oder andre Verderbnis" (1:722). Culture is what impedes access to this fount, what "die freie Würkungen der Natur hindert" (1:722), and idylls are "Gemählde aus der unverdorbenen Natur" (1:722). In a manner that anticipates Herder by some twenty years, Wieland seizes upon Theocritus as the naive poet of nature, the simple witness of a fading golden age, of the many "Überbleibsel der nicht gefabelten goldnen Zeit" (1:721). This modern Theocritus bids farewell to his incarnation as learned Hellenistic poet. He is the example of the quintessential bucolic poet who must have been "viel mehr durch Natur und durch solche Muster als durch besondere Regeln gebildet" (1:722). He paints "aus der würklichen Natur," which gives his idylls "eine Menge kleiner lebhaften Züge und naiver Wendungen" (1:722). Nature, and the immediate utterance of it, increasingly determines the bucolic.

As Theocritus becomes the poet of this nature, Virgil with his problematic eclogues develops into the representative of the pastoral contaminated by a false conception of art's relation to nature. This becomes clear with Heyne, Virgil's editor. With him the weight of traditional respect finally gives way before modern pastoral theory. In his introductory essay, *De Virgilii carminibus bucolis* (1767), Heyne completes the inversion of the proposition of Fontenelle and Rapin that art is the perfection of nature to the one that, in the bucolic, the least amount of art is the best means to represent nature, a distinction with respect to the late and learned

Hellenistic poet Theocritus that is elided in favor of him and the Greeks as giving direct expression to natural feeling. Heyne also addresses the generic status of the *Eclogues* in light of the dogma of the golden age as the synonym of the state of naive nature. His analysis focusing on these two points illustrates how unreadable the poems have become. His wish, in accordance with the stated principles of his edition, is to provide a critical reading of the poems so that in *ipsis his Eclogis multa rectius ac facilius intellegantur et sentiantur* (*O* 1:3; in the *Eclogues* themselves many points may be more correctly and easily understood and appreciated).[91] This means a normative analysis of the poems following the aesthetic precepts of modern opinion about the pastoral.

He begins with the familiar proposition that the unvarnished songs of shepherds cannot please and attributes to Theocritus the inspiration that *si arte paullulum polirentur* (*O* 1:5; if they are only slightly polished by art), then they become the vehicle *par excellence* for conjuring a golden age *tranquilitas, securitas, innocentia* (*O* 1:5; tranquillity, freedom from care and innocence) and also *delicias et gaudia numeris modisque adumbrando* (*O* 1:5; the charms and joys from their depiction in verse and meter). All of the lessons of *prodesse* are those of the golden age, all the pleasures of *delectare* are those of the exercise of taste. Just as for Fontenelle and Schlegel, these attributes of the bucolic cause an illusion, a "pleasing deception," a *fraus grata* (*O* 1:5) that captivates the mind of the reader. Heyne also agrees with Fontenelle that a "canvas," a *tabula*, on which *agri, greges, siluae descriptae exhiberentur* (*O* 1:5; the fields, flocks and woods described are displayed) is one *quod uix diu placere potest* (*O* 1:5; that can scarcely please for a long time). And, in a nod to Schlegel, he makes it one of the two modes of illusion available for the representation of the pastoral object. Unlike Schlegel, however, he draws a sharp distinction between the first kind, the description of "les choses purement rustiques" (the purely rustic things), and the second, the description of *locorum et temporis* (places and a time) that are of nature. The nature meant is the nature that corresponds to the feeling of beauty in nature in the mind of the beholder. In the second kind of pastoral the accent of the description rests on the feeling or "Empfindung" it evokes. When Heyne notes that the bucolic poets of antiquity rarely indulge in the sentimental description of nature, yet couches his observation as a baffling question, he neatly expresses the distance between the modern perspective on idyllic nature and the ancient one on the bucolic. The failure of the ancients to exploit this manner of description, to his mind so eminently suitable to the essence of the genre, does not result in the suspicion that, perhaps, the web of themes connected to the ancient genre necessitate a different understanding of the genre. The strength of the normative thinking, that is, the universality and immutability of the moral and psychological constitution of humanity, prevails.

Nonetheless his awareness of it does lead to an appreciation of Gessner on his part not shared by Schlegel, who tended to consider Gessner's rapture before nature a part of the Georgic poem's descriptive brief. For Heyne, Gessner even excels the Greeks: *frequentius, et in multis feliciter, eo Gesnerus usus est, suauissumus poeta, quem antiqua illa Graecia aut suum esse popularem credidisset, aut nobis inuidisset* (O 1:7; Gessner makes more frequent use of it than Theocritus, and is on many occasions more successful: a most delightful poet, whom ancient Greece itself would have begrudged us or thought one of its own). The ranking of Gessner here among the ancient poets, and for Heyne it is only a question of Theocritus and Virgil, is noteworthy. It suggests that Gessner may claim first place in the category of descriptive nature since Heyne also states that Theocritus surpasses Virgil in it. What precisely Heyne envisions under the proper use of descriptive nature is not entirely clear. He gives no examples from Theocritus. He only mentions in the footnotes the famous passage from *Idyll 7*, which describes a strong sense of well-being at the same time as the details of scene in nature are enumerated. In his text, however, he turns instead to the *Georgics*. As was the case for Rapin when attempting to sum up what was at issue in the pastoral it was the *Georgics* that acted as the lens through which the bucolic and Virgil were viewed, and now here for Theocritus as well. The citation Heyne chooses as an illustrative introduction to the discussion on the tranquil beauty of nature comes from the *Georgics* (*Ge.* 2. 467–71). What motivates the modern debate about the pastoral is not anything from the *Eclogues* or the *Idylls* but the Georgic golden age and its concomitant contrast between urban and rustic life, between sophisticated corruption and untainted simplicity.

Heyne's bucolic illusion of natural simplicity also includes a natural liberty both prior to and opposed to the *magnos hominum coetus* (O 1:8; large aggregations of humans). Intimations of simplicity and liberty linger on in the psyche of civilized man, the residue of an innate idea that the bucolic is composed to reinvigorate. The various elements of this view are not new; their combination, culminating in the phrase that this sort of subject matter *ad gratam illam, inhaerentem animo nostro, simplicitatis, libertatis et tranquillae felicitatis notionem reuocari potest* (O 1:9; can summon up that pleasing notion nestling within our souls of simplicity, freedom, and a peaceful happiness), is. It posits the same closer identity of man and nature as Herder in the same year also does in his consideration of Gessner and Theocritus.

It is therefore not surprising that Heyne makes the case against Virgil that Herder neglects to present, but assumes. The end result of Heyne's deliberations disputes the name of poetry for the *Eclogues* and begins to erode Virgil's right to a place among the first rank of poets: *Iam primum nisi alia essent, quibus Maro magni poetae nomen consequutus est, solis Bucolicis relictis uix eum incensum principium poetarum uenturum fuisse*

(*O* 1:17; In the first instance if there were no other poems with which Virgil has acquired the name of a great poet, if only his *Eclogues* remained, he would scarcely have come to be counted in the first rank of poets). Despite Heyne's disclaimer, the arguments he employs to dissect the *Eclogues* are not limited to these poems, but reach out to encompass the poet as well. The wording will also be echoed later by his student Friedrich Schlegel.

To accomplish his goal Heyne pursues two main lines of argument. The allegorical approach, now so patently absurd, does not merit serious consideration, only abuse. Heyne bases his first line of argument on the criterion of generic admissibility. On this criterion only *Eclogues* 3, 5, 7, and 8 are true bucolics, *bucolicae naturae* (*O* 1:17). These eclogues include the earliest and most closely imitative of Theocritus, *Eclogues* 3 and 5. One might expect to find *Eclogue* 2 in this list, but it is dismissed out of hand, presumably because it mentions homosexual love: *Nam ad illud genus, in quo uitae pastoritae libertas, innocentia, et simplicitas commendatur, id plane non pertinere, quis non uideat?* (*O* 1:11; For who would not see that it obviously does not belong to that genre that commends the freedom, innocence, and simplicity of the pastoral life?). *Eclogues* 7 and 8, both of a sophistication that argues a comparatively late date of composition, bear an unmistakable outward resemblance to the Theocritean idyll (only *Eclogue* 8 directly borrows material from Theocritus, notably *Idyll* 2).[92] And *reliqua ab eo aliena esset facile apparet* (*O* 1:9; it is readily apparent that the rest are foreign to the genre). The most distinctively Virgilian eclogues, and the ones most important to the later tradition, *Eclogues* 1, 4, 6, 9, and 10, are dismissed so that only the four most closely connected to Theocritus remain. To account for the rest, Heyne draws the obvious conclusion from the arguments of his predecessors about the simplicity of the pastoral golden age: namely, Virgil did not intend to write bucolics according to the proper conception of the genre.

This conclusion compels Heyne to entertain, though unwillingly, the notion of two sorts or species of pastoral. Virgil was a virtuoso whose *sollertia intra artis ac praeceptorum angustias uix coerceri potest* (*O* 1:10; ingenuity can scarcely be confined within the bounds of art and its rules). It drove him to devise new challenges simply for the display of his artistry, which in turn led to new genres. Examples of the first sort are *Eclogues* 4 and 6. In these the deviation occurs through the attempt to represent the golden age directly and not merely evoke the *imagines ac attributa* (*O* 1:10; the images and characteristics) of that age. *Eclogues* 1, 9, and 10 stem from the same wish to exhibit his virtuosity and the skill required to refer to contemporary events and personages while in the guise of a shepherd.[93] These eclogues are *tantum ad bucolicorum morem* (*O* 1:10; only in the manner of bucolics), an echo of Rapin's wording and ironic inversion of their meaning with the use of one word *tantum*.[94] To put a word in

Heyne's mouth — and to excuse it by noting that the use of *bucolicae naturae* begs its opposite — the primary distinction is between "eine Natur- und eine Kunstidylle." The "Kunstidylle" is only considered from the aspect of *sollertia* (ingenuity). The literary character of the *Eclogues* gains recognition but only as a presence alien to the "Naturidyll." It becomes the measure of the *Eclogues*' distance from nature. The creation of a new genre — and one will do since the objection to both sorts is in essence the same — to contain the awkward eclogues represents the outright rejection of the openly fictive character of the Virgilian eclogue and, by extension, of Alexandrian poetics. That Virgil should be made the poet of an artistic technique that has no more than a merely stylistic effect reflects the legacy of Rapin and Fontenelle. Simplicity remains the desired effect, but it is purged of ingenuousness. The deliberately non-naive treatment of the bucolic illusion they permitted is no longer countenanced, nor intelligible as other than a willful display of virtuosity.

Accordingly style forms the second general division of Heyne's argument. It addresses squarely the claims made on Virgil's behalf by Schlegel and Ramler. It is the more important of the two arguments, since the only aspect of Virgil's œuvre to retain a live interest is his facility for "ingenuous simplicity." Heyne too deems it the more momentous, to judge by length, since the discussion fills pages eleven to sixteen. The stylistic problem remains the same as ever. How does one represent a "demi-vrai," the *fraus grata* (pleasing deception), if one must exclude *quicquid, et si ipsam uitae rusticae ueritatem exprimit, ingratum tamen ad sensum ac molestum est* (*O* 1:11–12; whatever is displeasing and troublesome to our feeling, even if it does truly represent the rustic life), yet still render convincing the illusion of a place, an order, a world *qui nullus unquam nisi in hominum egregia imaginandi ui pollentium animis fuit* (1:12; that has never existed except in the soul of individuals of particularly powerful imagination): his answer, in a word, naturally. In contradiction to Schlegel, this means exactly that the eclogue should display the fewest concessions to the deformations of civilization. Heyne holds up Theocritus as the preeminent exemplar of the proper bucolic style. He is the good stylist, Virgil the bad stylist. Heyne seizes on Doric as the tongue *quantopere huic rerum generi apta et idonea sit, ut nec docta nec inculta et horrida. At Virgilius sermonis et dialecti suauitate destitutus* (*O* 1:13; so very suited to and appropriate for this kind of topic as it is neither learned nor coarse and uncouth. But Virgil is bereft of sweetness in language and dialect). The Latin language possesses an *asperitas* (a harshness) that precludes the sweet simplicity the genre demands (*O* 1:18). This linguistic disadvantage is only the first handicap under which Virgil labors. the second is the civility of his age, which Rapin and Scaliger deemed to be his greatest advantage. It compels him to improve on a more immediate simplicity of expression for the sake of *superbos Romanorum aures* (*O* 1:13; the proud Roman ears). The change of taste that Schlegel had noted now finds a judgment on its quality.

These comments merely enumerate the more conventional points of Heyne's position. At this juncture he departs from the earlier tradition and begins to define Virgil's poetic language as artificial, *docta*, and contrived in relation to the more natural poetic language for which Theocritus and his Doric stand:

> *Virgilio elegantiae laudem, dignitatis et doctrinae* **nemo invidebit;** *sed simplicitate et naturali aliqua venustate rerumque copia ac uarietate non minus cedit Theocrito, quam ars naturae.* (*O* 1:14)
>
> [*No one will begrudge* Virgil the fame of his elegance, dignity, and learning; *but* in simplicity, in a certain natural charm and in the range and number of his topics he yields no less to Theocritus than art does to nature.]

On a particular point he who labors *operose* (painstakingly) may surpass the effortless effusion of nature, but that art *iners et uana habenda est* (*O* 1:14; must be deemed ineffective and empty). Heyne reinterprets the Horatian praise of Virgil's verse as *facetus et mollis* (elegant and charming). *Facetus* refers to polish and elegance and is thus *ipso facto* undesirable. *Mollis* does refer to *suauitas* (charm), but the harshness of Latin, the cultivation of his age, the artfulness of Virgil's talent, all so undermine such charm that the question *utrum Virgilius Theocrito praestet* (*O* 1:14; whether Virgil is better than Theocritus) becomes easy to answer. These factors so vitiate the charm of the verse that Heyne finds incomprehensible the earlier praise of Virgil and judges critics such as Scaliger to be deluded *consuetudine fere, auctoritate, caecoque aliquo amore et impetu* (*O* 1:14; generally by habit, authority, or some hidden love and impulse). Their reasoning shows great inventiveness, but rests on *minutis nescio quibus et grammaticis rem rationibus* (*O* 1:14; points of such petty grammatical argument) — in short, pedantry and not critical discernment.

Given that the *Eclogues* have no redeeming merit with respect to the natural *Idylls* of Theocritus, Heyne faces the puzzle of Virgil's immense popularity in his, Virgil's, own day and subsequently with later poets. The source of his influence among poets arises simply from the fact that the artifact of art is simpler to reproduce than the creation of nature: *Artis scilicet semper facilior imitatio; naturalem uenustatem difficillime assequare* (*O* 1:16; doubtless the imitation of art is always easier, the pursuit of a natural charm the most difficult). But more important than this fact is that Virgil showed how to plagiarize the innate poet; he bequeathed a method for the talented but lazy poet and hack alike. Analysis shows that *sententiae autem et uerba magnam partem ex Theocrito sunt conuersa* (*O* 1:17; his ideas and words are largely taken from Theocritus); or alternatively: *Argumenta carminum . . . alia sunt ex Theocrito mutuata et interdum ieiune satis traducta aut e pluribus Idylliorum locis coagmentata, ut tertia et septima Ecloga* (*O* 1:17; the contents of other poems are adapted from

Theocritus, now and again fairly thinly altered, or stitched together from various passages in the *Idylls*, such as the third and seventh).[95] Heyne gives utterance on this point to the general feeling of the time. In an aside Ramler, as early as the 1740s, expressed the same opinion of Virgil, though less slighting in tone: "Ja er hat sich so sehr an ihn [Theocritus] gehalten, daß er seine Eclogen beynahe bloße Nachahmungen des Griechen sind. Einerley Materien, einerley Wendungen, sehr oft einerley Gedancken"; and Wieland likewise noted: "[Virgil] der selbst größentheils ein freyer Übersetzer des Theokrit ist."[96]

Following the demolition of Virgil's literary ability at the level of style, composition, and talent, and the denial of any intellectual interests deeper than the exhibition of a facility with language, there remains no avenue of approach open for a sympathetic reading of Virgil. Heyne draws the logical conclusion from this and makes his most radical claim, arguing that Virgil be removed from the bucolic canon. The imitation of the *Eclogues* should cease, as it is detrimental to the true interest of the genre and for the *nascentes poetae* (rising poets), who learn only to demonstrate their virtuosity while corrupting their feeling. Heyne diagnoses such misguided imitation as the cause for the failure of most ancient and modern bucolic poetry (*O* 1:15). A mark of the degree of Heyne's bafflement before the *Eclogues* may be found in his rather improbable suggestion that the inordinate fame of the poems is attributable solely to the approving reaction of the Romans to the surprising novelty of a tender plant unexpectedly surviving its transplant to inhospitable soil (*O* 1:18). The fame of novelty is usually passing, yet for some reason it did not wear off in the case of the *Eclogues*.

Herder represents the other side of the theoretical argument; that is, he makes plain its consequences for Theocritus. He forcefully elevates him to the role of champion of the new understanding of pastoral while making no more than passing mention of Virgil. He also at the same time represents the synthesis of the opposing arguments of Rapin and Fontenelle and their subsequent permutations. By fixing on a historical, non-fabulous age, Herder preserves the historicism of Rapin and the German tradition; by making the question of man's inner relation to nature the determining feature of a historical age, he preserves the subjective quality of Fontenelle and Schlegel; and by elevating this relation to at once an object of imitation and a source of inspiration, he forces the question of the status of this relation and thus prepares the way for Schiller's reflections on it.

His lavish praise of Theocritus's *Idylls* in the second collection of the *Fragmente über die neuere deutsche Literatur* (1767) does not greatly aid Theocritus, because he places him at an unbridgeable distance from the modern reader, in a time and place where man and nature communed more freely. Its residual effect confirms Theocritus's possession of the title of naïf. That Herder directs the animus of his criticism towards Gessner and not Virgil indicates that Virgil is no longer a formidable object to be overcome. He states bluntly what is at issue for the eighteenth-century reader in the successive stages of civilization from pastoral through to city and court. These stages represent an increasing separation from nature, which are measured by the progressive ossification of the capacity for direct feeling. "Erst Leidenschaft, denn Empfindung, denn Beschäftigungen, und endlich todte Malerey" (*HW* 1:353). Each stage accordingly produces an ever more derivative form of pastoral. And lest his reader should be in doubt of the far-reaching consequences of his claim, he continues with the claim that this change is parallel to the one that makes "aus der Homerischen Iliade eine Aeneide" (*HW* 1:353).

Herder's interest is to argue that nature expresses itself with an immediacy through the genius of Theocritus — and of Greek poets in general — that betrays the least possible amount of tampering on the part of civilization.

> Das Ideal des Schäfergedichts ist: *wenn man Empfindungen und Leidenschaften der Menschen in kleinen Gesellschaften so sinnlich zeigt, daß wir auf den Augenblick mit ihnen Schäfer werden, und so weit verschönert zeigt*, daß wir es den *Augenblick werden wollen*. (*HW* 1:356)

The success of the art is that is not recognized as art. The reader responds to it as he would to a scene before his eyes, as an object of attraction or repulsion, in this case a moment of rapture that assures the sentimental reader that he is at least in feeling, even if only for an instant, still a vicarious inhabitant of the state of nature. The fictive character of the bucolic may owe its entrancing illusion to its being a work of art, a "Verschönerung." Even despite Herder's recognition that Theocritus is "ein später Dichter" (*HW* 1:353), the latter portion of the essay, which sets forth the difference between Theocritus and Gessner, stresses the directness of the relation to nature, not the cultural mediation of art (see *HW* 1:356–60).[97]

Herder specifically rejects the notion of the golden age and any moralizing or idealizing qualities the bucolic may be supposed to have as a consequence; Theocritus "porträtierte aus dem Leben" (*HW* 1:357). Their rejection does not mean Herder succeeds in rejecting the bucolic golden age *in toto*; rather, he reformulates simplicity to be independent of the moral or ideal qualities of the Arcadian shepherd: "lauter Schäferlarven, keine Gesichter: Schäfer, nicht Menschen" (*HW* 1:358). True simplicity is an attribute of humanity nourished within nature. Its possession does not stem from any conscious acquisition: "Jenes Naivité ist eine Tochter der einfältigen Natur; die Naiveté im Geßner ist von der idealischen Kunst geboren" (*HW* 1:359).

However problematic the assumption of a full-fledged humanity within the bosom of nature may seem, its identification with the Greek world lends a strong element of historicism and primitivism to Herder's understanding of Theocritus. Whatever the Theocritean shepherds may engage in is innocent as they do it according to their nature, "die nach ihrem Zeitalter und nach ihrer Gesellschaft *unschuldig* ist" (*HW* 1:355). To put the matter another way, Theocritus does not project back into his rustics the aspirations of the Virgilian Georgic philosopher whom Herder quotes at this point: *Qui metus omnes et inexorabile fatum/ Subiecit pedibus* (*Ge.* 2. 491–92; "[who] hath laid all fears and immitigable Fate . . . under his feet; 321). The philosopher and the rustic are not comparable figures for Herder as they were for Virgil. This primitivism is historically conditioned and limited. It is not a mode of relation accessible to subsequent ages: "Wir, die von diesem Zeitalter der Natur so weit entfernt sind, daß wir fast niemals *wahre menschliche* Sitten, sondern *politische Lebensart* erblicken" (*HW* 1:357–58). He mentions here Fontenelle and Gessner, but he could as well mention Virgil. This view of primitivism means the rejection of the kind of feeling that only arises later with the awareness of no longer being within the culture of nature. For the estimation of Gessner, the nuanced "Empfindung" that Schlegel and Ramler along with the whole age of sentimentality so prized is now discredited as a token of alienation from nature. As this feeling, and the style that accompanied it, afforded some means of reading the Virgilian poems, its dismissal closes the last avenue of approach either to Virgil or to his poems.

Herder complements his pastoral historicism with his anthropological conception of the development of civilization. He identifies the pastoral age with the childhood of humanity, which soon becomes a commonplace of bucolic theory.[98] This not only gives the bucolic the new persona of the child to replace the increasingly implausible shepherd, but as a general condition it also preserves the naivety required for the idyll when extended to the inhabitants of the present-day village. As the child remains happily ignorant of the forces that shape his existence, so too does the village community. Herder's blithe assertion, "Theokrit schildert kleinere menschliche Gesellschaften" (*HW* 1:357), proves fateful, even if credit for the insistence on the smaller community as the locus of the pastoral belongs to Moses Mendelssohn. So powerful is the reconstitution of the idyll around a domestic bliss close to nature, or to use Jean Paul's aphoristic phrase, "Vollglück in Beschränkung,"[99] that it comes to form the conventional image called to mind at the mention of the word "idyll."[100] The truncated community formed on this notion of nature cannot include wider social and political relations.[101] The conception of a natural order of society outside the polis was alien to the ancient bucolic. From this modern perspective, the increasing intensity of the interpenetration of "nature" with social and political institutions in the *Eclogue*, the *Georgics*, and the *Aeneid* can find no echo. The integrity of the insight that animates them runs counter to the Enlightenment's conception of nature and man's relation to it.

Because of the very vitality of the genre and its accompanying theoretical debate, the rejection of the *Eclogues* is also an estrangement from the concerns that breathe life into the Virgilian poems. The versatility of the literary imagination of the ancient bucolic echoes, and echoes increasingly faintly, only in the recurrent demand for a guileless art. The discernment of nostalgia and its exploration moves inward to become a constitutive element of the human psyche and of pastoral theory, but not of pastorals themselves. Virgil's stature as a bucolic poet until the 1760s owes more to the inherited weight of tradition than to any vivid insight into his bucolics. The final break occurs once the various pastoral themes so coalesce about the idea of nature that that his poems seem to contradict the new expectations.

The debate about the pastoral is fittingly and ironically framed at either end of the century-long involvement with the ancient bucolic by quotations from the *Georgics*. At one end the sweet virtue of a lost age finds favor with Rapin. He cites a portion of Virgil's description of the golden age from the "Praises of the Country Life" (*Ge.* 2:467–71) as proof of the pastoral's concern for the golden age. At the other end, Herder quotes from the same passage of the *Georgics* (2:491–92) to deny the parallel Virgil had established between philosopher and farmer. The philosopher's relation to the countryside and the rustics has become essentially different; the two cannot be reconciled. It leads instead to a Gessner, one who projects his "knowing" feeling into the countryside in his idylls, but who succeeds better at deceiving himself than in returning to the feeling of the rustic. In these two instances the Georgic formulation acts as the lens through which the critics agree in looking back at the pastoral, and in this they are representative of the period as a whole.

The final step in the elevation of Theocritus and the corresponding demotion of Virgil follows only with Herder, who with Heyne represents the conclusion to the bucolic argument begun by Rapin and Fontenelle. The impetus the French critics gave to pastoral theory by restricting the issue of the reformed bucolic to a question of the interpretation of the works of Theocritus and Virgil is now exhausted. So too is the interest in the *Eclogues* and, as they are representative of the more general issues in the Virgilian œuvre, they foreshadow the fate of Virgil as a whole. Once the theorists sever the close link between the idyll, as the modern pastoral has now become, and the ancient-cum-Virgilian bucolic, the theoretical understanding of the genre rapidly develops along the lines suggested by the modern pastoral writers, notably Gessner and Voss. The former, though much maligned following Herder's critique, provides a modern starting point that easily extends to include Voss's *Luise* and Goethe's *Hermann und Dorothea;* a poetic form that is no longer an idyll, but an "idyllisches" or "bürgerliches Epos." Bucolic theory, once freed from the continual need to consider the example of Virgil, soon, with Schiller, transposes the treatment of bucolic harmony into a question of the attitude reflected towards a mode of feeling, in contrast to mere "Empfindung," into a question of naive and sentimental, or, in Humboldt's formulation, a question of an "Empfindungsweise." A writer can distill the essence of the idyll into the idyllic, which is an attribute, not a object. It becomes then suitable for an interlude or scene, but no longer for a genre. Hegel administers the *coup de grace* by insisting that the idyll, not having sufficient resources on its own, is compelled to join with epic, itself in turn a genre in the prosaic world of modernity rendered effete by constriction to the miniature world of the idyll.[102]

In the Enlightenment the theorists and the poets divide between themselves the dynamic contained within the confines of the ancient bucolic, but at the cost of rendering the genre insipid. The recognition of the limits of the new Arcadia occurs first within Schiller. The genre, stripped of all the devices and themes necessary for the exploration of the impulses to which it owes its origin and appeal, is defunct and must bore the reader. "Der Leser von Geist und Empfindung verkennt zwar den Wert solcher Dichtungen nicht, aber er fühlt sich seltener zu denselben gezogen und früher davon gesättigt" (*SchW* 20: 496). Schiller's recognition of the idyll as a late addition to poetry on account of its sentimentality in no way dissuades him from maintaining the paramount dogma that the idyll must always remain naive. As the idyll itself cannot legitimately question its own naivety, the only option for the genre lies in broadening the state of nature to include smaller forms of communal association, as in Voss's *Luise*. This extension is achieved only at the cost of rendering the lesser forms of community naive and so consistent with the notion of a life in nature.

Despite the disappearance of Virgil from the pastoral horizon, the development of the idyll to Voss's *Luise* and Goethe's *Hermann und Dorothea* suggestively parallels the development from the *Eclogues* to the *Georgics*. The transition from herdsmen to peasants is one parallel already noted. The other is its translation into the present. The significance of this lies in the removal of Arcadia from the dream world of the not-here and the not-now. Instead, the ideal habit of life it represents gains urgency and becomes a utopia, a moral appeal. One has now an idyll, "welche mit einem Wort, den Menschen, der nun einmal nicht mehr nach *Arkadien* zurückkann, bis nach *Elisium* führt" (*SchW* 20:472). These two parallels point to the affinities between the Virgilian model and the last third of the century. Virgil and his poems may have been swept from the canon, but that does not abolish the richness of the Virgilian devices for exploring the pastoral impulse, nor does it erase a striking word or image from the mind. German poets with a pastoral turn had read their Virgil, and, as good poets less than eager to produce works that would be uninteresting to Schiller's reader of "Geist und Empfindung," they are not above exploiting Virgil, despite critical disapproval. However, these Virgilian traces pass largely unremarked.

Notes

[1] To give only a brief list: Dante, Boccaccio, and Petrarch wrote Latin pastorals, a tradition that became part of the vernacular as is reflected in Spenser's *Shepheardes Calender* (1579). Sannazaro created the first modern pastoral novel with his *Arcadia* (1502, 1504). In Spain, Cervantes also wrote a pastoral novel, *Galatea* (1585), whose conventions he later spoofed, along with much else, in *Don Quixote* (1605, 1615). England could point to Sidney's *Arcadia* (1590, 1593) and France to the astonishingly successful *L'Astrée* (1607–25) by d'Urfé. In Germany, after having translated Sidney's *Arcadia*, Opitz in his turn produced *Schäfferey der Nimfen Hercinie* (1630). Pastoral drama also made its contribution with Tasso's *Aminta* (1573) and Guarini's *Il pastor fido* (1583).

[2] Thomas G. Rosenmeyer's *The Green Cabinet* (Berkeley: U of California P, 1969) is a distinctive example of this as well as highly influential in the study of the pastoral. With regard to the ancient bucolic, it should also be noted that Rosenmeyer attempts to shift the critical focus from the Virgilian *Eclogues* by recovering Theocritus's bucolic idylls for the pastoral tradition as more than simply a preface to Virgil's poems. For an assessment of Rosenmeyer's critical gesture, see Thomas K. Hubbard, *The Pipes of Pan* (Ann Arbor: Michigan UP, 1998), 2–3.

[3] With respect to pastoral criticism, this function of Schiller is most clearly underscored by David Halperin, *Before Pastoral: Theocritus and the Ancient Tradition of Bucolic Poetry* (New Haven: Yale UP, 1983), 42–49. Also in this regard see Paul Alpers, *The Singer of the Eclogues: A Study of Virgilian Pastoral* (Berkeley: U of California P, 1979), 204–9.

[4] A more generalized idyllic mode is the principle under which Renato Poggioli includes the topics of his later chapters on the pastoral; see *The Oaten Flute* (Cambridge: Harvard UP, 1975).

[5] William Empson, *Some Versions of Pastoral* (1935; rev. ed., New York: New Directions, 1974), *passim*.

[6] See Viktor Pöschl, *Die Hirtendichtung Virgils* (Heidelberg: Winter, 1964), 7–8.

[7] See Klingner, generally all of the essays dealing with Virgil, but especially "Virgil und die geschichtliche Welt" (298) and "Das erste Hirtengedicht Virgils" (312–26), in *Römische Geisteswelt*, 5th enlarged ed. (Munich: Ellermann, 1965).

[8] Bruno Snell, "Arkadien, die Entdeckung einer geistigen Landschaft," in *Die Entdeckung des Geistes: Studien zur Entstehung des europäischen Denkens bei den Griechen* (Hamburg: Classen & Goverts, 1946), 233–58; repr. in *Wege zu Vergil: Drei Jahrzehnte Begegnungen in Dichtung und Wissenschaft*, ed. Hans Oppermann, Wege der Forschung 19 (Darmstadt: Wissenschaftliche Buchgesellschaft, 1963), 338–67. Snell's essay is readily obtainable as it has been much reprinted and also translated into English.

[9] Poggioli's study includes many other elements, but the imaginary landscape of Arcadia remains his starting point, as the first sentence illustrates: "The psychological root of the pastoral is a double longing after innocence and happiness, to be recovered not through conversion or regeneration but merely through a retreat"

(1). The 1957 article "The Oaten Flute" becomes the first chapter of the 1975 book of the same name. Alpers points out the proximity of Snell's position to Schiller's (*The Singer of the Eclogues*, 204).

[10] Thomas G. Rosenmeyer, *The Green Cabinet*.

[11] See David M. Halperin, *Before Pastoral*.

[12] It is the general thrust of the argument in the first chapter and is summarized in its conclusion: Michael C. J. Putnam, *Virgil's Pastoral Art: Studies in the Eclogues* (Princeton: Princeton UP, 1970), 81.

[13] Charles Segal, *Poetry and Myth in Ancient Pastoral* (Princeton: Princeton UP, 1981), 6–7.

[14] See Hubbard, *The Pipes of Pan*, introduction. Programmatic in the sense that he accepts intention in the sense of an artistic persona shaped according to Bloom's notion of anxiety of influence (11–13).

[15] A recent token of Theocritus's emancipation from the pastoral is the shift from the fixation on the bucolic idylls to the more detailed study of the non-bucolic idylls: e.g. Frederick T. Griffiths, *Theocritus at Court* (Leiden: Brill, 1979) and Richard L. Hunter, *Theocritus and the Archaeology of Greek Poetry* (Cambridge: Cambridge UP, 1996).

[16] Rosenmeyer, for instance, uses Schiller to exemplify aspects of the early modern pastoral (*The Green Cabinet*, 210) or to modify the understanding of the golden age with respect to the Greek bucoliasts (222); see also Poggioli, *The Oaten Flute*, 4. As previously noted, the most extensive and critical engagement occurs in Halperin's *Before Pastoral*.

[17] For a brief treatment of this transition using the diminishment of allegory as the marker of the change, see Klaus Garber, "Arkadien und Gesellschaft: Skizze der Sozialgeschichte der Schäferdichtung als utopisicher Literaturform Europas," in *Utopieforschung: Interdisziplinäre Studien zur neuzeitlichen Utopie*, ed. Wilhelm Vosskamp (Stuttgart: Metzler, 1982), 2:37–81.

[18] The tendency to emphasize the realistic aspects of Theocritus, particularly when reading him next to Virgil, remains strong. When considering the difference between the two poets, Büchner states, "Aber viel stärker sind die Unterschiede. Vor allem der, daß Theokrit wirkliche Hirten in ihrer Realität voller Abstand und mit lächelnder Überlegenheit schildert. Seine Ordnung ist nicht die selbstgeschaffene und selbstentdeckte einer liebenden Seele, sondern die objektive Ordnung des Hirtenlebens, des Hirtengesangs, des Sommertages" (Büchner, *Dichter der Römer*, 239).

[19] For information on Theocritus I have relied on A. S. F. Gow's two-volume edition with a translation and commentary, *Theocritus* (Cambridge: Cambridge UP, 1950) and Theocritus, *Select Poems*, ed. K. J Dover (London: Macmillan, 1971), For a detailed discussion of the external and internal evidence about Theocritus's life see Gow's introduction (1:xv–xxii).

[20] See Gow, *Theocritus*, 1:lx.

[21] See Hunter, *Theocritus and the Archaeology of Greek Poetry*, 1–37, Griffiths, *Theocritus at Court*, 1–8, and Hubbard, *The Pipes of Pan*, 19–44.

22 On occasion it even behaves as a dramatic meter with one line divided between two or more speakers (*Idd.* 14 and 15). Among the bucolic idylls this feature is rare, yet still present (*Idd.* 4. 45; 5. 66; 10. 16).

23 In *Idyll* 8 the song is given in elegiacs, not in hexameters, one reason to suspect this idyll's authenticity.

24 Dover, in Theocritus's *Selected Poems*, lvii.

25 For a more detailed discussion of the various dialects Theocritus writes in, see Gow, *Theocritus*, 1:lxxii–lxxx and also Dover, *Select Poems*, xxvii–xlv.

26 Richard Hunter, *Theocritus: A Selection* (Cambridge: Cambridge UP, 1999), 62 and 78.

27 See Segal, "'since Daphnis Dies': The Meaning of Theocritus' First Idyll," in *Poetry and Myth in Ancient Pastoral* (Princeton: Princeton UP, 1981), 29–31, as well as Hubbard, *The Pipes of Pan*, 21–22 and Hunter, *A Selection*, 76–77.

28 For a consideration of "realism" and its tension with lyrical and mythical aspects in Theocritus, see Charles Segal, "Landscape into Myth: Theocritus' Bucolic Poetry," in *Poetry and Myth in Ancient Pastoral*, 210–30.

29 So allusive and complex is Theocritus's invoking of the myth that it is not precisely clear what the reader is to understand about the cause of Daphnis's suffering: see Dover, *Select Poems*, 83–86, Hunter, *A Selection*, 63–66, and Segal, "The Meaning of Theocritus' First Idyll," 35–36.

30 There are three main arguments put forward when attempting to place the eclogues in the order of their composition. The eclogues dependent on Theocritus not merely for their themes and motifs but also for their treatment of them, such as *Eclogues* 2 and 3, are universally agreed to be the earliest. Dispute arises when the skin may be old but not the wine, as in *Eclogues* 7 and 8. Another line of argument depends on the reference to external events, the date of which other sources confirm. This helps date *Eclogues* 1, 4, 8, and 9. Internal evidence provides the third source of information. This category is a hotchpotch. It ranges from conclusions deduced from Virgil's penchant for self-citation to references to figures in other eclogues. In view of Virgil's often elliptical manner of expression, ample room remains for scholarly interpretation. The tenth eclogue offers the other fixed point of departure, since the opening line announces, *extremum hunc, Arethusa, mihi concede laborem*, that it is the last poem. The variety possible is evident from the two arrangements taken from Karl Büchner (2, 3, 5, 9, 1, 6, 4, 8, 7, and 10 [*Dichter der Römer*, 234]); and Robert Coleman in his commentary to Virgil's *Eclogues* (Cambridge: Cambridge UP, 1977) (2, 3, 5, 4, 7, 8, 9, 1, 6, and 10 [19]). They both agree in placing the most Theocritean bucolics earliest (*Ecs.* 2, 3, and 5). Coleman adheres more closely to the principle that those eclogues more imitative of Theocritus are first in composition, allowing only *Eclogue* 4 to interrupt them, whereas Büchner, because of their Arcadian setting, among other reasons, argues for a later date of composition, after that of the Roman eclogues, 1, 4, and 9. The common point of their arrangement is the placing of *Eclogue* 6 after *Eclogues* 9 and 1. For a detailed discussion see Büchner, *Dichter der Römer*, 231–35, and Coleman, *Eclogues*, 14–21.

31 To seek the origin of Virgil's Arcadia in the historical Arcadia described by Polybius is pointless. As Snell observes, the Virgilian Arcadia has no resemblance

to the Arcadia in Greece; see "Arkadien, die Entdeckung einer geistigen Landschaft," in *Wege zu Vergil*, ed. Hans Oppermann, Wege der Forschung 19 (Darmstadt: Wissenschaftliche Buchgesellschaft, 1963), 338–39. It is distinguished by a combination of its mythical links with Pan, who appears in *Idyll* 1. 123–26, and its capacity to absorb the associations with which Virgil's imagination sought to endow it. See also Coleman, *Eclogues*, 207–9.

[32] Wendell Clausen stresses the slight presence of Arcadia in the Virgilian bucolic and warns against the importation of the full range of meaning and associations it later acquires: "Arcadia conceived as an ideal or symbolic landscape, 'la pastorale Arcadia,' is the invention of Jacopo Sannazaro and Sir Philip Sidney — that is, a feature of the pastoral tradition — and should not be imposed retrospectively on Virgil"; see Clausen, *A Commentary on Virgil: Eclogues* (Oxford: Clarendon Press, 1994), 289.

[33] Translations from the *Eclogues* are from C. Day Lewis, *The Eclogues of Virgil* (London: Jonathan Cape, 1963).

[34] Brooks Otis advances the notion of a subjective style and traces it back to the *Eclogues:* see *Virgil: A Study in Civilized Poetry* (Oxford: Clarendon Press, 1963), 105–19.

[35] Michael C. Putnam argues for the *Eclogues* as the poet's protest against the disorder of the Roman state that threatens the root of the poetic imagination in its attack on individual liberty: "it depends upon a concomitant personal liberty to create in an atmosphere of integrity and order"; see *Virgil's Pastoral Art*, 9. He states that *Eclogues* 4 and 5 claim for poetry the capacity to effect a reconciliation between the estranged individual and society (18).

[36] For a strong reading of the importance of departure to the Virgilian pastoral, see Eleanor Windsor Leach, whose study of the poems explores the premise that "the poet of the *Eclogues* does not leave the pastoral reluctantly with expressions of sorrow and loss, but deliberately, as if a period of controlled poetic experimentation had reached its limit and timely conclusion" *Vergil's 'Eclogues': Landscapes of Experience* (Ithaca: Cornell UP, 1974), 50.

[37] An example of the manner in which Virgil can be viewed as "sentimental" and the degree to which it may be considered like, similar to, or approaching a modern, Western attitude of mind is explored by Haecker. The title of his book alone — *Vergil, Vater des Abendlandes* — suggests the direction of his argument. He emphasizes those aspects of Virgil that resonate most powerfully in the Christian and medieval world and culminate in the phrase, *anima naturaliter christiana* (a soul naturally Christian). See also Snell, "Arkadien, die Entdeckung," 358–59, and Büchner, *Der Dichter der Römer*, 241–43.

[38] In these two instances Day prefers a looser translation of these lines (58–59 and 62–63):

> I picture myself already, scaling the crags, halooing
> Through the wide woods, . . .
> words and woods mean nothing to me now. (45–46)

[39] Again Day's translation omits the precise phrase: "the Golden Age/ Returns" (23).

40 Hans-Joachim Mähl traces the permutations of the golden age from antiquity to Romanticism in *Die Idee des goldenen Zeitalters im Werk des Novalis* (Heidelberg: Carl Winter, 1965).

41 All translations from the *Georgics* are taken from J. W. Mackail, trans., *Virgil's Works*, intro. Charles L. Durham, The Modern Library (New York: Random House, 1934).

42 Friedrich Klingner, "Die Einheit des virgilischen Lebenswerkes," in *Römische Geisteswelt*, 5th enlarged ed. (Munich: Ellermann, 1965), 279. The thought is a general and important one to the German school of interpretation. Hans Oppermann, for instance, also makes the experience crucial to Virgil's development as citizen and poet: "Sinn seines Daseins und Sinn seines Dichtens dankt er dem Jüngling, . . . Von nun an ist Vergils Schaffen an sein Volk und an dessen jungen Führer gebunden, nicht mehr der neoterische Artist, der römische Dichter spricht" ("Vergil," 108).

43 Gow, *Theocritus*, 2:129.

44 Undoubtedly our understanding of the reason for Virgil's use of these myths would change if we knew the sources he refers to here. Clausen speaks of a "neoteric *ars poetica*" (*A Commentary*, 176). The prominent figure of Gallus, both here and in the tenth eclogue, and the extent of Virgil's reworkings of his verse cannot be satisfactorily determined as we have only one fragment of his poetry; see N.B. Crowther, "C. Cornelius Gallus: His Importance in the Development of Roman Poetry," in *Aufstieg und Niedergang der römischen Welt*, ed. Wolfgang Haase (Berlin: de Gruyter, 1983), 30/3:1622–48.

45 Erwin Panofsky, "*Et in Arcadia ego:* Poussin und die elegische Tradition," in *Europäische Bukolik und Georgik*, ed. Klaus Garber, Wege der Forschung 355 (1955; repr. Darmstadt: Wissenschaftliche Buchgesellschaft, 1976), 271–305.

46 Panofsky, *Et in Arcadia ego*, 262.

47 For the quotes by King George and Dr. Johnson, see Panofsky, *Et in Arcadia ego*, 271.

48 There are two possible candidates for the title of successful love: that of Tityrus and Amaryllis in the first eclogue and the Amaryllis of *Eclogue* 8, who wins her Daphnis back from the city. Although we are told that Amaryllis has a more beneficial effect on Tityrus than Galatea (*Ec.* 1. 30–32), and he is singing of her to the woods, his precise standing with her is neither clear nor the main focus of the poem. As Tityrus is the fortunate shepherd, we may perhaps be justified in assuming that things go well between him and Amaryllis. Of the other Amaryllis, she is only able to turn her shepherd's heart by resorting to magic.

49 Klaus Garber explores the richness of the German species during the Baroque in *Der locus amoenus und der locus terribilis: Bild und Funktion der Natur in der deutschen Schäfer- und Landlebendichtung des 17. Jahrhunderts* (Cologne: Böhlau, 1974). Of particular interest is the section dealing with the motif of the *aetas aurea*, 214–25. Making a distinction between the age of the Patriarchs as an age of the past as opposed to the future of the golden age in *Eclogue* 4, he states; "Das Motiv des goldenen Zeitalters ist in der deutschen Bukolik eine Seltenheit

geblieben.... Das in der Wiederkehr des goldenen Zeitalters verhießene Glück wurde also an das Schäfertum delegiert (von *Ec.* 1). So auch in Deutschland. Hier hatte die räumliche wie ständische Begrenzung der Eintracht auf das Schäfertum zudem den Vorteil, daß sie ander als der Mythos vom Goldenen Zeitalter nicht so stark in Konflikt mit der Wirklichkeit geriet" (223).

[50] For the briefest of sketches of Rapin's entrance into German pastoral writings see Renate Böschenstein, *Idylle*, Sammlung Metzler 63 (Stuttgart: Metzler, 1967), 42–43.

[51] See Werner Krauss, "Über die Stellung der Bukolik in der Theorie des Humanismus" (1938), repr. in *Europäische Georgik und Bukolik*, ed. Klaus Garber, Wege der Forschung 355 (Darmstadt: Wissenschaftliche Buchgesellschaft, 1976), 152–54.

[52] Scaliger, *Poetices libri septem*, 1:94.

[53] Scaliger, *Poetices libri septem*, 1:96.

[54] Scaliger, *Poetices libri septem*, 1:96.

[55] Scaliger, *Poetices libri septem*, 4:324.

[56] Scaliger, *Poetices libri septem*, 4:350.

[57] Rapin sees himself having "a hard task, since I have no guide, neither Aristotle nor Horace to direct me, for both they, whatever was the matter, speak not one word of this sort of Verse" (16). The pagination refers to the English translation by Thomas Creech. He used it as the introduction to his *Idyllums* of Theocritus in 1684. It is cited according to *The Augustan Reprint Society* 3 (July 1947). The reason for the frequent double pagination is that Creech's translation does not always follow Rapin's prolix Latin, which leads to some modifications. Creech also omits the *pars quarta* of Rapin's treatise and the last portion of *pars tertia*. Accordingly I have also on occasion either cited directly from Rapin's text or given the location of the corresponding passage in his text. Rapin's text is cited from *Eclogae sacrae cum dissertatione de carmine pastorali*, rev. and enlarged ed., vol. 1 (Paris: 1723) and given in the form of volume number followed by the pagination in Roman numerals: here 1:xxxvj.

For an appraisal of Creech's translation see J. E. Congleton, *Theories of Pastoral Poetry in England 1684–1798* (New York: Haskell House Publishers, 1968), 62. This translation was largely responsible for the effect that Rapin had on English theory and practice, and most notably on Pope: see Congleton, *Theories*, 77–83; on Rapin and Fontenelle, see Annabel Patterson, *Pastoral and Ideology: Virgil to Valéry* (Berkeley, Los Angeles: U of California P, 1987), 200–206.

[58] When speaking of the Humanists, whom Helmut Schneider considers Rapin to have summed up (*Deutsche Idyllentheorien im 18. Jahrhundert* [Tübingen: Gunter Narr, 1988]), 27, he argues that the notion of a historical golden age was not taken seriously, as may seen by the fact "daß kein Widerspruch zum allegorischen Gehalt gesehen wurde" (24). This does not do justice to the role of the golden age in Rapin. He certainly does not consider it a known quantity, as he would, for example, the world of Rome under Augustus; he even says, if it ever existed, it did so in "fabulous times" (15; 1:xxxv). It is however more than just an acknowledged fiction, or a purely abstract assumption for the sake of argument. It is, for Rapin,

an ideal, Christian truth that can be seen in his repeated appeals to its moral essence, its simplicity or elegance, or from the doctrine of the imitation of an action, but most easily by looking at his own eclogues in which from out of the mouths of shepherds come pearls of Christian revelation. See also E. Kegel-Brinkgreve, *The Echoing Woods: Bucolic and Pastoral from Theocritus and Wordsworth* (Amsterdam: J.C. Gieben, 1990), 560–64. Thus Schneider's subsequent statement about the novelty of the initial German theoretical position — "Denn im Unterschied zu den humanistichen Vorgängern meint er [Gottsched] nicht mehr das goldene Zeitalter der Imitatio, sondern einen historischen Idealzustand *jenseits und außerhalb der klassichen Texte* [his emphasis]" (43) — cannot be accepted without modification.

⁵⁹ The argument tying biblical patriarchs and other mythical figures to the pastoral and thus closely intertwining the Christian conception of history with the bucolic genre is not original with Rapin: see Krauss, "Über die Stellung," 146–47.

⁶⁰ The Latin is more circumspect in its wording: *Tantae autem simplicitatis quae viget apud pastores forma, quid prae se fert aliud, quam primae hominum innocentiae auream aetatem, et beatam imaginem illorum temporum, quibus candor, innocentia, pax, otium, faustitas ruri regnare videbantur?* (1:xxiv). Böschenstein gives for the German of this the phrase, "vollkommener Spiegel der Unschuld," likewise less tentative than the Latin (*Idylle*, 43).

⁶¹ In another instance of the importance of the *Georgics* for an increasingly moral view of the pastoral, Rapin cites the passage in the second book about *Iustitia* being the last of the gods to leave earth at the end of the golden age, to support his contention that it is a time of *pastores . . . simplices, ingenui, candidi, justitiae amantes* (1:xcij; [not translated by Creech] shepherds, simple, free, honest, lovers of justice).

⁶² For this reason, he argues, Servius deemed only seven of Virgil's *Eclogues* to be true pastorals, and accepted only ten of Theocritus's thirty *Idylls* (27). See Rapin, 1:xlvij–xlviij. There is an odd discrepancy in the translation. Rapin states: *et ex triginta sex idyllis Theocriti decem tantum numeret [Servius] pure pastoralia* (1:xlvij), which Creech renders as, "and only ten of *Theocritus*'s thirty, to be pure pastorals" (27). Where Rapin got the number 36, or whether it is an error peculiar to this edition, I do not know.

⁶³ He scolds Mantuan for the former and, for the latter, the Italians in general. It too sets a pattern. Each nation will affect to find the pastoral of the neighbor deemed to be a literary rival either affected or coarse. Herder and Gottsched, for instance, agree in finding Fontenelle's shepherds too courtly.

⁶⁴ The first instance occurs on the proper expression of low or "mean" subjects and reads: "for ingenuous simplicity both of Thought and Expression is the natural *Characteristick* of *Pastoral*" (57; 1:lxxix); the same phrase occurs again, two pages later, this time to distinguish pastoral diction from an overly ornate and clever diction. "Ingenuous simplicity" obviously describes a stylistic middle ground.

⁶⁵ Theocritus' Doric becomes for Rapin that *quid exprimit ad rusticitatis simplicitatem sic idoneum: ut nihil, quod ingenio pastorali magis conveniat, excogitari posset* (1:cvj; [not translated by Creech] which expresses rustic simplicity so fittingly that nothing more suitable to the nature of the pastoral could be supposed). He brushes

aside the evidence of *Idyll* 14 that Doric sounded to the cultivated Greek ear like the *stridor turturum* (the racket of the turtle-dove) with the argument that it cannot be so since it was also spoken in Corinth, the *urbs . . . Graeciae plenissima urbanitatis* (1:cvij; the city . . . with greatest degree of Greek refinement).

[66] This is one of only three passages in which Rapin comments on love in the pastoral, although a serious concern for love is predicated of the golden age shepherd. The others mention love as one of the chief preoccupations of the shepherd (25; 1:xlv) and that it be innocent and pure (25 and 67; 1:xlv and xciij).

[67] Georg Christoph Lichtenberg, *Aphorismen, Essays, Briefe*, ed. Kurt Batt, Sammlung Dietrich 260 (Bremen: Schünemann, 1963), 279.

[68] Bernard le Bouvier de Fontenelle, "Discours sur la nature de l'eglogue," in *Oeuvres complètes*, ed. Alain Niderst (Paris: Fayard, 1989–2001), 2:385. Once again Congleton provides the standard survey of Fontenelle's views (*Theories of Pastoral Poetry*, 65–71). See Schneider for a consideration of the questions of taste and reality with regard to Fontenelle's essay (*Idyllentheorien*, 30–33). In the following paragraphs, references to Fontenelle's work will be by volume and page number alone.

[69] In the same vein: "les chèvres et les brebis ne servent de rien: mais comme il faut choisir entre la campagne et les villes, il est plus vraisemblable que cette scène soit à la campagne. . . . nouvelle preuve que l'agrément de l'Eglogue n'est pas attaché aux choses rustiques, mais à ce qu'il y a de tranquille dans la vie de la campagne" (2:392).

[70] Congleton approaches the matter from the opposite end: "The resulting theories of Rapin and Fontenelle, however, do not differ so widely as their diametrical methods and assumptions" (*Theories of Pastoral Poetry*, 70). What is surely more striking, and a tribute to the compelling power of Rapin's theoretical statement, is that the notion of simplicity, once harnessed to the rigor of rationalism, attains a life of its own in bucolic theory. It is this assumption along with its stylistic corollary that is of cardinal importance.

[71] See also Fontenelle, *Discours*, 36 for another oblique reference to Rapin. One might also see a silent tribute to Rapin in the fact that Fontenelle discusses the whole question of loftiness only in relation to Virgil, without any mention of Theocritus's non-bucolic idylls that Rapin had discussed in this context and ruled out for their lack of pastoral garb. His choice of Virgil for this purpose might also be further explained by the fact that that it was to Virgil that Rapin looked for his example of the proper introduction of lofty matters.

[72] On the final page of his essay Fontenelle makes an explicit and approving reference to Perrault and the *Querelle*, which began the year previously in 1687.

[73] Patterson views the relation of eighteenth-century theory to the pastoral as an example of symbolic displacement and of false consciousness (*Pastoral and Ideology*, 199–200). This leads her to seek the motivation for Rapin's and Fontenelle's speculations in either conscious or unconscious personal, political, and class aspirations. Unquestionably it places the pastoral in its wider historical context by emphasizing those interests that may dispose an individual to consider some arguments and not others. On the other hand, it fails either to concede a coherence to the material addressed or to recognize the effects of the Rationalist impulse to make all branches of human activity accessible to reason. Neither the systematic and

historical intent of Rapin nor the normative subjective psychology of Fontenelle is recognized. Rapin's two-part definition of the pastoral is, she argues, disingenuous, since he, in common with Fontenelle, wishes to "exclude the Virgilian dialectic, along with the 'high' subjects of history, prophecy, and metaphysics" (*Pastoral and Ideology*, 206). This characterization of Rapin's enterprise does not acknowledge Rapin's critical intent in his search for an object of imitation although it does accurately assess its effect. It also leaves Rapin's own *Eclogae sacrae* in an embarrassing want of an explanation. Likewise it is difficult to conceive why Fontenelle should be thought of as "insinuating" a personal interest into the pastoral: "Je suis berger" could not be more open. That the pastoral is wholly dependent on the interests of the "I" is his insight, even if one may well quibble about the assumptions of what those interests are.

[74] See Schneider, *Idyllentheorien*, 33–42.

[75] Alexander Pope, *The Poems of Alexander Pope*, ed. E. Audra and Aubrey Williams (London: Methuen, 1961), 1:25. The notes on the text of Pope's introduction to his *Pastorals* detail his use of both Rapin and Fontenelle. See Congleton, *Theories of Pastoral Poetry*, 75–96, and also Patterson, *Pastoral and Ideology*, 207–14.

[76] See John Chalker, *The English Georgic: A Study in the Development of a Form* (Baltimore: Johns Hopkins P, 1969); and more recently Anthony Low, *The Georgic Revolution* (Princeton: Princeton UP, 1985).

[77] Cited according to *The Pastoral Mode*, ed. Bryan Loughrey (London: Macmillan, 1984), 69.

[78] Gottsched, *Ausgewählte Werke*, 6/2:76. References to Gottsched's writings in the next pages are by volume and page number alone.

[79] "Capacious" because Harsdörffer is descriptive rather than normative with regard to the pastoral. He has room for the more courtly version of the pastoral with its personages of rank in the guise of shepherd (100), for a Georgic variety (101), and also for a golden age one (102). See Georg Philipp Harsdörffer, *Poetischer Trichter* (1647–53; facsimile repr., Hildesheim: Georg Olms, 1971), part 2.

[80] The question of "Hütte und Palast" is closely connected with the generic problem of separating the "Landgedicht" from the "Ekloge." Friedrich Sengle traced the opposition between town and country to this debate in his "Wunschbild Land und Schreckbild Stadt: Zu einem zentralen Thema der neueren deutschen Literatur" (1963); repr. in *Europäische Bukolik und Georgik*, ed. Klaus Garber, Wege der Forschung 355 (Darmstadt: Wissenschaftliche Buchgesellschaft, 1976), 432–60. Burghard Dedner approaches the same problem from the side of how the utopian idealization of "das Landleben" leads to a neglect of the conditions on the land and a weakening of the Enlightenment impulse to engage in reform and improvement. In "Vom Schäferleben zur Agrarwirtschaft: Poesie und Ideologie des 'Landleben' in der deutschen Literatur des 18. Jahrhunderts," 1972; repr. in Gerber, *Europäische Bukolik und Georgik*, 347–90; he too ties the German formulation of these themes to Gottsched and the ensuing debate about the pastoral.

[81] The challenge of definition unleashed a prodigious flood of ink and ingenuity in Germany during the middle decades of the century, which Gerhard Hämmerling

sets forth in his book, *Die Idylle von Geßner bis Voß: Theorie, Kritik und allgemeine geschichtliche Bedeutung*, Europäische Hochschulschriften, Reihe 1, Deutsche Sprache und Literatur (Frankfurt am Main: Peter Lang, 1981).

[82] Hämmerling discusses the relation of the middle style, naivety, and "Zärtlichkeit" to the bucolic (*Die Idylle*, 41–60). He puts forward the argument that Gottsched envisions a stylistic synthesis of Virgil and Theocritus.

[83] For a brief summary of the dispute see Böschenstein, *Idylle*, 46–47.

[84] Schneider, *Idyllentheorien*, 115. All quotations are from the reprint of the 1759 edition of Schlegel's translation of Batteux in Schneider's *Idyllentheorien*, 111–54. Schneider does not reprint the treatise in its entirety. A few passages devoted to a defense of Fontenelle's eclogues are omitted.

[85] With an eye on the earlier pieces, Mähl lays emphasis on Schlegel's use of the Swiss critics to champion the right of the imagination to combine elements of "Wirklichkeit" according to its own light and in the service of a Rococo sensibility; see *Die Idee*, 154–56.

[86] See Schneider, *Idyllentheorien*, 143–44 and Böschenstein, *Idylle*, 48.

[87] Carl Wilhelm Ramler, trans., *Einleitung in die schönen Wissenschaften*, by Charles Batteux (Leipzig: 1756), 1:137, "la vie champêtre." For information on the somewhat complicated evolution of Batteux's text as well as the scope of its German reception, see the introduction to his *Les Beaux-Arts réduits à un même principe*, ed. Jean-Rémy Mantion (Paris: aux amateurs de livres, 1989). Johann Georg Sulzer, *Allgemeine Theorie der schönen Künste* (1771; repr. Leipzig: Weidmanns Erben & Reich, 1773), 1:719.

[88] Sulzer, *Allgemeine Theorie der schönen Künste*, 1:721. Further references to Wieland's article will refer to Sulzer's work by volume and page number alone.

[89] This observation is from Böschenstein, *Idylle*, 47.

[90] Schneider suggests the year 1753 as the most likely (*Idyllentheorien*, 162), as does Bernhard Seuffert, "Prolegomena zu einer Wieland-Ausgabe VI," *Abhandlungen der königlichen preussischen Akademie der Wissenschaften*, Abhandlung 1 (1909): 107. However a later date seems more plausible. In February of 1756 Wieland was invited to contribute to Sulzer's *Allgemeine Theorie der schönen Künste*, a task that he completed by the end of the year; see Seuffert, "Prolegomena," 51 and also Thomas C. Starnes, *Christoph Martin Wieland: Leben und Werke aus zeitgenössischen Quellen chronologisch dargestellt* (Sigmaringen: Thorbecke, 1987), 1:115. This gives an *ante quam* of late 1756. Some of the articles he had written as early as 1753, in particular the "Abhandlung vom Naiven" (Seuffert, "Prolegomena," 40). For this reason, Seuffert recommends that the article on the "Idylle" be placed among the other pieces of doubtful authorship from the same year (see 36–38, and 107). This serves as a *post quam*. Internal considerations point to a date towards the end of the period. The difficulty of an early dating is Wieland's explicit praise of Gessner's "Idyllen" (Sulzer, *Allgemeine Theorie*, 1, 722), unless one assumes it is a later editorial addition. Although Gessner had written "Die Nacht" (published 1753) and "Der Frühling" (published 1756 in *Idyllen*) and made Wieland's acquaintance by the end of 1752, 1753 was the year of his pastoral novel *Daphnis*. According to E. Theodor Voss, it was not until December 1754 that Gessner returned to the writing of idylls, which he completed

in June 1755, see Salomon Gessner, *Die Idyllen*, ed. E. Theodor Voss (Stuttgart: Reclam, 1973), 298. This more or less corresponds to the chronology in Starnes's compilation: in October 1753 there is a mention of a reading from a "Schäfergedicht," not an idyll, by Gessner — probably *Daphnis* — again in early 1754 (see Starnes, *Christoph Martin Wieland* 1:54 and 61), and in January 1755 a notice that seven idylls are complete (1:85).

[91] As this essay does not change between the first and second edition, all quotations are again from the second edition.

[92] For a discussion of the degree of similarity see Coleman, *Eclogues*, 225–26 and 253–55.

[93] Sulzer's straightforward statement, "es gibt eine Gattung der Hirtenlieder, die ganz allegorisch ist" (*Allgemeine Theorie*, 1:720), accepts at least one "new" genre of pastorals as established. In his estimation of it he is less deprecatory, mentioning Virgil's first and tenth eclogues as "fürtreffliche Beyspiele dieser Art" (1:721).

[94] *Eclogue* 4 is also classed under this heading because of the Pollio reference.

[95] *Eclogue* 7 in fact borrows very little from Theocritus directly. Heyne's opinion appears to have been based on Servius; see *Commentarii*, 1:82.

[96] Ramler, *Einleitung*, 1:370 and Wieland in Sulzer, *Allgemeine Theorie*, 1:722.

[97] Time tempered Herder's youthful enthusiasm for a naive Theocritus. In *Adrastea* (1801), he writes: "Theokrits Gedichte sind Kunstwerke. . . . Wahrscheinlich war es Bescheidenheit, daß der gelehrte Alexandriner, Er, in Wahl der Gegenstände sowohl als im Versbau ein wahrer Künstler, diesen Namen [eidullion] wählte" (*HW* 10:279).

[98] The connection between children and an innocence most at home in the countryside stretches back into antiquity with Longus's *Daphnis and Chloe* (late 2nd or early 3rd century A.D.) and reappears in the idylls of Gessner and Maler Müller, but Herder equates childhood with a stage of culture in *Auch eine Philosophie der Geschichte zur Bildung der Menschheit*, 1774, *HW* 4:11–19. The pastoral age is "das goldene Zeitalter der kindlichen Menschheit" (4:15). The timeliness of the connection is visible in the unopposed rapidity with which it becomes a standard formulation of bucolic theory. For the general importance of childhood and its innocence in relation to nature and naivety, see Schiller (*SchW* 20:415–19); and for its peculiar relation to the Idylle, both positive and negative, in the section entitled "Idylle" (*SchW* 20:467 and 472; and Jean Paul, "Vorschule der Ästhetik," in *Werke*, ed. Norbert Miller (Munich: Carl Hanser Verlag, 1963), 5:257–58.

[99] Jean Paul, *Werke*, 5:258.

[100] See E. Theodor Voss, "Arkadien und Grünau: Johann Heinrich Voss und das innere System seines Idyllenwerkes" (1968), repr. in Garber, *Europäische Bukolik und Georgic*, 399. He argues that the interpretation of Voss's *Luise* and *Siebzigster Geburtstag* is biased because they are "kanonisiert" by this unhistorical and enduring ideal of the idyll.

[101] Sengle begins his genealogy of "Bauerngeschichte" from the perspective of one looking back after the Nazi period to find the cultural and literary origins of the idealization of the rural life. He points to this conception of the bourgeois idyll as the progenitor of the "Dorfgeschichte" (see Sengle, *Wunschbild*, 436 and 441–42). Jeffery Herf also lists as one contributing strand to Fascist ideology the

enduring strength of what he calls "simple pastoralism" in *Reactionary Modernism: Technology, Culture and Politics in Weimar and the Third Reich* (Cambridge: Cambridge UP, 1984).

[102] *SchW* 20:466–472; Humboldt, "Über Goethes Hermann und Dorothea," in *Gesammelte Schriften*, ed. von der Königlichen Preussischen Akademie der Wissenschaften (Berlin: de Gruyter, 1968), 2:250–51; and Georg Friedrich Wilhelm Hegel, "Vorlesungen über die Aesthetik," in *Sämtliche Werke*, Jubiläumsausgabe, ed. Hermann Glockner (Stuttgart: Frommanns, 1928), 14:416–18.

5: The German Idyll and the Virgilian Muse

Salomon Gessner: The Modern Idyll and Sentimental Nature

THE GRADUAL TRANSFORMATION OF THE pastoral, as the cultural criticism of the German Enlightenment coalesces with the new feeling for nature, comes to a head in the wildly popular *Idyllen* (1756) of Gessner. So successfully does Gessner combine all the various strands into a coherent literary expression that the result is tantamount to "eine neue Gattung."[1] The astonishing appeal of Gessner to his age is today even less well remembered than that of Haller and his *Die Alpen* (1732). Yet Gessner was the first German writer to achieve literary renown beyond the borders of the German world and was only displaced by the success of Goethe's *Werther*. Rousseau, though seriously ill, read the French translation upon receiving it in one sitting, and Diderot politely asked permission to include two of his pieces in the French version of Gessner.[2] The works of Gessner and, to a lesser extent, Haller mark the beginning of the modern French interest in German literary and cultural life.[3]

Gessner's *Idyllen* also represent the continuation of many elements from the Rococo poetry of the preceding decades. In its mixture of themes and influences this poetry also had a Virgilian presence, which is very marked in such works as Haller's *Die Alpen* (1732). This poem not only exhibits a poetic technique, a structure, and particular passages taken from the *Georgics* but also strongly propels the pastoral Arcadia toward a Georgic world with its emphasis on work, family, and the community in nature. A looser and more occasional use of Virgilian pastoral topoi appears in such writers as Friedrich von Hagedorn, as, for example, in the infusion of the pastoral illusion into the motif of the dream, which belongs more strictly speaking to the Anacreontic tradition. A more explicit use of Virgilian devices again surfaces in the works of the Anacreontic poet Johann Peter Uz, who gives particular attention to Virgil's problematic sixth eclogue. For German Rococo poetry, Arcadia remained a palpable fiction, even if one sweetly or alluringly portrayed. Gessner by no means breaks with this Arcadia, nor with many of the features of Rococo verse, although he does clearly subordinate this inheritance to the desire to make the idyll the artistic expression of a new sentimental vision of nature. His shepherd no longer speaks out of character; the pastoral guise and the idyll are not transparent. For all the continuity with the Rococo version of Arcadia, the transformation to the modern idyll is complete in Gessner's *Idyllen,* with little overt trace of the earlier pastoral tradition.

Simplicity and naivety were the overwhelming impressions his *Idyllen* left upon the minds of his contemporaries after reading the *Idyllen,* and in the light of the Rococo Arcadia, it is a fair assessment of Gessner's effect.[4] It is, however, a judgment that dogs the critical reading of Gessner throughout the following centuries, despite Herder's best efforts. E. Theodor Voss still feels compelled to note in 1977: "Im Wege steht obendrein ein sehr traditioneller Gesichtspunkt, nämlich die Gleichsetzung von 'Idyllik' und 'Naivität.'"[5] Gessner absorbs into his bucolic a host of different strands: Enlightenment moralism, the didacticism of Gottsched, a historical golden age, the esteem for a simple life, social criticism, pastoral motifs, and the enthusiasm for nature; these all contribute to the impression of "Idyllik und Naivität." Herder characterizes this mixture by its most distinctive feature, calling it "die verschönerte Natur" in his comparison of Theocritus and Gessner (*HW* 1:351–60). One may consider the outbursts of enthusiasm that Gessner places in the mouths of his simple shepherds naive in two respects, the one conscious and the other unconscious. The conscious naivety consists in having a shepherd act and speak of his feelings and their importance in a way that conforms to the opinions of the Enlightened about simple nature (the observation that it also confirms these opinions leads to other considerations, which will not be dealt with here). For example, in "Damon. Daphne" Damon rhapsodizes as follows:

> Umarme mich Daphne, umarme mich! O was für Freude durchströmt mich! wie herrlich ist alles um uns her! Welche unerschöpfliche Quelle von Entzüken! Von der belebenden Sonne bis zur kleinsten Pflanze sind alles Wunder! O wie reißt das Entzücken mich hin! wenn ich vom hohen Hügel die weitausgebreitete Gegend übersehe, . . . — wenn ich die Wunder betrachte, dann schwellt mir die Brust, Gedanken drengen sich dann auf; ich kan sie nicht entwikeln, dann wein' ich und sinke hin und stammle mein Erstaunen dem der die Erde schuf! (32–33)[6]

So transparent a maneuver may seem so artificial that it must surely fail to achieve its intended effect, but the opposite is the case. It does fulfill Fontenelle's and Herder's demand for rapture; *et in Arcadia ego* becomes "I too am a shepherd," to judge from Mendelssohn's comment:

> Gessner ist Beispiel genug. . . . Die Empfindungen seiner Schäfer grenzen beynahe an das Erhabene, aber ihre Lebensart ist so ländlich, so gemein, und das so armseelig als in der Natur. Man wünscht sich mit seinem *Palemon* ausrufen zu können. . . .[7]

The question is rather: why is it so successful? It depends on an unconscious sense of naivety, which may best be explained with reference to Kant's conception of "das Schöne." For Kant, the only truly beautiful object is the natural object, untouched by human culture. The serendipitous feeling of beauty occurs through the chance recognition that the ordering categories of nature correspond exactly to those of the human intellect. Man finds himself at home in the world. The *sine qua non* of this revelatory experience is that the observer's relation to the object should be disinterested in all respects. Such disinterest attests, for Kant, the imagination's freedom as well as its playfulness, that is, the mind engages in spontaneous activity apparently in possession of its own self without the need of exterior mediation.

Gessner's shepherds live a life exactly conducive to such disinterest. They are free from want, which causes separation from nature, while the absence of any form of subjugation guarantees their liberty. As a consequence, "sie empfangen bey unverdorbenem Herzen und Verstand ihr Glück gerade aus der Hand dieser milden Mutter" (15). They live in harmony with nature pursuing their appointed tasks without compulsion and unmotivated by a sense of gain, with ample time to devote themselves to the cultivation of their private selves. Consequently time and again, overwhelmed by the munificence of nature, they enthuse spontaneously on its beauty. The deeper naivety consists in the belief that a particular perception and its attendant feeling may be subsumed so directly under the universal of beauty.

The confidence with which this occurs repeatedly in the *Idyllen* is a sign that the poetological pastoral space of Virgil or even the more forthrightly imaginative poetic Arcadia of the Rococo poets has become the Arcadia of utopia. It is the positive land of what truly is, albeit idealized, a fiction that does not need constant recourse either to the present world or to the tension between the two worlds to assure itself of its own validity. Arcadia has passed wholly over into the golden age of Elysium: "kurz, sie [die Ekloge] schildert uns ein goldnes Weltalter, das gewiß einmal da gewesen ist, denn davon kan uns die Geschichte der Patriarchen überzeugen" (15). The insistence on the historical veracity of this age, of the "gewiß einmal da gewesen[en]" and on its wider Christian intimations argues for the independence of the new Arcadia, in which, as E. Theodor Voss observes, "unschwer Vergils 'justissima tellus' aus dem Landbaugedicht wiederzuerkennen ist."[8] That it should have strongly Georgic traits comes therefore as no surprise. It is Georgic not merely in the sense of the regular and orderly rhythm of work and rest, love and death, of the natural cycle of the seasons, but also in the sense that it is an entire age, a world complete in itself, naturally without the Virgilian philosopher from "The Praises of the Country Life," as Herder was shortly to observe.

Daphnis (1753), Gessner's pastoral novel and his only major work before the *Idyllen,* already displays all of these features.[9] The natural world is transformed into a large garden through the same premise of naivety as in the *Idyllen*. In the novel it is more obviously the premise of the cultured. Gessner leaves it to a refugee from the city to speak of the naive feeling for nature and to translate his feeling directly into its universal import as he regards from a hill the landscape unfolding before him: "Welche Seligkeit! hub er izt an, welche Stroeme von Wollust! Ach! kaum fasst sie mein wallendes Herz! Ach Natur! Natur! wie schoen bist du! wie schoen in unschuldigen Schoenheit, wo dich die Kunst unzufriedener Menschen nicht verunstaltet!"[10]

The plot of the novel, so far as it exists, takes place in a Georgic society and follows the story of Daphnis and Phillis, a young couple of modest means, but of surpassing virtue. Each shepherd in this society lives according to the precepts of Gottsched's shepherds, having a small flock, a few fields, and a hut to live in, and given to singing sweetly modest songs in praise of Amor. In so perfect a society, set apart from the ills of civilization, there are only the barest of complications available to impede the successful courtship of Daphnis. The plot serves simply as an excuse for Gessner to present extended descriptions of nature, uplifting anecdotes of virtue, and pastoral episodes of feasting and of singing, leavened with philosophic sermons. The literary form of the pastoral novel ill suits these small episodes, sustained as they are by the sentimentality of their feeling. The shorter form of the idyll, which Gessner now begins to write in greater numbers, offers a more appropriate vehicle for concentrating the effect of this feeling.

Gessner is able to absorb the literary technique of the German Anacreontic with impunity. The most Anacreontic in feeling is his early piece entitled "Die Nacht" (1753), although in *Daphnis* there are a number of imitations of Hagedorn. His earliest idyll, "Der Frühling" (1752, published 1756) draws more explicitly on the Rococo tradition, being an imitation of the like-named poems by Ewald von Kleist and Uz as well as of Uz's "Silenus." The idyll falls into two halves; the first half, an extended description of nature as the *locus amoenus* in the manner of Kleist's "Der Frühling," serves as a frame to the second half. Just as in Uz's "Silenus," the narrator has the good fortune to spy on a Bacchic gathering, in this case Bacchus himself accompanied by Silenus, Amor, and Pan. It also contains a brief allusion to Galathea's seductive flight in *Eclogue* 3:

> *Malo me Galathea petit, lasciua puella,*
> *et fugit ad salices et se cupit ante uideri,* (64–65)

[Now Galathea throws at me an apple — she's a wanton maid. Off to the sally trees she do run wishing I spy whereto she's fled. (18–19)]

and:

> Ich wollte eine junge Nymphe umfassen, so sagt er [Bacchus], das Mädchen flog mit leichten Füssen über die Blumen weg, und lachte zurück. (61–62)

This tone, struck in many of the *Idyllen,* preserves much of the Anacreontic lightness and sensuality. But, in the later idylls, the more worldly and erotic associations of "Viel Unschuld, aber nicht zu viel" are kept at bay.[11] The conclusion is almost invariably decorous and touching. A secular vision of paradise shapes the new, secular vision of nature's golden age. Within this larger purpose, in both *Daphnis* and the *Idyllen,* the imitations of Virgil and Theocritus are legion. The "Schnitterlied" (1:26–27) in *Daphnis* traces its origins back to *Idyll* 10 with the faintest trace of *Idyll* 1. Reminiscent of Virgil, there is a grotto scene (1:38) introduced like the similar episode in book 4 of the *Aeneid* with the couple, like the love-sick Dido and Aeneas, compelled by a sudden storm to take shelter in an opportune cave and there to confront their love. Gessner further includes details such as those in an Anacreontic song mixed with reference to the Virgilian commonplaces of the bucolic tradition: e.g. a "Buchen-Tal" and a "brauner Hirt" (1:40), or individual phrases, such as, "jaehrlich dem Pan zween junge Boecke" (1:60) after,

> *ecce duas tibi, Daphni, duas altaria Phoebo.*
> *pocula bina nouo spumantia lacte quotannis*
> *crateresque duo statuam tibi pinguis oliui;* . . . (*Ec.* 5. 66–68)

> [Bring us luck, good Daphnis! Hear two altars for you and two for Phoebus, where I'll set two bowls of olive oil, two cups of creaming milk every year. (28)]

However, his description of a system of irrigation echoes instead the description of the flood from the *Georgics.* Gessner also makes liberal use of the bucolic tradition of describing the engravings on drinking cups (1:61 and 150).

In the *Idyllen* themselves there are many other direct adaptations from Virgil and Theocritus, and a great number of them contain some echo of one or other, if not both. Many of these details concern the structure of the idyll, its setting, the manner of the singing competition, or some other aspect of rural life. The structure of "Idas. Mycon" is reminiscent of *Idyll* 1, in which, for the reward of a cup, a goatherd begs a song of Thyrsis. Gessner's Mycon asks of Idas a song in return for a pipe made of nine reeds and wax, a description narrowly modeled after *Idyll* 1. 18–24, while the line, "O Pan! dieser Tag sei mir heilig," recalls *namque erit ille mihi semper deus* (*Ec.* 1. 7; one who will always be a god to me; 9). The story spun around this devout wish bears no relation to that sung by Theocritus's Thyrsis of Daphnis, save that Gessner's Idas sets up Palemon as a great hero among the shepherds, not for his loving and singing, like Theocritus's Daphnis, but for his Christian charity. The only connection to the Virgilian *Eclogues* is the praise for the source upon which the pastoral world depends; here it is not the political order of the polis but that of a divine nature. "Myrtil. Thyrsis" follows *Idyll* 1 even more closely. This time the lamp Thyrsis offers as payment for a song is described in the detailed manner of the cup from *Idyll* 1. Gessner also adopts the use of a refrain from *Idyll* 1 to punctuate Myrtil's song, which echoes both Theocritus and Virgil. They invite their muse or their song respectively to sing with them and then to cease. Gessner, appropriately, invites nature itself, the "Felsenklüfte," "Hain," and "Ufer," first to accompany and then to desist. The story, since it begins as a lament, seems similar in this respect too to *Idyll* 1, but it concludes with the safe return of this latter-day Daphnis. In its context the last refrain, "Klaget izt nicht mehr, ihr Felsenklüfte, Freude töne izt vom Hain zurük und vom Ufer," fits better with Virgil's *parcite, ab urbe uenit, iam parcite carmina, Daphnis* (*Ec.* 8. 109; no more spells, no more spells now — my Daphnis is near; 40), which likewise concludes with the return of a lost Daphnis. Similarly, Gessner's appeal to nature and the demand that it echo the emotional state of the song is more reminiscent of Virgil's echoing woods in *Eclogues* than it is of Theocritus's *Idyll* 1.

The same sorts of transformations may be observed in those idylls that bear a more obvious relation to Virgil. Gessner adapts only those elements of Virgil to which he can give a sentimental and happy turn. The situation of "Der zerbrochene Krug," for example, evokes the sixth eclogue. A number of young shepherds happening upon a drunken faun asleep seize him, truss him up, and demand a song of him in return for his release. The faun, as bid, sings a lament for the jug he let fall during his stupor. Each verse, again punctuated by a refrain, is devoted to the description of one of the cup's panels. These panels are all mythological: one is the story of the syrinx from *Eclogue* 2. 31–36, another the beginning only of the story of Europa, and the last is of Bacchus and his train. The subject matter is Anacreontic: wine, woman, and song, with only the Europa panel hinting at the tales of unnatural love that Virgil's Silenus favored. Gessner defuses the possible increase in scope offered by the example of Silenus's preaching on the creation of the world by turning it into the description of a jug. The refrain, "Aber er ist zerbrochen, er ist zerbrochen, der schönste Krug! Da liegen die Scherben umher," is both bathetic and "naive" in its childlike sadness. The concluding scene with the shepherds standing in innocent wonder around the shards of the jug is sweet and trivial to the extent that it makes the whole idyll read as unintended parody.

Gessner's attention to the setting of his idylls, the *locus amoenus,* also bears witness to the same sentimental feeling as his other adaptations of the ancient bucolic. As Heyne remarks, Gessner makes much more extensive use of the *locus amoenus* than either of the ancient poets. Theocritus, although he introduced the *locus amoenus* in the first idyll, rarely paints the scene in full, preferring instead to mention small details of nature during the course of an idyll. Virgil makes much greater use of it, placing a fully drawn *locus amoenus* at the beginning of four eclogues (*Ecs.* 1. 1–3; 2. 1–4;

5. 3–7; 7. 1 and 10–12).[12] Gessner lengthens and elaborates the *locus amoenus,* as in "Milon," "Idas. Mycon," "Lycas und Milon," and "Myrtil. Thyrsis," for example. Nature is not so much the setting of the idyll as it is its subject. In many of these instances Gessner mixes in scenes strongly reminiscent of the classical *locus amoenus.*

The accomplice to Gessner's vital nature is love. Human love is here both a reflection and a form of unconscious communion with the animating force of nature. Long descriptive passages on nature may either begin with the love of shepherd and shepherdess for one another or move to that conclusion. In the two aetiological idylls, "Lycas, oder die Erfindung der Gärten" and "Die Erfindung des Saitenspiels und des Gesanges," the happy moment of invention hinges on love. In the former, the good shepherd, overwhelmed by feeling following the mutual confession of love between himself and his Chloe, sanctifies the site of this confession by grouping about the stand of trees numerous species of flowers gathered from the neighboring fields. In inventing the garden he introduces an artificial order into nature; yet one consonant with nature, since nature in being summoned to commemorate love commemorates only itself. In the latter idyll, nature and love are more directly connected. The production of "harmonischere Töne" by the shepherdess issues from a surfeit of feeling or "Entzückung" before the splendor of nature in its "Morgenroth" (53–55). The observation and example of the singing birds lead her to the spontaneous discovery of song. Just as the shepherdess hits upon song while enraptured by nature so does the shepherd hit upon the lyre while enraptured by the beauty of her song and of herself. The fitting consummation of this natural education is that "izt gieng der Jüngling mit dem Mädchen unter das Dach" (56), there to instruct all the other youths and maidens in singing and music.

The domain of Gessner's natural love also extends to the reordering of human relations. The extension of the idyll to include familial and social relations represents its ultimate fusion with the Georgic concern. In the *Idyllen* of 1756, this interest is muted in comparison to the collection of 1762 and the *Neue Idyllen* of 1772. In them, children make their frequent appearance in the idyll, where they appear as the manifestation of a life led in accordance with the rhythms of nature: "Ungesegnet ist das Haus wo keine Kinder sind. Ein zerstümmelt Bildgen des Amor hattest du gefunden" (92). Still in the *Idyllen* of 1756, the habits of life as the manifestation of the harmony of nature do come to the fore. In "Tityrus. Menalkas," Tityrus, the youngest son, happens upon his aged father, Menalkas, lying in the autumnal sun surveying the scene spread out before him "voll sanften Entzükens" (51). The son, unannounced, beholds the two of them, his father and the panorama, "lang mit stiller Freude" (51), before begging of his father a song. The song that follows merely glosses the dynamic of familial feeling presented in the foregoing tableau. It begins with nature and moves rapidly to the philosophic breadth of the *Georgics*. It echoes the perspective and conclusions of "The Praises of the Country Life" from book 2 (458–540), which it calls to mind with its imagery of the contented life from pagan antiquity (52). It differs by eschewing any reference to the ills of the city; such reference forms a prominent part of the contrast in Virgil and in Haller's later adaptation of it in *Die Alpen*.

The other idyll that concerns itself with this matter, "Palemon" (1754), draws the connection between the proper habit of life, love, and nature even more directly. Once again an old man gives a reckoning of his life by enumerating its various stages and joys. He summons his family, including the smallest grandchild, to a last festival in honor of the gods. At its end Palemon reveals himself to be a Philemon as he is metamorphosed into a tree in reward for his life of idyllic virtue. He does not die but returns to nature, and those who sit beneath the tree experience "ein heiliges Entzüken" and spill "eine fromme Träne" (43).

For these reasons, it cannot be said that the idyll of Gessner bears any real resemblance to the ancient bucolic, of either the Theocritean or Virgilian variety. Gessner aims for a naivety of feeling untainted with any hint of the reflection necessary for a life in civilization. The arts of civilization that do gain admission, gardening, song, and music, do not do so on account of their origin in conscious, purposive activity, but because they are the spontaneous effusions of those enraptured before nature.[13] The enthusiasm for nature wholly absorbs the Virgilian golden age, which was preeminently a divine order encompassing both nature and culture, not one sanctioning their division. Gessner's nature subsists without any obvious need for such external mediation, and what society he does admit is constructed out of nature as its immediate excrescence and not out of any incompleteness. Whatever Georgic impulse is left stops well short of larger social and political relations: Gessner's shepherds live as Gottsched envisaged without the need of law, like the Latins of *Aeneid* 7. Gessner's truncated Georgic prepares the way for the development that occurs in Maler Müller and Voss, in the latter of whom the idyll as a genre becomes an idealized mirror of bourgeois private life and settles into the modern, Georgic site of the village as its appropriate form of community.

This, however, is to anticipate. The question remains: in what sense may one speak of a Virgilian influence? E. Theodor Voss would have it that "Sein Verfahren besteht darin, gleichsam das 'Natürliche' Theokrits mit Vergils 'literarischer' Art in Einklang zu bringen, eine Verbindung, die immer wieder als Eklektizismus des seiner selbst vermeintlich nicht sicheren Geßner mißverstanden worden ist."[14] This may well be an accurate statement of Gessner's intention and wholly intelligible in light of the pastoral theory of the age, in which Theocritus is nature and Virgil is art. Virgil stood for the French style of eclogue, contrived, artificial, and courtly; the problematic eclogues justified every excess of "un-naive" sentiment. Theocritus, on the other hand, was nature in the raw, vigorous, and in the plain dialect of the countryman. However, neither of these positions serves as an accurate description of the *Idyllen* as they appear. They avoid the literary reflection common to both of the ancient poets and are as much devoid of Theocritus's scatological spoof and farce as they are of Virgil's more explicit self-reflection. Gessner may cast the *Idyllen* in ancient garb, but the use to which he puts the resultant hodge-podge of motifs, themes, and settings is completely different. Only those elements that will sustain a sentimental interpretation find an echo. Is then the influence of Virgil reducible to a mass of accidental borrowings and echoes, of no deeper significance?

In his preface, *An den Leser,* Gessner famously appeals to Theocritus for his model of natural simplicity:

> Ich habe den Theokrit immer für das beste Muster in dieser Art Gedichte gehalten. Bey ihm findet man die Einfalt der Sitten und der Empfindungen am besten ausgedrükt, und das Ländliche und das schönste Einfalt der Natur. (17)

There is no reference to, nor room for, Virgil in this categorical statement. Yet what Gessner knew of Theocritus is difficult to say. As he was unable to read Greek, he had to read Theocritus in translation, in all probability in French.[15] Likewise he was unable to read English. For both these influences, that of Theocritus and that of James Thomson's (1700–1748) popular poem *The Seasons* (1730), and more important, for his opinion of them, he most likely relied on Wieland and Kleist (the latter of whom he met and befriended when Kleist spent the last few months of 1752 in Zurich on a recruiting tour). Some indication of how Gessner read Theocritus may be gleaned from the final sentences of his preface:

> Zwar weis ich wol, daß einige wenige Ausdrüke und Bilder im Theokrit, bey so sehr abgeänderten Sitten uns verächtlich worden sind; dergleichen Umständgen habe ich auszuweichen getrachtet. Ich meyne aber hier nicht der gleichen, die ein französischer Übersetzer in dem Virgil nicht ausstehen konnte; die ich meyne, hat Virgil, der Nachahmer des Theokrit, selbst schon weggelassen. (18)

Gessner means that, in some sense, he wishes to use Virgil as his guide to Theocritus and read him as Virgil did. That, in his mind, does not extend to the exclusion of those examples of rustic bad taste that offended Gresset, the above-mentioned French translator, in the *Eclogues*. Rather he means most probably the sexually explicit language of Theocritus and his open reference to homosexuality. These elements are much reduced in Virgil, with only the second eclogue open to the objection of moral turpitude. This conclusion is merely negative: it tells us only that he looked to the *Eclogues* when deciding what not to write about. It does not address the question of what he may have taken from them for his purposes.

Although unable to read Greek and English, Gessner was able to read Latin, though how well remains unclear.[16] That his facility with the language extended to more than the ability merely to grasp the gist of what he read in Virgil is clear from the one unmistakably Virgilian turn of phrase that he adopts. In "Die Nacht" he employs "gegossen" in the same manner as Virgil did *fusus* to refer to an individual draped on the ground, grass, or some other such object: "Dort ist es, wo ich einst am blumichten Ufer beym Mondlicht das schönste Mädchen fand, es lag da in Blumen hingegossen (8).[17] It is most likely known to him from "The Praises of the Country Life" in the *Georgics* (2. 527).

It is a small point, but one that gives rise to a great bit of rather indirect and obscure comment that testifies to the wide readership the *Idyllen* enjoyed and also to the acuity of its sensitivity to Virgilian intimations. In his 1758 essay "Von der Sprache der Poesie," Klopstock, when considering the criteria for judging the borrowings from the ancients by those who aspire to make good some lexical deficiency of German's poetic idiom, states that one may object either that the image in German displeases or that the German author inserts it into an inappropriate context. He then continues without mention of Gessner with the comment: "Ist keine von beiden seine Ursache; so ist er verdreißlich darüber geworden, daß, *fusus*, hingegossen, im Deutschen heißt." As Klopstock now returns to his original argument again, it is unclear what displeases him about "hingegossen"; whether it is its sound or metrical properties in German, or disapproval of the direction in which the success of Gessner's prose poems may push the development of literary German. However, that it is an unsatisfactory attempt at "Verdeutschung" is clear. More curious is that it is also the only example he gives to illustrate his point in the whole section, while the only ancient poets mentioned as sources for such borrowings are the epic Dioscuri, Homer and Virgil. The inference is that Klopstock reads "hingegossen" in Gessner as the Virgilian *fusus*.

Herder revisits the question in his first collection of fragments from 1767. Footnoting Klopstock, Herder argues that failed idioms offer the chance "das Genie der Sprache zu untersuchen, und dasselbe zuerst mit dem Genie der Nation zusammen zu halten" (*HW* 1:193). To illustrate his point he chooses to explain why "sun" in German is feminine, the "moon" masculine, and the phrase *fusus in herba* (*HW* 1:193) forever foreign in German. The "alten Urväter" delighted to meet by night in the woods, there to debate war, bang their swords, and acclaim their decisions with the cry, "der Mond ist Zeuge! Eben daher ist das: im Grase *hingegossen* [Herder's emphasis] wohl ein zu wohllüstiges Bild für das waldigte kalte Deutschland, wie es vormals gewesen" (*HW* 1:193). As an explanation this is specious nonsense; as myth making, brilliant. Herder takes the notion of a language's development through time and grafts onto it the supposition that the motive and marker of this development is an accompanying and continuous sense of national spirit, with the result that the reaction of the contemporary German, here Klopstock, becomes a reflex of the distant past. The reflex does not merely confirm the continuous presence of nation- or peoplehood; it also allows the contemporary, in this case Herder, to assure himself that his sense of an influence as friendly or foreign is neither a personal foible nor a fad of the age, but inherent in the nature of the given language and people itself. What the example also illustrates is the sensitivity to Virgilian echoes that the long schooling in the Virgilian poems has left on the imagination of the educated in the eighteenth century, and, in the case of Herder, the determination that no moon-tongued, latter-day Herman should swallow a Virgilian-tipped eagle standard.[18]

No less than in the case of Klopstock or Herder, such an acquaintance with Virgil seems likely to have left some deeper impression on Gessner. He states his dependence on Virgil more forthrightly in a letter to Ramler dated 23 December 1755, that is, shortly before the publication of the *Idyllen,* yet after their composition:

> Freylich hab ich zu meinen Idyllen den Theokrit gelesen; ihn alein und den Virgil, bey diesen alein ist diese Dichtarth in ihrer Volkommenheit; die verzärtelten Franzosen hab ich nicht gelesen, sie sind zu sehr von ihm abgewichen.[19]

In the letter, Gessner restores the Virgilian eclogue to the parity with the Theocritean bucolic that his preface argued against. He acknowledges, *sub rosa* as it were, that for him Virgil is neither identical to the French idea of him, nor is he less a master of the genre than Theocritus. Since Gessner could read Latin, though "mühsam," one would expect him to retain a more lively impression of the Virgilian eclogue than merely the recognition that it was less offensive than the Theocritean bucolic.

In yet another letter of slightly more than a year earlier this time to Gleim, Gessner again states that he sought his "Regeln allein in Theokrit und Virgil, und las den Longus" (the last is the author of a pastoral romance from late antiquity). He also offers the following characterization of the bucolic world of Theocritus that suggests some hint of such an effect:

> Er [Theokrit] ist göttlich, aber er hat für Leute von andern, vielleicht bessern Sitten gesungen; ich kann den Käse und die Nüsse im Gedicht auch nicht zu oft ausstehen.[20]

Nuts and cheese do appear in Theocritus, but along with other such pastoral concerns as herding, sacrificing, and milk and honey: merely a part of the rustic clutter, not as the quintessential attribute. Their selection as the epitome of pastoral life stems rather from the concluding lines of Virgil's first eclogue:

> *sunt nobis mitia poma*
> *castaneae molles et pressi copia lactis,*
> *et iam summa procul uillarum culmina fumant*
> *maioresque cadunt altis de montibus umbrae.* (80–83)
>
> [You're welcome to taste my mellow
> Apples, my floury chestnuts, my ample stock of cheese.
> Look over there — smoke rises already from the rooftops
> And longer fall the shadows cast by the mountain heights. (*Ec.*1. 12)]

These lines of Virgil are remarkable for the mood they evoke. A few succinct details leave the impression of the serene progression of life in harmony with the rhythms of nature: a supper of cheese, nuts, and apples as smoke rises from the chimney tops and the shadows grow long on the hills. It is in the evocation of mood that Gessner approaches closest to Virgil.

Virgil frequently uses the time of day to evoke mood in his *Eclogues*, usually dusk, and only once dawn. Apart from its literal meaning, the reader comes away with a strong sense of closure, both in the sense that the bucolic world seems complete within itself and in the sense that it separates him from that world as he remains looking back at it. The resultant feeling is strongly elegiac. An example of this is the passage cited above (also *Ecs*. 6. 84–86; 9. 56–67; and 10. 75–77), and all the instances are in the problematic eclogues 1, 6, 9, and 10. The solitary evocation of dawn occurs in the only eclogue with a happy ending, *Eclogue* 8. 14–16. In all of these cases it is possible to draw a connection between the action of the eclogue, its emotional charge, and the time of day. Of equal interest for the purposes of the argument here is the observation that this mastery of composition occurs in the later *Eclogues*, that is, those least dependent on Theocritus and most concerned with delineating the pastoral space more clearly. Theocritus, more interested in satire, makes no more than an incidental use of time.[21]

In often choosing to set his *Idyllen* at dawn or dusk, Gessner exploits to the fullest the sentimental associations of the Virgilian technique, on occasion with little subtlety:

> O laß uns in zärtlicher Umarmung den kommenden Morgen, den Glanz des Abendroths und den sanften Schimmer des Mondes, laß uns die Wunder betrachten. (33)

The two mains uses of time are present in this example, that of love and that of wonder. In the former case, the love intimated is often Anacreontic as in "Daphnis. Chloe," "Daphnis," or "Der Faun." In the last-named, the time of day heightens the mood of the idyll, strengthening the sympathy of feeling between man and nature. The invention of song and of the lyre occurs at dawn, and the onset of evening accompanies the confession of love that leads to the discovery of the garden. Tityrus and Menalk have their talk in the evening of the year, the fall. The "Palemon" idyll begins at daybreak and ends with the "stille Abend." Gessner lessens the ambiguous elegiac sense of the Virgilian original; instead the sense of continuity dominates. What remains is the sentimental contemplation of it for the reader.

Another of the sentimental traits in Virgil that Gessner is able to use for his own purposes is Virgil's farewell to Arcadia, the *concedite silvae*, from *Eclogue* 10. 63 (farewell, you woods). In common with Gallus in the tenth, an anonymous shepherd in "Der veste Vorsatz" takes leave of the pastoral world with mock pathos. He pauses to remember each of his former loves, bidding each "Lebe wohl." In this idyll, Gessner is at once more Anacreontic and more blatantly sentimental: "einsiedlerisch will ich in deinem Schatten ruhen, melancholischer Wald" (59). The pathetic fallacy of the "melancholische Wald" parallels the *sonantis lucos* (*Ec.* 10. 58; sounding groves), among which Gallus sought consolation. The ending, however, shows the difference between the two in their use of sentiment. In the Virgilian eclogue, Gallus and the poet bid farewell to the bucolic world with the recognition that its poetry may assuage though not banish *crudelis amor*. Neither Gessner nor his shepherd makes any reference to the art of poetry. His shepherd, on the contrary, quickly finds cause enough to turn from thoughts of a hermit's retirement from the pastoral world to a return to it. The sight of a shepherdess's footprint causes him to cut short his lament in mid-flow as his mind hastens to trace the footprints to their owner. Whatever affliction love may visit upon Gessner's shepherds, it not sufficient to drive them beyond the borders of the pastoral world.

Gessner encapsulates his bucolic world by marking the frontiers in traditional style in the first and the last idylls of the collection of 1756. "An Daphnen," the first, closely imitates Uz's "Der Frühling." He begins, as does Uz, with an address to his muse and the traditional bucolic comparison of the larger epic with the smaller bucolic world:

> Nicht den blutbesprizten kühnen Helden, nicht das öde Schlachtfeld singt die frohe Muse; sanft und schüchtern flieht sie das Gewühl, die leichte Flöt' in ihrer Hand. (19)

Gessner settles the ambiguity present in Uz's muse, of whether it was merely engaged in a poetic apprenticeship before graduating to the larger world, or if it found in the green cabinet the true calling of poetry. Gessner's muse finds there stories enough, "von Großmuth, und von Tugend, und von immer frohen Unschuld" (20). He drives home this message in the concluding idyll, "Der Wunsch." This idyll is more properly a "Landgedicht," drawing on the tradition both of Horace's second Epode and of "The Praises of the Country Life" from the second Georgic. These both, with their reflection on the merits of rural life and the demerits of urban life, allow for a more philosophic treatment. With respect to this pronounced philosophic tone, Gessner's "Der Wunsch" differs markedly from his other idylls. It introduces the question of the bucolic world's relation to the present, seen here significantly as a matter of the poet's relation to the two of them. The author speaks directly using the "I" form and calling his vision a dream: hence the idyll's title, "Der Wunsch." Once again the Anacreontic motif of the dream resurfaces, with Gessner's vision of the pastoral world repeatedly being recognized in this concluding idyll as a dream. Despite the frequent and disruptive intrusions of the outside into his dream world, Gessner does not abandon it but concludes that it must be dreamt the harder. In effect the dream must become inseparable from his inner self, and hence no longer a dream, but an ideal directing his life. Like Uz before him, he stands Virgil on his head. In the first half of the fourth Georgic, Virgil portrays through the extended simile of the bees how the human state ought properly to order its affairs. It is a simile that looks forward, out of the rural world, to embrace the entire sweep of society. For Gessner, the bees' thriving presence signifies rather the place where the bucolic dream is properly dreamt, "wenn wahr ist, was der Landmann sagt, daß sie [die Bienen] nur da wohnen, wo Fried und Ruhe in der Wirtschaft herrscht" (66). He shuns the simile's larger implications.

Gessner distinguishes his pastoral dream on two points from the world of the present. One who lives the pastoral dream is not like the country gentleman: "Aber fern sei meine Hütte von dem Landhaus, das Dorantes bewohnt, ununterbrochen in Gesellschaft zu seyn" (67). This country gentleman merely transfers the life of the city to the country, spending his time in an unending round of entertaining, setting his table with every outlandish delicacy, and discussing at table matters of international politics and science: "Er eilt auf das Land um ungestört rasen zu können" (67). This form of imagining nature is false not merely because of its failure to appreciate its unadorned simplicity, but also because it fails to allow the pursuit of the modest life of labor necessary for those who would listen to the voice of nature. Following Gottsched on this point, and introducing a note of social critique, Gessner observes that the landed gentry of this sort can only sustain their manner of life by condemning the "Landmann" to an existence of brutish and brutalizing poverty:

> Weit umher ist der arme Landmann dein gepeinigter Schuldner; nur selten steigt der dünne Rauch von deinem umgestürzten Schorstein [*sic*] auf, denn solltest du nicht hungern, da du deinen Reichthum dem weinenden Armen raubest! (68)[22]

By turning the bucolic dream into the ideal of true virtue, Gessner makes unavoidable the tension between the idyll and the present age: this is more true the more the conviction of nature, even if only of an inner, subjective character, is sincerely held. Thus what seems entirely nostalgic, the "gewiß einmal da gewesen[e]," gains a utopian air, and Arcadia becomes implicitly a question of Elysium, as Schiller will later demand.

Gessner's disentangling of the modern idyll from its ancient model and reformulation of it about an unadulterated nature, at once naive and simple, result in so clear an expression of the new Arcadia that it in turn immediately gives rise to the question of its relation to the present. The concerns about society, history, and poetics so integral to the earlier pastoral now reoccur. They are, however, precisely those concerns that the pastoral theorists of the Enlightenment found so disturbing and had gradually removed from the understanding of the genre. They are not constitutive elements of the genre but alien intrusions. Their reemergence following Gessner's successful reformulation of the genre is one that occurs with this understanding. The successful depiction of an idyllic world free of these contaminations may engender the need to explore the relation of this new Arcadia to the present, but this undertaking should not puncture or intrude too closely on the idyllic world. The tension between these two contradictory impulses propels the subsequent development of the modern genre. Gessner's idyll becomes the new starting point for its development in Maler Müller, Voss, and Goethe. The Virgilian bucolic fades away behind it. Nonetheless, interesting parallels, even influences, can be observed as these poets grapple with the conundrum of how, within the constraints of naivety and simplicity, the idyll may take account of the tension it provokes.

Maler Müller and Voss: Georgic "Realism" and Self-Reflection

If Gessner's *Idyllen* point toward a fusion of an ideal of nature and the cultivation of emotion within the subject, then Maler Müller's idylls begin with this premise. The difficulty now confronting the idyll is the question of how the individual, confident in the claims of his emotional life and of its naturalness, is to conceive of the exterior world as permitting its expression. This beginning point transforms the idyll into a naive conception that only acquires clarity in relation to a notion of the sentimental. The contradictory impulses contained in the insistence that nature of a sort was temporally the prior state of both the individual and society, while yet still remaining even today, logically, the true state of both, progressively reshape the genre. In comparison to the bucolic of the Rococo, this tension results in a marked turn to the present in the idylls of Maler Müller, whether he seeks to grapple with it in theme, language, or setting. The remote and dreamlike air of the earlier bucolic fades as the realization of the tension between inner ideal and present circumstance sharpens. One critic observes, "das Transzendieren von poetischer Realität zum real-utopischen Zukunftsentwurf in der Haltung des Idyllischen, ist in allen Idyllendichtungen des Maler Müller nachzuvollziehen."[23] The resulting "realism" of his idylls in comparison with those of Gessner is, at first reading, their most self-evident difference. With Maler Müller, the idyll that Goethe and Herder had called for is at hand. Theocritus is its guiding figure, not however as the inspiration of an idyll that is remote and alien to the present, but as a contemporary inspiration whose example of rustics living according to nature in the historical age of ancient Sicily offers the modern writer the hope of emulation. Müller plans to take the idyll that is "so griechisch, daß man sie für ein Original eines alten Griechen geben könnte," strip it of its ancient garb, and dress it up "in Mützen rhein-ländischer Bauren."[24] Theocritus's Doric, long understood by the theorists as the authentic, pungent language of the countryside now comes into its own. It is the great sign of the authenticity of Theocritus's shepherds.

Müller depends on a different device in each of his three different sorts of idyll, ancient, biblical, and Palatinate, to bring his rustics so close to his readers that they might seem "real." Making them "real" involves making them "naive," and in his three types of idyll Müller explores three different ways of configuring naive and sentimental for his readers. In this context he refashions some of the techniques from the ancient bucolic. The satyrs and shepherds of his ancient idylls are blunt, crude, ridiculous, and sexually explicit, just like those of Theocritus, but also like some of Shakespeare's ruffians, notably Falstaff. In his biblical idylls, he depicts his figures with a psychological exactness that is immediately appealing and intelligible to his contemporary public. His Palatinate idylls take Gessner's Georgic society and set it in the village of the present day, as if in answer to Goethe's lament on Gessner's *Neue Idyllen* in 1772: "O hätt er nichts als Schweitzer-Idyllen gemacht! dieser treuherzige Ton, diese muntre Wendung des Gesprächs, das Nationalinteresse!" (*GSW* 1/2:348). The word "Nationalinteresse" and its synonyms occur regularly in reference to Müller's Palatinate idylls as a means of capturing the way in which Müller's "realism" culminates in "eine volksdeutsche Idylle," as one critic argues in 1939.[25] However "Volks- und Heimatdichtung" and "Volkspoesie" seem to later critics to lead easily to a misrepresentation of the "realism" in Müller's idylls.[26] They prefer to stop short of so reductive a term to emphasize instead how Müller, drawing on new linguistic levels and new social and thematic settings, introduces a highly differentiated view of society into the genre of the idyll. Yet since Müller does not begin with a dogma of realism, the end product is not easily absorbed into a notion of realism fashioned more with an eye to the nineteenth and twentieth centuries and the genre of the "Dorfgeschichte" than to the eighteenth and its idyll. What is elided in the concentration on the term realism is the degree to which other features of the idyllic tradition serve as a counterpoint to it;

or, for want of an example, how it is "utopian," to quote his editor Peter Erich Neuser. At issue is not the way in which idyllic and realistic reciprocally condition one another: that topic has been variously broached elsewhere; it is rather to consider whether the resulting amalgam bears any relation to Virgil's pastoral poems, and if so, in what manner does Virgil contribute to the formulation of naive and sentimental in the genre.

The easy order of Müller's idylls suggested above, first from "ancient" to "biblical," and then from "biblical" to "Palatinate," is deceptive. The date of their publication does not reflect the order of their composition. The "ancient" idylls, "Der Faun," "Der Satyr Mopsus," and "Bacchidon und Milon" were all published in 1775, as was the first Palatinate idyll "Die Schaaf-Schur." The second, "Das Nuß-Kernen" did not appear until 1811, when "Ulrich von Coßheim," a "deutsche Idylle" according to the title page, was also published. The first biblical idyll, "Der erschlagene Abel" was also published in 1775, but the second and better known one, "Adams erstes Erwachen und erste seelige Nächte" (in reality many idylls strung together by a narrative frame) falls in between the two extremes of 1775 and 1811 with a publication date of 1778. To further complicate the matter, a quick glance at the apparatus Neuser provides reveals that the initial composition of the idylls reaches back to Müller's time in Zwiebrücken, from 1766/67 to 1775, although it is not possible to determine the date of their final form.[27]

If the external evidence is inconclusive, the internal is no less unhelpful. It rests on the degree to which Müller frees himself from Gessner, a standard that depends on the perspective of the critic.[28] Nonetheless, it does offer a starting point. What Müller takes from Gessner, apart from external details such as setting, ancient names for his fauns, and the pagan machinery, is the acceptance of an essentially sentimental frame of mind. In his "Der Faun," for example, Müller transforms the lament for a dead shepherd from *Idyll* 1 and *Eclogue* 5 into the funeral dirge for the departed wife of the faun, a scene, in its sentiment of a touching domesticity, wholly consistent with Gessner's example. The faun approaches the funeral pyre to sing his wife's praises, "ein munteres Weib; redlich, treu und an Freundlichkeit giebts doch wenig deines gleichen" (10), all attributes equally at home in an idyll by Gessner. His characterization of these attributes under the Theocritean spell is considerably more direct and less refined than it would be in Gessner:

> Hast mir Treu erwiesen in allen Stücken; Buben zur Welt gebracht, groß und starck, voll heisser Eßlust, also, daß ich nicht weiß, woher nehmen, ihren Gaumen zu füllen. — Dein werd ich gewahr werden, du Fette, im Schmalztopf und im Keller: denn du warest nahrhafter als eine Heerde; einträglicher als ein Hügel, worauf Schnitter und Winzer ruht. (11)

The fluid rhythmic prose of Gessner yields to the broken grammar, the fragmentary sentences, the breathless rush typical of the Storm and

Stress. Equally typical of Müller is the concentration on the corporeal impulses of human behavior. His figures speak directly of their appetites and the gratification others afford them. The faun's children are "voll heisser Eßlust," his wife "einträglich." The sentimental approbation of this δαίμων of the body expresses itself through devices familiar from Gessner, the use of the time of day and of children. As the light departs from the day and the dew settles, the mourners light the pyre, and so send her corporeal remains from the light into the darkness as the moon rises in the sky. One of the younger offspring, uncomprehending, thinks he has only to tell his mother of his need for her and she will return, to which another, still smaller child responds: "Ja, ja! schrie der noch kleinere und purzelte über noch zwey ganz unmündige, die im Gras lagen —" (12). The sentence and the image of the weeping wee one and the babes beside him could have been written by Gessner, with the exception of "purzeln."

All of these features are found again in "Der Satyr Mopsus," but in a more consistent manner and combined with other Theocritean and Virgilian influences. Its direct antecedent is "Die ybel belohnte Liebe" from Gessner's collection of 1762. One night a satyr, accustomed to singing of his sincere love for a nymph, is set upon, wrapped up in a net, and tumbled down into the reeds by the nymph and her helpers, who then make off laughing into the night. Müller follows the outlines of Gessner's story, which in turn recalls the situation in Theocritus's third idyll. To it he also adds *Idyll* 11, in which Polyphemus sings of his love for Galathea. As the Cyclops boasted of his fine broad forehead with its single eye, Müller's Mopsus compares his own cheeks to those of the north wind Boreas in a carving:

> Du soltest's nur selbst sehen, wie wohl das geschnitzelt ist und wie groß und herrlich seine windvolle Backen hervorhangen, daß sie einer in der Ferne vor zwey Dudelsäcke nimmt. — — — Ja, du liebes! du, betrachte mich recht, was lustigen Ansehens ich bin.— (21)

The same essentially sentimental attitude as before takes from it the sharpness of Theocritus's humor, as it does the degrading quality of the more explicitly sexual language. Both Müller's humor and his language turn his Mopsus into a figure of the burlesque, a hale and hearty character given to earthy expressions that the reader understands stem more from his exuberant innocence than from the violence of any blind appetite. He is the sentimental comic counterpart to Gessner's sentimental earnest shepherd.

Only rarely does the sentimental burlesque of the portrayal threaten to yield to the violence implicit in the language. Mopsus and his followers capture the nymph with the intention of punishing her both for the humiliation she has inflicted on Mopsus and for her hard-hearted scorn of his sincere love. Mopsus now prepares to wreak his revenge:

> Pfeifstu nun so, Vögelgen! spricht Mopsus, indem er eine Gerte ablaubte; pfeifstu nun so? — — — Wart, wart, will dich — — — Nein! gehauen mustu mir werden; — — Ey, was! dass kann nicht anders seyn! — Dann tritt er vor sie hin, zerret ihr den Schleyer vom Busen, reißt ihren schönen Gürtel los, befiehlt ihr sich herum zu drehen, damit er sie rechtschaffen treffe. (33)

At the very moment the violence of his language threatens to become physical violence, the sentimental stripe of his heart shows itself. He succumbs to tears at her accusation that he has become more "grausam" than the wild animals. Unable to continue despite himself he releases her, professing his love all the while, and extorting a promise of love from her in return. Once released, she sings a lengthy mythological song in imitation of Virgil's Silenus (*Ec.* 6), before skipping off, laughing, to her cave.

With the nymph's song the character of the idyll changes radically and without transition to become a more explicit interpretation of the Virgilian tradition, albeit one that takes up that established by Uz and Gessner. The name "Mopsus" comes from *Eclogue* 5 and probably appealed to Müller for the pun with the German "Mops," a small- to medium-size breed of dog with a stubborn and surly appearance, hence also of stupid and surly individuals. Already at the outset of the idyll, in the first of its three "Gesängen" (Müller's word), Müller had invoked Virgil's Silenus eclogue when he described the discovery of Mopsus by the other satyrs in a manner reminiscent of Virgil's Aegle and her companions' discovery of Silenus. Müller lets fall the parallel until the nymph's song, which begins with the formulaic allusion to the "higher" song of the fourth eclogue. In this instance the golden age and *maiora canamus* become, "Die goldne Saiten erklangen . . . prächtig erhaben nun" (35). By and large the song follows the course for the German Silenus laid out by Uz. The nymph mentions first the birth of the gods, then the taming of chaos, and the creation of the cosmos and man, before passing on to the song of mythological creatures, and finally to the music of humanity with the figure of Orpheus. Departing from Uz and turning to Virgil, Müller's nymph concludes with Cymodoce's pathological love for Proteus, a tale that parallels the similar story of Pasiphae in *Eclogue* 6.

Other parallels can be traced between the structure of Müller's song and Virgil's. The common importance of cosmology, of the transfigured poet, and of pathological love, has been pointed out by Böschenstein. She also notes that "wie aufschwollen zum ersten Strale neugeschaffen die Hügel" (36) adapts *iamque nouum terrae stupeant lucescere solem* (*Ec.* 6. 37; and then the earth was dazed by unfamiliar sunshine; 31).[29] In addition to adopting Virgil's "referierende" structure for reporting the successive myths, Müller also employs the same additive stylistic device of "dann," or some such equivalent to introduce each new myth in the nymph's song. He begins with a "zuerst" and follows on with a "dann" for each of the next five myths before concluding with a "zuletzt." Virgil begins with a *namque canebat* (*Ec.* 6. 31; for he was singing), followed by a *hinc* (*Ec.* 6. 41; thereupon), a *his adiungit* (*Ec.* 6. 43; to these he adds), two *tum canit* (*Ec.* 6. 61 and 64; then he sings), and concludes with a summarizing *omnia, quae . . ., ille canit* (*Ec.* 6. 82–84; he sings all the songs that . . .) as Vesper announces the advent of night. Müller is more regular in his choice of connectives, as he is in the punctuation of beginning, middle, and end. Yet he also heightens the sense of magical rapture and closure by tying the conclusion of the song to the cycle of the day, except this time it is the dawn star rather than the evening star that marks the end of the song.

The same wish to concentrate the vatic intensity of a myth appears in his adaptation of the Orpheus story from the fourth book of the *Georgics*. It and the Praises of book 2 are the most widely cherished passages from the *Georgics*, to judge from the frequency of their translation. Müller takes from Virgil those details that indicate the magical quality and intensifies them. Virgil mentions that all the shades of Hell are *cantu commotae* (*Ge.* 4. 471; startled by his song; 350), and that:

> *quin ipsae stupuere domus atque intima Leti*
> *Tartara caerulosque implexae crinibus anguis*
> *Eumenides, tenuitque inhians tria Cerberus ora,*
> *atque Ixionii uento rota constitit orbis.* (*Ge.* 4. 481–84)
>
> [Nay, the very halls of death and Hell's recesses were amazed, and the Furies with livid serpents twined in their tresses; Cerberus held his triple jaws agape, and Ixion's whirling wheel hung motionless on the wind. (350)]

Müller too goes through all of these stages: his Cerberus sinks down in sleep at the feet of Orpheus, the tortures of Hell cease, "und inne halten alle Räder der Verdammnis, der Wuth" (36). The power to enrapture lies in the power of his song to be "keine wieder einander streitende Harmonie." Müller finds in the Furies the most potent image of this harmony, "daß mitleidig sich küssen die Schlangen auf der Erinys schröcklichem Haupte" (36). The word "mitleidig" fulfills the same sentimental function as was observed above: namely, that momentarily, in song, one glimpses the ideal unity within the order of creation; even the instruments of blind revenge, the snakes of the Furies in Hell, are momentarily turned from their appointed task. The scope of this vision matches that of the fourth eclogue and easily lives up to its promise, "Die goldne Saiten erklangen . . . prächtig erhaben nun" (35). The implicitly Christian origin of this beneficent view of the pastoral world comes clearly to the fore at this point. What the song momentarily banishes in Hell is "Verzweifelung" (36). Müller continues his story, not, as in Virgil, with the tale of Orpheus's vain attempt to retrace his steps to the light with his love Eurydice at his heels; rather he allows his Orpheus to address Hell and speak of love. The dead are dead because they lack the opportunity to love; "Verzweifelung" is the absence of love. Orpheus's descent and momentary taming of Hell mirrors the descent of Christ into Hell and its Harrowing following the Crucifixion. Müller's Orpheus concludes his dithyramb to love with the Kyrie, "O, ihr Götter, erbarmet euch unser!" (37). Müller's syncretism of pagan and Christian myth foreshadows the Romantic aestheticization of religion. His Orpheus/Christ figure is symbolic, not the historical figure of the devout. It implies that salvation, to continue the analogy, will henceforth be effected by the poet and his song, if at all.

Although the traditional interpretation of the fourth eclogue as a pagan prophecy of the birth of the Messiah sanctions Müller's insertion of a redemptive myth into the idyll, it offers little aid in determining how the content of the myth relates to the rest of the nymph's song and to the piece as a whole. Nor does it indicate how the idyll, if it is to indulge in such mythical speculations, will preserve the naivety essential to the modern conception of the idyllic. In what manner does Müller effect "eine wieder einander streitende Harmonie" between the sentimental desire to possess a naive simplicity within the bounds of an idyllic nature and the recognition that doing so renders this nature false? One simply observes that the Orpheus episode begs the question of the relation of the poet to idyllic nature, and of poetry to idyllic inspiration. A comparison between the plot of the nymph's final myth and that of the idyll offers the easiest approach to this matter (the Orpheus story is only the antepenultimate myth in the song). The final story tells of Cymodoce's vain love for Proteus. She, compelled to avail herself of Amor's magic to turn her obdurate lover's affections towards her, resorts to magic, in imitation of the anonymous enchantress in *Eclogue* 8 (and in *Idyll* 2), to secure her wayward Daphnis. If one reads Mopsus's deluded ambition to possess the nymph in the light of these two mythological stories, then a parallel can be observed. Just as the comic Mopsus fails to win the nymph, so do Orpheus and Cymodoce both ultimately fail; Orpheus, despite quelling Hell, does not retrieve Eurydice, and Cymodoce enjoys only an induced love, not a voluntary expression of affection. Thus both the "naive" idyll of the satyr and the "sentimental" idyll of the "grander songs," the *carmina maiora*, prove themselves to be illusive.

Müller also differs from Virgil in his use of the framing device. The naive "Mopsus" idyll acts as the frame for the very un-naive inset songs. Müller declines to comment directly on the question of the status of the idyllic by touching on the matter within the frame in the form of an explicit reference to the idyll's own generic and literary status. The reference to "die goldne Saiten erklangen . . . prächtig erhaben nun" seems to imply this question; but for the reader to observe that a "Stilbruch" occurs is a very different matter from the poet's telling the reader that he is now about to witness a "Stilbruch." To do so would make the entire idyll that follows too openly a literary construct, exactly the admission inimical to the modern insistence on the veracity of the naive condition. Nonetheless, Müller creates the faint expectation of such a frame at the beginning of the idyll by introducing Mopsus in a manner reminiscent of the sixth eclogue only to allow that expectation to wither to the point that his nymph's imitations of *Eclogues* 4 and 6 appear "out of context." Müller employs heterogeneous elements of the bucolic tradition without a clear sense of how he wishes to relate them artistically to the idyll as a whole. It is not evident in what manner the reader is to regard the naive frame and the un-naive inset song as an instance of "wieder einander streitende Harmonie," in other words in what way naive is to be understood through what is not naive. The use of Schiller's sentimental seems inappropriate here, since it looks back at what is naive; whereas here the nymph's songs are encased within the naive Mopsus's narrative. The songs do not look back on Mopsus, that is, beyond the naive setting, though they imply some comment by their complexity.

Although Müller declines to explore the literary and generic associations of the framing device as a vehicle for such reflection, this diffidence does not prevent him from giving it a new function. He transforms it into a straightforward narrative device. In essence, Müller's frame is not a proemium; it does not introduce an idyll. "Der Satyr Mopsus" is not one idyll but three, bound together by a narrative. Maler Müller's idylls with their dialogue, songs, and above all their episodes have a much more markedly dramatic character, or, since the use of a narrative suggests it, a much greater epic character. By adopting Gessner's "innocent" use of the bucolic frame, yet not his limitation of the idyll to one short piece, Müller sets the German idyll on the path to the idyllic epic of Voss and Goethe.

Müller's second approach to the question of self-reflection within the genre occurs in the biblical idylls. Here there is no hint of a recourse to Virgil for aid in considering his problem, since he resorts to the wholly modern perspective of psychology to articulate the relation between a previous "naive" state and the subsequent "sentimental" one. "Adams erstes Erwachen und erste seelige Nächte" still owes much to Gessner for its inspiration, in this case *Der Tod Abels* (1758). The division in this idyll lies between the narrative present of the postlapsarian first family, replete with Abel and the troublesome Cain, and the narrative past of the prelapsarian Adam in Eden. The earlier Adam only exists in the recollection of the later Adam. In the recollections of the later Adam about his younger self, Müller ties the two aspects of the naive and the sentimental nature together in the psychology of one individual. Although it may be objected that the Adam of the patriarchal age is an established theme for the idyll, the point is that the idyll of the Edenic Adam, as an idyll within an idyll, constitutes a reflection within the idyll on the idyllic. However, this is so only to the degree that Adam's recollections represent a reflection on the psychological origins of the idyllic. In effect, Müller substitutes the generic frame of Virgil's problematic eclogues for a psychological frame. The Adam of the Garden is unable to give an account of himself; the postlapsarian Adam must tell his listeners of the feelings and thoughts of the first Adam. This earlier naive Adam only gains a distinct consciousness through the recollections of the later Adam, who distinguishes the two states chiefly by impressing upon his audience the inability of his words to convey the qualitative difference of the two states, either by declaring this directly or by indulging in ecstatic outbursts. The naive idyll becomes for the sentimental observer not merely a designation for a relatively unreflective existence, but also a constitutive element in the observer's understanding of himself as one occupying a sentimental position. It also becomes largely ineffable, best apprehended as the negation of any current sentimental discomfort.

With the Palatinate idylls, Müller gives the problem of the relation of naive to sentimental a third formulation. Having passed from an antique mythological conception to a psychological one, he now moves to a historical dimension. Along with his other innovations, Müller takes the Gessner's Georgic village with its domestic society and puts it into the present of his native corner of Germany, the Palatinate. "Die Schaaf-Schur, eine pfälzische Idylle" and "Das Nuß-Kernen, eine pfälzische Idylle" are both idyllic mimes consisting entirely of dialogue interspersed with songs and the occasional tale. If their length (46 and 71 pages respectively in the edition of 1811, and 35 and 55 pages in the Reclam) mocks the claim to the title of idyll and the use of a chorus and of stage directions argue for that of drama, the subject matter and the interspersed songs and stories nonetheless identify them recognizably, though somewhat tenuously, as "idylls." The peasant, Walter, is the protagonist of both. In "Die Schaaf-Schur," he calls on those helping with the shearing of the sheep to pass the time by each singing a song in turn. Walter is a patriarchal figure and, like Mopsus, tyrannical to the point of violence in his enthusiasms. His chief enthusiasm, the singing of the old songs hallowed by tradition, is matched by his belligerent antipathy towards any fashionable modern effort that smacks of the French Rococo, in effect Gessner. The proponent of this modish creation is the hitherto most un-idyllic figure of the schoolmaster. He is also the conduit of most of the disturbing Enlightened comment in the idyll and therefore the object of the naive Walter's particular attentions. Walter roundly abuses him throughout, while merely browbeating the other participants to produce in turn a song according to his dictates.

Walter fits the term naive with respect to his attitude towards tradition. Only those songs and tales make it into his canon that are vouchsafed by some personal memory of the village's collective cultural traditions. The first song he learnt from a "Gesangbuch" (68), another is "ein uraltes Ding" from his "Kinderjahren" (73), the next "auch ein uralt Ding" (78), and the "Mährgen" is, as the word suggests, set in the Middle Ages among the knights and their ladies. For the pedigree of the tale he presumes on the oral tradition: "Versteht ihr mich, vom Fräulein von Flörsheim will ich nun erzehlen, die so weltberühmt wegen ihrer Schönheit war" (90). On his side then, stand those genres and themes vouchsafed by personal recollection as part of the religious and oral patrimony of his village. The only connection between them is that they are well known to him from his daily life, which they also help to shape, a circumstance that is Georgic rather than bucolic.

When challenged by the schoolmaster, Walter is unable to give any account of his preferences beyond the insistence that, as they appear good to him, their merit is self-evident, although he is aware such likes are not shared by others and so are in need of argument. The schoolmaster points out the weakness of this empirical fallacy, making it clear that intuitive immediacy must not be confused with persuasive explanation:

Schulmeister. . . . Warum gefällts ihm so wohl? Nur dieß.
Walter. Potz Stern! — hab ichs ihm denn nicht schon zehn tausendmal explicirt warum. — — Just weil so grad drin hergeht, wie mans denkt, und — — Blizt meynt er, er hab seine Buben vor sich?
Schulmeister. Ich merk, was er sagen will; er will sagen Herr Gevatter, weils so natürlich ist, nicht wahr?
Walter. Nu ja doch! (87)

He continues by making the simple point that what exists in time allows the comparison of before and after and hence gives rise to the need for study and consideration, and eventually a tradition. He puts his finger on the circularity of Walter's argument: personal associations cannot provide the standard of judgment as well as guarantee the authenticity of the tradition at the same time and in the same way.

Yet in making his point the schoolmaster engages in a species of Georgic creep. Gessner expended great effort to have the singer burst into song with the least amount of art possible, as a spontaneous eruption while in the rapturous thrall of nature's ecstasy. The schoolmaster is ready to grant the folk ways of the village the status of instinct and call them "natürlich." Yet songs from a hymnal are in origin hardly that. They only become "natural" by their continued existence in the oral tradition present to Walter's memory. The term "natural" or "naive" is only bestowed by one who feels himself not to be, or not fully so, part of this tradition. The schoolmaster's tradition is one of books, of bourgeois culture. He comes to experience what this means through his confrontation with Walter. By calling Walter's position "natural" the schoolmaster suggests that he, the outsider, has attained a sentimental position. He has understood the limitations of Walter's outlook, and has surpassed it and does not feel it poses any threat to his own culture since Walter is unable even to grasp the nature of his objections.

However, the schoolmaster is a somewhat hapless figure. He is not yet the pastor of Voss's *Luise*. He persists in the attempt to persuade, to "enlighten," Walter, as if a more or less equal exchange could occur between them. This Walter is an opponent, a challenge to the schoolmaster, who reveals himself to be the champion of Enlightenment poetics and the learned poet. The study of a poetic tradition requires the attention to rules and the cultivation of learning, of which the schoolmaster heartily approves. Fundamentally he is not at odds with Gottsched's project of a normative poetics, although he supports the Rococo brand of poetry. He criticizes Müller's songs for their rhyme (74) and speaks, in an oblique reference to Gessner, of "Idyllen" (70) instead of Walter's "Schäfers-Stückgen" (90). His attempt to read to Walter from a book, it is to be noted, ends in the anticipated disaster when Walter, echoing the earlier words of Gottsched and Gessner to the opposite effect, demands to know where such carefree, merry shepherds are to be found. The only song unapproved by Walter, a parody of Anacreontic verse, is offered by Walter's brother-in-law, who has it from "eine[r] Adliche[n]" (89) — a class of suspiciously un-idyllic loftiness — and introduces it with the disclaimer, "Ich meines Theils, versteh kein Wort davon" (89).

The two sides confront each other in this idyll over a chasm of mutual incomprehension. On the one side is an Enlightenment rationality, concerned only with its universal rules, and producing an ideal poetry that is bloodless and abstract to the degree that it measures itself by the rules and neglects its origin in "nature"; on the other side, an inarticulate Georgic immediacy that contradicts the Enlightenment simply by persisting obstinately in its time-honored habits. The poetry of the upper classes and the culture of the printed book oppose the poetry of the lower classes, of the church, and of the oral tradition. Only at the end do the two come, in some measure, together.

Alongside this *de facto* literary quarrel at center stage there runs a subplot. Throughout the idyll Lotte, Walter's daughter, is strangely discomforted, a discomfort that increases every time there is mention of the impending departure of the young man Veitel from the village. Walter, oblivious of the connection, receives no satisfactory reply to his repeated demands for the cause of her indisposition, until Veitel in the last song proposes to Lotte by promising not to go if she will marry him. The idyll concludes with Walter recommending this event to the schoolmaster for the subject matter of an idyll: "Aber Herr Gevatter Schulmeister, sag er, könnt man nicht aus dem Dings da all miteinander eine vortreffliche Idylle machen — he?" (58).

Gerhard Kaiser argues that a character in an idyll capable of recognizing the literary element of his own existence oversteps the premise of the idyll as a genre: "Eine Idyllenfigur, die sich als solche erkennt und ausspricht, ist keine mehr."[30] Kaiser concludes that the reflexivity involved in the perspectival consciousness of nature negates the ground on which the genre stands; this conclusion is valid only on the premise that idyllic nature may not contain an explicit reference to its character as idyllic. This premise is, however, only synonymous with the concept and word "idyll" following the Enlightenment's reformulation of the genre. It does not belong to the ancient idyll in which the division between "Natur" and "Kunst," "Bewußtsein," or "Geschichte" (58) is not central to the tension on which the ancient eclogue rests. Virgil does contrast his Arcadia to "Kunst," "Bewußtsein," and "Geschichte," but his Arcadia is not a nature conceived of with an independence sufficient to allow it to serve as one pole in so exclusive a contrast. Rather the opposite: only through the use of art, consciousness, and history do the contours of Virgil's Arcadia become visible. Virgil transgresses a stylistic convention to delineate, but not to isolate, the pastoral Arcadia. Maler Müller uses the same technique; most of the idyll touches on these matters through the "debate on literary matters," and Kaiser judges it in the same manner as the eighteenth century did the same violation in Virgil: the destruction of the illusion necessary for the idyll. Yet what Walter's statement points to is the assumption on the part of the reader that idyllic nature can only be naive. The naive Walter does not suddenly become sentimental at the end. He does not renounce his allegiance to the old songs and take up the schoolmaster's book. Walter merely fits the explanation of the idyll that the schoolmaster offered, a love tale of country folk with a happy ending, to the scene before his eyes. It is the reader, rather, who feels himself brought up short by the notion that the representation of naive and idyllic nature is a literary fabrication. It makes the same point as recollection did in "Adams erstes Erwachen": that idyllic nature only has meaning in relation to a sentimental attitude that it at once defines and constitutes. However, it does so in a slightly different manner. The idyll moves back and forth between the pre- and postlapsarian worlds of Adam. It does not contain a description of the transition between the two, the "peri- or circumlapsarian" world. Müller accomplishes this transition more neatly with the shock administered to the reader by Walter's use of the word "Idylle."

Similarly, Kaiser elides two different concepts of history in the statement: "Setzt die Theokritische und Vergilische Idylle eine Differenz von Natur und Geschichte voraus, so holt Maler Müller den geschichtlichen Charakter wie den Kunstcharakter der Idylle in sie ein."[31] This elision may be understood by observing that, if one holds to the difference of nature and history for Virgil and Theocritus, then it can only refer to a very different relation of the two in Müller. In the ancient bucolic, the relation of the poet-shepherd to his world is at issue, and in Virgil the historical sphere enters most forcefully with the state and politics. For Müller, history enters when he places his Georgic community into the present. His village, like that of Virgil's *Georgics,* is regulated by the cycle of work, adherence to traditional piety, and life within the family (the emphasis on song in Walter's life is the legacy of the more strictly idyllic strand of the golden age). As both are communities that exist in time, their elements are subject to a historical interpretation. For Virgil, there is no suggestion that either a Georgic or bucolic life can be conducted apart from the political order, with which the very conception of historical mediation is inseparable. For Gessner's rustics safely ensconced in a land whose place and time cannot be determined in relation to the present, the historical dimension can remain safely in abeyance. By placing his party of sheep-shearers in the present, Maler Müller simply allows these historical elements to make themselves felt again.

This similarity of initial position being granted, it does not follow that the result is the same. Rather, since they arrive at a historical conception of the Georgic community from different assumptions, the historical relation to this community also looks different. Müller's community does work with the assumption of a contrast between nature and art, and nature and history; namely that a nature and a more innocent apprehension of it persist in the face of the successive deformations of civilization. The clash between the two in the idyll allows the Enlightenment's golden age and idyllic nature to emerge with a clarity that begs the categorization of naive at the same time as it furthers the explication of the attitude of mind capable of looking back upon a nature that it itself no longer enjoys. Walter is aware of himself within a tradition of the hymnal and folktales, but it would not occur to him conceive of that tradition as a historical development. He inhabits a timeless world in the sense that it is, for him, ahistorical, or simply what he remembers. Walter is as ignorant of the wellsprings of human actions as he is blind to any hint of his dependence on a larger external order. He fails utterly to realize what moves his daughter, even revealing at the end that he thought the young Veitel's assiduous attentions to his house in the past weeks were a mark of esteem for his own person. These attitudes do not change as a result of Walter's statement at the end; rather that statement confirms his character as a figure of the modern idyll. Walter intends the word "Idylle" in the sense put forward in the literary quarrel in the idyll, in the sense of Gessner and the Rococo. For this poetics and for the enlightened schoolmaster, Walter remains a purveyor of barbarism and superstition, an impediment to progress. For the reader of the word "Idylle," Walter is more a naive than a formidable figure, comically unaware of this limitation, and one in relation to whom the reader experiences himself as sentimental. The naive here, as also in Schiller, is in contrast or opposition to the sentimental, but it is not its contradiction or antinomy.

In arriving at this position Müller avails himself of the subtleties of self-reflection that Virgil explored as he enunciated his vision of Arcadia. That they can be used to very different effect, in the one instance to articulate a distinction of naive and sentimental, and in the other delineate the seductive unreality of the poetic Arcadia, disputes neither their suitability, nor their provenance. Müller adapts the fourth and sixth eclogues for his own purposes in "Der Satyr Mopsus," somewhat in the established manner of Uz and Gessner. In "Die Schaaf-Schur," the extensive canvassing of literary matters is a bucolic technique that goes directly back to Theocritus and Virgil, as does the essentially ironic treatment of the idyll. The insertion of a direct reference to the literary fiction of the genre is a specifically Virgilian twist that Müller borrows, as is the more open questioning of the status of the pastoral world it invites.

The side of Virgil conspicuously absent from Müller's idylls, the insistence on the political order and the reinauguration of the golden age to come as the result of political reform, comes instead to the fore in Voss's idylls. The transfer of idyllic nature to the present in Voss causes the emphasis on the utopian element to shift from Arcadia, a land of the past, to Elysium, the world of the future. Kaiser notes: "Bei Voß hebt die Geschichte die Idylle auf und die Idylle die Geschichte, weil die Geschichte die Idyllennatur liefern muß, aber auch nichts sonst als eine statische Vernunftnatur hervorbringt, die vermeintliche Naturformen von Gesellschaft als Vernunftsformen in die Zukunft projiziert."[32] Voss regards idyllic nature, which proved so fissile under Müller's sensitive pen, much more concretely. He insists that the present organization of the world must correspond to the ideal of nature represented in the idyll. Such a view at once less historical, even almost ahistorical, ensures an extreme clash between the historical and the idyllic worlds. That Voss, a member of the "Göttinger Hainbund" and a passionate advocate of the Enlightenment and of freedom, should find Virgil amenable to his cause is incongruous at first glance, as once again, in keeping with his age, the young Voss's heroes are Theocritus and Homer.

Voss arrived at the university in Göttingen in 1772, where he remained until 1775. There he became a member of the "Göttinger Hainbund," a student club that united commoner and noble in devotion to Klopstock and freedom. Among its better-known members were the young Storm and Stress poets Ludwig Christian Heinrich Hölty (1748–76), Heinrich Christian Boie (1744–1806; whose sister Voss later married), the Stolberg brothers, Christian and Friedrich Leopold (1748–1821 and 1750–1819), and, on its fringes, Gottfried August Bürger. In a sense he remained a lifelong member of the club. He never departed from its enlightened ideals: the promotion of "Vernunft" through "Bildung" as the means to elevate the individual to a proper sense of his human dignity, an education that would in turn lead, it was hoped, to the gradual betterment of society. This project involved, for Voss, a passionate, if somewhat short-sighted, political espousal of

"Freiheit" in whatever English, French, or American form that it might take. In its social aspect, he conceived of freedom as the lifeblood of virtue, an incentive to lead an orderly and productive life in the family and community. At the personal level, freedom appears as the brotherhood of the "Hainbund," a form of friendship, perhaps, even more important to Voss than the tradition of effusive friendship in the eighteenth century might suggest, because it allowed one from a lowly class — and Voss was overly self-conscious of origins, especially his own — to associate with nobility on equal terms.

For Voss the enjoyment of freedom remains inseparable from the possession of all of its attributes. During his student days he wrote odes that vigorously extolled these ideals, such as "An Treuthart" (1772), an exhortation to youth to labor in the service of "Freiheit und Vaterland."[33] His expansive view of freedom and humanity allows the ode to be rewritten from the general to the particular individual: "Stolberg, der Freiheitssänger." Excessive praise slips into an equally overwrought satire on the oafish contentedness that impedes the progress of freedom in "Der Sklave" (1776, even more pointedly called "Der zufriedene Sklave").[34] These ideals, to which Voss the "Aufklärer" remained truer throughout his long life (1751–1826) than did all others of his generation, argue against his having much use for Virgil. The support given in all of Virgil's works to the imperial "tyranny" of the Augustan settlement does not recommend him to an ardent lover of freedom.

Yet the bucolic genre does appeal to Voss on two accounts. First, the genre, as it has come to be shaped during the eighteenth century in the hands of Gessner, offers a perfect match with Voss's interests. With the banishment of the Rococo pastoral and its poet-shepherds in favor of the Georgic community with its ordered life, and of its "pre-political" freedom, its natural as opposed to cultured humanity, the pastoral need not represent the golden age of a bygone Arcadia. The golden age may equally well bear a utopian emphasis, as Voss realizes. The all-encompassing breadth of Voss's conception of freedom, allowing for little room between the ideal and its embodiment, easily conceives of the idyll as a tool for the propagation of the Enlightenment: "Ich glaube, daß diese Dichtungsart großen Einfluß auf das Glück der Menschen haben kann."[35] Freedom and humanity confer an activist appeal on the idyll. Like Müller, Voss insists the idyll become more "realistic" and satirical. Unlike Müller, Voss does not intend by this shift to sharpen the tension between naive and sentimental in the idyll. He accepts the idyllic view of humanity and wishes only to mobilize it for his own ends. His "realism" is calculated to release the idyll's power to reform so that it may be put into harness for the Enlightenment.

Second, the composition of idylls permits Voss to give free rein to the love of all things Greek that animates the new philology at Göttingen. Just after the composition of his first two idylls, which promote the emancipation of the serfs, "Die Leibeigenen" (1774) and "Die Freigelassenen" (1775, both published in 1775 as the "Leibeigenschaft"), he writes in a letter (20/3/75) to his friend Brückner:

> Ich habe noch eine Idylle ["Die Freigelassenen"] gemacht, die zum Gegenstand einen mecklenburgischen Baron hat, der seine Bauern freigegeben . . . Ich denke zuweilen so stolz, daß ich durch diese Gedichte Nutzen stiften könnte. Welch ein Lohn, wenn ich zur Befreiung der armen Leibeignen beigetragen hätte! . . . Theokrit hat mich zuerst auf die eigentliche Bestimmung dieser Dichtungsart aufmerksam gemacht. Man sieht bei ihm, nichts von idealischer Welt und verfeinerte Schäfern. Er hat sicilische Natur und sicilische Schäfer, die oft so pöbelhaft sprechen wie unsere Bauern. Der Römer, Nachahmer in der Idylle sowohl als im Heldengedicht, stahl die besten Stellen, setzte sie nach seiner Fantasie zusammen, mischte etwas italienischen Sitten und Umständen hinzu, und so entstand ein Ungeheuer, das nirgends zu Hause gehört.

In the footsteps of Gessner, Voss makes Theocritus the model for a writer of idylls. Theocritus's shepherds are the authentic inhabitants of his native Sicily; his language the rough and ready speech of the Sicilian countryside: in short, we have Theocritus the modern "realist." Voss justifies his use of the Low German dialect in "De Winterawend" (1776) by citing in his notes Theocritus's use of Doric as well as the lines from *Idyll* 14 about Dorians being permitted the use of Doric.[36] Voss's idyll itself reasserts the traditional structures of the genre: the use of ekphrasis, the negotiation of the payment for a song, the song itself, the bucolic mime with its dramatic dialogue, and the new German hexameter. The song, however, is more in the tradition of the eighteenth century with a criticism of the vices of urban life. Another idyll, "Das Ständchen. Eine Junkeridylle" (1777), borrows even more directly from Theocritus with its combination of the plaintive song before the lover's obdurate door from *Idyll* 3 and the Polyphemus motif of the misguided ugly lover from *Idyll* 11. Voss also preserves the tone of these Theocritean idylls, insofar as "Das Ständchen" is intended satirically.

These similarities aside, the differences are equally great. Unlike Theocritus, or Müller, Voss has no interest, or sympathy, in making his own habits and those of his friends the object of ridicule. His bucolic mimes do not repeat the scatological ribaldry of *Idyll* 5, nor do they mock the rituals of courtship as in *Idylls* 3 or 6 — it is the conceited behavior of the Junker class, not the practice of serenading that is satirized in "Das Ständchen" —, and above all they do not draw attention to their literariness. In Voss's idylls there is no room, either conceptually or practically, for the shepherd as poet. This does not mean that he does not incorporate numerous literary references into his idyll; rather, his aim is not to satirize the fashionable literary conventions of his day. His purpose is very different: the promotion of a manner of life conducted in obedience to the principles of nature. Voss employs his satire to ensure this eventuality. What excites his vitriolic fits is the "Junker" as a class. In a good number of his idylls he intends some direct social or political criticism, as of the institution of serfdom in "Die Leibeigenen," or, in "De Geldhapers" (1777), of the ruinous effect of gambling on the poor, or some indirect criticism, by presenting a picture of the benefits of the Georgic life reformed along enlightened lines, as in the "Die Freigelassenen," which shows how the serfs would live once freed.

The further one moves from the mid-1770s, the milder Voss's idylls become. "Die Bleicherin" (1776), "Die Kirschpflückerin" (1780), and "Die Heumahd" (1784; Voss's version of Theocritus's reapers, *Id.* 10), all present the more traditional image of rural life passed in work, song, and love with none of the discomforting undertones of the earlier idylls, nor the imaginary haze of the Rococo pastoral.[37] In this sense they fulfill the promise of "Die Freigelassenen." Voss's peasants, occasionally crude as befits rustics, are invariably modest and diligent, as befits such children of nature. He even revives some of the motifs from the Rococo pastoral, such as a neckerchief in "Die Bleicherin" as a gift of love familiar from Christian Fürchtegott Gellert's (1715–69) pastoral drama, *Das Band* (1744); or the reappearance of birds in "Die Heumahd": the linnet, the goldfinch, and even the bird in the cage as a symbol of love, again reminiscent of Gellert's *Das Band*. The common thread between these and the earlier idylls is the close attention paid to the mimic situation as well as an eye for detail and the distancing use of the hexameter. The liveliness of the dialogue recedes in favor of the rich description of details, of an "akkumulierend-verdinglichenden Tendenz," in the words of Helmut Schneider.[38] This trait reaches its height in "Der siebzigste Geburtstag" (1780), although it is still very much present in his idyllic epic, *Luise* (1795).[39] In the former, Voss presents a verbal Dutch interior, a "Stilleben," a loving portrayal of bourgeois domesticity without any hint either of Rococo playfulness or of his earlier reforming satire.[40]

This transition to the earnest monumentality of epic owes its origin in part to Voss's increasing involvement with Homer. The translation of the *Odyssey,* begun in 1777, did not appear until 1781, and the *Odyssey* and *Iliad* together only in 1793. It does not seem then that there is any room for Virgil in this progression. Voss's idylls stand under the star of Theocritus, his epic *Luise* under that of Homer.[41] These are the two genres and poets that may recover Greek nature for the present. The temptation to accept Voss's characterization of the Theocritean idyll as well as the relation of that idyll to his own as valid remains enormous. Siegfried Streller summarizes the relation of Voss and Theocritus thus:

> Voß versucht, Theokrit nachzuahmen, indem er wie dieser einerseits die ländliche Wirklichkeit in ihrer Härte unbeschönigt zeichnet, andererseits

aber Möglichkeiten schön entfalteter Menschlichkeit gerade dort entdeckt, wo ein einsichtiger [Mensch] Freiheit gewährt und die Verhältnisse dadurch ändert.⁴²

Maria Erxleben, who holds a similar view of Theocritus's bucolic idylls as a "reale ländlich-einfache Hirtenwelt," repeats the eighteenth century's and Voss's equally typical characterization of the Virgilian eclogue: "sie (d.i. eine 'in überfeinerten Genüssen sich langweilende[.] höfische[.] Gesellschaft') glaubte Abbilder ihrer sehnsüchtigen Vorstellungen und einer ihrem Geschmack angepaßten verfeinerten Natur vor sich zu haben."⁴³ Nevertheless, as was the case with Gessner, Maler Müller, and Winckelmann, the matter is not so straightforward.

While Voss discloses in his letter to Brückner that Theocritus is his acknowledged model of unadorned rustic nature and Virgil the author of a bucolic monstrosity, he resorts to Virgil's first and ninth eclogues for the artistic means that will allow him, without detriment to the genre, to combine the prized attributes of Theocritus with his Enlightenment ideals.⁴⁴ He finds there an example of political and social comment within the bucolic that is applicable to his own situation. In "Die Leibeigenen" (originally entitled "Die Pferdeknechte"), one stable hand, Michel, complains to the other, Hans, that the seigneurial lord, the ubiquitous "Junker," having first promised to free him from feudal service upon his marriage and the payment of a certain sum, reneges on this agreement, inventing spurious obligations and charges. Hans, though sympathizing with Michel, restrains his friend from setting fire to his master's buildings in his frustrated rage, to the extent that by the end of the idyll his arsonist's fury contents itself with the lighting of a pipe of tobacco to ward off the evening mosquitoes.

Voss takes the general situation from *Eclogue* 1. Both he and Virgil present a discussion of disorders in the pastoral world and the solution to these disorders through the conversation between two rustics, one sad and one more or less contented. Obviously the democrat Voss does not share the political direction of the young god Octavian's solution in the Virgilian eclogue, as Octavian will shortly put an end to the Republic as Augustus, but he does make use of the notion that the betterment of society is dependent on the action of the upper classes. Similarly Voss can adapt such details from the eclogue as the purchasing of one's freedom from servitude by giving it quite a different context. Virgil's happy shepherd Tityrus informs the unhappy shepherd Meliboeus that he failed for so long to buy his *libertas* from slavery because he had an extravagant lover who, for whatever reason — and there is no indication the delay was disagreeable to Tityrus as it was to Voss's Michel — caused him to empty his purse as fast as he filled it (*Ec.* 1. 27–35). Voss's rustic, though he too is in love, seeks in contrast to gain his freedom so that he may be free to love and marry, and the impediment is now his lord's refusal. The similarity extends to more than just the presentation of the disordered pastoral community and the search for the remedy of that condition.[45] Voss favors the specific reference to the present of the Virgilian eclogue over the temporal indeterminacy of the Theocritean bucolic or of Gessner's idyll. The larger issue of social justice, implicit though unstated in the moral view of Georgic nature adopted by Gessner and Gottsched, emerges here with unmistakable virulence in the clash between the historical present and the idyllic truth. Voss does not quibble with the ability of nature to serve as a sufficient principle of human society; rather he takes this truth of the Georgic golden age and asks what prevents its realization in the present. Arcadia must step out of the past and into the present to become Elysium.

The matter becomes clearer in observing the difference in the parallel pointed out by Schneider between *Meliboee, deus nobis haec otia fecit* (*Ec.* 1. 6; O Meliboeus, a god has given me this ease; 9) and "Seit der Baron uns die Freiheit geschenkt, singt alles im Dorf" in "Die Freigelassenen."[46] Virgil's god grants leisure and returns one specific individual to his love and song; Voss's patron is not a god but a lord and his act of mercy bestows freedom on the entire community. In the further variation on *Eclogue* 1. 6, "Die Freiheit schenkt uns solchen Mut" (2. 2), freedom replaces Virgil's princeling god and grants to the individual the invigorating courage of self-determination, not the lassitude of leisure as in Virgil's eclogue. The song of Voss's village is merely one of the beneficial effects flowing from the restoration of justice, not the essential attribute of the rustic as it is in the ancient bucolic. Henning in the second of the two serfdom idylls "Die Freigelassenen" is contented and diligent in his work; he can marry Sabine, and the entire village can join together at their wedding feast to present the "Junker" and his wife with the "Ährenkranz" of the idyll's original title, all of the things denied Michel in "Die Leibeigenen." Voss's titles argue the same point. Contrary to the long-established tradition of antiquity and the example of Gessner, they do not name the idyll's interlocutors. Instead they are frequently named after either objects such as the "Ährenkranz," an activity, "Heumahd," or a position, "Pferdeknechte," "Bleicherin," which are all symbols of the Georgic order. A symbolic trait typical of communal order defines the individual rather than he it.

The use that Voss makes of the Virgilian texts for his social criticism is thus only partial. He directly appropriates eclogues 1 and 9 for this purpose but avoids the explicit literary self-reflection involved in making the shepherds preeminently poets; hence the ninth eclogue with its talk of the loss of the great shepherd-poet Menalcas in the rural upheavals is less favored than the first.[47] To sharpen the point: Voss's first two serf idylls might bear rechristening as the "Meliboeus" after the Virgilian shepherd exiled from Arcadia, and the "Tityrus" for the Virgilian shepherd restored to Arcadia, a pastoral "Paradise Lost" and "Paradise Regained" in Voss's strong contrast.

This concern remains central to Voss's later idylls. The agreeable tableau of rural life in "Die Freigelassenen" recurs again and again in the subsequent idylls, which are different in tone, but not in content. Even *Luise*, although it enlarges the pastoral world to include the pastor of the village in the guise of the noble hero of Homeric epic, does not alter the conservative and paternalistic benevolence underlying the social order of "Die Freigelassenen." Voss's view of rural life only confirms the essentially bucolic origins of the notion of idyllic nature with which he is working. The strong identification of the golden age with the age of biblical patriarchs by Gottsched and the German tradition also suggests more of a restoration rather than a revolution, if one is inclined to take that age seriously.[48] As E. Theodor Voss argues, one should not view the development that occurs in Voss's approach to the idyll as indicating a fundamental change in his estimation of the genre or of the image it represents.[49] At the same time as he revises *Luise*, he also writes the satirical idyll, "Junker Kord" (1795), that is no less scathing in its criticism of the barbarity of the country "Junker" than "Die Leibeigenen" or "Das Ständchen." And he returns to the subject of his youth more directly in 1800, when he writes a third idyll in the "Leibeigenschaft" series. "Die Erleichterten," falling between the earlier two, presents the debate between the "Herr" and the "Frau" that culminates at the end of the idyll in their decision to grant freedom to their serfs.

The change that transforms the progressive and socially critical author of the "Leibeigenschaft" idylls into the petty bourgeois, even "Biedermeier," author of "Luise" is less one of substance than of tone. As early as 1783 Voss began work on his translation of the *Georgics* that appeared in 1789. Likewise his involvement with the *Eclogues* stretched from 1788 and the periodic publication of the translation of individual eclogues in the early 1790s until the publication of all ten in 1797, two years after the republication of *Luise*.[50] The world of the village Grünau in *Luise* is the *iustissima tellus* of the *Georgics* (2. 460; "Earth . . . most just; 320) as it appears once the interests of the Storm and Stress have absorbed the transformation of the idyll by Gessner. The golden age of Gessner's "gewiß einmal gewesene" is moved firmly to the present, a transfer of the scorned "idealism" of Gessner to the true or "real" nature of the present. Grünau retains Gessner's and Haller's insistence on a life lived according to the inborn precepts of nature within the family and the community. It dispenses with the last vestiges of the imaginary Arcadia. The characters are given German not Greek names, they are not poets, and their songs are folk songs, not literary constructs. Any hint of the larger political framework in the Virgilian poems is dissipated through the assimilation of the social order first in Gessner to nature and then in Voss to the domesticity of the bourgeois class as the historical representative of this nature. Nonetheless the Virgilian eclogue, despite Voss's stated preference for

Theocritus, provides him with the structure necessary to bring the captivating power of Arcadia to bear on the present, and the *Georgics* and its associations remain in his mind as he rewrites the idylls of *Luise*.[51]

The cumulative effect of these changes is the exclusion of any element that might undermine the idyllic fiction. For the achievement of grafting the imaginary Arcadia convincingly onto the German present, Schiller classifies *Luise* in the "naiven Geschlecht" and argues that it "muß mit griechischen Mustern verglichen werden," and exclusively so (*SchW* 20:471–72, fn.). Voss's adaptation of the Rococo pastoral, first in the more activist "Leibeigenschaft" idylls and, then in the gentler bourgeois golden age of Grünau, is one strongly influenced by Virgil throughout. However, Virgil's influence has markedly different effects in his works and in Müller's. Voss is inspired by Virgil to insinuate naive, idyllic nature into the present until the two become inseparable, until the ideal of nature seems indistinguishable from its historical embodiment, in Kaiser's view. Voss does share with Müller the formal tendency to move the pastoral towards the expansiveness of the larger narrative to accommodate the idyllic microcosm. Although Müller arrives at essentially the same formal conclusion as Voss, the effect is very different. The scope of the larger narrative offers him the opportunity to explore the configuration of the naive in relation to the sentimental. He twice turns to Virgil for the literary means to accomplish this end, although in doing so he shows the limits of the continued utility of the Virgilian solution. His poet-shepherds, as well as his undisguised literary and generic transgressions, run counter to the notion of a naive idyll. They confront the modern idyllic world too directly for it to retain the residual independence it must have for it to serve as a reflection of the sentimental. Similarly, Voss, for the same reason, cannot countenance the appearance of the state in his rural Elysium.

Goethe: A Final Farewell to Arcadia

In Goethe's poems of an idyllic hue, Arcadia becomes historical not by moving into the rural present but by moving into the "ancient" present. The modern's approach to idyllic nature is thus, as was also the case for Werther, a drawing near to an ancient nature. In the first two works considered here, "Der Wandrer" (1772, published 1774) and the *Römische Elegien* (1788–90, published 1795), Goethe replaces the figure of Werther with that of the "Wandrer," who, as a traveling visitor, is even less properly an inhabitant of the idyll than the hapless Werther. Again as in *Werther*, it is the outsider's reflections that constitute as idyllic the scene before both him and the reader. He only experiences himself as sentimental by making this scene manifest as a world in which he and, through him, the reader do not share. The separation of the wanderer's sentimental perspective from the naive perspective of the idyll's inhabitants continues the division between them essential to the German idyll. However, Goethe's explicit concentration in the wanderer's ruminations on the relation between the two, and so consequently on the reader's sense of the proper boundary between the two, shifts the focus from the pastoral scene or idyll to the wanderer's reflections. The concrete particulars of the by-now-standard rural nature recede increasingly from view to be replaced by the viewer's perception of it, or by a mood in its presence.

Only in "Der Wandrer" is the setting recognizably idyllic. The dynamic of the modern present and its search for an accessible "ancient" nature propels the wanderer to leave the bounds of Arcadia. In the *Römische Elegien* we move from the countryside to the city, Roma, and bid farewell to the external trappings of pastoral. However as the importance of the palindrome "Roma-Amor" to these poems makes clear, we by no means forsake the pastoral's age-old preoccupation with love. The return to the city does, however, place these poems under the auspices of a different, though still suitably ancient, poetic deity, namely, the Roman elegy. Goethe's choice is appropriate and made easier by the genres' shared traits: both genres, bucolic and elegy, flourished at the same time in antiquity — with elegy by far the more intensively cultivated — and both share the preoccupations of love and art.

The wanderer's removal to the city is made necessary by the modern idyll's banishment of the poet from the pastoral, for in the *Römische Elegien* the wanderer reveals himself to be a poet. His return to the city answers the difficulty posed by the spontaneous effusions of Gessner or the bucolic rhapsodies of Werther, the latter of which only insist that neither word nor image can grasp for the imagination what is present to the self in feeling. As the imagination could proffer no object adequate to its feeling within the limits of the idyll, the subject could only variously count the ways in which the imagination failed it. The self possessed not a confirmation of its completion and fulfillment in the idyllic scene, but only a sense of its loss at its exclusion and longing that made the self the more sentimental the more keenly it was felt. The poet's readmission permits the wanderer in the *Römische Elegien* finally to effect a reconciliation between an ancient idyllic nature and the modern sentimental present through the mediation of art. The poet figure and the thematization of art grant admission to explicit reflection. Both the ancient past and the modern present become the products of the human consciousness, though historically conditioned, the one naive and idyllic, and the other modern because it is sentimental. This fusion of the two, tenuous and privileged though it is, because it rests on an arduous cultural "Bilding" for its coherence, nonetheless enables a new version of classicism. As did Winckelmann before him, Goethe too travels to Rome and through the Latin heritage to gain entrance to a usable Greek past. Once again it is an engagement not with Greek poets but with the Latin heritage that has led to this most desired of results, the assimilation of an ancient Greece.

Although we may find some loose reminiscences of the pastoral in the *Römische Elegien*, of far greater importance for their understanding is their interaction with the Roman elegists. The poems find a place in this study for their farewell to Arcadia. The reformulation of the pastoral into the modern idyll around the exclusive division between a naive and a sentimental nature raises an absorbing and deeply rooted issue of German culture and aesthetics, yet it deprives the genre of the tools for exploring it by outlawing the devices of the problematic eclogues from the genre. The wanderer must leave Arcadia in order to regain them. The second reason for the inclusion of *Römische Elegien* is the dismal failure of Goethe's attempt to return to an idyll that bears a more obvious resemblance to the ancient bucolic. It confirms the wisdom of his choice in turning to the city and the elegy as the site for his classical reconciliation. In 1797 he published the poem "Alexis und Dora" and labeled it "Idylle." Neither his contemporaries nor subsequent critics could accept Goethe's designation of it as an idyll, a judgment he himself accepted when he republished it as one of his elegies in the collection of his works in 1800, a reclassification much aided by its elegiac meter and the theme of love common to both ancient genres. His attempt in "Alexis und Dora" to return to the issue of *crudelis amor* and his use of a frame and a narrator to insert the Hydra's head of art into the idyll garnered only bafflement and rejection. The interpretative aporia that resulted for this idyll can, however, best be approached by considering its relation to the ancient bucolic.

The first of the poems under consideration here, "Der Wandrer," is an example of the dynamic between naive apperception and sentimental reflection similar in many respects to that of *Werther*. The wanderer is a wanderer precisely because the idyll is not his to gain possession of: he may not remain in the idyll; and the idyll is an idyll precisely because the wanderer apprehends it, revels in this apprehension, and passes on. The moment of departure finally constitutes the idyll by consigning it not quite to the past, nor yet welcoming it to the present. Like Maler Müller's "Adams erstes Erwachen," Goethe's "Wandrer" contains the separation between naive and sentimental within the awareness of one figure; the wanderer is the "Bewußtseinsträger" of the idyll, as Kaiser argues in making the same point.[52] The novelty of Goethe's "Der Wandrer" is the introduction of a sentimental figure directly into the idyll. This innovation makes the sentimental perspective in the constitution of the idyll a matter capable of treatment within the poem rather than placing this burden solely on the reader, as was previously the case. Despite this, the wanderer remains an outsider.

This dynamic shapes the poem as it does the adaptation of some traits familiar from the pastoral. It is a mime between the wanderer and a woman, without out any inset songs as such, but in their place four larger dithyrambic ecstasies. After one of these, and a number of similar asides, the woman resumes their conversation as if nothing out of the ordinary had occurred, apparently oblivious of her companion's distraction.[53] The split in "Der Wandrer" into the prosaic world of the woman and the poetic vision of the wanderer, elided somewhat by the continual movement between these two levels without the aid of any clear demarcation, is one form of this dynamic. Only the wanderer and the reader who follows him back and forth are aware of the two distinct levels, a realization that the course of the poem with its movement back and forth presents as an "Erlebnis" rather than the statement of a more explicit frame.

These two levels correspond to a similar split of idyllic nature into past and present. The present is a deft image of Georgic nature that Gessner would have cherished: the family, consisting of a young woman with a small child and an unseen husband, an "Ackermann" presently out among the fields, lives in a bucolic hut on a spot hallowed, in good Gessnerian tradition, by the life and death of the woman's father "in unsern Armen." The idyllic past appears in the form of a ruined temple, an object of pastoral Arcadia more familiar from the pictorial tradition.[54] The temple raises the question of both art and history in the idyll. Art does not appear explicitly as poetry, but in the more general aspect of a pastoral cultural artifact. The temple is on the one hand a symbol for those products of human design that vainly attempt to escape from the grasp of nature by erecting a lasting monument against its unceasing ebb and flow. In the first version of the poem, writing even appears as a subordinate and decorative part of the temple. The wanderer is able to make out that there is an inscription on the temple to Venus, but the text in its entirety is illegible, its words are "weggewandelt." On the other hand, as the temple of the goddess of love it is a thoroughly pastoral artifact. If we think of the scene before the wanderer's eyes as a tableau, then the temple of Venus both parallels and is a substitute for the gravestone of the earlier modern pictorial tradition of the pastoral. The gravestone was formerly the referent for the understanding of *et in Arcadia ego,* as death too was present; the temple of Venus refers rather to the more modern translation of it, namely, that each individual is/was psychologically an inhabitant of this happy state.[55] This accomplishment of human artifice remains subordinate to nature in the wanderer's reflection. It appears as a mere outgrowth of nature, as did artifice in Gessner, rather than the instrument of man's separation from nature:

> Schätzest du so Natur
> Deines Meisterstücks Meisterstück?
> Unempfindlich zertrümmerst
> Du dein Heiligtum
> Säst Disteln drein. (*GSW* 1/1:202–8, verses 74–79)

Art gains admittance in the idyllic nature of "Der Wandrer" only as a cultural artifact external to the wanderer, instead of the infinitely more problematic reflection of a more inward relation, which it would become if the wanderer were to conceive of his reflective dithyrambs as art. In this exclusion of any direct reference to poetry, Goethe is in accordance with his contemporaries Gessner and Voss. They all share the common belief in the persistence of an originally idyllic nature.

The only form of inner reflection that occurs in the poem is the temporal one of history. Yet this too is obscured. The context of the ruins, their relation to nature and to the present, is accomplished by the wanderer's musings about them. For the woman they are simply useful stones:

> *Frau*
> . . .
> Droben sind der Steine viel
> Um meine Hütte.
> . . .
>
> *Frau*
> Das ist meine Hütte.
>
> *Wandrer*
> Eines Tempels Trümmern! (44–51)

His own role in making this connection historical remains unobserved by the wanderer. He attributes it rather to nature with the notion that the temple is the masterpiece of nature's own masterpiece humanity. Just as nature subordinated the temple as artifact, so does it sublimate the temple in its historical guise; its unceasing decay and regeneration put an end to the "Meisterstücks Meisterstück." The easy assertion of the universality of nature and likewise of its highest perfection in ancient Greece is familiar from Winckelmann.[56] Before the temple, the wanderer innocently recollects these facts and rescues them from the oblivion of the present.

A final, slighter form in which the dynamic of naivety and reflection expresses itself is the correspondence of the outer time of day with the inner reflection of the wanderer. The time of the encounter between the wanderer and the woman is evening, the twilight period that is neither night nor day. In this early evening hour the idyllic image of nature draws closest to the wanderer in his reverie, before his "Leb wohl!" brings the idyll to a close. In bidding farewell to the present idyll of the woman and the past idyll of antiquity, he creates the distance necessary for the modern idyll. The technique, however, of using sunset to heighten the sense of idyllic nostalgia has belonged to the repertoire of the German pastoral since Gessner and is an indirect example of the Virgilian sense of mood.

To this one might add a few other remnants of the pastoral tradition that Goethe employs to draw the boundary between naive idyll and the sentimental perception of it. The notion of respite beneath the shade of a tree — here an elm rather than the more familiar beech — belongs recognizably to the pastoral tradition. Furthermore, the association of travel, whether to or from the city, with the countryside, and the implications of being under way for the static state of Arcadia, as well as the idea of breaking a trip, are all familiar from the *Eclogues* 1 and 9 (even *Eclogues* 8 and 10 can be counted among the traveling eclogues), although it had not hitherto been part of the German idyllic inventory. Whether it is a matter of pure coincidence or not, both poets hit on the same circumstances to offset the sense of space in their poems — Arcadia on the one hand and the idyllic nature of the naive on the other. These coincidences are by themselves nothing more than superficial. They do not conceal the vast difference between the two.

Art and history might offer more promising prospects, for they both appear in Virgil's *Eclogues*. Yet, as already noted, Goethe's art is the artifice of culture more generally, and Virgil's art is the sophistication of the Neoteric poet-shepherd. In Goethe's poem, what poetry there is comes not from a figure within the idyll but is supplied by a figure from without. And again, Goethe's history is a conception of organic rhythm, whereas Virgil's history revolves around the political idea of Rome. And both of these concepts in Goethe's poems are related to one another through a notion of a vital, omnipresent nature that is absent from the *Eclogues;* Arcadia is there not a synonym for naive nature. In its place, there stands a political-religious order, which is in turn absent from Goethe's poem.

All the more interesting therefore is the place Goethe's more psychological perception of idyllic nature may find for the Virgilian use of prophecy. It can much more easily be assimilated to the expression of longing, which characterizes the fundamental attitude of the sentimental towards the naive. More interesting connections can be drawn by keeping *Eclogue* 4 and the sixth book of the *Aeneid* in mind. Towards the close of the poem the wanderer, on asking where the path over the mountain leads, discovers that it will take him to Cumae. Cumae is the spot where Aeneas lands in Italy to consult with the sibyl, in whose company he descends into the underworld and hears of Rome and its future greatness.[57] The appearance of Cumae, the site of prophecy and the seat of the seer, may be innocent of any Virgilian association, as the Cumaean sibyl was famous quite apart from her role in the *Aeneid*. This, however, seems unlikely, in view of the wanderer's third monologue. In it Goethe draws art and nature together by comparing the casual way nature disposes of its precious objects in its cycle of life to the human manner of living ignorant among the ruins of history.

> Die Raup umspinnt den goldnen Zweig
> Zum Winterhaus für ihre Brut.

> Und du flickst zwischen der Vergangenheit
> Erhabne Trümmer
> Für dein Bedürfnis
> Eine Hütte o Mensch! (133–38)

The simile may be understood without further reflection. Yet in the naturalness of the simile, of a caterpillar spinning a cocoon on a branch, the adjective "golden" is out of place. Further to put a golden branch in the way of one Cumae-bound is anything but innocent. It recalls the *aureus ramus* (*Aen.* 6. 187; the golden bough; 153) of Virgil that Aeneas had need of at Cumae in order to gain access to the underworld and there to learn of the secrets of time and the fates. Goethe's wanderer is however not at Cumae, which still lies along the path beyond the horizon on the far side of the mountain. For the wanderer, there is no prophecy. Nonetheless, the wanderer does engage in a form of prophecy at the end, when, in an inner vision, he imagines not the physical destination of his journey but that of his passage through life. At the conclusion to this wandering, he envisages a return to the idyllic scene he has before him. In this vision of the future the "golden" imagery occurs again:

> Und kehr ich dann am Abend heim
> Zur Hütte vergüldet
> Vom letzten Sonnenstrahl,
> Laß mich empfangen solch ein Weib
> Den Knaben auf dem Arm. (158–62)

With a delicate shift, the color gold now adorns the artifact of culture rather than that of nature, although it remains in nature's gift to bestow the honor. It is further now a possession of the wanderer as his imagination presents a family to him.

The other source for an evocation of prophetic intimations, and one associated with the pastoral, is the fourth eclogue. It too provides a connection with Cumae, the word "golden," and the poem's concluding image. The singer of the eclogue purports to see the fulfillment of the Cumaean prophecy in his *carmen cumaeum* (*Ec.* 4. 4), a song about the end of the present cycle of time in the birth of a child, and with him the inauguration of the next cycle heralding the return of the golden age.

Of greater significance is the final image. Like Goethe, Virgil concludes his poem with a forceful image of a Madonna-like mother and child pair. Although more readily associated with Goethe's idyll than the use of "golden" and Cumae, the image of the woman with a babe on her arm shows the same relation to the poem as the sibyl. The central image of present-day idyllic nature in the poem is that of woman and child whom the wanderer happens upon. He even cradles the sleeping child in his arms and gives it his blessing while its mother fetches him water. Just as the wanderer's vision transferred the gold of nature's branch to an object of human devising, to art, so too does this vision now promise to overcome the isolation of the wanderer from idyllic nature by transferring wife, child, and hut to himself. At every level in the final sequence of images, the cyclical nature in the wanderer's monologues reaches out to embrace him and to place him in harmony inwardly with what he beholds externally. As the caterpillar takes up golden nature, the hut, art and history, and the family, both nature and civilization by reaching out to include the wanderer in the vision, so too does the wanderer gather up all of his musings in the final verses. Even the time of the idyll and the time in his vision match; it is evening in both. In one sense his future is no different than the present and the past, since it merely repeats them. The difference lies in the inclusion of himself in idyllic nature at the end. In this sense his vision represents an Elysium, and, since it remains in his mind's eye alone, an object of sentimental longing.

The conclusion then is very different from the bucolic world of Virgil and confirms the modern, German perception of the idyll. In Virgil's Arcadia one moves from the personal concerns of poetry and love to their relation to the more general ones of social piety and civic order in the Roman universe. In Goethe's idyll, one assimilates art and history to nature, which is in turn assimilated for the individual to domestic privacy; or alternatively he to it through the family. It becomes a personal vision, an inner instrument for the articulation of sentimental desire. It is a change from explicit statement to implicit allusion in accordance with the greater concentration on the consciousness of the individual. Despite this difference, Goethe's structuring of the wanderer's reflections — if one accepts the web of associations presented above — around the Virgilian inventory of prophecy (Cumae, mother and child, a golden branch) points to the continued creative resonance of the Virgilian model. In this instance Goethe employs it to insert the sentimental vision that overcomes the wanderer's earlier separation from idyllic nature, while yet retaining this promised harmony of the imagination as unrealized.

To this poem Goethe's *Römische Elegien* serve as a counterpoint, as in them the vision does not remain unfulfilled. The problematic elements of the *Eclogues*, which found no place in the idyllic nature of "Der Wandrer," gain entrance in these poems. Once again these preoccupations remain firmly tied to the individual's perception. Art expands from an ill-defined artifice to include poetry explicitly, history from the general concept of cultural change to the political present and Rome, love from the idyllic family to sexual intimacy. None of these elements is the exclusive province of the pastoral. For Kaiser the elegies represent a continuation of the reflections touched on in the "Der Wandrer." The same wanderer from the north appears, only this time he stops in the city, Rome, to find there in the arms of Faustine that love is also the true muse of poetry. Kaiser gives a tight schematic progression to the *Elegien,* which leads to the ever closer assimilation of the idyllic attitude into the wanderer's perception of his daily existence. The idyll becomes real through its transformation into one of the constituents of an individual's own awareness of self.

The neatness of this progression obscures the heterogeneous character of the poems — mythological stories, priapic elegies, mime, narration, disdain for the world of action, the ineluctable grasp of Amor, and so on — the more immediate source of which is the Roman elegists, Tibullus, Catullus, and, above all, Propertius. Like them, Goethe sets his love affair in the bustling city; his Faustine berates her northern lover as tellingly as Cynthia does her Propertius; like them, he dwells on the relation of Amor and poetry.[58] Unlike them, Goethe integrates these elements into a psychological conception that proves to be so inescapably a part of the wanderer's self that he both experiences and reflects on the world through it.[59] The simultaneous presence of art and love are necessary to effect the long-sought direct communication between an ancient and idyllic nature and a modern sentimental estrangement: Roma, the ancient world, Amor the present, the world of sentiment.

Love becomes a supple and expansive condition, at once both a concept and an experience. Amor is the unfettered enjoyment of life in the round, the normative condition of humanity and the source of reflection. Amor connects nature, history, and art, a feat that in "Der Wandrer" had been accomplished by monologues and an unfulfilled vision. It is the vital fluid the pale modern shade must imbibe to gain eyes, ears, and tongue. The wanderer comes to Rome from a "graulichen Tag" (VII, 2) in the north, "farb- und gestaltlos, die Welt" (VII, 4), one sunk in enervating "Betrachtung" (VII, 6). Once in Rome, he dared to seize the rapture of the moment, "Gelegenheit," to act on feeling, and take a beloved. The description of "Gelegenheit" begins relatively neutrally and conventionally as a metaphorical image, but soon passes over into the real experience of "Umarmung" and "Kuß" (IV, 30). Immediately following this pivotal moment, the wanderer's relation to the world is transformed:

> Froh empfind' ich mich nun auf klassischem Boden begeistert,
>   Vor- und Mitwelt spricht lauter und reizender mir. (V, 1–2)[60]

He senses and is happy that he does so. What he senses pleasurably is his awareness of his own self, being in a heightened, almost mystic condition. To this condition is given both a specific time and place; it is now and also antiquity, an oxymoron spelt out in the pentameter with "Vor- und Mitwelt" The same point is made metrically in the hexameter. Beginning with "klassisch" the line is perfectly regular, that is, classical, two dactyls followed by a spondee. "Nun" sits in the middle of the line both metrically and visually, and may be scanned as either the arsis or thesis of the third foot, that is, as either with or without stress. The perhaps more natural reading of the line puts the stress on "nun" with a strong masculine caesura; in which case the weight of "froh empfinden" falls on the present moment, the "nun," which is strongly emphasized by the metrical stress and the pause in the flow in the line; that is,

    Fróh empfínd' ich mich nún// auf klássischem Bóden begeístert.

However, one may with equal justification read the line with the stress on "mich," which places the emphasis of "froh empfinden" on the subject (from a grammatical perspective) and throws the temporal emphasis onto the classical "Boden"; that is,

    Fróh empfínd' ich mích// nun auf klássischem Bóden begeístert.

On this reading, the transition from the modern present to the ancient past gains the added metrical piquancy that the first half of the line has a swift, vigorous, spondaic, "modern" alternation of stressed and unstressed syllables followed by the slow, tranquil, and stately measure of the ancient, "quantitative" dactyl, to which the repetition of the sibilant, particularly in "klassischem," adds a musical softness. This metrical pattern of modern to more classical is repeated in the pentameter: Goethe could easily have lengthened the first foot by adding "Welt-" to "Vor-," as he did in the earlier versions, had he wished to avoid the contrast.

    The same wish to insinuate through perpetual motion is also evident in his use of rhetorical terms. The two lines are chiastic: the hexameter begins with the modern subject and ends with classical ground, the pentameter begins with classical ground ("Vorwelt") but returns in its final word, "mir," to the modern subject. This subject, in turn, through polyptoton, throws us back to the beginning, from which we may notice the regular declension, through nominative and accusative to dative, from subject to reflexive object, and then to indirect object. The ancient world does what the Germans most fervently desired: it speaks to them through the medium of love. And finally, in contrast to the subject's metrical position in the "modern" portion in the opening of the distich, the "mir" occurs in the more "classical," that is, in the more dactylic half of the pentameter line. The effect of this continual metrical, rhetorical, and semantic interweaving is an insistence on the Eleatic wholeness of the experience.

    We are assured that the wanderer correctly hears the ancient voice whispering to him through love by the awakening in him of the impulse to art in a suitably ancient guise, which is put forward in two striking images:

    Und belehr ich mich nicht? wenn ich des lieblichen Busens
        Formen spähe, die Hand leite die Hüften hinab?
    Dann versteh ich erst recht den Marmor, ich denk und vergleiche,
        Sehe mit fühlendem Aug', fühle mit sehender Hand.
    . . .

Oftmals hab' ich auch schon in ihren Armen gedichtet
Und des Hexameters Maß, leise, mit fingernder Hand,
Ihr auf den Rücken gezählt, Sie atmet in lieblichem Schlummer
Und es durchglühet ihr Hauch mir bis ins Tiefste die Brust.
(V, 7–18)

The two branches of art representative of ancient, that is Greek, excellence, statuary and epic, appear in these distichs. Their understanding and imitation, however, depend on the vital experience not of the past, but of the present, an assertion that could not be more graphically driven home than by the image of his mistress's body (see also XIII). The assurance that the sensations of the present provide accurate insight into the art of antiquity is given in the belief that the experience of love, or, to use the imagery of the *Elegien*, the worship of Amor, is an experience common to both ages. It restores the sentimental subject to the dominion of the pastoral *amor vincit omnia* and does so with the modern omission of the adjective *crudelis*. The physical enjoyment of love unites the "naive" Faustina and the "sentimental" wanderer, without, however, making either her "sentimental" or him "naive." This normative view of Amor permits Goethe to overcome the divide of historical distance. He can claim that he and the ancient poets, sharing a common experience, also practice intrinsically the same craft:

Amor schüret indes die Lampe und denket der Zeiten,
Da er den nämlichen Dienst seinen Triumvirn getan. (V, 19–20)

In the *Römische Elegien*, Amor assumes the ordering role that nature played in "Der Wandrer"; now art and history appear as Amor's offshoots rather than those of nature. The advantage of this change is to allow the wanderer to experience more inwardly what was only a vision at the end of the previous poem. It transfers from reflection to life the sentimental yearning for naivety. The removal of idyllic nature from center stage matches the similar abandonment of the modern idyll's more moral, Georgic view of love. This wanderer does not desire the idyllic family; he is content to seize what measure of love the moment offers. It is enough for him to enjoy life with a mistress, untroubled by the opinion either of the world or of her family. This resolution of the naive and sentimental represents the abandonment of the by now traditional "ethical" nature of idyllic love. The detachment of the longing for the naive from the idyllic nature of modernity returns the question of this longing and of its treatment and resolution to the sphere from which it originates: namely, that of culture. Goethe may return to the central themes of the ancient bucolic of art and love and their relation to the poet, yet, as it is a constellation of themes no longer permitted according to the modern dogma of the idyllic, he must do so outside the borders of the idyll proper in the sphere of the elegy, also an ancient genre in which these themes found a home.

Goethe's Rome becomes a cultural landscape fixed in the artist's imagination through the agency of love: "sie [die Liebe] bezeugt sich als urmenschliche schöne, untilgbare Lebens- und Naturformen, gerade in Rom."[61]

Goethe's later attempt in "Alexis und Dora" (written 1796, published 1797) to address once again through direct reference to art the themes of a naive nature, antiquity, and the sentimental self meets with little favor. General admiring applause greet the poem itself, but not its designation as an "idyll." Features from the previous two poems reappear. Goethe again uses travel and departure to bring the idyllic moment clearly into the focus of reflection. In a continuation of the *Römische Elegien,* Amor remains at center stage; love still conquers all and is still intimately connected with the psyche of the individual. In contradistinction to the two earlier poems, there is no chasm between the perspective of the two main figures of the idyll; Alexis is neither more nor less naive than Dora. Instead Goethe achieves the sentimental distance from naive immediacy through the use of recollection. As with Maler Müller's Adam, the reader only glimpses the formerly naive Alexis through his account of his previous state, which no longer exists. It ended the moment when he realized he was in love, which was also the very moment he had to leave. This moment becomes the object both of his happiness and of his despair:

> Nur Ein Augenblick war's, in dem ich lebte, der wieget
>   Alle Tage, die sonst kalt mir verschwinden, auf.
> Nur Ein Augenblick war's, der letzte, da stieg mir ein Leben
>   Unvermutet in dir, wie von den Göttern, herab.
>   (*GSW* 4/1:844–55, 15–18)

Schiller recognized in his letter of 3 July 1796 to Goethe that the entire idyll turns on this point:

> So ist mir die treffliche Stelle:
>
> > Ewig, sagte sie leise
>
> nicht sowohl ihres *Ernstes* [sic] wegen schön, der sich von selbst versteht, sondern weil das Geheimnis des Herzens in diesem einzigen Wort auf einmal und ganz, mit seinem unendlichen Gefolge, heraus stürzt. Dieses einzige Wort, an dieser Stelle, ist statt einer ganzen langen Liebesgeschichte, und nun stehen die zwei Liebenden so gegeneinander, als wenn das Verhältnis schon Jahre lang existiert hätte. (*SchW* 8/1:195)

In essence all the soulful musings of Alexis do little more than explain to the reader why this moment comes to hold such a position in his life. The idyll is a psychological one: the naive condition of the youth is compared to the emotional maturity of the adult who is aware of loss.

The adoption of the psychological perspective in the idyll along with the complete integration of the speaker Alexis into its action denies Goethe the complex reflections that art and history offered. It precludes the familiar pairing of antiquity and modernity in the more cultural and historical idyll of the *Römische Elegien* or "Der Wandrer." He compensates for this lack by inserting external details that give the impression of classical antiquity, such as the use of the Greek names for the gods. The Mediterranean setting of the idyll also suggests classical soil, even as the idea of a young man embarking on the unclassical career of a merchant would be a situation instantly familiar to a contemporary bourgeois reader (one need only think of Wilhelm's predicament at the beginning of *Wilhelm Meister*). The removal of the idyll to a distant, foreign, yet not unfamiliar place and to an indeterminate time close to the present compensates somewhat for this change. It also repeats the treatment of time and place in the ancient bucolic, particularly that of Virgil.

Similarly, and in a much more conscious fashion, Goethe avails himself of the ancient model to gain the subtleties that the intrusion of art affords. He employs a narrative frame to distinguish the voice of the narrator from that of Alexis. In the two earlier poems this was not the case. The narrative voice was identical to that of the "sentimental speaker," in a technical sense in the *Römische Elegien,* and in the vaguer sense of offering a larger perspective and distance in "Der Wandrer." The frame here allows the narrator both to comment on Alexis and to raise the question of the relation of art to the idyll. This latter question extends its purview to include the expectations of the reader in relation to the genre within its thematic sphere: again very much a trait of the ancient bucolic, but not of the modern idyll.

Goethe has no better luck with this ancient innovation than did Maler Müller with Walter's use of the word "Idylle." The generic status of the poem becomes contested. Both he and Schiller as well as others in their circle refer to the poem as an "Idylle."[62] It is also published in Schiller's *Musen-Almanach für das Jahr 1797* with the subtitle "Idylle." Yet eventually, with the publication of the *Neue Schriften* in 1800, the poem becomes an elegy and is included among the other elegies that follow the *Römische Elegien*. Goethe's readers found two passages perplexing in the sense that they offended against their expectations of a naive and idyllic pastoral. Schiller mentions the first in his letter of 18 June 1796:

> Daß Sie die Eifersucht so dicht daneben stellen, und das Glück so schnell durch die Furcht wieder verschlingen lassen, weiß ich vor meinem Gefühl noch nicht ganz zu rechtfertigen, obgleich ich nichts befriedigendes dagegen einwenden kann. Dieses fühle ich nur, daß ich die glückliche Trunkenheit, mit der Alexis das Mädchen verläßt und sich einschifft, gerne immer festhalten möchte. (*SchW* 8/1:175)

Violence of emotion has no place in the tranquillity of the idyll, at least since the time of Rapin. The second objection is to the lines:

> War es möglich, die Schönheit zu sehen und nicht zu empfinden?
> Würkte der himmlische Reiz nicht auf dein stumpfes Gemüt?

Klage dich, Armer, nicht an! — So legt der Dichter ein Rätsel,
   Künstlich mit Worten verschränkt, oft der Versammlung ins Ohr.
Jeden freut die seltne Verknüpfung der zierlichen Bilder,
   Aber noch fehlet das Wort, das die Bedeutung verwahrt;
Ist es endlich gefunden, dann heitert sich jedes Gemüt auf,
   Und erblickt im Gedicht doppelt erfreulichen Sinn.[63]

The intrusion of the narrator, the elaborate comparison to a riddle, and the mention of a poet in the midst of the young man's plaintive recollections destroy the idyllic fiction.[64] The whole lacks "psychologische Plausibilität" for his readers.[65]

In addition, one might add that the idyll is not about shepherds, nor is it even set in the countryside. It is set in the bustle of a small port city. The young hero, Alexis, is about to set off out into the world to make his fortune as a merchant. Between taking leave of his parents and arriving at the ship in the harbor waiting only for him to set sail, he is accosted by his lovely neighbor of long standing, Dora, whose gift of a basket of fruit beneath a myrtle tree in her garden leads to a mutual confession of love, sealed by Dora's promise of "ewig." The idyll itself only presents this sequence of events in the ruminations of Alexis, who stands next to the mast looking backwards to his past as he watches the shore and his beloved sink from sight, and not forward in the direction of the speeding ship and toward his future. He passes from despair at the thought of his impending long separation from his newly discovered beloved, to jealousy at the thought that Dora might give herself to another now that he is gone, and ends with his wish to die immediately in a shipwreck, the booty of the dolphins. At this point the poem breaks off and concludes with an abrupt comment of the narrator:

. . . —
Nun, ihr Musen, genug! Vergebens strebt ihr zu schildern,
   Wie sich Jammer und Glück wechseln in liebender Brust.
Heilen könnet ihr nicht die Wunden, die Amor geschlagen
   Aber Linderung kommt einzig, ihr Guten, von euch. (155–58)

So much for the idyll and its difficulties.

The first objection may be dealt with summarily. Goethe in a letter to Schiller (21–22/6/1796) justifies Alexis's jealousy on two accounts: first, that it is natural for one in the turmoil of emotion to suffer pangs of jealousy, and second, that a "pathetische[r] Gang" belongs to the idyll (*GSW* 8/1:179).[66] This adequately answers Schiller's only half-articulated reservation. He would not dispute the argument from nature; rather the argument from art would attract his attention, were he to think of the idyll as he does in *Naive und sentimentalische Dichtung*. He writes there of the idyll, "Die poetische Darstellung unschuldiger und glücklicher Menschheit ist der allgemeine Begriff dieser Dichtungsart" (*SchW* 20:467). Whatever thoughts Goethe may have had about the idyll, he does not include among them the opinion that the emotional condition of humanity in it should be different from that exhibited elsewhere. Indeed as it was precisely the insistence in the *Römische Elegien* that love unfold along the same emotional lines then and now that permitted the wanderer to fuse ancient and modern in the art of the present, Goethe would be disinclined to admit suspension of the constancy of love's effect on the psyche.

It is the second of the two difficulties outlined above that is the more interesting as it proves to be the more intractable. Recently, both Albrecht Schöne (1982) and Dieter Borchmeyer (1985) have sought to base their interpretations principally on this latter point. Schöne takes up F. P. Pickering's 1958 argument of the "versetzten Prolog," which states that Goethe, in order to preserve the poem's marvelously elegiac opening lines, inserted his original, but now ungainly, beginning, the prologue "Der Dichter legt ein Rätsel, . . ." into the spot where it now stands in the poem.[67] To stitch the two pieces together he resorted to a "so" (25), a comparative conjunction that suggests a simile between the riddling poet and lover Alexis. An unhappy resolution, in Schöne's view, as the simile does not compare like to like. He proposes to emend the text of line with an "es" for the "so" in a bid to restore the prologue, that is, "Es legt der Dichter ein Rätsel. . . ."

With the "es," all hint of a comparison dies, and the lines set forth instead the manner in which the succeeding poem ought to be read. The riddle, no longer limited to Alexis's condition, applies to the poem as a whole; once the reader solves the riddle, he will savor the poem in its entirety with its "doppelt erfreulichen Sinn." Schöne gives a two-part answer to the riddle, both of which involve mythological cleverness. The decipherment of the fruit basket yields the reading that Alexis slept with Dora. Such cleverness on Goethe's part seems pointless as it does not materially affect the interpretation of the poem that Schöne offers. A more convincing argument is his contention that the dolphins accompanying the ship at the outset of the poem "als flöhe ihnen die Beute davon" (4), as well as those dolphins to whom Alexis commends himself in his jealous despair at the end, are both to be read as the animals of Venus. His wish that the thunder of Zeus sink the ship represents now not a wish for suicide, but a fruitless acknowledgment of Venus's power and a desire to return to Dora. On this reading, "Alexis und Dora" continues the *Amor uincit omnia* theme of the *Römische Elegien*, but this time in a setting much more strongly reminiscent of its first occurrence in *Eclogue* 10. It restores the adjective *crudelis* and thus restores to the idyll the tension at the heart of the ancient bucolic.

Borchmeyer rejects both the emendation proposed and the first portion of the answer to the riddle. The "so" compares, instead, the previous and the present states alluded to in Alexis's rhetorical question (22–24) to the condition of an audience perplexed by an author's riddle. Just as the audience vainly strives to fit the pieces together until, with one word, the solution is given, and all the pieces suddenly make sense, so too did Alexis fail to see with his heart what his eyes daily disclosed to him until that final goodbye moment in the garden and Dora's pledge of "Ewig."[68] Borchmeyer explains the stylistic incongruity of the simile by observing that it represents Goethe's attempt at Homeric naivety. Homer often uses "situationsfremde Ausschweifungen," which are on that account judged naive. In this instance the "situationsfremde" element is the break in psychological plausibility. Goethe's motive for such a "naive" device is his delight in the parlor game of riddles, one of which he now inserts into the poem with the consequences indicated above.

Neither of these two answers satisfies. Schöne's argument proposes a considerable alteration to the text, as if Goethe were not the master of the tools of his trade. It also makes the entire poem hang on an awkward piece of pedantic cleverness at variance with the rest of the poem. Furthermore, the role of the dolphins, the use of the word "Beute," and the view of Dora as the gift of the gods work much better at the level of imagery of whose significance Alexis remains unaware, as Borchmeyer argues.[69] Alexis does sincerely wish that the ship founder, but it is Venus who intends that he should not die in the shipwreck. Nor does Borchmeyer's answer convince. The "doppelt erfreuliche[r] Sinn" of the riddle refers in this instance to Dora in Alexis's eyes, and no longer to the entire "Gedicht," as verse 30 states. And further, that Homer need not justify his similes psychologically follows from the fact that Homer had no conception of psychology as such. The reasons for his similes appearing inappropriate are different: they are often too long, a retarding moment; they also suggest a only a rough analogy that the plethora of details he provides does not bear out for the more exact mind of the reading as opposed to a listening public. But Goethe's simile does not offend in these ways. The eye does not slip over these few lines only for the mind later to realize that they do not quite fit. One is immediately brought up short and must reread the lines in an attempt to discover who speaks them and what they mean in a most elementary fashion. The result of Borchmeyer's argument is to turn a mountain into a molehill, to attempt to assimilate the simile or prologue to a "naive" conception for an unnaive purpose, the insertion of a puzzle.

If, however, one reads the "Stilbruch" neither as the result of formal ineptitude nor as a doubtful attempt at naive camouflage but as deliberate and intended, then one may add a level of meaning that complements the earlier levels of the psychological story and the symbolic imagery. As a "Stilbruch" it stands fully in the tradition of the ancient bucolic that did not pretend to represent a naive condition. Virgil employed the notions of the appropriate *modus dicendi*, of genre and subject matter to distinguish more sharply the contours of his poetic Arcadia. Goethe employs his "Stilbruch" to disrupt the anticipated illusion of a psychologically plausible naivety.

But the parallel between Goethe and Virgil does not end there. Unique among the extant ancient bucolic poets, Virgil introduces two riddles into the third eclogue (104–7), although they have neither the prominence nor importance in that work that Goethe's riddle does for his poem. Where the two examples of "Stilbruch" meet is that both turn on the question of art and its relation to what is depicted. As usual, Goethe prefers insinuation to direct statement. It is impossible to determine whether the words of the simile or prologue are spoken by Alexis or a narrator; or, even if one accepts the supposition of a narrator, exactly where he begins to speak.[70] It is only the intrusion of the idea of a poet, his audience, and the effect of his art on the audience, the "doppelt erfreulichen Sinn," that makes the notion of a narrator so appealing.

This entire matter might, perhaps, become clearer if one views the simile or prologue and the narrator's epilogue at the end as an instance of the bucolic framing device so beloved of the ancients. The unequivocal use of such a device at the end constitutes in itself an oblique allusion to the ancient model, an allusion that becomes explicit if one recollects that its content — the notion that poetry alone offers some alleviation of the pangs of love — comes directly from Theocritus's eleventh idyll, as Kaiser notes.[71] The idyll's last distich,

> Heilen könnet ihr [Musen] nicht die Wunden, die Amor geschlagen;
> Aber Linderung kommt einzig, ihr Guten, von euch,

repeats the first two and a half lines from *Idyll* 11:

> οὐδὲν ποττὸν ἔρωτα πεφύκει φάρμακον ἄλλο,
> Νικία, οὔτ' ἔγχριστον, ἐμὶν δοκεῖ, οὔτ' ἐπίπαστον,
> ἢ ταὶ Πιερίδες·
>
> [There is against love no other remedy, Nikias, neither balm nor bandage, so it seems to me, than the Muses.][72]

The thought may come from Theocritus, but the context of the two idylls is not comparable. After this bit of advice, Theocritus presents for his audience's amusement the lovesick ravings of the coarse and deformed Polyphemus against the injustices of the world and the fair Galathea. The burlesque of the piteous lover in no way corresponds to the tone of Goethe's poem that, if somewhat knowing, is not mocking. Rather the knowing sense that permeates the poem as well as the sympathy for Alexis's predicament is closer to Virgil, specifically to his tenth eclogue, in its sensibility.

Goethe's narrator interrupts Alexis's "pathetischen Gang" at the point it reaches the height of self-destructive madness:

> Treffe dein leuchtender Blitz diesen unglücklichen Mast!
> Streue die Planken umher und gib der tobenden Welle

> Diese Waren, und mich gib den Delphinen zum Raub!–
> Nun, ihr Musen, genug! Vergebens strebt ihr zu schildern,
> Wie sich Jammer und Glück wechseln in liebender Brust. (152–56)

The young Alexis is driven to jealousy, despair, and finally madness by love. Implicit in the imagery throughout the poem is the sense that Alexis could not have done otherwise, that he was fated to find himself inextricably enmeshed in the embrace of Amor. The dolphins here at the end point to Venus, and refer us back to the dolphins chasing their fleeing booty at the beginning of the poem. Likewise, at the beginning, Alexis's sense of their moment of love as an instant descended "wie von den Göttern herab" (18), the etymology of Dora's name, the gift of god, the basket of fruit, however deciphered, nonetheless presented under the bough of the myrtle and so under the aegis of Venus, all of these argue that falling deeply enough in love for the emotion to be violently wrenching was not something that Alexis could have avoided. The indirect return to this theme, unknown to Alexis, in his final words with "den Delphinen zum Raub" duplicates the same more forthright conclusion of Gallus's woe in Virgil:

> *'omnia uincit Amor: et nos cedamus Amori.'*
> *Haec sat erit, diuae, uestrum cecinisse poetam,* ... (*Ec.* 10. 69–70)

> ["All-conquering is Love — no use to fight against him."
> Muses divine, may you be satisfied with these verses
> Your poet has sung . . . (46)]

Love's power is not concealed from its victim in mythological imagery as it is from Alexis. The famous line on omnipotent love beginning *omnia uincit Amor* falls to the lovesick Gallus.

Virgil addresses the matter of Amor more straightforwardly from the outset when he has the various deities of Arcadia come to Gallus and variously demand or comment — *unde amor iste . . . tibi? . . . Galle, quid insanis?* (*Ec.* 10. 21–22; "What fired this passion of yours?"... "You have lost your senses, Gallus"; 44) — and, for this reason, on account of Gallus's mad infatuation, pronounce Amor to be *crudelis Amor* (*Ec.* 10. 29). There is no difference between the position of the narrator, that of the gods, and that of Gallus. In Goethe, the reader is only shown passion's madness as at first it germinates happily, then grows, and turns sour. The recognition that the hand of some larger power is at work only comes on reflection as one unravels the mythological imagery woven into the more powerful and immediately absorbing psychological narrative. This difference notwithstanding, the parallel between the two poets in the treatment of the theme as well as the uncanny similarity in the timing of the narrator's entrance is striking. Both signal the narrator's return with the same phrase: "Nun, ihr Musen, genug!" in Goethe's case, and in Virgil's, *Haec sat erit, diuae . . . Pierides* (10. 70–72; Muses divine, may you be satisfied with these verses; 46). Goethe gives a Virgilian setting to his Theocritean reference.

The parallel can be made more exact. But in order to do so the role of the naive in the poem and the question of how the frame relates to both the poem and the naive must be taken up again. That there is nothing naive in the *Eclogues* has been said before, though this does not deny that there is an awareness of the power of emotion that attaches a sense of longing to the idea of Arcadia. The matter is clearest in the tenth eclogue, where Virgil handles it with an urbane empathy, ironic yet understanding. Virgil's Gallus is a sophisticated man of the court and no longer a young man. Yet he still indulges, supposedly, in a ludicrous infatuation for Lycoris, which Virgil transposes to Arcadia. Although Virgil speaks tongue-in-cheek, he manages to imbue Gallus's yearning for a quiet and untroubled life together with Lycoris in Arcadia with a gentle and haunting quality. He achieves this effect through the insistent repetition of *crudelis amor* and the more subtle repetition of descriptions of the mountains and echoing woods of Arcadia, which parallels Goethe's repetitions of the Venus imagery. In the end Gallus realizes that, as much as he intensely wishes that Arcadia were real, he must return to the business of this world, in this instance, to the political world (*Ec.* 10. 44–45). Arcadia emerges at the end as an alluring yet imaginary space of poetry that allows occasional emotional release.

In Goethe's idyll, on the other hand, Alexis begins in Arcadia, which is to say, he lives happily for the moment in the modern naive condition, ignorant of his emotions and unaware that they may cause him to clash with the world. As has already been observed, he is not a figure of the traditional idyll of Gessner, nor even later of that of Maler Müller or Voss. He is not already or soon to be safely bound up in the cares of the family. He is not a static character like so many of his peers in the idyllic world; he will undergo an inner development, a "pathetischen Gang." He belongs to that other category of figures for the modern idyll, the child, who is more plausibly and readily discernible as a contemporary inhabitant of the naive realm than a serf or the pastor of Grünau. He will, however, in the course of the poem cease before our eyes to be a child. The only vestige of the more traditional bucolic imagery is the garden with its fruits and myrtle in which he and Dora meet. By virtue of his naivety, Alexis enters the garden as a legitimate inhabitant, unlike the wanderer or Werther, who enter but remain outsiders. In the garden Alexis begins the transition from a state of immaturity into that of emotional maturity.

However, the more proximate cause of this inner transformation is the exterior necessity of his departure. The world of commerce appears as this necessity. It is the "Waren" that Alexis curses at the end just as it is the playful banter about the necklace he is to earn for Dora that intrudes itself into their conversation in the garden.[73] What civil war and the political sphere is for Virgil's Arcadia, commerce is for Goethe's naive idyll. By bringing about the inevitable loss of Alexis's childlike innocence through the clash between the outside world and the realization of inner longing, Goethe duplicates the farewell that Virgil took from his Arcadia.

The position that the narrator assumes in each is remarkably close. In Virgil's tenth eclogue the recognition that Arcadia is a distinctive world of the imagination, given shape by the tension between longing and necessity, is an insight shared by both the poet and Gallus. They both acknowledge that Arcadia is the bewitching creation of those who first have experience of the world. In Goethe's idyll this is not the case. Alexis does not experience himself as naive, for were he to do so the bitterness of his first parting would not move him to consider following in Werther's footsteps. This knowledge is reserved for the narrator, and by extension for his audience, both of whom know about the balm of distance that time and poetry offer. It is only we who, because of this hindsight, might thus feel inclined to view Alexis's loss of innocence as sweetly naive. He, having no such acquaintance of first love and loss, has no distance from it. It is real and present to him, and its unfolding is shattering: from wild euphoria to equally low despair, then jealousy, and finally rage, in this instance turned inward against himself in the wish for suicide. By following this course Alexis will, should he quell the impulse to suicide, eventually join his sentimental audience.

It is perhaps precisely because the idyll presents one who is passing from a psychologically naive condition to the sentimental one that Schiller felt disquiet at the strength of Alexis's jealousy and Friedrich Schlegel viewed the "Mischung des Weisen und Sinnlich-Süßen mit der Leidenschaft" to be a "kleiner Verstoß" against truth. By presenting so abrupt a contrast between Alexis's "pathetischem Gang," psychological maturation, and the twofold intrusion of the narrator, Goethe suggests that the idyllically naive only becomes a state and an idea with clear definition and meaning in relation to what is sentimental, here the detachment of emotional maturity. The position of the first intrusion is finely calculated for this effect. Once the reader has been lulled into the belief of a psychologically realistic narrative, the extended simile badly shakes that impression, though it does not wholly destroy it. Only at the conclusion, with the renewed intrusion of the narrator, does the puzzling matter of his presence become unavoidable. For whom is the advice about the balm of the muses? Surely not for Alexis; but if for us, would not our readiness to read such a poem preclude our needing such advice? Perhaps, since Goethe's audience was not inclined to accept it as an idyll though it was more than prepared to read the poem as an elegy. Poetry may indeed present a psychological development, but it should not be allowed to shake one's conviction in the reality of idyllic nature.

Be that as it may, that Goethe should not only hit upon the device of the deliberate reference to the artistic fiction of the idyll within the idyll itself, but also use it to suggest the configuration of the naive in relation to the sentimental, as Virgil used it to allow Arcadia first to emerge, is an interesting parallel. He also develops it in the same way as Virgil. He puts his character in a distant classical place yet also in a situation recognizably modern, just as Virgil put figures from his present into the imaginary Arcadia. As Virgil used the Roman martial present to give contours to his Arcadia, Goethe uses his bourgeois, capitalist present to lend shape to Alexis's naive condition. In addition to whatever sense one wishes to give to "doppelt erfreulichem Sinn" with respect to Alexis, one may now add the play of the idyll as a whole upon the audience's expectation of a naive idyll that the frame introduces in a classical manner.

The earlier statement that the element of recollection creates the sentimental distance of the idyll also requires emendation. The "true" sentimental distance becomes the creation and function of the narrator. Only in relation to the narrative does recollection fulfill the task set it by Müller in his "Adams erstes Erwachen." In that poem recollection served to propel the reader from naive past to sentimental present without presenting the moment of Adam's transition. In "Alexis und Dora," Alexis's recollection presents exactly this transition: a real and dangerous enough "Gang" for him, but not to the narrator and his reader. A "naive" reader could first read the idyll naively, but would likely stumble enough that he would find himself compelled to read sentimentally, that is, he would have to begin to reflect that the naive, emotional immaturity of Alexis is known to him by his own sentimental, emotional maturity. He can then read Alexis both naively and sentimentally. If he pushed himself still further, he would realize that to restrict the naive and sentimental to Alexis only would mean to read the presence of the narrator only naively as one who simply relates a story without comment on it. If he were to read the narrator sentimentally, he would have to read himself, the reader, sentimentally too. He would have to realize that the categories of naive and sentimental exist only within the recollection provided by some form of cultural representation, in this instance poetry. In order to do so he would have to abandon the strict separation of the sentimental present from idyllic nature.

However, as it was the labor of the eighteenth century to anchor the conviction of an idyllic nature within the psychology of the sentimental subject and his continued relation through feeling to a state of nature and further to find in ancient Greece the closest historical approach possible within the realm of culture to this cherished state, such an admission would compel the wholesale reexamination of all of these contexts. Naturally an attendant undertaking would be the reconsideration of the relation of the Latin tradition to the German present, all of which the late eighteenth century is not prepared to contemplate. It prefers to label "Alexis und Dora" an elegy and to continue its beautiful dream of fair Greece.

Novalis: Virgil, a Romantic Muse?

With Novalis we truly enter upon the terrain of the repressed muse. His friendship with the Schlegels and familiarity with their views — Friedrich Schlegel particularly was in the process of stating clearly the conclusions of the preceding decades for the estimation of Virgil and the Latin heritage — makes all the more unexpected the receptiveness he shows for Virgil. The importance to Novalis of the idea of the golden age offers an easy bridge to the German pastoral tradition where the aura of the golden age in the form of Arcadia was a central image of the genre. This connection has been appreciated since Hans-Joachim Mähl's study of the historical development of the golden age and its role in Novalis's work, as have Novalis's translations of the fourth eclogue while a schoolboy.[74] The same triadic structure at work in Goethe's configuration of the idyll between naive and sentimental also recurs in Novalis's conception of the golden age, with, however, very different results. Goethe, in, for example, "Der Wandrer," used the reflective consciousness of the wanderer to allow idyllic nature to appear as present while yet, in the reflections of the wanderer, making it seem in some sense a prior state of the past and also, in a different sense, the desired state of the future. Depending on the attitude of the wanderer, nature seemed now Arcadian and now Elysian. Likewise, Novalis's golden age stretches across the spectrum of time, belonging to neither the past, the present, nor the future. In the vision of the poet it is both "Erinnerung" and "Ahnung."[75]

Unlike the golden age in the idyll at the hands of Goethe, or even Maler Müller, Novalis does not assimilate the image of golden age nature to the psychological consciousness of the private individual. He focuses instead on it as hieratic prophecy and explores its historical associations. The poet to whom this insight into the higher nature of time is granted is less the possessor of a private vision than he is the conduit of and participant in the odd simultaneity of the golden age. The overwhelming sense of urgency, of historical renewal on a vast scale, and of intense poetic vision in Novalis forms a link to Virgil's fourth eclogue. The strong religious feeling of that eclogue appeals to Novalis's own religious temperament, just as the Virgilian imagery and associations provide him with the poetic and intellectual vocabulary needed for its articulation. The radical difference between the Latin and the Romantic poet lies in the accomplishment of the golden age. The salvation of the Virgilian golden age will take place in the historical world through the agency of the state; but for Novalis the instrument of its accomplishment is the poet whose poetic activity creates, sustains, and furthers the progressive transfiguration of the prosaic world as it moves toward the golden age.

Yet this very difference indicates the degree to which the Virgilian text becomes susceptible to a highly Romantic interpretation by a sympathetic reader, that is, one who does not subscribe to the prejudice of his age. In a letter to Schiller on 7 October 1791, the young Novalis tells of his thoughts when reading Homer's *Odyssey* and Schiller's *Don Carlos*. He expresses himself with the usual Homeric enthusiasm of his day on nature and genius, on the perfection of an artless directness. However, he also distances himself from the reigning belief in the normative stature of Homeric epic: "Ossian und Homer, Milton und Ariost, Virgil und Klopstock, jeder ist, was er wollte und konnte: aber keiner wollte je ein infallibler, einziger Codex der Gesetze der Schönheit und Wahrheit seyn und ein Idol für alle Zeiten und Völker abgeben . . ."[76] Of equal interest in the above citation is the appearance of Virgil in Novalis's list of the canonical authors of epic (quite apart from his partner in the list). This picture becomes slightly murky as he continues his letter. Having praised all things that come from nature and, in vaguely Schillerian language, also "jede[n] großen Menschen, dessen Geist eine runde, vollendete Form ist," he continues by making the presence of this spirit the measure of great art: "So finde ich auch im Ariost, im Ossian, im Werther, im Don Karlos mehr Homerisches, mehr ächte Homerheit als im Apollonius Rhodius und andern Nachahmern Homers, in deren Hände der Göttliche eine Anthropomorphose ausstehen muß" (4:100). If Novalis is not to have contradicted himself within the space of a few lines, then one must conclude that he does not share the received wisdom of his day, which holds that the Neoteric poets are simply the belated Latin excrescence of the debased Alexandrians, the pale imitation of a bloodless shadow.

For whatever reason, he does not number Virgil among the hapless successors of Homer, but rather ascribes to Virgil some measure of the "Göttliche" that he deems so important. To put the matter another way: Novalis's own deep and capacious religious feeling forms the basis for his affinity to Virgil. Nor does he appreciably change the opinion he held as a young student at Jena after his encounter with Schiller. On the contrary, it leads to a sharper disagreement with the dogma of his day. Novalis's brief notes on his reading of Goethe's essay on Laocoon in 1798 reflect the argument of the essay with one notable exception. He reverses the aesthetic judgment passed on the two works of art, the statue and Virgil's description. Goethe's essay deals almost exclusively with the statue. Only at the end does he introduce the Virgilian episode to dismiss it as merely "ein rhetorisches Argument" (*GSW* 4/2:87). Novalis, on the other hand, again judges the aesthetic merit of the work according to the moral-religious sense it conveys. The statue is "ein unmoralisches Werk" — presumably because of the unmerited suffering of Laocoon. And he continues, "Virgils religioese Darst[ellung] des L[aocoon] ein glückl[icher] Kunstgriff aus dem Laocoon ein Opfer zu machen — oder eine Vertilgung d[es] Schädlichen durchs Schädliche" (3:412). Novalis's appreciation of the religious impulse in the Virgilian text gives him an insight into the epic unique in the eighteenth century. The notion that Virgil constructs a vision of the universe in which obdurately discrete occurrences become transparent in a higher plane, the sublimation of "das Schädliche durch das Schädliche," accords better with Novalis's Romantic sense of dissonance than does Homeric utterance as the natural epic of harmonious genius. Homeric epic presents too healthy an image of harmonious and unified existence, of the individual perfectly realized, for it to be of much use to the sickly patient of the modern age. With no knowledge of the illness that comes after it, it can offer little practical advice. On the other hand, the intimation of a higher infinite in Virgil's religious sense strikes a deep chord in Novalis's Romantic soul.

Still, an affinity of temperament and a fragmentary phrase may seem an implausibly slight foundation on which to build such large speculations on the relative appeal of primary and secondary epic to a Romantic poet, even if one is prepared to concede that this characterization of Homeric and Virgilian epic is a serviceable one. It does emphasize the tendency to regard Homeric song as epic that simply emerges, and to regard Virgilian epic as a work that is all too visibly constructed. Since Novalis does not elaborate his views further, a contrast may serve the purpose of explication. The same implicit distinction between secondary and primary epic, used to very different consequence, underlies the outlook of Novalis's contemporary and friend, August Wilhelm Schlegel.

In the same year that Novalis confided his thoughts on Laocoon to his *Allgemeines Brouillon,* Schlegel presented his views on Homer and Virgil in his review of Goethe's *Hermann und Dorothea.* Goethe has written, so runs Schlegel's argument, the epic Homer would have written were he still composing in Schlegel's day. This thesis leaves Schlegel with the necessity of explaining what true or Homeric epic is. He repeats all of the commonplaces about Homer:

> Denn was wir oben als wesentliche Merkmale des Epos angaben: die überlegene Ruhe und Parteilosigkeit der Darstellung; die volle, lebendige Entfaltung, hauptsächlich durch Reden, die mit Ausschließung dialogischer Unruhe und Unordnung der epischen Harmonie gemäß umgebildet werden; den unwandelbaren, verweilend fortschreitenden Rythmus: diese Merkmale lassen sich ebensogut an dem deutschen Gedicht entwickeln als an Homers Gesängen.[77]

He chooses Virgil as his example to demonstrate what epic is not: "Virgil schuf mit römischem Nachdrucke eine ganz eigne Art der Epopöe. An ihm, der den Neueren weit mehr Vorbild geworden ist als Homer, kann man den Unterschied der vermischten Gattung, der wir jenen Namen geben, von dem reinen ursprünglichen Epos auffallend zeigen."[78] In the consideration that follows this remark, Schlegel characterizes the Virgilian epic negatively by listing only what it is not — a list that is the inverse of the one cited above for Homer and Goethe — rather than by examining what it is. Novalis, however, makes a tentative step in this direction with his suggestion that the formal traits of Virgil's epic ought to be considered in relation to some animating idea or feeling.

Not only does Novalis hold an aberrant opinion; it is also an opinion of long standing. It appears both in the young student of 1791 and in the mature Novalis of 1798, at the beginning of his most creative period and after his acquaintance with the Schlegels and his intensive study of the idealist philosophy. The root of this opinion has long been known: Mähl has emphasized the importance of Virgil in the formation of the young Novalis, and pointed out that he turned to the task of translating the fourth eclogue with its prophecy of the child and the golden age not once, but three times, although only on the third attempt did he get beyond the proemium and complete the task. Yet he does not include Novalis's translations of the fourth eclogue or his translation of the first five lines of the sixth in the body of his text, but prints them in an appendix at the end with other unpublished juvenilia. While recognizing the general importance of the image of the child and the golden age in addition to that of vatic vision, Mähl does not draw any direct connection.[79] And later critics generally follow his lead in acknowledging Virgil as part of Novalis's general intellectual background, but not any nearer or creative connection.[80]

However, exactly such a connection occurs in the "Atlantis-Märchen" and, to a lesser extent, elsewhere in *Heinrich von Ofterdingen*. The "Märchen" form is itself for Novalis the Romantic version of the earlier idyll. It preserves the tension between Arcadia and Elysium.[81] "Hyazinth und Rosenblüte," the "Arion-Sage," and the "Atlantis-Märchen," all revolve around an Arcadia-like land in which nature discloses its secrets to man, and in the latter two tales it is man as poet who is most at home in this land. For his own purposes, Novalis takes up in his tales the strong sense in the Virgilian eclogue — and somewhat in Theocritus (see *Idyll* 1) — of a nature transfigured and apprehended only by the power of the poetic imagination that the Enlightenment discounted in favor of the nature so represented. The Virgilian poems that resonate most strongly with this tone are the fourth and sixth eclogues; and they, along with book 4 of the *Aeneid*, leave a discernible impression on the "Atlantis-Märchen."

Before attempting to judge the extent and character of this impression, some more exact knowledge of the way in which Novalis knew Virgil and how he reacted to him is advisable. From the middle of June 1790 until October of the same year, Novalis attended the "Oberprima" of the school at Eisleben. At that time the school enjoyed a considerable reputation because of its director, Christian David Jani, a gifted teacher and scholar best known for his annotated edition of Horace's *Odes* (1778–82). He was in addition a translator of Virgil. Under his tutelage Novalis translated not only from Virgil, but also from Horace, Theocritus, and Homer. His translations from the latter three poets are far fewer than those from Virgil, which include short translations from the *Eclogues*, three translations from the Orpheus episode (*Ge.* 4. 464–80), and two of the first ten lines from book 2 of the *Aeneid*. Such prominence, and even the choice of selections, in part reflect the traditional position of Virgil in the curriculum of the time. Personal preference also seems to play some role, since, if one is to judge by the list of books Novalis drew up to take with him to university at Jena (4:692–95), he did not avail himself of the first opportunity to be rid of the tiresome pensum; on the contrary, he took two translations of the *Georgics* as well as Johann Jacob Dusch's German version of Johann Martin's edition of the *Georgics*.[82]

In addition to Martin's edition of the *Georgics*, two grounds may be adduced to argue that the edition that Novalis knew best was that of Heyne, a matter of some importance since it determines how he read and understood the fourth eclogue as well as what he knew of Virgil more generally. The first argument is external: Jani, Novalis's teacher at Eisleben, used Heyne's text for his own translation of the *Aeneid*. The second is internal and depends on Novalis's rendering of the last four lines of *Eclogue* 4. Contemporary editions usually give the following version of the text:

Incipe, parue puer, risu cognoscere matrem
(matri longa decem tulerunt fastidia menses)
incipe, parue puer: qui non risere parenti,
nec deus hunc mensa, dea nec dignata cubili est. (*Ec.* 4. 60–63)

[Begin, dear babe, and smile at your mother to show you know her —
This is the tenth month now, and she is sick of waiting.
Begin, dear babe. The boy who does not smile at his mother
Will never deserve to sup with a god or sleep with a goddess. (25)]

Heyne, however, finds the image of a newborn grinning at its mother a somewhat egregious use of poetic license to express the delight and relief of the proud parent. For this reason he prefers the textually better attested *cui* for *qui*; that is, the parents smile at the infant: *Incipe, parue puer: cui non risere parentes.*[83] He does so despite noting in the apparatus that *qui* is the preferred reading of such *viri docti* (learned men) as Juan Luis de la Cerda, Peter Burmann, and Quintilian. In the second edition he strengthens this note with the insertion of the comment: *Sensu aut nullo aut parum commodo: at "cui" indubitate vera lectio* (*O* 1:81; in meaning in no way appropriate, not even a little; on the contrary, "at whom" is without a doubt the true reading). He devotes his commentary on these lines to arguing exactly this point. Line 60 may state that the child is to acknowledge its mother with a smile, but the sense of the line is that the poet has transferred the smile of the mother to the child. The *cui* of line 62 confirms this: *Exprimit id, quod iam dicendum erat: risum hunc matris ad puellum natum faustissimi ominis esse, a contrario; quae conversio rationi poeticae valde consentanea est* (*O* 1:47; It expresses by means of the opposite — namely, that it is a most auspicious omen for a mother to smile at her newborn child — what has just been said, an inversion wholly in accord with poetic reasoning). The penchant of the learned to think otherwise he mocks: *Vix dici potest, quantum, h l trepident interpretes, qui* (*O* 1:47; it can scarcely be said how this passage confuses the interpreters).

Novalis's translation reflects exactly this dispute:

Lieblicher Knabe beginne <im Lächeln zu begrüßen> die lächelnde
                                                                    Mutter zu kennen,
Der zehn zögernde Monde so manchen Ekel erzeugten.
Lieblicher Knabe beginn, <wem nimmer die Eltern gelächelt> wen
                                                lächelnd die Eltern nicht grüßten
Traun! den bewirthet kein Gott und keine der Göttinnen kost ihn.[84]

Heyne's influence manifests itself in the parentheses. The first parenthesis contains the more literal sense of the Latin that the rendering preferred by Heyne has displaced. Similarly the version in the second parenthesis again reflects the Latin (when read with *cui*), while the translation outside of it with the use of "grüßen" in place of *risere* argues the attentiveness of Novalis to Heyne's commentary.

Whatever the case may be, Novalis is thoroughly familiar with the image of a babe smiling at its mother and its portentous associations. Not only does the image of the golden age and the child conflate easily with that of the Madonna and Child in the syncretism of his *Geistliche Lieder* (1799), but a more direct repetition occurs early on in his poem *Orpheus* (1790?) and then again later in *Heinrich von Ofterdingen*.

Novalis's initial encounter with Virgil does not remain an obligatory exercise; the captivating power of the Virgilian imagination moves him to imitation in the Orpheus poem. All of his interest in Virgil and his translations from his works, the fourth and sixth eclogues and the Orpheus and Eurydice episode from the *Georgics*, come together in the poem. Richard Samuel numbers the poem incorrectly among Novalis's premature and fragmentary attempts "im Epos des großen Styls" (1:451). The only reason he gives for such a designation is the use of the "Homeric" dactylic hexameter: "Virgil mag Hardenberg dazu angeregt haben, die ganze Geschichte des Orpheus in homerischer Form zu erzählen" (1:452). It is, however, nothing of the sort. It is instead a complete and finished eclogue in the manner of Virgil, with a framing invocation of the muse, a double frame, a dirge, and an inset song. In inspiration, execution, and allusion, Novalis's *Orpheus* is Virgilian and a bucolic in the ancient style. The exordium turns on the contrast of the high, sublime tone of epic with the lower, gentler tone of the idyll just as in the first frame of *Eclogue* 6 — with an interesting twist. Novalis expands the contrast to include a historical survey of ancient and modern epic. He begins by referring to the sphere of epic with familiar words and images:

> Reiche dem blühenden Jüngling doch auch die epische Leier,
> Der die Helden besang und Mord und blutige Kriege,
> Rauschender Waffen Getös und Siege der Liebe und Ruhe,
> Wenige traten mit Glück in diese glänzende Laufbahn (1:547–48)

that echo both Uz and the sixth eclogue:

> *cum canerem reges et proelia, Cynthius aurem*
> *uellit et admonuit: . . .*
> *Nunc ego (namque super tibi erunt qui dicere laudes,*
> *Vare, tuas cupiant et tristia condere bella)*
> *agrestem tenui meditabor harundine Musam: . . . . (Ec.* 6. 3–8)
>
> [Next, kings and wars possessed me; but Apollo tweaked my ear,
> Telling me, . . .
> Since there'll be bards in plenty desiring to rehearse
> Varus' fame, and celebrate the sorrowful theme of warfare,
> I shall take up a slim reed-pipe and a rural subject. (30)]

The interesting twist occurs when Novalis, in listing Virgil after Homer, distinguishes between a "sublime" and a "gentle" epic:

> Und es folgte Virgil der Dichter, Latiens Größter,
> Ihn mit sanfterem Ton und nicht mit der erhabenen Stärke. (1: 548)

A few lines later, he uses the same adjective, "sanft," to characterize the type of song that he will sing in imitation of Orpheus, who, like the Virgilian Pan, first taught the shepherds to sing pastoral song (see 1:548; *Ecs.* 2. 31–37 and 4. 55–59). There is in this association no contradiction; the reasoning merely depends on the received opinion, at least since Scaliger, that the eclogue, though a minor species of epic, is the most ancient and primitive, hence its shared meter with the later, grander song. Not only does the young Novalis place himself on the same mythic plane with Orpheus at the very dawn of poetry, as did the anonymous singer of the fourth eclogue, but he also singles out Virgil as the great follower of Orpheus in epic. Homer's songs are simply too immense, too distant; they become "die unerreichbaren Lieder," and the poet himself an inimitable figure "hoch über d[en] Grenzen der Erde" (1:548).

To accomplish the turn from epic to idyll, Novalis exchanges the idea of Apollo pulling the ear of the recalcitrant poet in the sixth eclogue for the equally Virgilian notion of the favored smiling child from the fourth eclogue. He does so however in the manner of Heyne:

> Vater wie lächeltest Du, wie mich die Mutter geboren
> Nicht mit erhabenem Blicke, Du weihtest mich lächelndem Scherze
> Und den sanfteren Grazien, ländlich mit Blumen gekränzet,
> Sieh drum wählt ich mir auch zu singen den sanfteren Orpheus.
> (1:548)

The song that follows relates the tale of Orpheus and Eurydice from Virgil with strong Rococo overtones, as "lächelndem Scherze" suggests. Novalis even incorporates elements from the *Aeneid*, when his Venus comforts the grieving Orpheus as she once did Virgil's Aeneas in the passage also favored by Pyra and Klopstock:

> Die goldlockichte Venus, der Liebe mächtige Göttin.
> Sie erschien ihm im Traum und brachte die tröstende Ruhe
> mit sich, ihr wellten ambrosische Locken vom rosigen Nacken,
> Rosendüfte umgaben die schlanken Glieder der Göttin . . . (1:550)

> *Dixit et auertens rosea ceruice refulsit,*
> *ambrosiaeque comae diuinum uertice odorem*
> *spirauere; pedes uestus defluxit ad imos,*
> *et uera incessu patuit dea.* (*Aen.* 1. 402–5)

> [So Venus spoke, and as she turned away her loveliness shone,
> a tint of rose glowed on her neck and a scent of Heaven
> breathed from the divine hair of her head. Her grown trailed
> down to her feet; her gait alone proved her a goddess. (40)]

The poem culminates with an inset song, a dirge sung by the now joyous Orpheus as he stands by the fresh grave of his beloved. The last three of its eight stanzas concentrate not on the sadness of her loss but on his anticipated descent to Hades. There he will free her with his song as Venus had previously promised him in a dream. At this point both the song and the idyll end with a standard pastoral close, which looks like a reworking of the last lines of *Eclogue* 6 to suit Orpheus's circumstances:

> Siehe so tönte die Stimme zur Klage der bebenden Laute.
> Und ihn hörten die Musen, versammelt am hohen Parnasse,
> Ihn auch Luna, die schimmernde, und die Nymphen des Haines.
> Und vom Mitleid versank ihr himmlisches Schimmern in Dämmrung.
> (1:551)

omnia, quae Phoebo quondam meditante beatus
audiit Eurotas iussitque ediscere lauros,
ille canit, pulsae referunt ad sidera ualles;
cogere donec ouis stabulis numerumque referre
iussit et inuito processit Vesper Olympo. (Ec. 6. 82–86)

[All the song that of old time his favoured river, Eurotas,
Heard Apollo compose and made its laurels learn,
Silenus sang. The valleys caught this music and tossed it
Skyward. At last the Evening Star, unwelcome, rose
In heaven, bidding the boys drive home their sheep
   and count them. (32)]

The sense of closure achieved by the return to the frame and by reference to the change of day and night is typical of the Virgilian eclogue.

This poem holds greater significance than merely demonstrating the powerful impression that the Virgilian ideas and imagery made on the mind and imagination of the young Novalis. It also shows the very early connection between the Virgilian words and images and the preoccupations central to Novalis in his maturity. Both Rehm and Friedrich Hiebel have pointed out the importance of *Orpheus* for Novalis as he later grieved for his young fiancée Sophie von Kühn who died of tuberculosis.[85] Novalis's grief for Sophie is entirely personal, but the connection of death, love, and song comes entirely from the literary tradition. The lament in *Orpheus* stands fully in the ancient bucolic tradition of Theocritus's *Idyll* 1 and Virgil's *Eclogue* 5, while the notion of a fabled poet taming nature and Hades to recover the dead comes straight from the fourth Georgic. In this poem Novalis already, though with a light touch, gives an example of a poet whose poetic ability is suddenly matured by the death of a beloved, whose song both contains and bridges the distance between human and divine, whose love leads through death and the infinite to poetry. But the comparison may be extended even further. In some formal respects *Orpheus* anticipates the *Hymnen an die Nacht*. In it Novalis has already once placed beside a grave a figure who sings a song of death and return during the night. Likewise he has created a frame into which he set a song, as he does in *Hymnen an die Nacht* (1799) with its extended and regular alternation between song and frame.

The figure of mourning does not exhaust the literary utility of Orpheus; he is also an archetype of the poet. He is one of those mythical figures at the very dawn of time, when the imaginary and the real still mix promiscuously. His song has the power of divination and with it he can enrapture all of nature. All of these elements form a strong part of the bucolic tradition. The pathetic fallacy of nature, albeit ironically, stands at the beginning of the bucolic with Theocritus's first idyll, where all of nature is in sympathy with the great shepherd-poet Daphnis. Virgil employs it not merely as mourning nature in *Eclogue* 5, but also enlarges it beyond recognition to include the more intimate union of human and nature in the golden age in *Eclogue* 4, not to mention his predilection for echoing woods. For example, the wondrous power of song to penetrate to the very core of nature, both animate and inanimate, stands right at the beginning of *Eclogue* 8, where the songs of the competing shepherds causes the cattle to pause in their grazing and the flowing waters of the rivers to stay their flood (*Ec.* 8. 1–5). Alongside the pastoral Daphnis, Orpheus also appears in the company of other such mythical poets as Linus and Pan (*Ec.* 4. 55–59) in Arcadia. Perhaps, more important for Novalis, the more recognizably human shepherds also hope in the golden age to vie themselves with their mythic predecessors, including Arion:

> *nunc et ouis ultro fugiat lupus, aurea durae*
> *mala ferant quercus, narcisso floreat alnus,*
> *pinguia corticibus sudent electra myricae,*
> *certent et cycnis ululae, sit Tityrus Orpheus,*
> *Orpheus in siluis, inter delphinas Arion.* (*Ec.* 8. 52–56)

[The wolf may fly from the lamb, and the oak-trees bear fruit
  of gold;
Alders surprise us with sweet narcissus, and tears of amber
  down a tamarisk roll.
Let screech-owl's flyting be more delightful than swan-song,
  Tityrus in minstrelsy
With Orpheus vying [with Orpheus among the woods, with Arion
  among the dolphins] (38)[86]

When nature brings forth prodigies, poets will sing again in concord with nature, as Orpheus did of old among the trees and Arion among the dolphins. Novalis explores exactly these themes in his version of the Arion legend in his last and unfinished work, the novel *Heinrich von Ofterdingen* (1802).

> So sollen vor uralten Zeiten Dichter gewesen sein, die durch den seltsamen Klang wunderbarer Werkzeuge das geheime Leben der Wälder, die in den Stämmen verborgen Geister aufgeweckt, in wüsten, verödeten Gegenden den toten Pflanzensamen erregt, und blühende Gärten hervorgerufen, grausame Tiere gezähmt und verwilderte Menschen zu Ordnung und Sitte gewöhnt, sanfte Neigungen und Künste des Friedens in ihnen rege gemacht, reißende Flüsse in milde Gewässer verwandelt, und selbst die totesten Steine in regelmäßige tanzende Bewegungen hingerissen haben. Sie sollen zugleich Wahrsager und Priester, Gesetzgeber und Ärzte gewesen sein. (1:211)

These lines resonate with the images and words from the fourth, sixth, and eighth eclogues. Yet the Romantic spirit has transformed them thoroughly:

these effects are explicitly the effect of the poet; his power remains mysterious, as does the kaleidoscopic, whirling nature that he touches.[87]

The same holds true for Novalis's retelling in the novel of the marriage of Dido and Aeneas in the "Atlantis-Märchen." Novalis's king, possessing a peaceable realm and a daughter in need of marriage, allows pride in his origins to dismiss all possible suitors as unworthy. In the countryside not far from the palace, the princess happens upon an old man and his son, both devoted researchers of nature, and the son happily of marriageable age. Neither the notion of illicit love nor the manner of their courtship owes anything to Virgil, but the manner of their marriage does. Silenus-like, the son tells her of the cosmos's secrets, in return for which she begins to teach him song. On the very day that he escorts her back to the palace garden, a sudden storm overtakes them, forcing them from the path to the shelter of a cave, just as a similar storm conspired to isolate Dido and Aeneas in a cave so that they were able to confess their passion and call it marriage:

nec iam furtiuum Dido meditatur amorem:
coniugium vocat, hoc praetexit nomine culpam. (Aen. 4. 171–72)

[Dido . . . ceased to take any thought for secrecy in her love. She called it marriage; she used this word to screen her sin. (102)]

Although Virgil disapproves of their union by placing it away from any public witness, Juno does ensure that their purely private bond of passion is witnessed by the powers of nature:

prima et Tellus et pronuba Iuno
dant signum; fulsere ignes et conscius aether
conubiis summoque ululrunt uertice Nymphae. (Aen. 4. 166–68)

[Primaeval Earth and Juno, Mistress of the Marriage, gave their sign. The sky connived at the union; the lightning flared; on their mountain-peak nymphs raised their cry. (102)]

The notion of a marriage that does not need public recognition for its enactment but is sanctified and completed by the witness of nature appeals to Novalis. He thus inverts the Virgilian order and dwells upon the scene that Virgil passed over in a scant eight lines. The cave, mentioned simply as *spelunca* in Virgil without any qualifying adjective such as *opaca* (shady) or *uiridis* (green), expands to become a full-scale *locus amoenus*. It is filled with moss to rest on, a "Mandelstrauch" to eat, a "nahes Rieseln" to drink and, although there are no birds to sing, they bring with them a lute, the badge of the poet, for music (1:221). The *locus amoenus* has its wonted effect. However, Novalis draws out approvingly the idea of intercourse that Virgil both elided and commented on with the line *dant signum; fulsere ignes et conscius aether* ([they] gave their sign. The sky connived at the union; the lightning flared).

> Eine höhere Macht schien den Knoten schneller lösen zu wollen, und brachte sie unter sonderbaren Umständen in diese romantische Lage. Die Unschuld ihrer Herzen, die zauberhafte Stimmung ihrer Gemüter, und die verbundene unwiderstehliche Macht ihrer süßen Leidenschaft und ihrer Jugend ließ sie die Welt und ihre Verhältnisse vergessen, und wiegte sie unter dem Brautgesange des Sturms und den Hochzeitfackeln der Blitze in den süßesten Rausch ein. (1:221–22)

The image of a young couple confessing love in a cave during a storm is by no means unique to Virgil. However, the same cannot be said of the storm's wedding-song and the lightning's marriage-torch. Song and torch belong to the Roman wedding ceremony, and both figure in the Virgilian marriage, the one as nymphs singing and the other as lightning. Novalis glosses *fulsere ignes,* somewhat prosaically and pointedly, with "Hochzeitfackeln der Blitze" and transforms the nymphs' ululations into a "Brautgesang des Sturms." He could hardly have given a clearer indication of the passage he has in mind than through the use of the uniquely Virgilian phrase "Hochzeitfackeln der Blitze"; had he wished to communicate to the imagination of his readers simply the image of a marriage in nature, then some instantly recognizable feature from the Christian wedding ceremony would have more naturally suggested itself, such as, "die Hochzeitglocken des Donners," and not the totally unfamiliar torch.

Although Novalis reverses the judgment on the act, he does retain the simultaneity of marriage and physical union for which nature alone, with Virgilian storm and lightning, now provides a sufficient ceremony, and he does not omit the idea of a contrasting and restraining social convention. Similarly, just as the cave represents the moment of peripeteia in Virgil's story, so too is it the moment of crisis in Novalis's "Märchen." Again, the denouement is inverted; no longer does it introduce a tragic end, but rather the beginning of a glorious rise. What Virgil plainly states with *ille dies primus leti* (*Aen.* 4. 169; on that day were sown the seeds of suffering and death; 102), Novalis denotes with, "Er war in dieser Nacht um mehrere Jahre älter, aus einem Jünglinge zum Manne geworden" (1:222); that is, not merely has he come to sexual maturity but also that he has become decisive, filled with his "Plan," and finally ready to embark on that most Romantic course of action, namely, to take up the office of poet. Novalis's scene is beholden to the Virgilian account not merely for its details (the storm, cave, marriage, and nuptial lightning), but also for its central theme of a marriage in and of nature. The dramatic pacing of the narration as well as the pivotal role of the episode that Novalis accords the episode in the "Märchen" both reflect the Virgilian original.[88]

The Virgilian associations and the Romantic reworking of them continue in the rest of the "Märchen." Novalis assimilates elements of the fourth and sixth eclogues in the final episode of the "Märchen," in which the hitherto unknown young man discloses himself as a poet to the court and effects a reconciliation between the estranged father and daughter. By this reconciliation the land enjoys a life that "fortan nur *ein* schönes Fest war" (1:229), and so becomes Atlantis. The coincidence of the advent of the golden age with a youth coming into the possession of his mature powers forms a structural parallel with the fourth eclogue. Virgil's golden age also found its ultimate fruition in the child's attainment of its majority. And therein lies the difference: what Virgil attributed to his powers of governance, Novalis attributes to his powers of song. However, the stages by which Novalis accomplishes this indicate a continuing creative reshaping of Virgil along with the modern eighteenth-century idyll of Gessner.

The preparation for the transformation of the kingdom into Atlantis follows the course suggested in the earlier part of the "Märchen" and in *Eclogues* 4 and 6 with their blend of nature, poetry and love. Just prior to the cave scene, the young man, when revealing "Naturgeheimnisse" to the princess, found himself so moved by the telling of these holy truths that he was unable to restrain himself from breaking out into spontaneous song, much to the delight of the princess (1:220–21; rather like Gessner's young shepherds before them). Following his education through love, the young man introduces himself to the court with the same words, now however in the form of a song. Earlier he merely instructed like a Silenus: "Er lehrte ihr, wie durch wundervolle Sympathie die Welt entstanden sei, und die Gestirne sich zu melodischen Reigen vereinigt hätten" (1:220). Now he sings of the creation of the cosmos as Silenus did (*Ec.* 6. 31–42):

> Er handelte von dem Ursprunge der Welt, von der Entstehung der Gestirne, der Pflanzen, Tiere und Menschen, von der allmächtigen Sympathie der Natur, von der uralten goldenen Zeit und ihren Beherrscherinnen, der Liebe und Poesie, von der Erscheinung des Hasses und der Barbarei und ihren Kämpfen mit jenen wohltätigen Göttinnen, und endlich von dem künftigen Triumph der letztern, dem Ende der Trübsale, der Verjüngerung der Natur und der Wiederkehr eines ewigen goldenen Zeitalters. (1:225)

The order of creation from the cosmos to its stars up through the plants, animals, and humans matches the order laid out by Silenus. The latter portion of the song, however, takes up the themes and order of the fourth eclogue: the rejuvenation of nature from its present iron-age condition and the return of the golden age. Even the notion of maleficent conflict from the lines,

> *si qua manent sceleris uestigia nostri,*
> *inrita perpetua soluent formidine terras* (*Ec.* 4. 13–14)

> [mankind shall be freed from its age-long fear,
> All stains of our past wickedness being cleansed away (23)]

appears in this song as hate and barbarism.[89]

However, by opposing these evils to love and poetry, Novalis joins the inheritance of the eighteenth-century idyll to the ancient eclogue. Gessner made intimacy with nature the muse of poetry and the source of love most clearly in "Die Erfindung des Saitenspiels und des Gesanges." He first suggested that the excitement of innocent feeling in the face of nature would rouse the human soul to song. Novalis's youth repeats this awakening; the primacy of nature remains at the center of the "Märchen" as it had since Gessner's idyll.

The mixture of ancient eclogue and modern idyll leaves neither unaffected and results in something Romantic.[90] It introduces a dynamic principle into the static pastoral world of the idyll quite different from the psychological one Goethe sought to introduce. Love and poetry are not the effects of a communion with nature, but autonomous powers that coexist with nature. The youth, at first a researcher of nature, comes himself to the full appreciation of the "allmächtigen Sympathie der Natur" only through his own experience of love and its escort, poetry. Thus the generalizing terms of his song recapitulate the stages of his own "Werdegang" or "Bildung." What previously seemed only an inner personal experience becomes, in the telling, an external, universal truth, no longer limited to the private vision of the individual. On this point Novalis steps beyond the bounds of the eighteenth-century idyll to give to the idyllic a social scope that accords well with the Virgilian eclogue. In accordance with the injunction of the "Arion-Sage," the poet must shoulder the burden of taming the "Barbarei" through "Ordnung und Sitte" and of fostering "sanfte Neigungen und Künste des Friedens." Indeed if he has truly grasped the "allmächtige Sympathie der Natur," he should find himself incapable of doing otherwise; the activities are not separable. The young man in the "Märchen," then, becomes, to pursue the parallel with the fourth eclogue, the mature child who will, for the kingdom of Atlantis, inaugurate the golden age: *magnus ab integro saeclorum nascitur ordo* (*Ec.* 4. 5; a great new cycle of centuries/Begins; 23). His status as golden child is still more palpable a few sentences later: "Auch die Kinderunschuld und Einfalt seines Gesichts schien allen übernatürlich" (1:225).

However, the consummation of this transformation to the golden age depends on society's acceptance of the poet: a question of "gewöhnen," not of subjugation. The permanence of the golden age rests not on an individual but on the persistence in successive generations of what the poet represents. The poet must found a new *gens aurea* (golden race); he must gain recognition for his son, the child of his union with the king's daughter. The recognition of his son as the legitimate heir simultaneously effects the accession of the poet to the office of king. To achieve this result, Novalis resorts once again to a more concrete Virgilian image, that of the child. If Novalis's king recognizes his daughter's offspring, he recognizes her marriage. He does this in ancient style before the public by presenting the child to the heavens, that is, to the gods. The child represents the promise of things to come, and in his role as omen he appears, like Virgil's child, marked out by special signs for this task. When he appears before the assembled court on his mother's arm he looks "freundlich" at all and sundry, and in a repetition of the fourth eclogue, he smiles when stretching out his hands for the sparkling royal diadem, one day to be his (1:227).[91]

The final image of the story about life in Atlantis henceforth as "ein schönes Fest" Novalis owes to antiquity and, in particular, to the fourth eclogue. The ancients envisioned the life of the gods in Olympus as a permanent banquet among other diversions. In Homer, whom Novalis knew well, the gods are continually making merry and feasting. Great heroes fortunate enough to be elevated by the gods could look forward to one day mixing in that company. Virgil predicts exactly such a reward for his child toward the beginning of the eclogue (*Ec.* 4. 15–16) and repeats it in the final line with the image of table and bed. In making life in Atlantis one permanent banquet, Novalis gives an image of the final telos of the golden age wholly in accord with its depiction in the fourth eclogue.

In addition to its content, the concluding image again underscores its idyllic origins in its function. The bucolic device of returning to the frame following the inset song was familiar to Novalis from his own *Orpheus* and his reading of Virgil's *Eclogues*. The song that the youth sings at the end of the tale, especially when placed alongside the inset song of Novalis's own Orpheus poem, looks increasingly like an inset song from the bucolic tradition: a supposition that, taken together with the *locus amoenus* in the cave, the themes of the fourth and sixth eclogues, and the framing device, underscores Novalis's transformation of the traditional idyll into a Romantic tale.[92]

So completely has Novalis made the images from the Virgilian poems his own that they have seeped into the very marrow of his poetic imagination.[93] Virgil's golden age child is transported from its bucolic setting into a Romantic context. In Virgil's golden age, the child as the future ruler remained a person distinct from the poet; history and poetry remained separate spheres; Arcadia did not come to Rome. In Novalis's Atlantis, the historical world of barbarism and hatred will yield to the dominion of poetry; the Arcadian nature of the eighteenth-century idyll will succeed in encompassing the world of "Waffen Getös" that always opposed it, in Uz and Gessner, in Maler Müller and Goethe, and even in Novalis's own *Orpheus*; poetry will subordinate kingship.

If one accepts for argument's sake this characterization of the "Atlantis-Märchen" and the Virgilian-cum-idyllic footing on which it rests, then one may turn to the question of what relation the "Atlantis-Märchen" bears to the rest of *Heinrich von Ofterdingen*, what the ghost-like trace of Virgil in this reflection might be, and what value such a shadow might have. In addition to particular images, such as the marriage in nature from the *Aeneid*, the golden age, and the child, Novalis also gains from his reworking of the fourth and sixth eclogues the thematic parameters of the "Märchen": cosmology and the golden age, prophecy and the present, the coincidence of the gradual strengthening of the golden age with the growing up of a child to adulthood. All of these elements in their Romantic transformation structure the "Atlantis-Märchen" at the same time as they introduce in abbreviated form all of the novel's major themes, with the notable exception of the death of the beloved. In many senses of the word, the "Atlantis-Märchen" prefigures the rest of the work, not only in its general structure, but also in particular episodes.[94]

In broad strokes, Heinrich must repeat the "Bildung" of the youth in the "Atlantis-Märchen." He must acquire an intimate knowledge of nature, love, and poetry before he may present himself at court. The first part of the novel, "Die Erwartung," corresponds to the youth's experience in the first part of the "Märchen" up until his induction through love into the art of poetry.[95] The second, unfinished part of the novel, as far as one can tell, corresponds to the elevation of that personal insight into the more universal truths of poetry represented in the second half of the "Märchen." The final consummation of this ever increasing interpenetration of the mundane world by that of poetry would parallel the promise of an Atlantis at the fairy-tale's end. Both in the *Paralipomena* (1:342) and in Ludwig Tieck's *Bericht über die Fortsetzung,* an explicit mention of Atlantis occurs at the point where the real world passes over into the infinite, that is, into its final fulfillment.[96]

Lesser, but equally instructive, parallels can also be observed. As the youth married his princess, Heinrich also marries his Mathilde. The princess, as she became inseparable from the youth, behaved as a daughter towards his father the old man (1:220), and, after the engagement of Mathilde and Heinrich in the last lines of chapter 7, chapter 8 begins: "Nachmittags führte Klingsohr seinen neuen Sohn" (1:284). The chapter concludes with the actual marriage. In this instance, the ceremony is indoors, and not in a cave, although as before a simple exchange of vows without witnesses suffices. The rather more explicit language of the cave scene yields to understatement: "Eine lange Umarmung, unzählige Küsse besiegelten den ewigen Bund des seligen Paars" (1:290). At this juncture the narrative breaks off to resume in chapter 9 with a tasteful advance of the clock from the afternoon and the engagement to evening and a small "Hochzeitsfest" for the "Brautpaar" (1:290) — a device perhaps better known from its use by Theodor Fontane in *Schach von Wuthenow* (1883). These small differences aside, the rituals of courtship and marriage punctuate the young Heinrich's poetic education just as they did that of the youth in the "Atlantis-Märchen."

A final parallel occurs between the invocation of the "allmächtigen Sympathie der Natur" with its companions, love and poetry, and their opponents, hatred and barbarism, on the one hand, and the "Klingsohr-Märchen" on the other hand. Before his fairy-tale, Klingsohr takes up again explicitly the matter of a dynamic tension internal to nature in order to emphasize that nature is not unadulterated goodness. It also contains, as a proper part of itself, its own iron age that will not be overcome without a struggle. Of those who view nature as a beneficent poetic genius, he says: "Sie ist es nicht zu allen Zeiten. Es ist in ihr, wie in dem Menschen, ein entgegengesetztes Wesen, die dumpfe Begierde und die stumpfe Gefühllosigkeit und Trägheit, die einen rastlosen Streit mit der Poesie führen. Er wäre ein schöner Stoff zu einem Gedicht, dieser gewaltige Kampf" (1:284). The central problem in the "theogony" of the generations with which Klingsohr wrestles in his tale is the education of Eros and Fabel to their proper function. They must learn to cooperate if they are to restore their world to order. Nature, as the "Atlantis-Märchen" suggested, stands in need of the active agency of poetry and love if the promised regeneration is to occur.

No less apparent is that these repetitions of something earlier are always repetitions with a difference. Heinrich's education includes a host of subjects and gradations scarcely present in the "Atlantis-Märchen," and the same is true of the broad and bewildering sweep of "Die Erfüllung." Once we, the reader and Heinrich, have progressed through these differences, the image of the golden age offered in the "Atlantis-Märchen" appears only as a reflection of an earlier "Arcadian" golden age. The new golden age that is to come is not a simple return to the earlier one, but a higher, altered form of the same. The conclusion of the novel presents the unfolding of the "Elysian" golden age. The two extremes are related not as reflections in a mirror, but rather each is a refraction of the other. At the end one has returned to the beginning, not as in a circle where the two coincide, but in the sense of a spiral.

What separates the two ages the one from the other is the role of death. It is absent from Atlantis, or rather present only as death in the natural course of things, as part of the orderly succession of the generations. Untimely death, however, the rupture of the natural course, forms a crucial part of Heinrich's education and final transfiguration, as it does of Klingsohr's "Märchen," from which the following citation is taken:

> Das große Geheimnis ist allen offenbart, und bleibt ewig unergründlich. Aus Schmerzen wird die neue Welt geboren, und in Tränen wird die Asche zum Trank des ewigen Lebens aufgelöst. In jedem wohnt die himmlische Mutter, um jedes Kind ewig zu gebären. (1:312)

Despite the Christian overtones of the language and imagery, Novalis seems to have envisioned the realization of this penitential mortification as involving some sort of return to the family along the lines of the "Atlantis-Märchen." The novel, he mentions in one note, should conclude on this note:

Das Buch schließt just umgekehrt wie das Märchen — *mit einer einfachen Familie*
[Novalis's emphasis]

Es wird stiller einfacher und menschlicher nach dem Ende zu.
Züge aus Heinrichs Jugend. Erzählung seiner Mutter.
Heinrich und Mathildens wunderbares Kind.
Es ist die Urwelt, die goldne Zeit am Ende.
Saturn=Arctur.
Die Szenen im Feste sind Schauspiele.
Die entferntesten und verschiedenartigsten Sagen und Begebenheiten verknüpft. Dies ist eine Erfindung von mir.
(Elysium und Tartarus sind wie Fieber und Schlaf
beisammen.) (1:345)

Quite apart from whether these thoughts would have found their way into the final version of the novel's second part, the set of associations is in itself suggestive. The family reappears as at the end of the "Atlantis-Märchen," and not as at the end of the "Klingsohr-Märchen" — since Novalis himself referred only to Klingsohr's tale as a "Märchen," it is assumed that the "Märchen" ending not to be repeated is that of the "Klingsohr-Märchen" — as does the wondrous child and the golden age, complete with a feast. This time the feast seems to be a permanent enjoyment of poetry that revolves around the configuration of death and Elysium.[97]

If the Arcadian golden age and the Elysian golden age form the two poles around which the novel divides, then the means of their relation is temporal. The refraction occurs in a temporal medium. The "Arion-Sage" and the "Atlantis-Märchen" both belong to the past of antiquity.[98] They are both stories related in the narrative present, which is that of the Christian Middle Ages. The "Klingsohr-Märchen" at the close of the "Die Erwartung" and the second half of the novel both represent tales that move beyond the strictly Christian world. In them Christianity contributes only one strand of the mythologies that Novalis hoped to bind together. It sits side by side with those of pagan antiquity, India, and even Northern Europe; all the mythologies known to Novalis would find their place in it. The style of these tales differs also from the earlier ones as Novalis develops a Romantic symbolism to give coherence to the bewildering variety. The essentially symbolic movement of the "Klingsohr-Märchen" points towards the direction of the novel's second half. These three types of cultural epochs, ancient, Christian, and post-Christian, give a linear sense of history in strong contrast to the spiral motion of the golden age.

But the two movements do not remain simply opposed to one another. Novalis knits the two together through a tripartite conception of history equally familiar from Virgil and from Christianity. The ancient "Märchen" represents prelapsarian nature; Heinrich's medieval present, fallen nature in its iron age; and the world of the "Erfüllung," redeemed nature. In the earthly paradise of Atlantis untimely death was absent, though not time itself; death came as the natural completion of life, not something that cut it short. In that more naive age the youth did not find himself compelled to battle against a world under the sway of barbarism and hate. He sang to a court already steeped in the love of poetry. He merely assumed his place among the Saturnian children of Atlantis, who were predisposed by nature to the golden age. Division existed without rancor. Nonetheless this Atlantis of unknown location remains subject to the law of Chronos; the youth will in the course of time hand over to his son. In the fallen present, Heinrich confronts a world in which barbarism and hate confound any such easy triumph of poetry. And, most important, death, the curse of the expulsion, exists in the present as a grievous affliction that cruelly truncates the flow of life. In the second half of the novel, Heinrich will poeticize the world, his Mathilde is restored to him and, at the very end, in "Die Vermählung der Jahreszeiten," nature and humanity are released from the bonds of time.

In the tension between the golden age of the past and that of the future as well as in the sharp triadic structure of history, Novalis seizes on the Romantic potential for reflection present in Virgil. Into them he incorporates many other associations while, nonetheless, keeping Virgil present in his mind. His knowledge of Virgil is not merely a part of his general culture that recedes along with the memories of schoolboy drudgery, but something of which he makes creative use throughout his brief career. This provides a highly suggestive possibility for a more Romantic reading of Virgil and his conception of mythology and its relation to the poet and society.

Notes

[1] Böschenstein, *Idylle,* 51.

[2] These details taken from Böschenstein *Idylle,* 56.

[3] See Daniel Madelénat, "Allemagne," *Dictionnaire des littératures de langue française,* ed. Jean-Pierre de Beaumarchais, Daniel Couty and Alain Rey, 2nd ed. (Paris: Bordas, 1994), 1:34.

[4] For an assessment of the reaction to Geßner's idylls among readers other than simply the theorists, see Uwe Hentschel, "Salomon Geßners *Idyllen* und ihre deutsche Rezeption im 18. und beginnenden 19. Jahrhundert," *Orbis Litterarum* 54 (1999): 332–39, esp. 340–44, for which the following is representative: "Überblickt man die Äußerungen der Deutschen zu Geßner bis an das Ende des 18. Jahrhunderts, so zeigt sich, daß Engels Einschätzung aus dem Jahre 1772, die Lektüre der Idyllen lasse uns "alle des Elendes, aller der Unruhe, die durch das streitende Interesse der Menschen veranlasset wird," vollkommen vergessen durchaus zutreffend war" (342).

[5] E. Theodor Voss, "Salomon Geßner," in *Deutsche Dichter des 18. Jahrhunderts,* ed. Benno von Wiese (Berlin: Schmidt, 1977), 249–75; here, 255.

[6] All citations are from the critical edition of Gessner's *Idyllen,* ed. E. Theodor Voss (Stuttgart: Reclam, 1973), as is the unusual orthography. References to his works in the following paragraphs will be made in the text using the page number alone.

[7] Moses Mendelssohn. "Briefe, der neuesten Literatur betreffend" (nos. 85–86, 1760), *Gesammelte Schriften,* ed. Ev J. Engel (Stuttgart-Bad Cannstatt: Frommann-Holzboog, 1991), 5/1:147.

[8] E. Theodor Voss, "Salomon Geßner," 267.

[9] See Brigitte Peucker, *Arcadia to Elysium: Preromantic Modes in the 18th Century* (Bonn: Bouvier, 1980), 50–52.

[10] Salomon Gessner, "Daphnis," in *Sämtliche Schriften,* ed. Martin Bircher (1762: Zurich, Orell Füssli, 1972), 1:80–81.

[11] Friedrich von Hagedorn, "Der Jüngling" (1728), in *Poetische Werke* (Hamburg: Bohn, 1769), 3:94.

[12] Two of Theocritus's three set-piece *loci amoeni* are in fact parodies (*Id*.5. 31–34, and 45–49). Virgil also has a further instance of it in the body of the third Eclogue (55–57), but there, as in *Idylls* 1 and 5, before the start of the singing competition.

[13] If this seems reminiscent of the earlier comments about Werther, then designedly so, since he too is numbered among Gessner's receptive readers: see Elizabeth Powers, "The Artist's Escape from the Idyll: The Relation of Werther to Sesenheim," *Goethe Yearbook* 9 (1999): 47–76, esp. 53–59.

[14] E. Theodor Voss, "Salomon Geßner," 261.

[15] See W. Creizenach, "Salomon Geßner," *Allgemeine deutsche Biographie* (1879: Berlin: Duncker & Humblot, 1968), 9:122; Böschenstein, *Idylle,* 53. I am unable to discover what translations Gessner read, but that they would have given a very different picture of Theocritus than a reading of the original Greek seems certain in view of the preconceptions of the time and the manner of translation.

[16] August Wilhelm Schlegel attributes Gessner's scruple, less charitably, to ignorance in his review of "Salomon Geßner" by Johann Jakob Hottinger, in *Kritische Schriften,* ed. Emil Staiger (Zurich: Artemis Verlag, 1962), 114–26. He considers it likely that Gessner read Greek texts in Latin translation and takes as evidence of this Gessner's failure, as Herder had argued, to perceive the distance "zwischen schöner Darstellung individueller Natur und einer ganz selbstgeschaffnen Idyllenwelt, zwischen naiver Einfalt . . . und sittlicher Idealität" (119).

[17] Compare with: *nec prius absistit quam septem ingentia uictor/ corpora fundat humi et numerum cum nauibus aequet* (*Aen.* 1. 192–94); *fusi per moenia Teucri/ conticuere* (*Aen.* 2. 252); and *ipse dies agitat festos fususque per herbam.* (*Ge.* 2. 527).

[18] I take it as granted that *fusus in herba* refers to Virgil, although the closest Virgilian wording is *fusus per herbam*. The commentary in the Deutscher Klassiker Verlag gives the source as Ovid, *Met.* 3. 838 (*HW* 1:1047), which makes the wording and its context difficult to check since book 3 only has 733 lines. Even should it be the case that the wording favors Ovid, I remain skeptical on the grounds that *fusus in herba* is a more natural remembrance of the Virgilian phrase because *in*

with ablative is the more expected combination with the participle *fusus*. It is however a trait of Virgil to use prepositions and cases with his verbs that run counter to the expectations of spoken or prose language; and if Herder is citing from memory (since the entire phrase is certainly not given in the Klopstock essay he refers to in his footnote), then such a correction is to be expected. However the matter cannot be definitively settled.

[19] For the chronology of composition, see E. Theodor Voss, "Geßner," 297. The letter to Ramler is cited in a footnote by Voss (18–19).

[20] Gessner an Gleim, 29 Nov. 1754; see Wilhelm Körte, ed., *Briefe der Schweizer: Bodmer, Sulzer, Geßner; aus Gleims litterarischem Nachlasse* (Zurich: Heinrich Gessner, 1804), 217–18.

[21] In *Idyll* 11, Polyphemus would sing away the whole day, from dawn onwards, of his recalcitrant Galatea. More usually an idyll begins at noonday (*Idd.* 1 and 6), or there is no explicit mention of the time (*Idd.* 3, 4, 5, 8, and 9). One merely assumes it is sometime during the heat of the day.

[22] Recent scholars are at pains to stress the degree of social criticism present in Gessner's *Idyllen*, see: E. Theodor Voss, "Geßner," esp. 263–65; and more generally for the relation of the idyll to the social relations of the age, Helmut Schneider's afterword to *Idyllen der Deutschen*, ed. H. Schneider (Frankfurt am Main: Insel, 1978), 355–68.

[23] Peter-Erich Neuser, Nachwort to Friedrich (Maler) Müller, *Idyllen*, ed. Peter-Erich Neuser (Stuttgart: Reclam, 1977), 358.

[24] Müller, *Idyllen*, 45. References to his idylls in the following pages will be made in the text using the page number alone.

[25] Klemens Möllendorf, "Die Idyllen des Maler Müllers," *Euphorion*, 40 (1939), 154. Möllendorf uses the phrase in relation to *Der Christabend* (published 1914). The article orders Müller's idylls according to a notion of "realism" of which the final, culminating manifestation is "eine volksdeutsche Idylle."

[26] Respectively from: Renate Böschenstein, "Maler Müller," in Benno von Wiese, *Deutsche Dichter des 18. Jahrhunderts: Ihr Leben und Werk*, 641; and Mix York-Gothart, "Zum Problem des Realismus in Friedrich (Maler) Müllers Idylle 'Die Schafschur,'" in *Maler Müller in neuer Sicht*, ed. Rolf Paulus, Gerhard Sauder, and Christoph Weiß (St. Ingbert: Röhrig, 1990), 53.

[27] These represent only a small portion of Müller's complete idylls, which were first edited by Otto Heuer, *Idyllen*, 3 vols. (Leipzig: K. Wolff, 1914).

[28] Möllendorf considers them in the order of biblical, ancient, and Palatinate ("Die Idyllen des Maler Müllers"), as does Böschenstein in both *Idylle* and in "Maler Müller"; Neuser prefers the order ancient, biblical, and Palatinate. Despite Böschenstein's caveat — "Die Unsicherheit der Datierung verbietet es, die verschiedenen Genera, wie naheliegt, als Entwicklungsschritte in der Aneignung und Umformung einer Gattungstradition zu sehen" ("Maler Müller," 651) — each sort of idyll displays a difference of treatment and emphasis, in addition to the superficial one of subject matter, that begs the interpretative question of their relation.

[29] For a sensitive consideration of this "Gesang" see Renate Böschenstein, "Grotte und Kosmos: Überlegungen zu Maler Müllers Idyllen-Mythologie," in Sauder,

Paulus, and Weiß, *Maler Müller in neuer Sicht,* 9–30; for a discussion of Virgil's relation to Müller, 11–16.

[30] Gerhard Kaiser, *Wandrer und Idylle: Goethe und die Phänomenologie der Natur in der deutschen Dichtung von Gessner bis Gottfried Keller* (Göttingen: Vandenhoeck & Ruprecht, 1977), 31.

[31] Kaiser, *Wandrer und Idylle,* 31–32.

[32] Kaiser, *Wandrer und Idylle,* 36.

[33] All the dates given refer to the date of composition, not of publication, and are taken from *Der Göttinger Dichterbund: Johann Heinrich Voss,* ed. August Sauer, Deutsche National-Litteratur 49 (Berlin: Spemann, n.d.), vol. 1. The numerals in parentheses do not refer to volume and page number but Sauer's numbering of the poem and line. The phrase "Freiheit und Vaterland" is from *Stolberg, der Freiheitssänger.*

[34] Voss wrote the ode in response to a review by Wieland of his *Trinklied für Freie* and the "Leibeigenschaft" idylls (Teutsche Merkur, January 1776). Voss seems to have taken particular affront, a lifelong weakness of Voss's, at Wieland's not inaccurate complaint about the "heisere Geschrei nach Freiheit"; see Sauer, *Voss,* 4. 14; and also E. Theodor Voss, "Arkadien und Grünau: Johann Heinrich Voss und das innere System seines Idyllenwerkes," in *Europäische Bukolik und Georgik,* ed. Klaus Garber, Wege der Forschung 355 (Darmstadt: Wissenschaftliche Buchgesellschaft, 1976), 401–4.

[35] From a letter dated 20 March 1775 to his friend Brückner, cited in Maria Erxleben, "Voß' Idyllendichtung und ihre Beziehung zu Theokrit und Homer," in *Federlese: Beiträge zu Werk und Wirken von Johann Heinrich Voß,* ed. Volker Riedel (Neubrandenburg: Literaturzentrum Neubrandenburg, 1989), 22.

[36] Sauer gives the note in its entirety in his apparatus to the idyll, *Voss,* 2. 7.

[37] Sauer views this change approvingly, observing in relation to *Die Elbefahrt* (1776), "Das Leben hat die Phantasiewelt ganz und für immer verdrängt" (introduction, *Voss,* li).

[38] Schneider, *Idyllen,* 399.

[39] Although the three idylls of *Luise* appeared separately in the years 1783 and 1784, it was not until their revision and republication as one poem in 1795 that the work made its great impression on Schiller and Goethe. As a result, the book version is the one most often cited from.

[40] Sauer, introduction, *Voss,* liv. Sauer also calls this idyll the "Höhepunkt" (lv) of Voss's idyllic production.

[41] Again one may cite Sauer as representative of this view. He writes of *Luise:* "Der Kundige entdecke überall den tiefen Kenner Homers, er könne Stellen des alten Barden aus diesen deutschen Dichter verstehen lernen" (introduction, *Voss,* lviii).

[42] Siegfried Streller, "Zeitkritik und bürgerliches Selbstbewußtsein in Voß' Idyllendichtung," in Riedel, *Federlese: Beiträge zu Werk und Wirken von Johann Heinrich Voß,* 13–14.

[43] Erxleben, "Voß' Idyllendichtung," 20. The opinion is of long standing. Wilhelm Herbst, a nineteenth-century scholar and author of a large monograph on

Voss, repeats Voss's "Ungeheuer." The Virgilian eclogue is the "entstellte Form des Idylls" that forsakes the "Volksleben" in favor of "Culturinteressen"; cited in E. Theodor Voss, "Arkadien und Grünau," 414.

[44] See Helmut J. Schneider, who provides the only extensive examination of the connection in "Johann Heinrich Voss," in Benno von Wiese, *Deutsche Dichter des 18. Jahrhunderts: Ihr Leben und Werke*, 793–96.

[45] Kaiser in *Wanderer und Idylle*, 107–26, gives the most detailed and nuanced interpretation of the first two idylls of the 'Leibeigenschaft.' He too interprets *Die Leibeigenen* in the light of the eighteenth-century conception of the idyll: "Als Form vollkommenen naturhaften Lebens verweist die Idylle in den 'Leibeigenen' doppelt eindringlich auf die Verstörung der Menschen; es entsteht eine Parodie des Idyllenschemas. Die natürlichen Lebensformen des Idyllenpersonals sind infrage gestellt: die Familie wird zerstört, die Liebe kann sich nicht erfüllen" (110). It is churlish to observe that neither the bucolic idylls of Theocritus nor the eclogues of Virgil readily lend themselves to the support of family values, nor to successful love. By crediting "natürliche Lebensformen" to the bucolic genre, Kaiser presents the new, eighteenth-century view of the idyll, the result of the labor of a century, as the normative view of the idyll, in relation to which the Virgilian eclogue must appear as a "Parodie" in Voss's imitation of it.

[46] Schneider, *Idyllen*, 397.

[47] See also Schneider, "Johann Heinrich Voss," 796.

[48] Against the criticism of Voss on this point by Kaiser, *Wanderer und Idyllen*, 120–25, and in Hedwig Voegt, introduction to Johann Heinrich Voss, *Werke in einem Band*, selected by Hedwig Voegt (Berlin; Weimar: Aufbau Verlag, 1972), xiii–xiv, one may object that his attempt to persuade all "right thinking" people, including the landowning nobility, to free the serfs corresponds to the manner in which serfdom was abolished in Germany, and thus represents a more advantageous expedient to someone genuinely interested in the condition of the serfs than the advocation of an outright revolution, which flatters the proponent's intense ideological sincerity more than it does his concern for the well-being of others.

[49] E. Theodor Voss, "Arkadien und Grünau," 391–431.

[50] See E. Theodor Voss, "Arkadien und Grünau," 408–15.

[51] E. Theodor Voss is even more emphatic in his estimation of Virgil's role in Voss's thinking and writing. He argues, "daß der Versuch, den Dichter . . . beim Wort zu nehmen, . . . über seine unmittelbaren Äußerungen hinaus geschehen muß, um auch die erst im Gefüge der Mittelbarkeiten eines Gesamtwerkes zur Erscheinung kommenden Elemente, hier das hochbedeutsame Element Vergil, ernstnehmen zu können" ("Arkadien und Grünau," 428).

[52] Kaiser, *Wandrer und Idylle*, 37. The same situation reoccurs in Goethe's *Die Leiden des jungen Werther*, particularly in the earlier letters; see also the letters of the 15th, 26th, and 27th of May (*GSW* 2/2:353–54, 357–58, and 358–60).

[53] There is a moment of perhaps unintended comedy. In reply to his lengthy praise of the "keimende Natur" that concludes with "Leb wohl, du glücklich Weib!," she asks, "Du willst nicht bleiben?"

54 Walter Rehm, *Griechentum,* 128; and also Rehm, *Europäische Romdichtung* (Munich: Hueber, 1960), 175.

55 In the less familiar later version of 1789, the wanderer merely notes that once there were words but he is unable even to begin to decipher them.

56 A premise that forms the basis for Rehm's inclusion of the poem in *Griechentum,* 117–18.

57 See Kaiser, *Wandrer und Idylle,* 40.

58 For Goethe's relation to the Roman elegiac poets on matters of form and content, see Theodore Ziolkowski, *The Classical German Elegy, 1795–1950* (Princeton: Princeton UP, 1980), 67–75.

59 Klingner examines the sense in which the inwardness of the Roman poets does represent some sense of the spiritual depth of the individual but is far removed from the tighter unity supposed by a psychological conception of the individual, in "Liebeselegien: Goethes römische Vorbilder," in *Römische Geisteswelt,* 5th enlarged ed. (Munich: Ellermann, 1965), 419–29.

60 This line is cited according to Johann Wolfgang Goethe, *Goethes Werke,* ed. Erich Trunz, 2nd ed., Hamburger Ausgabe, v. 1 of 14 (Munich: Beck, 1981), 160, and not from *GSW* as usual. The reason for this is that the "Münchener Ausgabe" reprints on facing pages the text from the manuscript of 1791 entitled *erotica romana* and also that of the first printing of the elegies as a cycle in the *Horen* in 1795. With the exception of the word order in the pentameter, and of a comma at the end of the hexameter in place of the earlier exclamation mark, the distich is the same in both.

> Froh empfind' ich mich nun auf klassischem Boden begeistert!
> Lauter und reizender spricht Vorwelt und Mitwelt zu mir.

In this instance the version of the "Ausgabe letzter Hand" printed in the "Hamburger Ausgabe" is preferable because of its greater metrical and rhetorical complexity. The pentameter above is merely perfectly classical in its scansion. All other quotations are from the "Münchener Ausgabe," 3/2. The Roman numeral refers to the number of the elegy and the Arabic numerals that follow to the verse.

61 Walter Rehm, *Romdichtung,* 176.

62 Albrecht Schöne, *Götterzeichen, Liebeszauber, Satanskult: Neue Einblicke in alte Goethetexte* (Munich: Beck, 1982), 64; and Dieter Borchmeyer, "Alexis und Dora (1797)," in *Goethes Erzählwerk: Interpretationen,* ed. Paul Michael Lützeler and James E. McLeod (Stuttgart: Reclam, 1985), 192, fn. 1.

63 Goethe, "Alexis und Dora," 23–30. Further references to this poem are cited in the text using verse numbers only.

64 In particular one might refer to Friedrich Schlegel's letter to his brother August Wilhelm from 15 June 1796, in which he notes a "kleine Ungeschicklichkeit" by which he means that Alexis should be so calm as to introduce the simile of a riddle. The resulting "Mischung des Weisen und Sinnlich-Süßen mit Leidenschaft," he regards as a "kleiner Verstoß" against the truth. This is cited from documents that accompany the commentary to this poem (*GSW* 4/1:1197).

65 Schöne, *Götterzeichen*, 68.

66 Goethe returns to this criticism, and to his reply to it, in Eckermann's *Gespräch mit Goethe* (25 December 1825; GSW 4/1:1201).

67 F. P. Pickering, "Der zierlichen Bilder Verknüpfung: Goethes 'Alexis und Dora' 1796," *Euphorion* 52 (1958): 341–55.

68 Borchmeyer goes through Alexis's memory of Dora bringing her products to market, of her walk, of her neck, and the return of these same features again in their encounter in the garden; "Alexis," 201–7, esp. 203.

69 Borchmeyer, "Alexis und Dora (1797)," 209.

70 Borchmeyer makes this point to different effect when he concludes, "Letzten Endes ist es aber gleichgültig, ob hier der Erzähler oder Alexis redet; ob dieser selbst oder ob der 'Dichter' jenen Vergleich zieht, bleibt für den Sinnszusammenhang irrelevant. Goethe hat möglicherweise mit Absicht unbestimmt gelassen, wer da redet" ("Alexis," 199–200). It does seem that Goethe has intentionally left the matter in doubt, and it is irrelevant for the interpretation that Borchmeyer proposes. However, if this passage is read in conjunction with the final lines of the idyll, then the interpolation of the narrator's voice is not irrelevant to the meaning of the poem as a whole.

71 Kaiser, *Wandrer und Idylle*, 53. Kaiser's reference to Theocritus does not seem to have found favor among later critics, who refrain from discussing it. It is not even mentioned in the commentary to "Alexis und Dora."

72 These lines are cited according to the text of K. J. Dover, Theocritus, *Select Poems* (London: Macmillan, 1971), and not as usual from Gow since this page is missing from the edition of Gow at my disposal.

73 Schöne explores this point in detail in *Götterzeichen*, 99–101.

74 Mähl, *Die Idee*, 145–86.

75 Mähl, *Die Idee*, 401–4, and thereafter *passim* in the chapter.

76 Novalis, *Werke, Tagebücher und Briefe Friedrich von Hardenbergs*, ed. Hans-Joachim Mähl and Richard Samuel, 5 vols. (Munich: Hanser, 1978–87), 4:99, Nr. 32. Further references in the next few pages to Novalis's works are cited in the text using the volume and page number alone.

77 August Wilhelm Schlegel, "Hermann und Dorothea," 250. See also Novalis's letter from 12 January 1798 to A.W. Schlegel (4:244–47, Nr. 113).

78 A. W. Schlegel, "Hermann und Dorothea," 231.

79 See Mähl, *Die Idee*, 362–71.

80 Friedrich Hiebel notes in the second edition of his *Novalis: Deutscher Dichter, europäischer Denker, christlicher Seher* (1951; Bern: Francke, 1972): "Hans-Joachim Mähl sieht in seinem Werk über *Die Idee* . . . die Fragmentsammlung *Glauben und Liebe* als die für die Romantik entscheidende Staatsauffassung an und bringt die Gedanken im Zusammenhang mit dem abendländischen Ideengut, das sich seit Virgils Verkündigung des goldenen Zeitalters (in der vierten Ekloge), der Weltfriedensidee des staufischen Kaisertums und Dantes *De Monarchia* bis in die neuzeitliche Entwicklung des pietischen Chiliasmus und Kants *Zum ewigen Frieden* entfaltet hat" (163). A more recent critic, Josef Haslinger, doffs his hat in a similar

fashion in Mähl's direction, "Novalis beschäftigte sich 1790 eingehend mit der berühmten vierten, 'messianischen,' Ekloge Vergils. Er fertigte davon eine vollständig überlieferte Übersetzung an. Fasziniert daran hat ihn offenbar die Idee eines goldenen Zeitalters" (*Die Ästhetik des Novalis,* ed. Friedbert Aspetsberger and Alois Brandstetter, Literatur in der Geschichte, Geschichte in der Literatur 5 [Königstein/Ts.: Hain, 1981], 29).

[81] H. A. Korff, *Geist der Goethezeit* (Leipzig: Hirzel, 1949), argues that the "Märchenroman" of Novalis with its medieval setting represents the romantic version of the idyll: "Es sind, in ein anderes Klima versetzt, die Menschen der Gessnerschen Idyllen, des Idyllenideals des 18. Jahrhunderts, die Menschen eines goldenen Zeitalters, das jetzt nur nicht mehr in einem arkadischen Nirgendwo gesucht, sondern gefunden wird im 'romantischen Mittelalter'" (3:589). Mähl objects that this misrepresents both the intention and the effect of the Middle Ages in the novel. The transparency of the fable serves rather to accentuate the "sort" of way a poet, and with him society, must set out on in order to bring about a golden-age transformation. The emphasis falls not on the solidity of an earlier historical reality but on it as means of articulating the import of inner longing (see *Die Idee,* 417–18). One might further object that the linking of the poet's inner vision to a larger social transformation in time results in a conception and a form that bursts the boundaries of the slighter genre; the golden age is the central theme of only one eclogue, not the framework for the composition of idylls *per se*. This difference represents both a quantitative and a qualitative change. However, the smaller "Märchen" do look more recognizably like the earlier idyll insofar as they, like mirrors reflecting the larger whole, depend for their effect on the tension between Arcadia and Elysium.

[82] The translations are those of Bock and Voss. A complete list of the editions, so far they are known, is given in 4:1045–57.

[83] Publius Virgilius Maro, *Opera,* ed. Christian Gottlob Heyne, 1st ed. (Leipzig: Fritsch, 1767), 1:47.

[84] Mähl, "Anhang: Unveröffentlichte Jugendlyrik von Novalis," in *Die Idee,* 431.

[85] Rehm provides an excellent account of the terms "Wahrsager und Priester, Gesetzgeber und Arzt" in relation to Orpheus but conflates Orpheus with Arion in *Orpheus: Der Dichter und die Toten* (Düsseldorf: Schwann, 1950), 57–65. Hiebel discusses generally the figure of Orpheus in relation to the death of Sophie and the passage from Virgil's *Georgics,* and Virgil as a descendant of Orpheus in Dante's *Divine Comedy* (*Novalis* 57–60).

[86] Day's line continues: "With Orpheus vying or with Orion —" (38).

[87] The one odd association in this chain occurs in the list of the poet's attributes at the end, in which one may see a further association with Virgil. Priest, prophet, and lawgiver follow from the description, but doctor seems a less evident association. It may have suggested itself to Novalis from his knowledge of Virgil. Virgil offers, unlike mythic poets, the example of a human poet who lays strong claim to all of those attributes, at least according to the *vitae*. In addition to his familiarity with Virgil as the pagan prophet in the fourth eclogue, Novalis was probably familiar with the *vita* by Donatus, since Heyne reprints it with his own commentary on it in the first volume of his edition, the same volume that

contains the *Eclogues* and the *Georgics*. It contains stories of the prodigies surrounding Virgil's birth, his great moral purity, his great knowledge of *medicinae et mathematicae*, as well as his healing of Augustus's horses and advice to Augustus on the constitution of Rome. Heyne's comment on such "facts" is usually sparse and along the lines of, *unde ineptissima narratio profluxerit, nondum assequi potui* (*O* 1:cxx). Pierre Bayle's *Dictionaire historique et critique,* which Heyne recommends among others, provides a more copious and useful supply of anecdotes: useful because an edition of the *Dictionnaire* appears in Novalis's book list; copious because Bayle devotes considerable space in footnote I to the refutation of the more outlandish tales of magic and of the charge: "un insigne Enchanteur & Necromantien et de ce qu'il avoit faict une infinité de choses esmerveillables par le moyen de Magie," 3rd ed. (Rotterdam: Michel Bohm, 1720), 4:2828.

[88] Martin Schneider, "Novalis und Karamsin: Eine These zur Herkunft des Atlantis-Märchens im 'Heinrich von Ofterdingen,'" *Arcadia: Eine Zeitschrift für vergleichende Literaturwissenschaft* (1984), 19: 285–87, argues that the German translation (1800) of a story by the Russian author Nicolai Michailovich Karamsin provided Novalis with his source for the "Atlantis-Märchen," in particular the courtship and wedding of the pair. The similarity argues rather that Karamsin could read Virgil as well as Novalis could. His observation that in Karamsin's version thunder and lightning express the "Empörung der Natur" at the union of the lovers points instead to his close dependence on the Virgilian original. Furthermore, the chronology is difficult. Even if one accepts that the translation, as was not uncommon, circulated before the date of publication on its title page, the time still seems relatively short, since Novalis wrote the first five chapters in January and February of 1800 (*Werke, Tagebücher und Briefe,* 1:185). Finally, the presence of a book in Germany does not put it in the hands of Novalis; nor does Novalis seem elsewhere to demonstrate a familiar and fond acquaintance with Russian literature.

[89] Virgil himself returns to these same themes with similar worlds in book 6 of the *Aeneid,* in which he, perhaps mindful of his earlier poems, begins with the order of creation that culminates in the reestablishment of the golden age under Caesar Augustus. Because of the likeness of theme and wording, the passage (*Aen.* 6. 724–96) may also have suggested itself to Novalis.

[90] Richard Samuel characterizes specifically the cave episode as a "Waldidylle" but leaves the matter at that in "Novalis," in *Der deutsche Roman vom Barock bis zur Gegenwart: Struktur und Geschichte,* ed. Benno von Wiese (Düsseldorf: Bagel, 1963), 1:271.

[91] Homer provides a further possible source for this image, although an inverted one. When Hector bids farewell to Andromache at the Scaean Gate, she has with her their child Astyanax. The child takes fright at the sight of his father. His father's flashing helmet causes him to weep. Hector then takes his son into his arms to pray to the gods that his son might become the lord, defender of the city (ἄστυ ἄναξ), as his father before him(*Iliad* 6. 466–81). Homer's child shrinks back in fright at his gleaming birthright, Novalis's reaches out eagerly to grasp his gleaming birthright with the Virgilian smile of welcome at his destiny. Further, both Hector and the king perform the act of acknowledgment by taking the babe into their arms

and, in the one instance, calling on the gods to bless the child, and in the other presenting it to heaven.

[92] Erika Voerster notes Novalis's use of a frame to inset the song, but relates it to the more general interest of the Romantics to favor devices that form a reflection within the text: "Auch hier hat Novalis die romantische Theorie der Verschachtelung im dichterischen Werk erfüllt" (*Märchen und Novellen im klassischen-romantischen Roman* [Bonn: Bouvier, 1966], 128).

[93] A later example of a free association occurs in the "Klingsohr-Märchen" in the passage concerning the treasure chamber, which turns out to be a wondrous garden. Among its wonders are sheep: "Große Herden von Schäfchen, mit silberweißer, goldner und rosenfarbner Wolle irrten umher" (1:299). In Virgil, they appear as:

> *nec uarios discet mentiri lana colores,*
> *ipse sed in pratis aries iam suaue rubenti*
> *murice, iam croceo mutabit uellera luto;*
> *sponte sua sandyx pascentis uestiet agnos.* (*Ec.* 4. 42–45)

In Novalis's translation, they appear as:

> Dann lernt Wolle nicht mehr mit bunten Farben sich zu schmücken
> Sondern auf Wiesen schmückt dann selbst das Fell sich der Widder
> Bald mit rosigen Purpur und mit dem Golde des [Strich?]krauts
> Und willfährig bekleidet die weidenden Lämmer die Sandyx.
> (Mähl, *Die Idee*, 431)

[94] Both Samuel and Voerster have considered the importance of the "Atlantis-Märchen" for the novel as a whole. Samuel's treatment is cursory, with only brief mention of explicit references to the tale in chapter 5 and in the *Paralipomena* ("Novalis," 271–72). Voerster presents a much more detailed analysis that considers the three tales primarily as a triadic cycle, but does not omit the relation of the individual tales to the novel (*Märchen*, 142–50).

[95] Voerster also points out these parallels between Heinrich and the Atlantis youth (*Märchen*, 147) and, before her, Samuel observed Heinrich's recollection of the tale in chapter 5 when he meets the "Bergmann" ("Novalis," 1:271).

[96] Ludwig Tieck, *Bericht über die Fortsetzung*, in *Werke, Tagebücher und Brief*, 1:368.

[97] Maler Müller also used the bucolic to introduce the specifically Christian account of the vanquishing of death in connection with Orpheus in an earlier lightly "Elysian" touch.

[98] The characterization is not intended in so unromantic a sense as absolutely definitive since the carbuncle in the story is an image from the Christian tradition.

Conclusion: Proximity and Estrangement

Though the strongest reception of Virgil occurs within German idyllic literature, this is ultimately of little consequence. Virgil's reputation and the expectation of finding a Virgilian muse in eighteenth-century literature stands and falls on the epic, the *Aeneid*. Only once Heinze squarely readdresses the issue of the Virgilian epic, reaching the conclusion that it is not a derivative, plagiarized, non-poem, and restores to it the status of an original and creative work of art, albeit non-Homeric, does a new approach to the Latin poet become possible for the Germans. Only then do the consequences of the estrangement from Virgil in the eighteenth century begin to unravel. At the close of the eighteenth century, such is the distance from Virgil and the absence of any expectation of finding in its literature a Virgilian muse that we may plausibly speak of a repressed muse. At the point of the greatest apparent remove, a sense of possible proximity appears in Novalis's sympathetic reworkings. A more disquieting sense of a romantic proximity also occurs in the unpublished writings of Friedrich Schlegel. It is all the more piquant in him as he is so prominent among the public champions of the new view of the Latin heritage. However, his very disinclination to take further the affinities he observes in his notes illustrates the scale of the hindrances inhibiting any reconsideration of the issue.

Famously in his *Gespräch über die Poesie*, Schlegel places in the mouth of Ludoviko a speech on mythology. Ludoviko argues that mythology is the muse of poetry and states as a fact that "wir haben keine Mythologie" (*KFS* 2:312). He assigns to the modern age the task of making good this want. The modern must "consciously" "eine [Mythologie] hervorbringen" (*KFS* 2:312). It must be "das künstliche aller Kunstwerke" (*KFS* 2:312). The success of this enterprise must remain doubtful, as he also holds that a mythology is "ein solches Kunstwerk der Natur" (*KFS* 2:312). The properties formerly attributed to Greek culture — it is both nature, yet also art, and at once necessity, yet no less freedom — now become the prized attributes of the new mythology. The attitude of the viewer before a work which he knows to be a product constructed by human endeavor, though he professes it to be a work of nature, must contain a strong dose of irony. Ludoviko prefers to call it "idealism" and confidently sees in it the power to undertake such a project.

In Antonio's later speech on the novel, the reader learns, among many other things, that the old poesy fed so entirely off mythology that it was oblivious of history, which now has become the "Grund" of romantic poetry, a ground that has as its premise the real of history and the imaginary of mythology. The novel is the genre that accomplishes this subtle negotiation and so acquires the mantel of the quintessential form for romantic literature. It is also a form of epic, and so may lay claim to its totality by containing within itself the other genres, that is, their modes and perspectives, so that it becomes "gemischt aus Erzählung, Gesang und andern Formen" (*KFS* 2:336).

In addition, in Schlegel's famous Athenäum fragment, the reader discovers that "die romantische Poesie ist eine progressive Universalpoesie" (*KFS* 2:182). This poetry consists of the perpetual transgression of all manner of boundaries, which historical change and the perception of it continually throw up. By this means poetry becomes "gleich dem Epos ein Spiegel der ganzen umgebenden Welt, ein Bild des Zeitalters" (*KFS* 2:182). Poetry is not the reflection itself, but rather a species of "unmoved mover," the "unreflected reflection" present within the work, which begs for an "endlose Reihe von Spiegeln" (*KFS* 2:182–83).

If so cavalier a treatment of some of Schlegel's best-known texts seems one-sided, then designedly so, for the aim is to sharpen the possible connection to Virgil's *Aeneid*. As an epic, it too may lay *prima facie* claim to the metaphor of the mirror and hence the honor of being "like" romantic poetry. Indeed, many of those faults that Heyne, Herder, and Schlegel himself found so objectionable in Virgil's works seem to be the virtues of romantic poetry. Schlegel lamented that Virgil did not confine himself to the old Latin legends of heroic ancestors, but mixed his epic up with contemporary concerns: namely, that in one work he combined mythological (that is, imaginary) and recorded (that is, real) history. Yet Antonio made the tension between mythology and history the distinctive trait of the new poetry, and therefore scarcely a matter of reproach. Furthermore, Virgil by transposing his history into the past transforms it into a prophecy, a transposition that opens up a space for nuanced reflection, for the device of mirroring, and not straightforward representation, regardless of whether we give it an Augustan reading or a more oppositional one. To give an example: what does the contemporary Roman make of the parade of great Roman figures from the future, presented by Anchises to his son in the underworld, yet which concludes with a dead figure from the present? Or what of Aeneas's exit from the underworld by the Ivory Gate of false dreams? That the dream of the future may be true for Aeneas, but a false "future" for the contemporary Roman, since it his past? Even the citation practice of the learned style represents another form of reflection as it places Virgil's work within an "endless" chain of a romantic intertextuality.

Schlegel writes that no one can consider the *Aeneid* a true epic because "das Rhetorische und Tragische hat man im ganzen und im einzeln oft bemerkt, und die lyrischen Stellen bieten sich auch sichtbar und zahlreich genug dar" (*KFS* 1:490). If this is true, then Virgil has produced an epic which, in addition to incorporating history and mythology, also includes the rhetorical mode of writing as well as the modes proper to the other two branches of literature as they were known in his day, and which together with epic remain the basis for ordering German aesthetic thought about literature in the eighteenth century. If verse epic cannot bear the multiplicity of the modern genre of epic, then perhaps the title of "novel" might more accurately designate the work that Schlegel describes.

And on the point of mythology: Virgil's position prefigures that of Ludoviko and his companions. They, oppressed by their exclusion from the myths of the older, principally Greek, poetry, seek refuge in a new mythology that will confer on them the benefits of the bygone, older one. Similarly, the Romans too did not enjoy — as Herder and Schlegel are at pains to point out — the sort of mythology that gave rise to Greek literature. Virgil's solution to this difficulty is to create for the Romans their own mythology, one that aims to be universal in scope for them. Virgil selects not Greek mythology, but, by assuming the perspective of the defeated Trojans, the mythology of their Asian opponents (see *Aen.* 2. 557), from the outset a rewriting of Homer with a difference. This people from the "Morgenland" voyages to the new West, the "Abendland," where it will fuse with a young, and somewhat barbarous, people to form a new, third people — neither side, neither Trojan nor Latin, "wins." Even the Greeks in the form of Diomedes refrain from continuing the old animosity with the new people. Aeneas's war in Latium prefigures the Roman domination of Western Europe not as conquest with a sole victor, but as colonial war with a civilizing mission. Eventually the subject peoples are incorporated into the Roman people and gain full civic rights, a process of which Virgil, an Italian provincial, was highly conscious in light of the century's long series of civil wars undermining the Republic and leading to the grant of citizenship to the Italic peoples. The new community becomes a universal community, embracing within the Roman world all the peoples and cultures of antiquity, the older ones of Asia, Africa, and Greece as well as the newer one of Italy. Virgil, to complicate matters further, adds a romantic spiraling twist to his epic history. The story of Aeneas's voyage to Latium is also the story of his return to the obscure origins of his family in Italy, to the site of an earlier golden age, and at the same time a step toward a very different future with the founding of the Roman people and the setting in motion of its history toward a new would-be golden age.

However, dubious this "Nationalgedicht" may seem, the Romans of Virgil's day found the resulting mixture of myth and history so convincing that they readily made it the storehouse of their national mythology. Quibbles at its transparently invented nature, at such anachronistic fabrications as Dido living in the same age as Aeneas and meeting him, are toothless before the animating power of its vision. The epic fulfilled, on the point of its acceptance, exactly the effect Ludoviko envisions for a new mythology. St. Augustine, for example, stubbornly and passionately clings to the ideal of the universal community, and Dante honors Virgil as the singer of the city from which was destined to come the universal empire and church.

Schlegel himself seems to have sensed a possible closeness of Virgil to some of his theories but to have been reluctant to examine this proximity further. In his fragments from the years 1797–1803, he makes a number of statements that contrast strongly with those to be found in his published works: "Das moderne Epos fängt mit Virgilius an" (*KFS* 16: V, 276),[1] "Auch *Virgil* hat eine συστ [systematische] Tendenz" (V, 959), "Zur συστ [systematischen] π [Poesie] außer Dante, Virgil, d[en] Trag.[ödien], Guar[ini's] auch D[on] Q[uixote]" (V, 1024), "Die ganze φσ [Philosophie] und Hist[orie] der π [Poesie] in *Ein* Gedicht von Virgilisch-Dantisch epischer Form" (VI, 10), "Virgil, Horaz, Ovid sind offenbar *romantische Naturen*" (VII, 86; cf. also VII, 80), "Die Aeneide als Versuch einer neuen Muthologie ist didaktisch" (IX, 69), "*Virgilius* als Versuch einer römischen Mythologie sehr hoch zu setzen" (XII, 229). "Die Geschichte der romantisch[en] Poesie ist überhaupt schon mit *Ovidius und Virgilius* anzufangen und Homer wenigstens zu erwähnen" (XIII, 117). For a failed poet, Virgil keeps good company, company that Schlegel commonly holds in high regard, such as Dante and Cervantes. In Schlegel's published works, Virgil is not admitted into their company; Dante, not Virgil, appears alongside Homer in the *Gespräch über die Poesie*. Furthermore, if Virgilian epic form has nothing to recommend it, why the notion of a Virgilian-Dantean poem for his own presumably most romantic of compositions? And what does it mean to say that the *Aeneid* is the beginning of the modern epic — in what way modern? And again, what is the significance of recognizing that Virgil attempts a "neue Mythologie," which is also a Roman one and "sehr hoch zu setzen"? And finally, what does Schlegel understand by the repetition of Virgil as a romantic poet?

The point is not that these associations remain rare, fragmentary and unexplored, but rather that Schlegel should entertain them at all. In this the Janus-like position of Rome first noted in Herder appears again. The dominant paradigm elaborated by Winckelmann, Heyne, Herder, Schlegel himself, and others, constructs the Latin world as the opposite pole to the Greek world; in order to explore the depth of the Greek Homer one shows the superficiality of the Latin Virgil. He and Rome negate the felicitous world of Greece and so bring antiquity to a close by rupturing it. The Latin heritage becomes a barrier behind which the happy coincidence of nature and art are known to have given rise to the normative culture of Greece. Yet sadly the modern individual may only peer back historically at this antiquity over the Latin barrier that excludes him from a more direct communication with it. The modern individual experiences himself as romantic and ancient Greece as classical through the disruptive mediation of Rome. This notion facilitates the articulation of three separate cultural identities: "das Griechische," "das Romanische" and "das Germanische," two of which show a great likeness and stand within the hallowed circle, while the third, with its later offspring, does not; to the nationalist tendencies of the succeeding century an appealing constellation, but one which need not be fiercely jingoistic. Sellar, preparing his general treatment of Virgil for Victorian England, accepts these theoretical categories, acknowledging three types of imagination, Greek, Italian, and Germanic. He notes their divergence thus: "The genius of the ancient Latin race is further removed from that of the modern Germanic race, than either is from the genius of ancient Greece."[2] The sharpness of the distinctions depends on whether Sellar would number the modern-day French, Italians, and Spanish among the Germanic race by virtue of the "Völkerwanderung" at the fall of the Western Empire, or regard them, rather, as the modern descendants of the Latins — the English, as Anglo-Saxons, are safely within the pale of Germanic.

Happily, the modern may find an antidote in nature to this ailment of history. The same nature confronts him today as faced the ancient Greek, and he may, by consulting his feeling and tending it carefully, fashion the key that will crack open the barrier and gain him readmittance of a kind to the garden of "das schöne Natur" in Greece. The paradigmatic contrast of Greece-Rome is so tightly intertwined in the vital concerns of the eighteenth century — history, the beautiful, freedom, nature, sentiment, and a sense of Germanness — that for Schlegel to pursue the similarities to the Virgilian epic he senses would be for him to deconstruct the pole so carefully constructed during the century. It would explode the sharp division between classical and romantic and the condition of longing if Rome were to present a more fluid cultural continuum, if it were suddenly to seem at once potentially quasi- or proto-romantic and also a vestigial, fading classical. The beautiful, inimitable perfection of Greece, which the modern may yearn for, requires the barrier of historical remoteness that Rome provides as its negation. The weakening, or even removal, of the barrier over which Greek and modern comfortably commune would compel a fundamental reevaluation of the mediating term; and Schlegel could only entertain so radical a notion were he also willing to rethink the two terms related through this mediation, namely, the Greek and the modern, that is, the Germanic. Yet it has been the labor of the century to endow Greece with every possible beneficial signification, to find its trace and its continued importance in every human undertaking, so it is hardly to be expected that Schlegel alone should pursue such a line of thought.

In the light of these considerations it is all the more surprising, then, that Schlegel should even associate Virgil, modern epic, mythology, and romantic, and that Novalis should sense so strongly the mythical and religious impulse in Virgil. For Novalis, Virgil can be one source among many that he dips into and takes from for his own purposes, one tessera in his own universal and progressive mosaic. Novalis's use of Virgil casts doubt on the notion of him as a historical anomaly, for it restores the Latin poet to the continuity of culture on which the Romantic feeds and reflects. It is also a latently more historical attitude. However, its exploration will only occur gradually, as will likewise any lessening of the sense of Rome as a "Dämongeschichte" and a culture without its own literary expression. It is a process dependent on the restoration of Greece to the corrosive flux of history so that Greece moves from the column of "the" to perhaps merely "a" "schöne Natur," a shift which stretches well into the twentieth century.

Virgil inspires as a romantic muse only insofar as he strikes the chords of myth-making poet, nature, and prophecy. Novalis fixes his attention only on certain elements in the Virgilian texts. He can sense a mythological and religious affinity, adapt prophecy, turn the romantic potential of the golden age to spiral and circular possibilities, deck out nature with various motifs from the Virgilian repertoire, and convert the figure of the bucolic poet into the far grander romantic poet. The service that Virgil's myth-making provides to the Roman state and any reflection on it hold no interest for Novalis. Presumably this aspect of Virgil, to judge by the comment of Schlegel and others, is an embarrassment, as it seems only to aid the destruction of freedom.

If this Virgil is notably absent from the later eighteenth century, it is a Virgil to whom German scholars in the wake of Heinze will devote great attention. Nor is it a concern that remains simply a scholarly peculiarity, as two examples from writers of the former German Democratic Republic show. For both Heiner Müller and Christa Wolf, assertions such as that of Haecker about the centrality of Virgil to the West, "Vergil, Vater des Abendlandes," have sufficient currency for them to respond to it critically. In *Germania Tod in Berlin* (1977), Müller argues that the Western Allies' defeat of Nazi Germany and the foundation of the Federal Republic of Germany repeats the imperialist settlement of Augustan Rome. The replacement of one regime by another perpetuates, in Müller's eyes, the basic structures of the previous one, notwithstanding the official "Virgilian" propaganda hailing the birth of the new regime as a new beginning. This is rather for Müller a symbolic execution of Germania. He casts this event as the end of the iron age and the inauguration of the golden age with an abbreviated, free translation of the fourth eclogue:

SCHON ENTSTEIGT EIN NEUES GESCHLECHT DEM ERHABENEN HIMMEL
SCHLIESST DIE EISERNE ZEIT UND BEFREIT VOM SCHRECKEN DIE
   LÄNDER.
SEHT WIE ALLES ENTGEGEN ATMET DEM NEUEN JAHRHUNDERT
DAS GEFLÜGELT HERAUFKOMMT MIT GESCHENKEN DER ERDE;
SANFT MIT ÄHREN WIRD VON SELBER VERGOLDEN DIE FLUR SICH

AUCH AM WILDERNDEN DORN WIRD ABHANGEN DIE TRAUBE
AUS HARTSTÄMMIGEN EICHEN WIE TAU WIRD TROPFEN DER HONIG
ZU VERSUCHEN DAS MEER IM GEBÄLK, ZU SCHIRMEN DIE STADT MIT
MAUERN, DEN GRUND MIT DER FURCHE ZU SPALTEN IST DA KEINE
NOT MEHR.[3]

The reader should, however, bear in mind that Müller's prophet is not a poet, but a "Schädelverkäufer."

The same sense of the questionable continuity of the Virgilian text as one of the West's core narratives also appears in Christa Wolf's *Kassandra* (1983). She rewrites the two foundational pagan narratives of the Western, humanist tradition from the female perspective of Cassandra, the daughter of Priam and Hecuba, who was doomed to foretell the future and never to be believed. Wolf's comment on Homer, the Iliadic hero, and the carnage of the *Iliad* is succinctly enough stated by the change of Achilles' epic epithet to "Achill, das Vieh."

Her Virgilian figures are more surprising and interesting. She includes in her tale not merely Aeneas but also Anchises, his father. Anchises appears as one of the few sympathetic male figures: "Alles wurde leichter mit Anchises."[4] Cassandra concludes that he honors her mother not as the Queen of Troy but for herself (105), and the Amazons permit him, a man, to remain in their presence, contrary to their custom (134). The unusual ability of Anchises to find acceptance both in the male world of the Trojan citadel and among the excluded women who form their own society outside the masculine city also appears in his son. Cassandra places him on the same level as herself insofar as she loves him (149). Even as she sits awaiting her death, she frequently interrupts her tale to address him directly, as if her recollections were a conversation with him. What separates the two is their different relation to the future and what it portends (108). When they parted, they quarreled, as she refused to flee Troy with him and failed to make her reasons understood; she talks of Aeneas "der mich nie bedrängte, der mich immer gelten ließ, nichts an mir biegen oder ändern wollte, bestand darauf, daß ich mit ihm ging. Er wollte es mir befehlen (156). What she fears for Aeneas is exactly this — command. She fears that familiarity with the habit of command, born of the people's desire for a leader, will transform the earlier Aeneas into yet another "Held," another idol for a new people; and of heroes Cassandra has seen sufficient at Troy. She views her death as the shock needed to provoke an inner questioning in Aeneas, "wenn er der ist, den ich liebe" (109). Earlier she had said she loved Aeneas "mehr als mein Leben" (149), which manner of speaking she now makes literal with her death — "Um deinet- und um meinetwillen" (156). Wolf's *Kassandra* represents an oppositional, feminist narrative to the canonical, male ones of the humanist tradition.

The reading of Virgil by these writers, as well as by other writers and scholars of the twentieth century, be they approving or critical, corrects his dismemberment in the eighteenth century by acknowledging the Virgilian texts as an integral part of the German cultural tradition.

Notes

[1] Unlike other citations from Schlegel, these are listed according to division (the Roman numeral) and the fragment number given in the *Kritische Ausgabe*, not the page number. Side by side with these fragments are others that repeat such points as Virgil is a failed poet, with many comparisons to French poets (see XII, 237, 243, 248; XIII, 119), and also that he failed to choose the true, proper Roman mythology (see XIV, 77).

[2] Sellar, *The Roman Poets*, 88.

[3] Heiner Müller, *Germania Tod in Berlin* (Berlin: Rotbuch, 1977), 57–58.

[4] Christa Wolf, *Kassandra* (Darmstadt: Luchterhand, 1983), 105. Further references to this work are made in the text using the page number alone.

Works Cited

Allgemeine Deutsche Biographie. Auf Veranlassung Seiner Majestät des Königs von Bayern herausgegeben durch die historische Commission bei der königlichen Akademie der Wissenschaften. 56 vols. 1875–1912. Facsimile repr. Berlin: Duncker & Humblot, 1967–71.

Alpers, Paul. *The Singer of the Eclogues: A Study of Virgilian Pastoral*. Berkeley: U of California P, 1979.

Andreae, Bernard. *Laokoon und die Gründung Roms*. Kulturgeschichte der antiken Welt 39. Mainz: Zabern, 1988.

———. *Laokoon und die Kunst von Pergamum: Die Hybris der Giganten*. Frankfurt am Main: Fischer, 1991.

Anger, Alfred. *Literarisches Rokoko*. Sammlung Metzler 25. Stuttgart: Metzler, 1962.

Baeumer, Max L. "Klassizität und republikanische Freiheit in der außerdeutschen Winckelmann-Rezeption des späten 18. Jahrhunderts." In *Johann Joachim Winckelmann, 1717–1768*, ed. Gaehtgens, 195–220.

Baridon, Michael. "Historiography." In *Cambridge History of Literary Criticism*, ed. H. B. Nisbet and Claude Rawson, 4:282–301. Cambridge: Cambridge UP, 1997.

Baswell, Christopher. *Virgil in Medieval England*. Cambridge: Cambridge UP, 1995.

Batteux, Charles. *Les Beaux-Arts réduits à un même principe*. Edited by Jean-Rémy Mantion. Paris: aux amateurs de livres, 1989.

Bayle, Pierre. *Dictionaire historique et critique*. 3rd ed. Vol. 4. Rotterdam: Michel Bohm, 1720.

Behagel, Otto. *Deutsche Syntax: Eine geschichtliche Darstellung*. 4 vols. Heidelberg: Winter, 1923–32.

Beißner, Friedrich. "Afterword." In Wieland, *Ausgewählte Werke*.

Bender, Hermann. "Geschichte des Gelehrtenschulwesens in Deutschland seit der Reformation." In *Geschichte der Erziehung vom Anfang an bis auf unsere Zeit,* ed. Karl Adolf Schmid, 5/1:1–337.

Bender, Wolfgang. "Johann Jacob Bodmer und Johann Miltons 'Verlohrnes Paradies.'" *Jahrbuch der deutschen Schillergesellschaft* 11 (1967): 225–67.

Bodmer, Johann Jacob. *Vier kritische Gedichte*. Edited by Jakob Baechtold. Deutsche Litteraturdenkmale des 18. Jahrhunderts in Neudrucken 12. Stuttgart: G. J. Göschen, 1883.

Boileau-Despreaux, Nicolas. *Oeuvres Complètes*. Introduction by Antoine Adam. Edited by Francoise Escal. 2 vols. Bibliothèque de la Pléiade 188. Paris: Gallimard, 1966.

Bollacher, Martin. "Geschichte und Geschichtsschreibung in Herders 'Ideen zur Philosophie der Geschichte der Menschheit.'" In *Johann Gottfried Herder: Academic Disciplines and the Pursuit of Knowledge,* ed. Koepke, 168–77.

Borchardt, Rudolf. "Vergil." *Corona* 1.3 (1930): 296–309. Repr. in Oppermann, *Wege zu Vergil: Drei Jahrzehnte Begegnungen in Dichtung und Wissenschaft,* 199–210.

Borchmeyer, Dieter. "Alexis und Dora." In *Goethes Erzählwerk: Interpretationen,* ed. Paul Michael Lützeler and James E. McLeod, 192–215. Stuttgart: Reclam, 1985.

Böschenstein, Renate. "Grotte und Kosmos: Überlegungen zu Maler Müllers Idyllen-Mythologie." In *Maler Müller in neuer Sicht,* ed. Sauder, Paulus, and Weiß, 9–30.

———. *Idylle.* Sammlung Metzler 63. Stuttgart: Metzler, 1967.

———. "Maler Müller." In *Deutsche Dichter des 18. Jahrhunderts: Ihr Leben und Werk,* ed. Benno von Wiese, 641–57.

Braitmaier, Friedrich Jacob. "Über die Schätzung Homers und Virgils von C. Scaliger bis Herder." *Korrespondenz-Blatt für Gelehrten- und Realschulen Württemburgs* 32 (1885): 454–68, 502–3; and 33 (1886): 84–92, 121–29, 271–94, 364–73 and 525–33.

Brandt, Reinhard. ". . .ist endlich eine edle Einfalt, und eine stille Größe." In *Johann Joachim Winckelmann, 1717–1768,* ed. Gaehtgens, 41–54.

Bräutigam, Bernd. "Poetizität und der Ursprung literarischer Ästhetik im 18. Jahrhundert." In *Neuere Studien zur Aphoristik und Essayistik,* ed. Giulia Cantarutti and Hans Schumacher, 223–49. Berliner Beiträge zur neueren deutschen Literaturgeschichte 9. Frankfurt am Main: Lang, 1986.

Breitinger, Johann Jacob. *Critische Dichtkunst.* Afterword by Wolfgang Bender. 2 vols. 1740. Facsimile repr. Stuttgart: Metzler, 1966.

Brosin, Oskar. *Parallelstellen aus modernen Dichtern zu Virgils Aeneis.* Progr. Nr. 163. Liegnitz: H. Krumbhaar, 1880.

Browning, Robert. *German Poetry in the Age of the Enlightenment.* University Park and London: Pennsylvania State UP, 1978.

Büchner, Karl. *P. Vergilius Maro: Der Dichter der Römer.* Stuttgart: Druckenmüller, 1957.

Bursian, Conrad. *Die Geschichte der classischen Philologie in Deutschland von den Anfängen bis zur Gegenwart.* 2 vols. Munich & Leipzig: Oldenbourg, 1883.

Butler, E. M. *The Tyranny of Greece over Germany.* New York: Macmillan, 1935.

Calinger, Ronald. *Gottfried Wilhelm Leibniz.* Troy, NY: Rensselaer Polytechnic Institute, 1976.

Chalker, John. *The English Georgic: A Study in the Development of a Form.* Baltimore: Johns Hopkins P, 1969.

Clausen, Wendell. "An Interpretation of the *Aeneid*." In *Virgil: A Collection of Critical Essays*, ed. Commager, 75–88. Englewood Cliffs, NJ: Prentice Hall, 1966.

———. *A Commentary on Virgil: Eclogues*. Oxford: Clarendon Press, 1994.

Coleman, R., ed. *Eclogues*, by Publius Vergilius Maro. Cambridge Greek and Latin Classics. Cambridge: Cambridge UP, 1977.

Coleridge, Samuel Taylor. *Collected Letters of Samuel Taylor Coleridge*. Edited by Earl Leslie Griggs. 6 vols. Oxford: Clarendon Press, 1956–71.

———. *The Collected Works*. Edited by Kathleen Coburn and Bart Winer. 6 vols. London, Princeton: Routledge & K. Paul, Princeton UP, 1969–.

———. *Specimens of the Table Talk of the Late Samuel Taylor Coleridge*. Edited by H. N. Coleridge. 2 vols. New York: Harper & Brothers, 1835.

Commager, Steele, ed. *Virgil: A Collection of Critical Essays*. Englewood Cliffs, NJ: Prentice-Hall, 1966.

Comparetti, Domenico Pietro Antonio. *Vergil in the Middle Ages*. Translated by E. F. M. Benecke. 1895. Repr. with a new introduction by Jan Ziolkowski. Princeton: Princeton UP, 1997.

Congleton, J. E. *Theories of Pastoral Poetry in England, 1684–1798*. 1952. Repr. New York: Haskell House Publishers, 1968.

Creech, Thomas, trans. *De carmine pastorali*, by René Rapin. Affixed as preface to *Idylliums*. Theocritus. Thomas Creech. 1684. Repr. with an introduction by J. E. Congleton in *The Augustan Reprint Society* 3 (1947).

Creizenach, W. "Salomon Geßner." In *Allgemeine deutsche Biographie*. 1879. Repr. Berlin: Duncker & Humblot, 1968.

Crowther, C. B. "C. Cornelius Gallus: His Importance in the Development of Roman Poetry." In *Aufstieg und Niedergang der römischen Welt*, ed. Hildegard Temporini and Wolfgang Haase, 30/3:1622–48. Berlin: de Gruyter, 1983.

Curtius, Ernst Robert. *Europäische Literatur und lateinisches Mittelalter*. Bern: Francke, 1948.

Cysarz, Herbert. "Klassik." In *Reallexikon der deutschen Literaturgeschichte*, ed. Paul Merker and Wolfgang Stammler, 2:92–100. Berlin: de Gruyter, 1926–28.

Dacier, Anne Madame de. *Des Causes de la Corruption du Goust*. 1714. Facsimile repr. Geneva: Slatkine Reprints, 1970.

Daltrop, Georg. *Die Laokoongruppe im Vatikan: Ein Kapitel aus der römischen Museumsgeschichte und der Antiken-Erkundung*. Xenia: Konstanzer Althistorische Vorträge und Forschungen 5. Constance: Universitätsverlag Konstanz, 1982.

Dann, Otto. "Deutsche Nationsbildung im Zeichen französischer Herausforderung." In *Die deutsche Nation: Gesichte — Probleme — Perspektiven*, ed. Otto Dann, 9–23. Vierow bei Greifswald: SH-Verlag, 1994.

Day Lewis, C., trans. *The Eclogues of Virgil*. London: Jonathan Cape, 1963.

Décultot, Élisabeth. *Johann Joachim Winckelmann: Enquête sur la genèse de l'histoire de l'art.* Paris: Presses Universitaires de France, 2000.

Dedner, Burghard. "Vom Schäferleben zur Agrarwirtschaft: Poesie und Ideologie des 'Landleben' in der deutschen Literatur des 18. Jahrhunderts." *Jahrbuch der Jean-Paul-Gesellschaft.* 7 (1972): 40–83. Repr. in Garber, *Europäische Bukolik und Georgik,* 347–90.

Deitz, Luc, and Gregor Vogt-Spira. Introduction. In Scaliger, *Poetices libri septem.* 1:xi–lxxiv.

Deutsches Wörterbuch. Edited by Hermann Paul. 5th ed.

Donatus, Tiberius Claudius. *Interpretationes Vergilianae.* Edited by Heinrich Georg. 2 vols. Bibliotheca Scriptorum Graecorum et Romanorum Teubneriana. Stuttgart: B.G. Teubner, 1969.

Dover, K. J. ed. *Select Poems,* by Theocritus. London: Macmillan, 1971.

Dryden, John. *The Works of John Dryden.* Edited by Edward Niles Hooker and H. T. Swedenberg, Jr. 20 vols. Berkeley & Los Angeles: U of California P, 1956–2000.

Duden: Grammatik der Gegenwartssprache. 4th ed. Vol. 4. Mannheim: Dudenverlag, 1984.

Eliot, T. S. *What is a Classic?* London: Faber & Faber, 1945.

Empson, William. *Some Versions of Pastoral.* Rev. ed. New York: New Directions, 1974.

Erxleben, Maria. "Goethe und Vergil." In *Vergil: Antike Weltliteratur in ihrer Entstehung und Nachwirkung,* ed. Johannes Irmscher, 131–48. Amsterdam: Hakkert, 1995.

———. "Voß' Idyllendichtung und ihre Beziehung zu Theokrit und Homer." In *Federlese: Beiträge zu Werk und Wirken von Johann Heinrich Voß,* ed. Riedel, 20–28.

Ferris, David. *Silent Urns: Romanticism, Hellenism, Modernity.* Stanford: Stanford UP, 2000.

Finsler, Georg. *Homer in der Neuzeit von Dante bis Goethe.* Leipzig & Berlin: Teubner, 1912.

Fontenelle, Bernard le Bouvier de. "Discours sur la nature de l'eglogue." In *Oeuvres complètes,* ed. Alain Niderst, 2:383–409. 8 vols. Paris: Fayard, 1989–2001.

Fontius, Martin. *Winckelmann und die französische Aufklärung.* Berlin: Akademie, 1968.

Fowler, Peta G., and Don P. Fowler. "Virgil." In *The Oxford Classical Dictionary,* ed. Simon Hornblower and Antony Spawforth, 1602–7. 3rd ed. Oxford: Oxford UP, 1996.

Friedrich, Wolf-Hartmut. "Heyne als Philologe." In *Der Vormann der Georgia Augusta: Christian Gottlob Heyne zum 250. Geburtstag; Sechs akademische Reden,* 15–31. Göttingen: Vandenhoeck & Ruprecht, 1980.

Fuhrmann, Manfred. "Die Querelle des Anciens et des Modernes, der Nationalismus und die deutsche Klassik." In *Brechungen: Wirkungsgeschichtliche Studien zur antik-europäischen Bildungstradition*, 129–49. Stuttgart: Klett, 1982.

Fumaroli, Marc de. "Les Abeilles et les araignées." In *La Querelle des anciens et des modernes*, ed. Anne-Marie Lecoq, 7–218. Paris: Gallimard, 2001.

Gaehtgens, Thomas W., ed. *Johann Joachim Winckelmann, 1717–1768*. Hamburg: Felix Meiner, 1986.

Gail, Anton. "Im Schatten der Griechen: Die augusteische Dichtung, vor allem Vergil und Horaz im deutschen Schrifttum um 1800." In *On Romanticism and the Art of Translation: Studies in Honor of Edwin Hermann Zeydel*, ed. Gottfried F. Merkel, 141–62. Princeton: Princeton UP, 1956.

Garber, Klaus. "Arkadien und Gesellschaft: Skizze der Sozialgeschichte der Schäferdichtung als utopischer Literaturform Europas." In *Utopieforschung: Interdisziplinäre Studien zur neuzeitlichen Utopie*, ed. Wilhelm Vosskamp, 2:37–81. Stuttgart: Metzler, 1982.

———. *Europäische Bukolik und Georgik*. Wege der Forschung 355. Darmstadt: Wissenschaftliche Buchgesellschaft, 1976.

———. *Der locus amoenus und der locus terribilis: Bild und Funktion der Natur in der deutschen Schäfer- und Landlebendichtung des 17. Jahrhunderts*. Cologne: Böhlau, 1974.

Geschichte der Erziehung vom Anfang an bis auf unsere Zeit. Edited by Karl Adolf Schmid. 5. vols. Stuttgart: J. G. Cotta'sche Buchhandlung, 1884–1902.

Gessner, Salomon. *Die Idyllen*. Edited by E. Theodor Voss. Stuttgart: Reclam, 1973.

———. *Sämtliche Schriften*. Edited by Martin Bircher. 3 vols. 1762. Facsimile repr. Zurich: Orell Füssli, 1972.

Gibbon, Edward. *The Memoirs of the Life of Edward Gibbon with Various Observations and Excursions by Himself*. Edited by George Birkbeck Hill. London: Methuen, 1900.

Gillot, Hubert. *La Querelle des anciens et des modernes en France*. Paris: Édouard Champion, 1914.

Gleim, Johann Wilhelm Ludwig. *Sämmtliche Schriften*. 4 vols. Amsterdam: 1770.

Goethe, Johann Wolfgang. *Goethes Werke*. Herausgegeben im Auftrage der Großherzogin Sophie von Sachsen. Ser. 4, vol. 14. 1893. Facsimile repr. Tokyo: Sansyusya Publishing; Tübingen: Max Niemeyer, 1975.

———. *Goethes Werke*. Edited by Erich Trunz (Hamburger Ausgabe). 2nd ed. 14 vols. Munich: Beck, 1981.

———. *Sämtliche Werke nach Epochen seines Schaffens*. Edited by Karl Richter with the assistance of Herbert G. Göpfert, Norbert Miller, and Gerhard Sauder (Münchener Ausgabe). 21 vols. Munich: Hanser, 1985–98.

Gottsched, Johann Christoph. *Ausgewählte Werke*. Edited by Joachim and Brigitte Birke. Ausgaben deutscher Literatur des XV bis XVIII Jahrhunderts, ed. Hans-Gert Roloff. 12 vols. Berlin: De Gruyter, 1968–.

Gottsched, Johann Christoph. Preface to *Des Publius Virgilius Maro Hirtengedichte,* by Publius Vergilius Maro. Translated by Johann Daniel Overbeck. Helmstaedt: Weygand, 1750.

Gow, A. S. F., ed. and trans. *Theocritus.* With a commentary by the editor. 2 vols. Cambridge: Cambridge UP, 1950.

Grafton, Anthony. "Germany and the West, 1830–1900." In *Perceptions of the Ancient Greeks,* ed. K. J. Dover, 225–455. Oxford: Blackwell, 1992.

Graves, Robert. "The Virgil Cult." *Virginia Quarterly Review* 38 (1962): 13–35.

Griffin, Jasper. "Virgil." In *The Legacy of Rome: A New Appraisal,* ed. Richard Jenkyns, 125–50. Oxford: Oxford UP, 1992.

Griffiths, Frederick T. *Theocritus at Court.* Leiden: Brill, 1979.

Grosses Vollständiges Universal Lexikon. Vol. 13. Leipzig and Halle: Zedler, 1735.

Grumach, Ernst. *Goethe und die Antike: Eine Sammlung.* 2 vols. Berlin: Walter de Gruyter, 1949.

Haecker, Theodor. *Vergil, Vater des Abendlandes.* Leipzig: Hegner, 1931.

Hafner, German. *Die Laokoon-Gruppen: Ein gordischer Knoten.* Akademie der Wissenschaften und der Literatur 5. Stuttgart: Steiner, 1992.

Hagedorn, Friedrich von. *Poetische Werke.* 3 vols. Hamburg: Bohn, 1769.

Haller, Albrecht von. *Die Alpen und andere Gedichte.* Selected by Adalbert Elschenbroich. Stuttgart: Reclam, 1965.

Halperin, David. *Before Pastoral: Theocritus and the Ancient Tradition of Bucolic Poetry.* New Haven: Yale UP, 1983.

Hammer, A. E. *German Grammar and Usage.* Baltimore: Arnold, 1983.

Hämmerling, Gerhard. *Die Idylle von Geßner bis Voß: Theorie, Kritik und allgemeine geschichtliche Bedeutung.* Europäische Hochschulschriften, Reihe 1: Deutsche Sprache und Literatur. Frankfurt am Main: Peter Lang, 1981.

Hardenberg, Friedrich von (Novalis). *Schriften.* Edited by Paul Kluckhohn and Richard Samuel. 5 vols. Stuttgart: Kohlhammer Verlag, 1960–88.

Harrison, S. J. "Some Views of the *Aeneid* in the Twentieth Century." In *Oxford Readings in Vergil's "Aeneid,"* ed. S. J. Harrison, 1–20. Oxford: Oxford UP, 1990.

Harsdörffer, Georg Philipp. *Poetischer Trichter.* 3 vols. in 1. 1647–53. Facsimile repr. Hildesheim: Georg Olms, 1971.

Haslinger, Josef. *Die Ästhetik des Novalis.* Literatur in der Geschichte, Geschichte in der Literatur 5. Edited by Friedbert Aspetsberger and Alois Brandstetter. Königstein/Ts: Hain, 1981.

Hatfield, Henry. *Aesthetic Paganism in German Literature: From Winckelmann to the Death of Goethe.* Cambridge: Harvard UP, 1964.

———. *Winckelmann and His German Critics.* Morningside Heights, NY: King's Crown, 1943.

Heck, Eberhard, and Ernst A. Schmidt, eds. *Res humanae — res divinae.* Heidelberg: Winter, 1990.

Heeren, Arnold Hermann Ludwig. *Christian Gottlob Heyne.* Göttingen: Johann Friedrich Röwer, 1813.

Hegel, Georg Friedrich Wilhelm. "Vorlesungen über die Aesthetik." In *Sämtliche Werke,* ed. Hermann Glockner. Jubiläumsausgabe. Vol. 14. Stuttgart: Frommanns, 1928.

Heinze, Richard. *Virgils epische Technik.* 3rd ed. 1915. Facsimile repr. Darmstadt: Wissenschaftliche Buchgesellschaft, 1982.

Hentschel, Uwe. "Salomon Geßners *Idyllen* und ihre deutsche Rezeption im 18. und beginnenden 19. Jahrhundert." *Orbis Litterarum* 54 (1999): 332–39.

Herder, Johann Gottfried. *Sämtliche Werke.* Edited by Bernhard Suphan. 33 vols. 1877–1913. Facsimile repr. Hildesheim & New York: Georg Olms Verlag, 1967.

———. *Werke.* Edited by Martin Bollacher, Jürgen Brummack, Christoph Bultmann, Ulrich Gaier, Gunter E. Grimm, Hans Dietrich Irmscher, Rudolf Smend, and Johannes Wallmann. 10 vols. Frankfurt am Main: Deutscher Klassiker Verlag, 1985–2000.

Herf, Jeffrey. *Reactionary Modernism: Technology, Culture and Politics in Weimar and the Third Reich.* Cambridge: Cambridge UP, 1984.

Hermand, Jost, and Reinhold Grimm. *Die Klassik-Legende.* Frankfurt am Main: Athenäum, 1971.

Heuer, Otto. Introduction to *Idyllen,* by Maler Müller. Edited by Otto Heuer. Vol. 1 of 3. Leipzig: K. Wolff, 1914.

Heyne, Christian Gottlob, ed. *Opera,* by Publius Vergilius Maro. 1st ed. 4 vols. Leipzig: Fritsch, 1767–75.

———, ed. *Opera,* by Publius Vergilius Maro. 2nd rev. ed. 4 vols. Leipzig: Caspar Fritsch, 1787–89.

Hiebel, Friedrich. *Novalis: Deutscher Dichter, europäischer Denker, christlicher Seher.* 2nd rev. ed. Bern: Francke, 1972.

Hilliard, Kevin. *Philosophy, Letters, and the Fine Arts in Klopstock's Thought.* London: Institute of Germanic Studies, U of London, 1987.

Hölderlin, Friedrich. *Sämtliche Werke.* Edited by Friedrich Beissner. Stuttgarter Ausgabe, im Auftrag des württembergischen Kultministeriums. 8 vols. Stuttgart: J. G. Cottasche Buchhandlung Nachfolger, 1944–85.

Homer. *Opera Iliadis.* Edited by David B. Monro and Thomas W. Allen. 3rd ed. 2 vols. Oxford Classical Texts. Oxford: Oxford UP, 1920.

Horcheimer, Max, and Theodor Adorno. *Dialektik der Aufklarung.* 1944. Repr. Amsterdam: Querido, 1947.

Horsfall, Nicholas, ed. *A Companion to the Study of Virgil.* Leiden: Brill, 1995.

Hubbard, Thomas K. *The Pipes of Pan.* Ann Arbor: Michigan UP, 1998.

Hugo, Victor. *Oeuvres Complètes.* Edited by the Centre National des Lettres and Jacques Seebacher et al. 15 vols. Paris: Robert Laffont, 1985–.

Humboldt, Wilhelm von. *Gesammelte Schriften*. Edited by der Königlichen Preussischen Akademie der Wissenschaften. 17 vols. 1903–36. Facsimile repr. Berlin: de Gruyter, 1968.

Hunter, Richard L. *Theocritus: A Selection*. Cambridge: Cambridge UP, 1999.

———. *Theocritus and the Archaeology of Greek Poetry*. Cambridge: Cambridge UP, 1996.

Irmscher, Johannes, ed. *Winckelmanns Wirkung auf seine Zeit: Lessing, Herder, Heyne*. Stendal: Winckelmann Gesellschaft, 1988.

Jauss, Hans Robert. "Ästhetische Normen und geschichtliche Reflexion in der 'Querelle des Anciens et des Modernes.'" In *Parallèle des anciens et des modernes en ce qui regarde les arts et les sciences*, by Charles Perrault, ed. Max Imdahl, Wolfgang Iser, Hans Robert Jauss, Wolfgang Preisendanz, and Jurij Striedter, 8–65. Munich: Eidos, 1964.

———. *Literaturgeschichte als Provokation*. Frankfurt am Main: Suhrkamp, 1970.

———. "Schlegels und Schillers Replik auf die 'Querelle des Anciens et des Modernes.'" In *Literaturgeschichte als Provokation*, 67–106.

Johnson, Samuel. "On Pastoral and Country Life." In *The Pastoral Mode: A Casebook*, ed. Bryan Loughrey, 67–71. London, Macmillan, 1984.

Johnson, W. R. *Darkness Visible*. Berkeley: U of California P, 1976.

Justi, Carl. "Ein Manuscript über die Statuen im Belvedere." *Preussische Jahrbücher* 28 (1871): 581–609.

———. *Winckelmann und seine Zeitgenossen*. Edited by Walter Rehm. 5th ed. 2 vols. Cologne: Phaidon, 1956.

Kaiser, Gerhard. *Klopstock: Religion und Dichtung*. Gütersloh: Mohn, 1963.

———. *Wandrer und Idylle: Goethe und die Phänomenologie der Natur in der deutschen Dichtung von Geßner bis Gottfried Keller*. Göttingen: Vandenhoeck & Ruprecht, 1977.

Kallendorf, Craig. *In Praise of Aeneas: Virgil and Epideictic Rhetoric in the Early Italian Renaissance*. Hanover and London: UP of New England, 1989.

Kant, Immanuel. *Gesammelte Schriften*. Edited by the Königliche Preußische Akademie der Wissenschaften. 29 vols. Berlin: Georg Reimer, 1902-.

Kegel-Brinkgreve, E. *The Echoing Woods: Bucolic and Pastoral from Theocritus and Wordsworth*. Amsterdam: J. C. Gieben, 1990.

Keller, William Jacob. "Goethe's Estimate of the Greek and Latin Writers." *Bulletin of the University of Wisconsin*. Philology and Literature Series 6 (1916): 1–129.

Kennedy, Duncan F. "Virgilian Epic." In *The Cambridge Companion to Virgil*, ed. Martindale, 145–54.

Klemperer, Victor. "Romanische Literaturen." *Reallexikon der deutschen Literaturgeschichte*, ed. Paul Merker and Wolfgang Stammler, 3:74–107. Berlin: de Gruyter, 1928–29.

Klingner, Friedrich. "Die Einheit des virgilischen Lebenswerkes." *Mitteilungen des Deutschen Archäologischen Instituts, Römische Abteilung* 45 (1930): 43–58. Repr. in Klingner, *Römische Geisteswelt*, 274–92.

———. "Das erste Hirtengedicht Virgils." *Hermes* 62 (1927): 129–53, Repr. in Klingner, *Römische Geisteswelt*, 312–26.

———. "Liebeselegien: Goethes römische Vorbilder." In *Römische Geisteswelt*. Friedrich Klingner. 3rd enlarged ed. Munich. H. Rinn, 1956. Repr. in Klinger, *Römische Geisteswelt*, 419–29.

———. *Römische Geisteswelt*. 5th enlarged ed. Munich: Ellermann, 1965.

———. *Virgil*. Zurich and Stuttgart: Artemis, 1967.

———. "Virgil und die geschichtliche Welt." In *Römische Geisteswelt*. Friedrich Klingner. 2nd enlarged ed., 155–76. Wiesbaden: Dieterich, [1952]. Repr. in Klingner, *Römische Geisteswelt*, 293–311.

———. "Virgil: Wiederentdeckung eines Dichters." In *Das neue Bild der Antike,* ed. Helmut Berve, 219–45. Leipzig: Koehler and Amelang, 1942. Repr. in Klingner, *Römische Geisteswelt*, 239–73.

Klopstock, Friedrich Gottlieb. *Ausgewählte Werke*. Edited by Karl August Schleiden. Afterword by Friedrich Georg Jünger. Munich: Hanser, 1962.

———. *Sämmtliche Werke*. Edited by A. L. Back and A. R. C. Spindler. 18 vols. Leipzig: Fleischer, 1823–30.

———. *Werke und Briefe*. Edited by Adolf Beck et al. Hamburger Klopstock-Ausgabe. 13 vols. Berlin: Walter de Gruyter, 1974-.

Knight, W. F. Jackson, trans. *The Aeneid*. Virgil. Baltimore: Penguin, 1958.

Koepke, Wulf. "*Kulturnation* and Its Authorization through Herder." In *Johann Gottfried Herder: Academic Disciplines and the Pursuit of Knowledge,* 177–98.

———, ed. *Johann Gottfried Herder: Academic Disciplines and the Pursuit of Knowledge*. Columbia, SC: Camden House, 1996.

Kohl, Katrin. *Friedrich Gottlieb Klopstock*. Sammlung Metzler 325. Stuttgart: Metzler, 2000.

Korff, Hermann August. *Geist der Goethezeit*. 5 vols. Leipzig: Hirzel, 1923–57.

Körte, Wilhelm, ed. *Briefe der Schweizer Bodmer, Sulzer, Geßner: aus Gleims litterarischem Nachlasse*. Zurich: Heinrich Gessner, 1804.

Kortum, Hans. "Die Hintergründe einer Akademiesitzung im Jahre 1687." In *Antike und Moderne in der Literaturdiskussion des 18. Jahrhunderts,* ed. Krauss and Kortum, lxi-cxi.

Krauss, Werner. "Die französische Aufklärung und die deutsche Geisteswelt." In *Perspektiven und Probleme: Zur französischen und deutschen Aufklärung und andere Aufsätze,* 121–265. Luchterhand: Berlin, 1965.

———. "Der Streit der Altertumsfreunde mit den Anhängern der Moderne und die Entstehung des geschichtlichen Weltbildes." In *Antike und Moderne in der Literaturdiskussion des 18. Jahrhunderts,* ed. Krauss and Kortum, ix–lx.

Krauss, Werner. "Über die Stellung der Bukolik in der Theorie des Humanismus." *Archiv für das Studium der Neueren Sprachen* 174 (1938): 68–93. Repr. in Garber, *Europäische Georgik und Bukolik*, 140–64.

Krauss, Werner, and Hans Kortum, eds. *Antike und Moderne in der Literaturdiskussion des 18. Jahrhunderts.* Berlin: Akademie Verlag, 1966.

Leach, Eleanor Windsor. *Vergil's "Eclogues": Landscapes of Experience.* Ithaca: Cornell UP, 1974.

Lessing, Gotthold Ephraim. *Gesammelte Werke.* Edited by Wolfgang Stammler. 2 vols. Munich: Hanser, 1959.

———. *Werke und Briefe.* Edited by Wilfried Barner together with Klaus Bohnen, Gunter E. Grimm, Helmuth Kiesel, Arno Schilson, Jürgen Stenzel, and Conrad Wiedemann. 12 vols. Frankfurt am Main: Deutscher Klassiker Verlag, 1985–2003.

Leventhal, Robert S. *The Disciplines of Interpretation: Lessing, Herder, Schlegel and Hermeneutics in Germany, 1750–1800.* Berlin: De Gruyter, 1994.

Lewis, C. Day. *The Eclogues of Virgil.* London: Jonathan Cape, 1963.

Lewis, C. S. "Virgil and the Subject of Secondary Epic." In *A Preface to Paradise Lost.* Oxford: Oxford UP, 1954. Repr. in *Virgil: A Collection of Critical Essays*, ed. Commager, 62–67.

Lichtenberg, Georg Christoph. *Aphorismen, Essays, Briefe.* Edited by Kurt Batt. Sammlung Dietrich 260. Bremen: Schünemann, 1963.

Low, Anthony. *The Georgic Revolution.* Princeton: Princeton UP, 1985.

Mackail, J. W., trans. *Virgil's Works.* Introduction by Charles L. Durham. The Modern Library. New York: Random House, 1934.

Madelénat, Daniel. "Allemagne." In *Dictionnaire des littératures de langue française*, ed. Jean-Pierre de Beaumarchais, Daniel Couty, and Alain Rey, 1:33–36. 2nd ed. Paris: Bordas, 1994.

Mähl, Hans-Joachim. *Die Idee des goldenen Zeitalters im Werk des Novalis.* Heidelberg: Carl Winter, 1965.

Marchand, Suzanne L. *Down from Olympus: Archaeology and Philhellenism in Germany, 1750–1970.* Princeton: Princeton UP, 1996.

Martin, Dieter. *Das deutsche Versepos im 18. Jahrhundert.* Berlin: de Gruyter, 1993.

Martindale, Charles, ed. *The Cambridge Companion to Virgil.* Cambridge: Cambridge UP, 1997.

———. "The Classic of All Europe." Introduction: to *The Cambridge Companion to Virgil*, 1–18.

———. Introduction to *Virgil and His Influence: Bimillenial Studies,* ed. Charles Martindale, 1–24. Bristol: Bristol Classical P, 1984.

Mayer, Hans. "Wielands 'Oberon.'" In *Zur deutschen Klassik und Romantik.* Pfullingen: Neske, 1963. 30–47, 359. Repr. in Schelle, *Christoph Martin Wieland*, 189–204.

McCarthy, John A. *Christoph Martin Wieland.* Twayne World Author Series 528. Boston: Twayne Publishers, 1979.

Meinecke, Friedrich. *Die Entstehung des Historicismus.* Edited by Carl Hinrichs. 1936. Repr. Munich: Oldenbourg, 1959.

Mendelssohn, Moses. "Briefe, der neuesten Literatur betreffend" (nos. 85–86, 1760). In *Gesammelte Schriften,* vol. 5, ed. Eva J. Engel, 138–47. Stuttgart-Bad Cannstatt: Frommann-Holzboog, 1991.

Mettler, Werner. *Der junge Friedrich Schlegel und die griechische Literatur.* Zurich: Atlantis, 1955.

Miller, Norbert. "Winckelmann und der Griechenstreit: Überlegungen zur Historisierung der Antiken-Anschauung im 18. Jahrhundert." In *Johann Joachim Winckelmann, 1717–1768,* ed. Gaehtgens, 239–64.

Milton, John. *Paradise Lost: A Poem in Twelve Books.* Edited by Merritt Y. Hughes. Indianapolis: Odyssey, 1962.

Möllendorf, Klemens. "Die Idyllen des Maler Müllers." *Euphorion* 40 (1939): 145–57.

Moritz, Karl Philipp. *Werke.* Edited by Jürgen Hahn. Bibliothek deutscher Klassiker. 2 vols. Berlin and Weimar: Aufbau-Verlag, 1973.

Morrison, Jeffery. *Winckelmann and the Notion of Aesthetic Education.* Oxford: Clarendon Press, 1996.

Müller, Friedrich (Maler). *Idyllen.* Edited with an afterword by Peter-Erich Neuser. Stuttgart: Reclam, 1977.

Müller, Heiner. *Germania Tod in Berlin.* Berlin: Rotbuch Verlag, 1977.

Muncker, Franz. *Friedrich Gottlieb Klopstock: Geschichte seines Lebens und seiner Schriften.* Berlin: Behr, 1893.

———. "Über einige Vorbilder für Klopstocks Dichtungen." *Sitzungsberichte der philosophisch-philologischen und der historischen Klasse der königlichen bayerischen Akademie* 6 (1908): 3–33.

Niebuhr, Barthold Georg. *Vorträge über die römische Geschichte an der Universität zu Bonn gehalten.* Edited by Myer Isler. 3 vols. Berlin: Reimer, 1846–48. In English, *Lectures of the History of Rome from the Earliest Times to the Fall of the Western Empire.* Edited and translated by Leonhard Schmitz. 1844. Rev. 4th ed. London: Lockwood, 1873.

Nietzsche, Friedrich. *Sämtliche Werke.* Kritische Studienausgabe. Edited by Giorgio Colli und Mazzino Montinari. 1967–77. 15 vols. Repr. Munich: Deutscher Taschenbuch Verlag; Berlin; New York; de Gruyter, 1999.

Nitchie, Elizabeth. *Vergil and the English Poets.* New York: Columbia UP, 1919.

Norden, Eduard. *Die Geburt des Kindes: Die Geschichte einer religiösen Idee.* Leipzig: Teubner, 1924.

Norton, Robert E. *Herder's Aesthetics and the European Enlightenment.* Ithaca, NY: Cornell UP, 1991.

Oesterlen, Theodor. "Vergil in Schillers Gedichten." In *Studien zu Vergil und Horaz,* 6–15. Tübingen: F. Fues, 1885.

Oppermann, Hans. *Vergil.* Frankfurt am Main: Verlag Moritz Diesterweg. Repr. in *Wege zu Vergil: Drei Jahrzehnte Begegnungen in Dichtung und Wissenschaft,* 93–176.

Oppermann, Hans. ed. *Wege zu Vergil: Drei Jahrzehnte Begegnungen in Dichtung und Wissenschaft*. Wege der Forschung 19. Darmstadt: Wissenschaftliche Buchgesellschaft, 1963.

Otis, Brooks. *Eclogues, Virgil: A Study in Civilized Poetry*. Oxford: Clarendon Press, 1963.

Panofsky, Erwin. "*Et in Arcadia ego:* Poussin und die elegische Tradition." In *Meaning in the Visual Arts: Papers in and on Art History*, 295–320. New York: Doubleday, 1955. Repr. in Garber, *Europäische Bukolik und Georgik*, 271–305.

Parker, Kevin. "Winckelmann, Historical Difference, and the Problem of the Boy." *Eighteenth Century Studies*. 25.4 (1992): 523–44.

Parry, Adam. "The Two Voices of Virgil's *Aeneid*." *Arion*. II.4 (Winter 1963). 66–80. Repr. in Commager, *Virgil: A Collection of Critical Essays*, 107–23.

Patey, Douglas Lane. "Ancient and Moderns." In *The Cambridge History of Literary Criticism*, ed. H. B. Nisbett and Claude Rawson, 4:32–74. Cambridge: Cambridge UP, 1997.

Patterson, Annabel. *Pastoral and Ideology: Virgil to Valéry*. Berkeley, Los Angeles: U of California P, 1987.

Paul, Jean. *Werke*. Edited by Norbert Miller. 6 vols. Munich: Carl Hanser Verlag, 1959–63.

Paulsen, Friedrich. *Geschichte des gelehrten Unterrichts auf den deutschen Schulen und Universitäten vom Ausgang des Mittelalters bis zur Gegenwart*. Edited by Rudolf Lehman. 3rd enlarged ed. 2 vols. Vol. 1. Leipzig: Veit, 1919; vol. 2. Berlin & Leipzig: Walter de Gruyter, 1921.

Perrault, Charles. "Le Siècle de Louis le Grand." In *Parallèle des Anciens et des Modernes*. 2nd ed. 1692–97. Facsimile repr. Geneve: Slatkine Reprints, 1971.

Peucker, Brigitte. *Arcadia to Elysium: Preromantic Modes in the 18th Century*. Bonn: Bouvier, 1980.

Pfeiffer, Rudolf. *History of Classical Scholarship: From 1300 to 1850*. Oxford: Oxford UP, 1976.

Pfotenhauer, Helmut, Markus Bernauer, and Norbert Miller with the assistance of Thomas Franke, eds. *Frühklassizismus: Position und Opposition: Winckelmann, Mengs, Heinse*. Bibliothek der Kunstliteratur 2. Frankfurt am Main: Deutscher Klassiker Verlag, 1995.

Pickering, F. P. "Der zierlichen Bilder Verknüpfung: Goethes 'Alexis und Dora — 1796.'" *Euphorion* 52 (1958): 341–55.

Poggioli, Renato. *The Oaten Flute*. Cambridge: Harvard UP, 1975.

Pope, Alexander. *The Poems of Alexander Pope*. Edited by John Butt. 11 vols. London: Methuen, 1939–69.

Pöschl, Viktor. "Das befremdende in der Aeneis." In *2000 Jahre Vergil: Ein Symposium*, ed. Viktor Pöschl. 175–88. Wiesbaden: in Kommission bei Otto Harrassowitz, 1983.

———. *Die Dichtkunst Virgils: Bild und Symbol in der Äneis*. 2nd rev. ed. Darmstadt: Wissenschaftliche Buchgesellschaft, 1964.

Pöschl, Viktor. *Die Hirtendichtung Virgils.* Heidelberg: Winter, 1964.

Potts, Alex. *Flesh and the Ideal: Winckelmann and the Origins of Art History.* New Haven: Yale UP, 1994.

Powers, Elizabeth. "The Artist's Escape from the Idyll: The Relation of Werther to Sesenheim." *Goethe Yearbook* 9 (1999): 47–76.

Preiß, Bettina. *Die wissenschaftliche Beschäftigung mit der Laokoongruppe.* Bonn: VDG Verlag, 1992.

Propertius, Sextus. *Elegies I–IV.* Edited by Lawrence Richardson. Norman: U of Oklahoma P, 1976.

Putnam, Michael C. J. *The Poetry of the Aeneid.* Cambridge: Harvard UP, 1965.

———. *Virgils Pastoral Art: Studies in the "Eclogues."* Princeton, NJ: Princeton UP, 1970.

Pyra, Immanuel Jacob, and Samuel Gotthold Lange. *Freundschaftliche Lieder.* Edited by August Sauer. Deutsche Litteraturdenkmale des 18. und 19. Jahrhunderts in Neudrucken 22. Stuttgart: G. J. Göschen, 1885.

Rach, Alfred. *Biographien zur deutschen Erziehungsgeschichte.* Weinheim and Berlin: Beltz, 1968.

Ramler, Carl Wilhelm, trans. *Einleitung in die schönen Wissenschaften,* by Charles Batteaux. Vol. 2. Leipzig: 1756.

Rapin, René. *Eclogae sacrae cum dissertatione de carmine pastorali.* Rev. and enlarged. ed. Vol. 1. Paris: 1723.

Rehm, Walter. *Europäische Romdichtung.* Munich: Hueber, 1960.

———. *Griechentum und Goethezeit: Geschichte eines Glaubens.* Leipzig: Dieterich'sche Verlagsbuchhandlung, 1936.

———. *Orpheus: Der Dichter und die Toten.* Düsseldorf: Schwann, 1950.

Reill, Peter Hanns. *The German Enlightenment and the Rise of Historicism.* Berkeley: U of California P, 1975.

Richter, Simon. *Laocoon's Body and the Aesthetics of Pain: Winckelmann, Lessing, Herder, Moritz, Goethe.* Detroit: Wayne State UP, 1992.

Riedel, Volker. *Antikerezeption in der deutschen Literatur vom Renaissance-Humanismus bis zur Gegenwart.* Stuttgart: Metzler, 2000.

———, ed. *Federlese: Beiträge zu Werk und Wirken von Johann Heinrich Voß.* Neubrandenburg: Literaturzentrum Neubrandenburg, 1989.

Rigault, H. *Histoire de la querelle des anciens et des modernes.* 1859. Repr. New York: Burt Franklin, 1965.

Rosenmeyer, Thomas G. *The Green Cabinet.* Berkeley: U of California P, 1969.

Rüdiger, Horst. "Winckelmanns Geschichtsauffassung: Ein Dresdner Entwurf als Keimzelle seines historischen Denkens." *Euphorion.* 62.2 (1968): 99–116.

Sainte-Beuve, Charles Augustin. *Étude sur Virgile.* Edited by Calmann Lévy. Paris: Lévy Frères, 1891.

Samuel, Richard. "Novalis." In *Der deutsche Roman vom Barock bis zur Gegenwart: Struktur und Geschichte,* ed. Benno von Wiese, 1:252–300. Düsseldorf: Bagel, 1963.

Sandys, John Edwin. *A History of Classical Scholarship*. 2nd rev. ed. 3 vols. Cambridge: Cambridge UP, 1906–8.

Sauder, Gerhard, Rolf Paulus, and Christoph Weiß, eds. *Maler Müller in neuer Sicht*. Saarbrücker Beiträge zur Literaturwissenschaft 24. St. Ingebert: Röhrig, 1990.

Sauer, August, ed. *Der Göttinger Dichterbund: Johann Heinrich Voss*. Deutsche National-Litteratur 49. Vol. 1 of 3. Berlin: Spemann, 1886.

Scaliger, Julius Caesar. *Poetices libri septem*. Edited by Luc Deitz and Gregor Vogt-Spira. 5 vols. Stuttgart: Friedrich Frommann Verlag, 1994–98.

Schadewalt, Wolfgang. "Goethes Beschäftigung mit der Antike." In *Goethe und die Antike: Eine Sammlung,* ed. Ernst Grumach, 2:971–1050. Berlin: Walter de Gruyter, 1949.

Schelle, Hansjörg, ed. *Christoph Martin Wieland*. Wege der Forschung 421. Darmstadt: Wissenschaftliche Buchgesellschaft, 1981.

Schelling, Karoline. *Caroline: Briefe aus der Frühromantik*. Edited by Erich Schmidt. 2 vols. Leipzig: Insel, 1913.

Schiller, Johann Christoph Friedrich. *Schillers Werke*. Nationalausgabe, im Auftrag des Goethe- und Schiller-Archivs, des Schiller-Nationalmuseums und der Deutschen Akademie. Gen. ed. Julius Petersen and Gerhard Fricke. 35 vols. Weimar: Böhlaus Nachfolger, 1943-.

Schindel, Ulrich. "C. G. Heyne." In *Classical Scholarship: A Biographical Encyclopedia,* ed. Ward W. Briggs and William M. Calder III, 176–82. Garland Reference Library of the Humanities 928. New York: Garland, 1990.

———. "Johann Matthias Gesner, Professor der Poesie und Beredsamkeit 1734–1761." In *Die Klassische Altertumswissenschaft an der Georg-August-Universität Göttingen,* ed. Carl Joachim Classen, 9–27. Göttingen: Vandenhoeck & Ruprecht, 1989.

Schlegel, August Wilhelm. *Kritische Ausgabe der Vorlesungen*. Edited by Ernst Behler. 1 vol. Paderborn: Schöningh, 1989.

———. *Kritische Schriften*. Edited by Emil Staiger. Zurich: Artemis Verlag, 1962.

Schlegel, Friedrich. *Kritische Friedrich-Schlegel-Ausgabe*. Edited by Ernst Behler with the assistance of Jean-Jacques Anstett and Hans Eichner, vols. 1–14, 16–25, 29–30, 33, 35. Munich: F. Schöningh, 1958-.

Schlegel, Johann Adolf, trans. "Von dem eigentlichen Gegenstand der Schäferpoesie." *Traité des beaux arts reduits à un même principe,* by Charles Batteux. 2nd rev. ed. Leipzig: Weidmannische Buchhandlung, 1759. Repr. in *Deutsche Idyllentheorie im 18. Jahrhundert,* ed. Helmut J. Schneider, 111–54. Tübingen: Narr Verlag, 1988.

Schmidt, Thomas. "Deutsche National-Philologie oder Neuphilologie in Deutschland? Internationalität und Interdisziplinarität in der Frühgeschichte der Germanistik." In *Internationalität nationaler Literaturen,* ed. Udo Schöning, 311–40. Göttingen: Wallstein, 2000.

Schneider, Helmut J. "Johann Heinrich Voss." In *Deutsche Dichter des 18. Jahrhunderts: Ihr Leben und Werke,* ed. Benno von Wiese, 782–815.

Schneider, Helmut J., ed. *Deutsche Idyllentheorien im 18. Jahrhundert.* Deutsche Text-Bibliothek 1. Tübingen: Gunter Narr Verlag, 1988.

———, ed. *Idyllen der Deutschen.* Frankfurt am Main: Insel, 1978.

Schneider, Karl Ludwig. *Klopstock und die Erneuerung der deutschen Dichtersprache im 18. Jahrhundert.* Heidelberg: Winter, 1960.

Schneider, Martin. "Novalis und Karamsin: Eine These zur Herkunft des Atlantis-Märchens im 'Heinrich von Ofterdingen.'" *Arcadia: Eine Zeitschrift für vergleichende Literaturwissenschaft* 19 (1984): 285–87.

Schöne, Albrecht. *Götterzeichen, Liebeszauber, Satanskult: Neue Einblicke in alte Goethetexte.* Munich: Beck, 1982.

Schulenburg, Sigrid von der. *Leibniz als Sprachforscher.* Veröffentlichungen des Leibniz-Archivs 4. Frankfurt am Main: Klostermann, 1973.

Schulz, Eberhard Wilhelm, "Winckelmanns Schreibart." In *Studien zur Goethezeit: Erich Trunz zum 75. Geburtstag,* ed. Hans-Joachim Mähl and Eberhard Mannack, 233–55. Heidelberg: Carl Winter, 1981.

Segal, Charles. "Landscape into Myth: Theocritus' Bucolic Poetry." *Ramus* 4 (1975): 115–39. Repr. in Segal, *Poetry and Myth in Ancient Pastoral,* 210–30.

———. *Poetry and Myth in Ancient Pastoral.* Princeton: Princeton UP, 1981.

———. "'since Daphnis Dies': The Meaning of Theocritus' First Idyll." *Museum Helveticum* 34 (1974): 1–22. Repr. in Segal, *Poetry and Myth in Ancient Pastoral,* 25–46.

Seibt, Gustav. "Die unnachahmlichen Nachahmer: Das seltsame Verhältnis der Deutschen zu den Griechen; Wie eine verspätete Nation den Zauber der Frühe suchte." *Die Zeit.* Zeitliteratur, Sonderbeilage, 4. Oct. 2001 (41), 55.

Sellar, W. Y. *The Roman Poets of the Augustan Age: Virgil.* 2nd ed. Oxford: Clarendon, 1883.

———. "Virgil." In *Encyclopaedia Britannica.* 9th edition. 24:248–55.

Semrau, Eberhard. *Dido in der deutschen Dichtung.* Stoff- und Motivgeschichte der deutschen Literatur 9. Edited by Paul Merker and Gerhard Lüdtke. Berlin & Leipzig: De Gruyter, 1930.

Sengle, Friedrich. "Von Wielands Epenfragmenten zum 'Oberon.'" In *Festschrift Paul Kluckhohn und Hermann Schneider, gewidmet zu ihrem 60. Geburtstag,* ed. their Tübingen students, 266–85. Tübingen: J. C. B. Mohr, 1948. Repr. in Schelle, *Christoph Martin Wieland,* 45–66.

———. *Wieland.* Stuttgart: Metzler, 1949.

———. "Wunschbild Land und Schreckbild Stadt: Zu einem zentralen Thema der neueren deutschen Literatur." *Studium Generale.* 16 (1963): 619–31. Repr. in Garber, *Europäische Bukolik und Georgik,* 432–60.

Servius, Grammarius. *Servii Grammatici qui feruntur in Vergilii carmina commentarii.* Edited by Georg Thilo and Hermann Hagen. 3 vols. Leipzig: Teubner, 1881–1902.

Seuffert, Bernhard. "Prolegomena zu einer Wieland-Ausgabe VI." *Abhandlungen der königlichen preussischen Akademie der Wissenschaften.* Phil.-historische Klasse. Anhang, Abhandlung 1 (1909): 1–110.

Snell, Bruno. "Arkadien, die Entdeckung einer geistigen Landschaft." In *Die Entdeckung des Geistes: Studien zur Entstehung des europäischen Denkens bei den Griechen*, 233–58. Hamburg: Classen & Goverts, 1946. Repr. in Oppermann, *Wege zu Vergil: Drei Jahrzehnte Begegnungen in Dichtung und Wissenschaft*, 338–67.

Spargo, John Webster. *Virgil the Neocromancer.* Cambridge: Harvard UP, 1934.

Staiger, Emil. "Wieland: 'Musarion.'" In *Wieland: Vier Biberacher Vorträge 1953*, 35–54. Wiesbaden: Insel Verlag, 1954. Repr. in Schelle, *Christoph Martin Wieland*, 93–108.

Starnes, Thomas C. *Christoph Martin Wieland: Leben und Werke aus zeitgenössischen Quellen chronologisch dargestellt.* 3 vols. Sigmaringen: Thorbecke, 1987.

Streller, Siegfried. "Zeitkritik und bürgerliches Selbstbewußtsein in Voß' Idyllendichtung." In *Federlese: Beiträge zu Werk und Wirken von Johann Heinrich Voß*, ed. Riedel, 13–19.

Suerbaum, Werner. "V. Maro, P." In *Der neue Pauly: Enzyklopädie der Antike*, ed. Hubert Cancik and Helmuth Schneider, 12/2:42–60. Stuttgart; Weimar: Metzler, 2002.

———. *Vergils "Aeneis": Beiträge zu ihrer Rezeption in Gegenwart und Geschichte.* Bamberg: Buchners Verlag, 1981.

———. *Vergils "Aeneis": Epos zwischen Geschichte und Gegenwart.* Stuttgart: Reclam, 1999.

———. "Vita Vergiliana — accessus Vergiliani — Zauberer Virgilius." In *Aufstieg und Niedergang der römischen Welt*, ed. Hildegard Temporini and Wolfgang Haase, 31/2:1156–262. Berlin: Walter de Gruyter, 1981.

Sulzer, Johann Georg. *Allgemeine Theorie der schönen Künste.* 5 vols. 1771. Repr. Leipzig: Weidmanns Erben & Reich, 1773.

Szondi, Peter. "Antike und Moderne in der Ästhetik der Goethezeit." In *Poetik und Geschichtsphilosophie* 1, ed. Senta Metz and Hans-Hagen Hildebrandt. Frankfurt am Main: Suhrkamp, 1974. 2:1–265.

Tennyson, Alfred. *The Poems of Tennyson.* Edited by Christopher Ricks. Berkeley: U of California P, 1987.

Theocritus. *Select Poems.* Edited by K. J. Dover. London: Macmillan, 1971.

———. *Theocritus.* Edited with a translation and commentary by A. S. F. Gow. 2 vols. Cambridge: Cambridge UP, 1950.

Thomas, Richard F. *Virgil and the Augustan Reception.* Cambridge: Cambridge UP, 2001.

Turner, Frank M. "Why the Greeks and not the Romans?" In *Rediscovering Hellenism: the Hellenic Inheritance and the English Imagination*, ed. G. W. Clarke, 61–82. Cambridge: Cambridge UP, 1989.

Uhlig, Ludwig. "Schiller und Winckelmann." *Jahrbuch für internationale Germanistik* 17.1 (1985): 131–46.

Uz, Johann Peter. *Sämtliche poetische Werke.* Edited by August Sauer. Deutsche Litteraturdenkmale des 18. und 19. Jahrhunderts in Neudrucken 33. Stuttgart: G. J. Göschen'sche Verlagshandlung, 1890.

Vance, Norman. "Virgil and the Nineteenth Century." In Martindale, *Virgil and His Influence: Bimillenial Studies,* 169–92.

Vergilius Maro, Publius. *A Commentary on Virgil, Eclogues.* Edited by Wendell Clausen. Oxford: Clarendon, 1994.

———. *Eclogues.* Edited by R. Coleman. Cambridge Greek and Latin Classics. Cambridge: Cambridge UP, 1977.

———. *Georgics.* Edited by Richard F. Thomas. Cambridge Greek and Latin Classics. 2 vols. Cambridge: Cambridge UP, 1988.

———. *Opera.* Edited with a commentary by John Conington and Henry Nettleship. 3 vols. London: Whitaker, 1858–71.

———. *Opera.* Edited with a commentary by Christian Gottlob Heyne. 1st ed. 4 vols. Leipzig: Fritsch, 1767–75.

———. *Opera.* Edited with a commentary by Christian Gottlob Heyne. 2nd ed. 4 vols. Leipzig: Fritsch, 1787–89.

———. *Opera.* Edited by R. A. B. Mynors. Oxford Classical Texts. Oxford: Oxford UP, 1969.

Vida, Marco Girolamo. *The "De arte poetica" of Marco Girolamo Vida.* Translated with commentary by Ralph G. Williams. New York: Columbia UP, 1976.

Vitae Vergilianae antiquae. Edited by Giorgio Brugnoli and Fabio Stok. Rome: Typis Officinae Polygraphicae, 1997.

Voerster, Erika. *Märchen und Novellen im klassischen-romantischen Roman.* Bonn: Bouvier, 1966.

Voltaire. "Essai sur la poésie épique." In *The Complete Works of Voltaire,* ed. Ulla Köving, 3B: 415–98. Oxford: Voltaire Foundation, 1968.

Vormbaum, Reinhold, ed. *Evangelische Schulordnungen.* Vol. 3. Gütersloh: Bertelsmann, 1864.

Voss, E. Theodor. "Arkadien und Grünau: Johann Heinrich Voss und das innere System seines Idyllenwerkes." Afterword to *Idyllen,* by Johann Heinrich Voss. 1801. Facsimile repr. Heidelberg: Lambert Schneider, 1968, 29–79. Repr. in Garber, *Europäische Bukolik und Georgik,* 391–431.

———. "Salomon Geßner." In *Deutsche Dichter des 18. Jahrhunderts,* ed. Benno von Wiese, 249–75.

Voss, Johann Heinrich. *Der Göttinger Dichterbund: Johann Heinrich Voss.* Edited by August Sauer. Deutsche National-Litteratur 49. Vol. 1 of 3. Berlin: Spemann, 1886.

———. *Werke in einem Band.* Selected and introduced by Hedwig Voegt. Berlin, Weimar: Aufbau Verlag, 1972.

Waniek, Gustav. *Immanuel Pyra und sein Einfluß auf die deutsche Litteratur des achtzehnten Jahrhunderts.* Leipzig: Breitkopf & Härtel, 1882.

Wiedemann, Conrad. "The Germans' Concern about their National Identity in the Pre-Romantic Era: An Answer to Montesquieu?" In *Concepts of National Identity: An Interdisciplinary Dialogue; Interdiisziplinäre*

Betrachtungen zur Frage der nationalen Identität, ed. Peter Boerner, 141–52. Baden-Baden: Nomos, 1986.

———. "Römische Staatsnation und griechische Kulturnation: Zum Paradigmawechsel zwischen Gottsched und Winckelmann." In *Akten des VII. Internationalen-Germanisten-Kongresses,* ed. Albrecht Schöne, 9: 173–78. Göttingen: 1985.

Wieland, Christoph Martin. *Ausgewählte Werke.* Edited by Friedrich Beißner. 3 vols. Munich: Winkler, 1964.

———. "Oberon: Ein romantisches Heldengedicht in zwölf Gesängen." In *Ausgewählte Werke.*

Wiese, Benno von, ed. *Deutsche Dichter des 18. Jahrhunderts: Ihr Leben und Werke.* Berlin: Schmidt, 1977.

Williams, R. D. *The Aeneid.* Edited by Claude Rawson. Unwin Critical Library. London: Allen & Unwin, 1987.

Winckelmann, Johann Joachim. *Gedanken über die Nachahmung der griechischen Werke in der Malerei und Bildhauerkunst.* Edited by Ludwig Uhland. Stuttgart: Reclam, 1990.

———. *Geschichte der Kunst des Alterthums.* Wiener Ausgabe 1934. Repr. Darmstadt: Wissenschaftliche Buchgesellschaft, 1972.

———. "Ein Manuscript über die Statuen im Belvedere." Edited by Carl Justi. *Preussische Jahrbücher* 28 (1871): 581–609.

Wlosok, Antonie. "Vergil in der neueren Forschung." In Heck and Schmidt, *Res humanae — res divinae,* 279–301.

———. "Zur Geltung und Beurteilung Vergils und Homers in Spätantike und früher Neuzeit." In Heck and Schmidt, *Res humanae — res divinae,* 476–98.

Wohlleben, Joachim. "Germany 1750–1830." In *Perceptions of the Ancient Greeks,* ed. K. J. Dover, 170–202. Oxford: Blackwell, 1992.

Wolf, Christa. *Kassandra.* Darmstadt: Luchterhand, 1983.

York-Gothart, Mix. "Zum Problem des Realismus in Friedrich (Maler) Müllers Idylle 'Die Schafschur.'" In *Maler Müller in neuer Sicht,* ed. Sauder, Paulus, and Weiß, 49–65.

Ziolkowski, Theodore. *The Classical German Elegy, 1795–1950.* Princeton: Princeton UP, 1980.

———. *Virgil and the Moderns.* Princeton: Princeton UP, 1993.

Index

Addison, Joseph, 18, 85, 97
allegory, 18, 145, 151–52, 153, 160, 165, 171, 178
Apollonius of Rhodes, 254
Arcadia, ix, xiii, 27, 28, 31, 137–38, 145, 146–48, 149, 152, 153, 154, 155, 169, 182, 185, 198, 199, 200, 210, 212, 223, 224, 225, 226, 230, 231–32, 233, 234, 235, 237, 239, 247, 249–52, 253, 256
Argens, Marquis d', 22
Ariosto, Ludovico, 254
Aristotle, 17, 87, 157
Augustan reading of Virgil. *See* European School of Virgilian criticism
Augustus, xiii, 2, 3, 4, 7, 10, 32, 40, 43, 44, 45, 46, 47, 48, 107–8, 138, 151, 158, 171, 174, 229

Batteux, Charles, 168, 174, 175
Bion, 166
Blackmore, Richard, 97
Blumauer, Alois, 16, 17, 103
Bodmer, Johann Jakob, 97–98, 111–14, 115, 122, 171, 173
Boie, Heinrich Christian, 225
Boileau(-Despréaux), Nicholas, 6, 96, 102, 104
Borchardt, Rudolf, 13
Borchmeyer, Dieter, 246–47
Böschenstein, Renate, 216
Brandes, Georg, 80
Breitinger, Johann Jakob, 111, 112–14, 115, 171
Buchheit, Vinzenz, 10
Büchner, Karl, 10, 12
bucolic metaphor. *See* allegory
Bürger, Gottfried August, 17, 225
Burmann, Peter, 257

Bursian, Conrad, 85
Butler, E. M., x, 65

Caesar (Gaius Julius Caesar), 21, 43–45, 48
Calpurnius (Titus Calpurnius Siculus), 166
Camões, Luís (Vaz) de, 20, 98
Catullus (Gaius Valerius Catullus), 240
Cerda, Juan Luis de la, 257
Chapelain, Jean, 97
Chesterfield (Philip Dormer Stanhope, Earl of), 15
Chetwood, Knightly, 155–56
Cicero (Marcus Tullius Cicero), 4, 15, 21, 44, 64, 79, 82, 83, 85
Coleridge, Samuel Taylor, 22
Conington, John, 22
Creech, Thomas, 156

Dacier, Anne de, 6
Dante (Dante Alighieri), 3, 64, 284
Deshoulières, Madame, 155
Diderot, Denis, 198
Desmarets de Saint-Sorlin, Jean, 99
Donatus (Aelius Donatus), 74–75
Donatus (Tiberius Claudius Donatus), 28
Dover, K. J., 141
Dryden, John, 5, 18, 96, 155–56
Dusch, Johann Jakob, 257

ekphrasis, 106–7, 143, 162, 165, 202–3, 227
Empson, William, 136
epic, xiv, 1–3, 5, 29–30, 96–110, 119–20
Epicurus, 44
Erxleben, Maria, 229
Euripides, 31

308 ♦ INDEX

European School of Virgilian criticism, 4, 10, 11, 13, 138, 282

Fénelon, François de, 5
Fontane, Theodor, 268
Fontenelle, Bernard le Bovier de la, 26, 138, 139, 153, 155–56, 159, 168, 170, 171–73, 175, 176, 179, 181, 183, 184, 199; pastoral theory, 162–67
Friedrich, Wolf-Hartmut, 81, 82, 85
Friedrich II (the Great), 32

Gellert, Christian Fürchtegott, 228
Gessner, Salomon, xiv, 17, 26, 27, 101–2, 171, 172, 177, 181–84, 198–212, 213, 214–16, 220, 221, 222, 224, 225, 226, 227, 229, 230, 232, 235, 236, 250, 265–66, 267
Gibbon, Edward, 8, 77
Gleim, Johann Wilhelm Ludwig, 74, 208
Glover, Richard, 97
George III, 154
Goethe, Johann Wolfgang von, xiii, 14, 17, 18, 37, 70, 73, 85, 86, 100, 102, 212, 213, 219, 267
Goethe, Johann Wolfgang von, works by: "Alexis und Dora," 142, 234, 243–53; *Dichtung und Wahrheit*, 77; *Hermann und Dorothea*, 27, 30–31, 101, 128, 154, 184, 185, 255–56; *Die Leiden des jungen Werthers*, 24–26, 27, 29, 37, 232; *Römische Elegien*, 233–34, 239–43, 244, 246; "Über Laokoon," 69, 254; "Der Wandrer," 232–39, 242, 244, 253; *Wilhelm Meister*, 244
golden age, 11, 18, 28–29, 31, 46, 84, 97, 123, 128, 137, 145, 148–51, 153, 155, 237–39, 156, 158, 161, 162, 163, 164, 168–70, 172, 173–74, 175–76, 177, 178, 182, 184, 199, 200, 205, 216, 224, 225, 226, 230, 231–32, 238, 253–54, 256, 258, 262, 265–71, 283

Gottsched, Johann Christoph, 3, 26, 79, 83, 96, 97, 104, 107, 114, 153, 155–56, 168, 169–71, 172, 199, 201, 205, 211, 222, 230, 231
Gow, A. S. F., 151
Graves, Robert, 11
Gresset, Jean Baptiste, 172–73, 206
Guarini, Battista, 154, 284

Haecker, Theodor, 10, 12, 14, 286
Hagedorn, Friedrich von, 16, 198, 201
Haller, Albrecht von, xiii, 16, 18, 104, 106, 111, 113, 198
Halperin, David, 137
Harsdörffer, Georg Philipp, 169
Harvard School of Virgilian criticism, 3, 10, 11, 13, 138
Hegel, Georg Friedrich Wilhelm, 185
Heinze, Richard, 10, 12–13, 23, 281
Herder, Johann Gottfried von, xiii, 8, 14, 28, 38, 39–48, 86, 87, 100–101, 137, 153, 164, 168, 175, 177, 181–84, 199, 200, 207–8, 213, 282, 283, 284
Hesiod, 84, 98
Heyne, Christian Gottlob, xiv, 18, 74, 153, 168, 174, 184, 203, 257–58, 260, 282, 284; on the *Aeneid*, 80–82; on the *Eclogues*, 175–81; on the *Georgics*, 82–85; relation to Friedrich Schlegel, 86–87; schooling and early career, 75–77; Virgil edition and its neo-humanist purpose, 77–81
Hiebel, Friedrich, 261
Hilliard, Kevin, 110
history, xi, 282–83, 285; with respect to epic, 96–99, 107–9; with respect to the idyll, 28–29, 137, 149–50, 156–60, 163, 164, 167, 172–74, 181, 183, 223–25, 225–30, 232, 235–37, 239–40, 242, 244, 253, 267, 269–71; with respect to philhellenism, 34, 35, 36–39 (Winckelmann), 39–48 (Herder); with respect to the *Querelle*, 6–9; of Virgil in poetics, 1–5; of Virgilian scholarship, 9–13

Hohberg, Wolf Helmhardt von, 97
Hölderlin, Friedrich, xiii, 23
Hölty, Ludwig Christian Heinrich, 225
Homer, ix, xi, 1, 4, 5, 6–8, 16, 17, 19, 21, 29–30, 35, 36, 37, 38, 42, 48, 78, 81, 86, 96, 97, 98, 110, 111, 112–14, 115, 116, 117–18, 120, 141, 143, 225, 228, 247, 254, 255–56, 257, 259–60, 267, 283, 284
Horace (Quintus Horatius Flaccus), 5, 15, 16, 19, 21, 48, 64, 66, 82, 83, 87, 104, 116, 157, 158, 159, 210, 257, 284
Hubbard, Thomas, 138
Hudemann, Ludwig Friedrich, 98
Hugo, Victor, 21
Humboldt, Wilhelm von, 14, 30, 37, 74, 77, 185
Hume, David, 8, 15
idyll, xi–xii, xv, 25–31, 37; changes in understanding of, 152–55; characterization of the Theocritean idyll, 140–45; characterization of the Virgilian eclogue, 145–52; in literary production, 198–212 (Gessner), 212–25 (Maler Müller), 225–32 (Voss), 232–53 (Goethe), 253–71 (Novalis); problems of definition, 136–40; theory of, 155–62 (Rapin), 162–67 (Fontenelle), 169–71 (Gottsched), 171–74 (Johann Adolf Schlegel), 175 (Wieland), 175–81 (Heyne), 181–84 (Herder)

Jani, Christoph David, 257
Jean Paul (Johann Paul Friedrich Richter), 168, 183
Johnson, Dr. Samuel, 154, 169
Johnson, W. R., 13
Justi, Carl, 66

Kaiser, Gerhard, 111, 222–23, 225, 232, 234, 239, 248
Kant, Immanuel, 15–16, 25, 35, 72, 79, 200
Kleist, Ewald von, 201, 206

Klingner, Friedrich, 10, 12, 14, 137, 151
Klopstock, Friedrich Gottlieb, 17, 20, 97, 98, 100–101, 110–19, 207, 208, 225, 254, 260
Kühn, Sophie von, 261

Lachmann, Karl, 77
Laocoon. *See* Winckelmann
Leibniz, Gottfried Wilhelm, xiii, 5
Lessing, Gotthold Ephraim, xiii, xiv, 16, 18, 72, 80, 81, 85, 86, 107
Lewis, C. S., 20
Lichtenberg, Georg Christoph, 162
Louis XIV, xii, xiii, 4, 6, 7, 32, 46
Lucretius (Titus Lucretius Carus), 20, 44, 112, 159

Mähl, Hans-Joachim, 253, 256
Marlowe, Christopher, 154
Martin, Johann, 257
Mendelssohn, Moses, 183
Milton, John, 20, 99–100, 108–9, 110, 111–13, 120, 122, 254
Moritz, Karl Philipp, 75
Moschus, 166
Motte, Antoine Houdar(t) de la, 6
Müller, Heiner, 286–87
Müller, Maler (Friedrich), 17, 26, 205, 212–25, 226, 227, 229, 232, 234, 243, 244, 250, 252, 253, 267
Müsil, Robert, 33

naive and sentimental, x–xi, xv, 26, 37, 136, 139, 185, 212–14, 218–19, 223–25, 226, 232–39, 242, 250–53. *See also* sentimentality
neo-humanism, xiv, 35, 74, 76, 79–81, 85–86. *See also* philhellenism
Naumann, Christian Nicolaus, 98
Nettleship, Henry, 22
Neuser, Peter Erich, 214
Niebuhr, Barthold Georg, 14, 21, 23
Nietzsche, Friedrich, x, 35, 47–48
Norden, Eduard, 10
Novalis (Friedrich von Hardenberg), xiii, 17, 86, 253–71, 281, 285–86

Oppermann, Hans, 10, 13
Ossian, 254
Otis, Brooks, 11
Ovid (Publius Ovidius Naso), 18, 20, 86, 116, 284

Parry, Adam, 4
Perrault, Charles, 4, 6, 7, 46
Pfeiffer, Rudolf, 76
philhellenism, ix–x, 13–14, 16, 32–33, 34–37, 63–64, 86, 167, 233–34, 252–53, 284–85. *See also* neo-humanism
Pickering, F. P., 246
Pietsch, Johann Valentin, 97
Poggioli, Renato, 137
Pope, Alexander, 102, 104, 115, 155–56, 168
Pöschl, Viktor, 10, 12, 137
Postel, Christian Heinrich, 97
Propertius (Sextus Propertius), 2, 18, 86, 240
Putnam, Michael, 12, 138
Pyra, Immanuel Jakob, 16, 100, 111, 113, 114, 115, 119, 260
Pyra, Immanuel Jakob, works by: *Der Tempel der wahren Dichtkunst*, 103–10

Querelle des anciens et des modernes, xi, xiii, 4, 6–8, 15, 32, 35–36, 38, 99, 138, 155
Quintilian (Marcus Fabius Quintilianus), 2, 257

Racine, Jean, 19
Raleigh, Sir Walter, 154
Ramler, Carl Wilhelm, 174–75, 179, 181, 183, 208
Rapin, René, 26, 138, 139, 153, 168, 170, 171, 175, 177, 178, 179, 181, 184, 244; contrast to Fontenelle, 163–67; pastoral theory, 155–62
Rehm, Walter, 64, 73, 261
Ronsard, Pierre de, 97
Rousseau, Jean-Jacques, 23, 198
Rosenmeyer, Thomas, 137

Sadoleto, Jacopo, 70–71
Saint Beuve, Charles Augustin, 21, 23
Samuel, Richard, 258
Scaliger, Julius Caesar, 4, 28, 76, 156–57, 158, 179, 180
Scheyb, Franz Christoph von, 98
Schiller, Friedrich, xi, 8, 16, 17, 25, 26, 37, 46, 69, 72, 73, 122, 136, 138–39, 150, 168, 181, 184, 185, 212, 219, 224, 232, 243–45, 251, 254
Schlegel, August Wilhelm, xii, 11, 30, 35, 37, 77, 78, 86, 255–56
Schlegel, Caroline, 17
Schlegel, Friedrich, xii, xiii, 8, 17–21, 38, 42, 44–45, 48, 77, 86, 251, 281–86
Schlegel, Johann Adolf, 153, 168, 171–75, 176, 179, 183
Schneider, Helmut, 228
Schneider, Karl Ludwig, 110, 112–13
Schöne, Albrecht, 246–47
Scipio (Publius Cornelius Scipio Africanus), 44
Scudéry, George de, 97
Segrais, Jean Renaud de, 155
Seibt, Gustav, 13
Sellar, William Young, 22, 23, 285
sentimentality, 23–25, 27, 30, 31, 34, 39, 101, 136, 147, 153, 154, 176, 182, 183, 198–99, 200–201, 203, 205, 206, 210, 215–16. *See also* naive and sentimental
Servius (Marius or Maurus Servius Honoratus), 4
Shaftesbury (Anthony Ashley Cooper, Earl of), 15
Shakespeare, William, 33, 213
Snell, Bruno, 137
Sophocles, 72
Spinoza, Benedict de, 23
St. Augustine, 284
state of nature, xi, xii, 23, 26–28, 29, 37, 136, 154–55, 167, 168–69, 172, 174, 176, 182, 185, 235–37, 252
Stifter, Adalbert, 25
Stolberg brothers, Christian and Friedrich Leopold, 225

INDEX ♦ 311

Streller, Siegfried, 228
Suetonius (Gaius Suetonius Tranquillus), 2
Sulzer, Johann Georg, 174–75

Tacitus (Publius or Gaius Cornelius Tacitus), 97
Tasso, Torquato, 20, 97, 99, 158
Tennyson, Lord Alfred, 22, 23
Theocritus, xiv, 7, 136–39, 151, 153–54, 156–57, 199, 202, 223, 225, 256, 257, 261; characterization of the Theocritean idyll, 140–45; in pastoral poetry, 202–9 (Gessner), 213–15 (Maler Müller), 227–32 (Voss), 248–50 (Goethe); in pastoral theory, 157–63 (Rapin), 163–67 (Fontenelle), 171–73 (Johann Adolf Schlegel), 175 (Wieland), 175–81 (Heyne), 181–84 (Herder)
Theocritus, works by: *Idyll* 1, 142–44, 146, 147, 154, 162, 163, 165, 202–3, 214, 256, 261–62; *Idyll* 7, 151–52, 177, 181; *Idyll* 11, 142, 144–45, 147, 151, 165, 215, 227, 248
Thomas, Richard, 9
Thomson, James, 206
Tieck, Ludwig, 268
Tibullus (Albius Tibullus), 240

Uz, Johann Peter, 17, 198, 201, 210, 211, 216, 225, 259, 267

Vico, Giambattista, 8
Vida, Marco Girolamo, 2
Virgil (Publius Vergilus Maro), 4, 9–13, 13–14, 16, 31, 33–34, 38, 48, 63–65, 68–69, 70–71, 141, 143, 153–54, 244; characterization of the Virgilian eclogue, 145–52; Heyne's edition, 77–78; epic, 1–3, 5, 19, 36, 96–103; in pastoral poetry, 202–12 (Gessner), 214–25 (Maler Müller), 225–32 (Voss), 237–39, 244, 246–52 (Goethe), 256–71 (Novalis); in pastoral theory, 157–62 (Rapin), 162–67 (Fontenelle), 169–71 (Gottsched), 171–74 (Johann Adolf Schlegel), 175 (Wieland), 175–81 (Heyne), 181–84 (Herder); Latin literature, ix–x, 18, 20–21, 45; nature, xi–xii, 22, 23, 31; problematic eclogues, 145, 153, 157, 160, 170–71, 173–74, 175, 178–79, 205, 209, 248–50; relationship to the pastoral tradition, 137–39; style and rhetoric, 14–15, 18–23, 112–19, 156–58, 160–62, 164–66, 171, 173, 178–79
Virgil, works by: *Aeneid*, 2, 3, 5, 10–13, 16, 17, 18, 19, 22, 40, 45, 63, 66, 80–82, 83, 85, 87, 96, 98–101, 105–8, 111, 119, 120–29, 138, 182, 183, 237–38, 254–55, 256, 257, 260, 263–64, 281–87; *Eclogues* (*see also* Virgil, in pastoral poetry; Virgil, in pastoral theory), 3, 5, 17, 18, 27–28, 31, 40, 64, 82, 83, 107, 123, 138, 145–52, 155, 156–85, 202–10, 214–19, 229–30, 237–39, 246–52, 257–267, 286–87; *Ec.* 1, 138, 148, 151, 160, 171, 202, 203, 209, 229–30, 237; *Ec.* 4, 64, 122–23, 141, 148–49, 150, 152, 160, 216–18, 219, 237, 238, 253, 256, 257–60, 262, 264–67; *Ec.* 6, 145, 152, 160, 172–74, 198, 203, 206, 216–17, 219, 225, 256, 258–61, 264–65, 267; *Ec.* 10, 146–48, 149, 152, 154, 160, 209, 210, 237, 246, 249–50; *Georgics*, 3, 5, 6, 17, 18–19, 22, 27, 31, 40, 66, 82–85, 86–87, 104, 138, 149–51, 159, 174, 177, 183–84, 185, 205, 207, 210–11, 217–18, 231–32, 257
Voltaire (François-Marie Arouet), 8, 16, 46, 97, 114
Voss, E. Theodor, 199, 200, 205, 231
Voss, Johann Heinrich, 17, 18, 26, 30, 77, 85, 86, 102, 154, 184, 185, 205, 212, 219, 222, 225–32, 236, 250

Wieland, Christoph Martin, xiii, 17, 86, 99, 102–3, 168, 175, 181, 206
Wieland, Christoph Martin, works by: *Oberon*, 119–29
Wili, Walter, 23
Winckelmann, Johann Joachim, 27, 34, 35, 36–39, 40, 42–43, 46, 47, 48, 76, 80, 81, 85, 86, 229, 233, 284; interpretation of Laocoon, xiii–xiv, 16, 17, 38, 63–74
Wolf, Christa, 286–87
Wolf, Friedrich August, xiv, 14, 35, 76, 77, 85